# ROUTLEDGE LIBRARY EDITIONS:
# THE HISTORY OF ECONOMIC THOUGHT

Volume 8

T0299792

# NOBEL LAUREATES IN
# ECONOMIC SCIENCES

# NOBEL LAUREATES IN ECONOMIC SCIENCES

## A Biographical Dictionary

Edited by
BERNARD S. KATZ

Routledge
Taylor & Francis Group

LONDON AND NEW YORK

First published in 1989 by Garland Publishing, Inc.

This edition first published in 2017
by Routledge
2 Park Square, Milton Park, Abingdon, Oxon OX14 4RN

and by Routledge
711 Third Avenue, New York, NY 10017

*Routledge is an imprint of the Taylor & Francis Group, an informa business*

© 1989 Bernard S. Katz

*British Library Cataloguing in Publication Data*
A catalogue record for this book is available from the British Library

ISBN: 978-1-138-29250-5 (Set)
ISBN: 978-1-315-23288-1 (Set) (ebk)
ISBN: 978-1-138-28355-8 (Volume 8) (hbk)
ISBN: 978-1-138-28358-9 (Volume 8) (pbk)
ISBN: 978-1-315-27017-3 (Volume 8) (ebk)

**Publisher's Note**
The publisher has gone to great lengths to ensure the quality of this reprint but points out that some imperfections in the original copies may be apparent.

**Disclaimer**
The publisher has made every effort to trace copyright holders and would welcome correspondence from those they have been unable to trace.

# NOBEL LAUREATES IN ECONOMIC SCIENCES
## A Biographical Dictionary

EDITED BY *Bernard S. Katz*

*Garland Publishing, Inc.*
NEW YORK & LONDON 1989

Library of Congress Cataloging-in-Publication Data

Nobel laureates in economic sciences: a biographical dictionary / edited by
Bernard S. Katz.
    p. cm. — (Garland reference library of the humanities : vol.
850)
  Includes index.
  ISBN 0-8240-5742-2 (alk. paper)
  1. Economists—Biography.  2. Nobel prizes.  I. Katz, Bernard S.,
1932–  .  II. Series.
HB76.N63  1989
330′.092′2                                  89-1062
[B]                                            CIP

Design by Alison Lew

Printed on acid-free, 250-year-life paper

Manufactured in the United States of America

# CONTENTS

DEDICATED TO
MY WIFE AND DAUGHTER,
LINDA AND MERYL

# FOREWORD

Tom Sawyer had to apologize for eavesdropping on his own funeral. My doubts about introducing a book that included a chapter on me were overcome by the decision not to sample the symphonies for which I was writing an overture.

The contents of science must be judged and evaluated on their own intrinsic merits vis-à-vis the empirical reality. No mean task! Anecdotes about scientists—whether in their laboratories, nurseries, or boudoirs—are irrelevant from this point of view. The accuracy of the law of gravitation in describing dropped objects, discharged cannon balls, or the meandering of the perihelion of Mercury is quite independent of Newton's moment of discovery when contemplating in a Lincolnshire garden the fall of an apple. In this same regard, Freud's classifying the slow-to-publish Sir Isaac as an anal type is equally irrelevant.

Why then chop down trees to print books about economist scholars? Indeed, why pick out these particular scholars, who happened to be annointed by a Swedish committee of fallible human beings?

These are legitimate questions. And there is the further fundamental query: Even if the heroes of the present saga were certifiable as the true leaders and innovators of the discipline we call political economy, why add to the invidious differences of individuals' fortunes by creating new prizes and honors? As some tome says, "To him/her who hath shall be given. But, Oh Lord, why pile it on?"

Tom Sawyer cannot answer these questions, and I won't try. Science is an adventure with a growing number of players. Lay people and professionals are interested in its great game. Emeritus professors recall by the fireplace legends of great deeds performed when giants walked the earth. Working researchers never meet, even for innocent merriment and recreation, but what they gossip: gossip about themselves. Students, experience shows, are motivated into scientific careers by stories they've read about past leaders.

Here is one illustration. Sinclair Lewis wrote an enthusiastic novel about a biology researcher, Arrowsmith. The book sold well. But I recall hearing as a young student, newly arrived in Cambridge, Massachusetts, the disdainful view of Hans Zinsser. Zinsser, a remarkable scholar in the domains of medicine and biology, author of *Rats, Lice and History*, declared, "When genuine scientists read that high-fallutin' oath taken by Dr. Arrowsmith before the altar of SCIENCE, it makes them want to throw up." O.K.— Dr. Zinsser earned his right to be an intellectual snob, his right to tell the truth and shame the devil. Still, I can testify as a reader of the official short autobiographies of Nobelists that several of the recent decades' prize winners in medicine reported that the reading of Lewis's *Arrowsmith* contributed toward their choice of careers.

By good luck I've known all the prize winners in economics. The economics award was of course not in Alfred Nobel's will. It is not quite a proper Nobel Prize. The Bank of Sweden, to celebrate its 300th anniversary, funded a prize parallel with those in Physics, Chemistry, Medicine, Literature, and Peace once the Nobel Foundation and the Royal Swedish Academy of Science agreed to accept the new responsibility. One day in 1968, back at the very beginning, I was asked by the Royal Academy to suggest possible economists. Off the top of my head I wrote down the few dozen persons who presumably deserved serious consideration. Like the Lord, who took six times as long to do His work, after doing my duty that day I determined to rest. I don't know whether the discipline of economics is a science or an art, but over the years I have been able to notice the considerable overlap between my casual list and the historical record. A perfect correlation? No, that would make the story an unbelievable one. A few of my darlings have gone off to heaven before Stockholm made up its mind: Joan Robinson, Roy Harrod, Nicholas Kaldor, Abba Lerner, Michal Kalecki, are part of that group. And a few flowers whose fragrance I had not yet discerned caught the Nobel committee's infallible eye. But for that considerable subset of overlap, even the calculated Spearman rank-order-correlation-coefficient relating to when each received his (yes, alas, *his* not *his/her*) tap seems oddly high—a tribute to one or all of a) the Royal Swedish Academy of Science, b) economics as an objective science, or c) your humble servant.

Tolstoy never received the Nobel Prize and John Steinbeck did. Einstein and Planck got their prizes late. At least one scientist got his prize for treating a disease not now thought to exist. When insulin was developed for diabetes, Bantam so disapproved of having to share the prize with his boss that he gave half to his assistant; careful historians of that discovery believe those three persons—and a fourth!—merit credit for the achievement. One cosmologist is said to have been honored for an effect that bears his name but which he first denied when his female assistant called it out. I know a modest physicist who avers that a Berkeley committee secured him the prize when it granted him first crack on some new hardware. If these are authentic tales concerning the noneconomic Nobel Prizes, we must accept with a grain of salt the selection process in our domain that runs somewhere between hard science and crafty art.

They say at Fenway Park, you can't follow the game without a scorecard. In that same spirit I wish the reader joy in learning about those who left their tracks and egestions in the quicksands of evolving economics.

PAUL SAMUELSON

# INTRODUCTION

The prize in Economic Sciences in the memory of Alfred Nobel was first awarded in 1969, sixty-eight years after the first Nobel Prizes were given. The award for economic sciences has been the only addition to the initial five award categories established by the Nobel Foundation. It was made possible by a 1968 donation by the Central National Bank of Sweden to mark its 300th anniversary. The individuals chosen for the prize, its monetary value, which is the same as for the other sciences, and its administration are governed by the Swedish Academy of Sciences.

When Per Asbrink, the Governor of Sveriges Riksbank, first proposed the award, its appropriateness was questioned by a number of natural scientists in the Academy. Not only was there a natural hesitancy to extend the number of the awards, there was the more substantive question as to whether economics was sufficiently scientific. This latter doubt has dogged the award periodically.

The basis of the Nobel Prize in the natural sciences is to celebrate specific achievements rather than outstanding individuals. However, research in economics does not lend itself to individual scientific discoveries as does research in the physical sciences. This difference raises a number of concerns about the discipline and the intent of the award. For example, Keynes believed that economics depended as much on values, intuition, ethics, and introspection as it did on the scientific method. Gunnar Myrdal, a 1975 Nobel laureate in economics, has questioned the legitimacy of granting the award. An early supporter of the prize, in the mid 1970s he expressed his intent to introduce to the Academy a proposal as to how the Academy may divest itself of the charge of awarding the economics prize as if economics was a "hard" science. He argued that economics was a "soft" science as it had no "constant," no "laws of nature," and was a "confused admixture of science and politics." He also suggested that the Academy was in danger of politicizing the prize by awarding it to him jointly with Friedrich von Hayek. Myrdal believed that the joint award was but a gesture to balance his twentieth-century liberalism with the classical liberalism of Hayek.

Responding to these concerns, defenders are quick to point out that a number of the Nobel laureates are themselves natural scientists (physicists Tinbergen and Koopmans) and that Kantorovich and Debreu are respected mathematicians. In fact, they would argue, the preponderant majority of Nobel laureates in economics have fully incorporated the scientific method in their research.

Members of the Academy were sensitized to this "scientific" issue early in their deliberations, and their earliest choices for the prize were individuals whose work reflected one of the more "scientific" aspects of modern economics, that of quantitative methods, econometrics. Nevertheless, in reviewing the full gamut of Nobel laureates, it becomes evident that the Academy did not get too enmeshed in the "scientific" problem. The awarding of the prize has, without question, meandered across the discipline called economics. This latitude may be best exemplified by the award to Herbert Simon, who has maintained that economics is both a social and behavioral science. Simon's Nobel award was given for his work in administrative science, an area closely allied to business administration.

The objective of the Nobel award among the sciences has always been to award the prize for a specific achievement rather than to exceptional individuals. Nobel, in his will, directs that the award be given to "those who during the preceding year, shall have conferred the greatest benefit to mankind." While Nobel's directions have been followed in the main, members of the Academy have given breadth to their charge. They have sometimes honored an individual more than a specific work, and, as in the award to Simon, they have widened the definition of economics, expanding the boundaries of the science. The Nobel Prize cannot be awarded posthumously. Even working within this limitation, the Academy was initially faced with a long list of notable economists as they considered the first award. There were many individuals who, given the quality of

their work, could justly lay claim to the prize. For the first medal the Academy worked from a final choice of ten. In terms of age, speculation ran from the seventy-four-year-old Ragnar Frisch to the forty-eight-year-old Kenneth Arrow. Front runners included Paul Samuelson, Sir John Hicks, Jan Tinbergen, Leonid Kantorovitch, François Perroux, Simon Kuznets, Wassily Leontief, and Milton Friedman as well as Frisch and Arrow. Although Frisch of Norway and Tinbergen of the Netherlands were the Academy's first choices, all but François Perroux, who died in June, 1987, have eventually been awarded the prize.

Over the years, American economists have won most of the awards. By 1988 fourteen of the twenty-five recognized laureates have held U.S. citizenship. This record of American achievement is unequaled in any other field of the Nobel Prize. In all probability, however, had the award been given from 1901, as all other awards have been, the American record would not have the same glitter. Economists from Scandinavia, Great Britain and Austria would have dominated. Nevertheless, the harvest of prizes has been due, in large part, to the Academy's propensity to reward the role of math and econometrics in economic science.

The use of mathematics in economics was pioneered in Europe, a fact reflected in the Academy's first awards to the non-American econometricians. More recently, however, starting with the work of Paul Samuelson, the 1970 economic laureate who mathematized modern economics, many of the technical advances in mathematical economics and econometrics have been of American origin. Americans have been imaginative in broadening the application of economics' new tool to the far reaches of the discipline. They have mathematically conceptualized and measured economic phenomena and have been celebrated accordingly.

Since the inception of the Nobel Prize, joint awards have become rather commonplace. In the physical sciences two or more awards have been given to individuals whose work was unrelated. This has not been the case in economics. By 1987 there have been only six joint economic awards, and all have been given to those whose work is closely related, at least by the Academy's pronouncements. The joint award given to Friedrich A. von Hayek and Gunnar Myrdal in 1974 strains the definition of similarity in study and results. Myrdal has argued that their work and political views were disparate.

Any attempt to classify the economic prize awards among its recipients immediately runs into the problem of the multidimensionality of economic research. An argument has been made that the giving of the awards has followed a theme of "great issues." It is maintained that the Academy has seen the discipline's main concerns, as economic development, Keynesianism versus Monetarism, and the development of econometrics and has given the awards accordingly.

While this tripartite schema of great issues has its intellectual appeal, it is doubtful that it could be all-inclusive given the differences among the laureates. Moreover, it is doubtful that the Academy would significantly deviate from its charge of granting the award on the basis of specific achievements and give the award based on issues. If such a task were taken the Academy could be rightly accused of attempting to shape global values. In this regard it may be sufficient to indicate that Myrdal has already chastised the Academy for its attempts to seek political balance.

The need to group the vast body of Nobel laureate accomplishments into general categories appears compulsory. However, any classification would only hazard the criteria assumed by the Academy. What follows is a classification that leans heavily on suggestions by other writers.

A first category of prizes, an award for the theoretical application of economics, is one that best represents Nobel's original charge, that of rewarding individuals for specific contributions. Here one can point to the shared prize of Bertil Ohlin and James Meade for their work in international economics; Robert Solow for his contributions to the theory of economic growth; James Tobin for his work on financial markets and their linkages to employment, production, and prices; Franco Modigliani and his life cycle hypothesis of household saving and his contribution to the valuation of the firm; George Stigler and his studies on industrial structure; and Milton Friedman's contributions to consumption analysis and monetary theory. Awards for a specific subject are further represented by the shared 1979 prize given to Sir Arthur Lewis and Theodore Schultz for their work on economic development and the problems of less developed nations. For highly praised and analytically suggestive empirical contributions both Simon Kuznets and Lawrence Klein have received the Nobel Prize, Kuznets for his empirical research on economic growth and Klein for his further development and application of large scale econometric models.

A second category would be the prize for general economic theory. Here the listing would be led by Paul Samuelson for having developed contemporary static and dynamic economic theory, Kenneth Arrow and John Hicks in a joint award for their contributions to welfare and general economic equilibrium theory, Gerard Debreu for his reformulation of general equilibrium theory, and Maurice Allais for his work on the theory of markets and resource allocation.

The joint award given in 1974 to the apparently disparate economists Gunnar Myrdal and Frederich von Hayek creates an initial confusion, given their polarized research and political dispositions. However, the Academy recognized their contributions as embracing the interdependence of economic, social, and institutional phenomena. What they provided, along with James Buchanan and Herbert Simon, is a third category suggesting innovative methods for economic analysis. The award was given to Buchanan for his contributions in developing the theory of economic and political decision-making, more commonly known as "public choice theory," and to Simon for his contribution to the understanding of the decision-making process within economic organizations.

A final classification would be for pure economic analysis. In this last category would fall the prizes awarded to the first winners of the Nobel Prize, Ragnar Frisch and Jan Tinbergen, for their pathbreaking work on economic dynamics and econometrics, to Wassily Leontief for his input-output method of analysis, to Richard Stone for the development of the systems of national accounts, and jointly to Tjalling Koopmans and Leonid Kantorovich for their work on the theory of the optimum allocation of economic resources.

In the main, there has been a reduction in the backlog of individuals who well deserve the prize for their contributions over their lifetimes. In part the catching up has been fostered by the death of prizeworthy economists. There is now room for the Academy to grant the prize to individuals whose work has not been in the mainstream. This is as it should be. Economics is not a science dealing with irrevocable physical laws; it is about society, people, their habits, and their propensities. It is a science that thrives on differing points of view, and its Nobel Prize winners will reflect these differences as they all work to advance what we know about our world.

BERNARD S. KATZ
EASTON, PA

# NOBEL LAUREATES IN ECONOMIC SCIENCES BY YEAR

1969    Ragnar Anton Kittil Frisch (Norway) and Jan Tinbergen (The Netherlands)

1970    Paul Anthony Samuelson (United States)

1971    Simon Kuznets (United States)

1972    Kenneth J. Arrow (United States) and John Richard Hicks (Great Britain)

1973    Wassily W. Leontief (United States)

1974    Friedrich August von Hayek (Great Britain) and Gunnar Myrdal (Sweden)

1975    Leonid Kantorovich (Soviet Union) and Tjalling C. Koopmans (United States)

1976    Milton Friedman (United States)

1977    James Meade (Great Britain) and Bertil Ohlin (Sweden)

1978    Herbert Alexander Simon (United States)

1979    William Arthur Lewis (British West Indies) and Theodore Schultz (United States)

1980    Lawrence R. Kline (United States)

1981    James Tobin (United States)

1982    George J. Stigler (United States)

1983    Gerard Debreu (United States)

1984    Richard Stone (Great Britain)

1985    Franco Modigliani (United States)

1986    James McGill Buchanan (United States)

1987    Robert Merton Solow (United States)

1988    Maurice Allais (France)

# The Laureates

# MAURICE ALLAIS 1988

In 1988, Maurice Allais, a French professor, was selected as the Nobel Prize winner in Economic Sciences. He is the first French citizen to win the award since it was created in 1968. As reported in *The New York Times* (October 19, 1988), The Nobel Prize committee noted that international recognition of Allais's work has been slow in coming due partly to the volume, complexity, and length of most of his work and partly because he wrote in French. His major contributions to economic thought have been in the theory of markets and the efficient utilization of resources. However, he has also written extensively on capital and growth theory, money and business cycles, and risk analysis. He is probably best known as the founder of the Allais Paradox, which concerns the theory of individual choice in the face of uncertainty.

## From Engineer to Economist

Maurice Allais was born on May 31, 1911, in Paris to Maurice and Louise (Caubet) Allais. He received his early training in engineering at the Ecole Polytechnique and the Ecole National Supérieure des Mines de Paris and began his career in 1937 as an engineer at the Department of Mines and Quarries. During a visit to the United States, however, he observed at first hand the idle factories and unemployed workers created by the Depression, and this experience changed his life. Since that time his major motivation has been to improve the conditions of life, to try to find a remedy to many of the problems facing the world. This motivation led him to economics—a way of helping people. With his engineering background, Allais taught himself economics and introduced mathematical rigor into the French school of economics, which was mostly nonquantitative at the time.

From 1943 to 1948 he was the Director of the Bureau of Mining Documents. In 1944 he started his academic career as a professor of economic analysis at the Ecole National Supérieure des Mines de Paris. He later became a professor of economic theory at the Institute of Statistics at the University of Paris. Since 1944 he has been the Director of the Center for Economic Analysis. In 1949 Allais received his doctorate in engineering from the University of Paris. In 1954 he was appointed the Director of Research at the National Center of Scientific Research, and he has continued to the present in that position. From 1967 to 1970, he was a professor at the Graduate Institute of International Studies in Geneva, Switzerland. And since 1970 he has been the director of the Séminaire Clément-Juglar d'Analyze Monétaire at the University of Paris-X.

Allais married Jacqueline Bouteloup on September 6, 1960; they have one daughter, Christine. His leisure interests include history, physics, swimming, skiing, and tennis. In addition to his economic research, he has published articles on history and physics. He also frequently writes commentaries on economics for French newspapers.

## Early Economic Works

Allais's most influential works, done in the 1940s and 1950s, deal with market equilibrium and how best to allocate resource among consumers. These publications detail his theories and provide guidelines for pricing in monopolies and public sector planning. Two works, *A la recherch d'une discipline économique. Première partie: l'économique pure.* (*In Search of Economic Discipline*) (1943), which runs 900 pages, and *Economie et intérêt* (*Economy and Interest*) (1947), which is 800 pages long, established Allais's reputation as a conservative free-market economist and laid the foundation for the school of French economist-engineers. In the first publication, he provides rigorous detailed mathematical proofs that equilibrium prices are "efficient" in an abstract model of a market in which goods are traded between households and firms. In other words, nobody can become better off without making somebody else worse off. Though the assumptions under which these conclusions hold are not met in reality, Allais's results are important in the stream of economic thought as they represent an exhaustive analysis of equilibrium theory.

These writings may make Mr. Allais sound like the kind of economist who assumes a nonexistent can opener and attempts to open a can; but in fact, he has applied his work in the real world. In all of his work, even from the very beginning, we see a constant search for theories that actually do predict reality and a deep reluctance to accept any theory that does not reflect reality.

He has written about how to run public monopolies more efficiently, and it was this research that led him to figure prominently in debates on economic planning in France after 1945. His views were not popular in post-war France, a nation that tried to combine state intervention with market forces. He has remained a critic of the establishment throughout his career; and the establishment, as a result, has remained aloof from him. Jacque Lauteman of France's National Center for Scientific Research says Allais's work provides a very strong base for those opposed to government direction of the economy by establishing a link between the equilibrium of many individuals' decisions and maximum efficiency, similar to Adam Smith's "invisible hand."

## Allais's Impact

Though Allais did not publish in English until late in his career and has had relatively little influence among American and English economists, he is respected. His work has been said to parallel the work of two very well-known economists, Sir John Hicks of the United Kingdom and Paul A. Samuelson of the United States. Both of these writers were awarded Nobel Prizes,

Mr. Samuelson in 1970 and Sir John in 1972. Samuelson, currently of MIT, has called the Frenchman "a fountain of original and independent discoveries." He also has noted that if Allais's earliest writing had been in English, the evolution of economic theory may have taken a different course.

An old friend, 1976 Nobel laureate Milton Friedman of the Hoover Institution at Stanford, has remarked that Allais is "tenacious" and "a little bit of a nut," but also a "highly original thinker" who "derives very little of his work from the work of others." He has certainly influenced his students, several of whom have moved to major government jobs and two of whom have received the Nobel Prize, Gerard Debreu in 1983 and Kenneth H. Arrow in 1972. Gerard Debreu, who studied with Allais in the late 1940s, built upon Allais's work for his own study of the existence and stability of efficient markets. Debreu describes himself as a "disciple" of Allais and said his mentor well deserves this honor.

Allais's contribution to the economic sciences is in four major areas: general equilibrium and the efficient allocation of resources, capital and growth theory, money and business cycles, and decision-making under risky conditions.

# General Equilibrium Analysis

When Allais's 1943 book was published, it was one of the most detailed studies on general equilibrium and optimality theories. Many

compare it to Hicks's *Value and Capital* and Samuelson's *Foundations of Economic Analysis*. Among the three, Allais gives the earliest formalization of an intertemporal general equilibrium and, in particular, all the arbitrage conditions between capital goods and land are made explicit. He then provides the first results of global stability of Walrasian "tâtonnement" (Negishi, *Econometrica*, 1962). The book contains a complete report of optimality theory with respect to distributable surpluses and an accurate presentation of the two welfare theorems. Later, Allais's view of the importance of the Walrasian model changed dramatically (1971, 1981). He currently defines a state of general equilibrium as a position in which no distributable surplus can be obtained, and he also describes the whole motion of the economic system as governed by the continual search for surpluses. This new perspective can be seen as a merging of general equilibrium and optimum theory (1981).

Allais's initial professional work led him towards problems of applied economics and regulation. In France, the corps of mining engineers, one of the best-known and respected branches of the civil service, regulated the mining and energy industry and was very influential in the definition and control of public industrial policy. A large part of Allais's work has been devoted to applied economic studies which have always been supported by theoretical analysis. In "Méthode d'évaluation des perspectives économique de la recherche minière sur des grands éspaces. Application au Sahara Algerien" (1954) and *L'impôt sur le capital et la réforme monétaire* (1977) we see Allais applying economic risk and game theory to managerial decision-making.

After World War II, France nationalized many industries including electric utilities, railroads, and mining. Allais's research concluded that some type of pricing system rather than direct regulation would allocate resources more efficiently even in state-run monopolies. Consider as an example an electric utility that charges different rates at different times depending upon demand: high rates during peak-hours and lower rates at off-peak times. Such a rate structure gives customers an incentive to change their electricity usage to off hours; as a result, the amount of waste or underuse of electrical capacity is minimized. Several of Allais's students used these results in directing many state-run monopolies in France after the war. For instance, Marcel Boiteux managed the national electric company and employed a system of pricing based on Allais's research.

# Capital and Growth Theory

His main research contribution to capital, interest, and growth theory are put forth in *Economie et intérêt* (1947), "L'influence du coefficient capitalistique sur le revenue réel par tête" (1960), and "The Influence of the Capital-Output Ratio on Real National Income" (1962). He published his second major work *Economie et intérêt* in 1947. It was a

massive, original work on capital and interest. First, and sometimes preceding other economists by fifteen years, he worked out most of the results of so-called neoclassical theory of growth, including the famous "golden rule of accumulation," that is, to maximize real national income, the optimum rate of interest should equal the growth rate of the economy. He painstakingly detailed a complete theory of capitalistic processes with a vigorous formalization of the concept developed by Jevons in 1871. In other words, the distribution of past expenditures on primary inputs generates the present national income. Allais's systematic use of this idea made it possible for him to construct a theory of economic growth; but more importantly, its use was of even greater help in the analysis of capitalistic efficiency. The initial results imply that the optimum interest rate is zero percent in a stationary no-growth economy. Allais (1962) and other authors later generalized this outcome to the so-called golden rule of accumulations. Thus, Allais completed his theory of optimal allocation of resources with a theory of capitalistic optimum.

In another aspect of this research, Allais carefully tests the explanatory power of his capitalistic optimum theory by comparing growth processes in different countries and analyzing the difference between the optimal amount of capital and the real state of capital accumulation (1965b, 1966, 1967).

Allais's early accomplishments came in spite of being isolated from the rest of the world during World

War II. Paul Samuelson tells the following story about Allais, who was teaching at the French National School of Mines in 1944. When Paris was liberated by the Allies, Sir John and Lady Hicks were the first economists in the city. They made their way to an attic where, once their eyes adjusted to the dimness, they could see a group of students with miners' lamps on their heads listening to a lecturer at a board. The lecturer, of course, was Allais and he was talking about whether the interest rate should be zero percent in a stationary state. In the middle of the war, with very few resources, he worked out an elaborate modern theory of capital and interest.

## Monetary Theory

In the mid-1950s, Allais turned his attention to the study of money, and he must be considered a major influence in the revival of the quantity theory of money (1965a, 1966, 1969, 1974). The reduced form of his model explaining the dynamics of national monetary expenditure is not unlike Phillip Cagan's formulation. Allais claims his model is different because it includes an assumption about the psychological law of the perception of time. In explaining inflation as a response to money supply growth, people in a stable economy may take up to two years to react to an increase in the money supply by bidding prices higher. However, in a rapidly changing situation, such as hyperinflation, the adjustment time may be as short as a few days. Allais's original idea is that though chronological time is different in the two cases, the psychological time is the

same. From a psychological perspective, a year ago may seem like only yesterday when nothing has occurred, and last week may seem like last year when things are changing rapidly. Thus Allais's model is constructed around psychological time and this makes it possible for him to explain the local stability of a steady-state equilibrium, business cycles, and hyperinflation state with the same basic model.

## Risk Analysis

The fourth area of Allais's research is risk analysis, that is, the analysis of how individuals evaluate risks and benefits in decision-making. As usual, his approach is both theoretical and empirical. He builds his analysis on the basis of psychological tests performed in 1952 ("La psychologie de l'homme rationnel devant le risque: critique des postulats et axiomes de l'Ecole Américaine"). For Allais, the theory of choice evolved, chronologically, through four steps. At first, the natural evaluation of a lottery was assumed to be the mathematical expectation of the monetary gain. Second, the mathematical expectation of utility gained was used. The third step then considered subjective probabilities. The American School (Milton Friedman, Jacob Marshak, John Von Neumann, Oskar Morgenstern, Paul Samuelson, and Leonard Savage) takes into consideration only these three steps. Allais claims that a fourth step must be taken; the value of a lottery is a probability density function parameterized by the gains. In essence, he believes the expected utility hypothesis implies such a function. This last step seems very natural and logical to Allais (1953a, 1953b, 1979).

He has also criticized Bernoulli's writings on decision-making under risky conditions, arguing that they do not help to define rationality in an uncertain environment. Through specific examples, he convincingly disproves Savage's independence and Samuelson's substitutability axioms. The major argument is, in short, that when faced with a choice in the vicinity of certainty, a rational agent will prefer absolute safety. Allais proposes the following definition of rationality in risky situations: first, the set of choices must be ordered; second, an absolute preference axiom must be satisfied; and third, only objective probabilities must be considered. In fact, Allais argues that Bernoulli only takes into account the dispersion of the monetary gains whereas it is the dispersion of their psychological values, or utility, that is the important factor.

# The Allais Paradox

Though he was awarded the Nobel Prize for his work on markets and efficient resource utilization, Maurice Allais is probably best known in the United States for the so-called Allais Paradox. Allais constructed the paradox to disprove an axiom of decision-making behavior supported by Von Neumann and Morganstern. The paradox illustrates how individuals evaluate risks and rewards when making decisions. In 1944, Von Neumann and Morgenstern proposed their independence axiom stating that a rational choice be-

tween two alternatives should depend only on how those two alternatives differ, not on any factor that is the same for both choices. Allais disagreed with their axiom and presented the following experiment to show how it failed to predict decision-making accurately.

Consider the following two scenarios. In the first, an individual is asked to choose between two alternatives, X or Y. If she chooses X, she will receive $1 million. If she chooses Y, she has a 10 percent chance of receiving $2.5 million. Most people would choose X because it is a sure thing, though Y is "rationally" the better choice because it maximizes the average payout. For example, given 100 such choices, a person consistently choosing X will get $100 million while a person choosing Y will, on average, receive $114 million. The preference for X, however, is well-understood and predictable.

The second scenario is also a choice between two alternatives, X and Y. Alternative X means that a person has an 11 percent chance of getting $1 million and an 89 percent chance of receiving nothing. While alternative Y means that a person has a 10 percent chance of getting $2.5 million and a 90 percent chance of receiving nothing. In this situation, most people would choose Y because they perceive little difference between and 10 and 11 percent probability and a big difference between $1 and $2.5 million. Y is also the "rational" choice. Given 100 such decisions, the payoffs would be $11 and $25 million respectively for X and Y.

The independence axiom of Morganstern and Von Neumann

would predict if X is chosen over Y in the first case, then X would be chosen over Y in the second. To fully understand why this should be, Robin Davies gives the following example in the Oct. 28, 1988, issue of *Science*. Suppose the payoff in each scenario is a result of a random drawing of one ball from a group of 100 of which 89 are red, 10 blue, and 1 black. In the first scenario, the drawer will receive $1 million under alternative X regardless of what color ball she draws. Choice Y means that she will receive $1 million if a red ball is drawn; $2.5 million, blue; nothing, black.

The outcomes in the second scenario are somewhat different. Under alternative X, if a red ball is chosen, the person will receive nothing; blue, $1 million; black nothing. Whereas alternative Y yields the following: red, nothing; blue, $2.5 million; black, nothing.

Each scenario yields the same alternatives or choices with the following exception: in the first case, the drawer will receive $1 million whenever she draws a red ball regardless of her choice between X and Y. While in the other case, a person will receive nothing if she draws a red ball regardless of her choice between X and Y. Thus, the outcome in both situations are identical if she chooses a red ball no matter if she chooses X or Y. Following this reasoning, the independence axiom implies that the choice between X and Y depends only on the outcome if she chooses a blue or black ball, it does not depend on the outcome when a red ball is chosen.

The Allais Paradox, however, contradicts this conclusion of Von Neumann and Morganstern's axiom. In the first scenario, most would choose X over Y whereas in the second, the choice would be Y over X. The results of such an experiment definitely imply that people are taking into consideration more than how the two choices are different. They are also taking into account the payoff from drawing a red ball. Thus, we can conclude that the independence axiom does not hold, thus a paradox.

## Other Honors

In addition to this most recent honor, Allais has received many distinguished honors throughout his career. A sample includes Chevalier de la Légion d'Honneur, Officier des Palmes Académiques, Chevalier Ordre de l'Economie Nationale, the Lanchester Prize, a Gold Medal from both the American Society for Operations Research and the Société d'Encouragement pour Industrie Nationale, the Robert Blanché Prize, and the Zerilli Marumó Grand Prize from the National Center of Scientific Research.

When told he had won the award, Dr. Allais said he was "shocked" and it was "mind-boggling" according to major news sources. He knew that the Nobel Prize committee had had him under consideration, but he no longer expected the honor. The prize money, currently valued at approximately $400,000 will enable him to continue with his advanced research, though at 77 he is well past the official retirement age. "I'm happy to have the Nobel Prize to show how absurd this

situation is," he said at a news conference in Paris. "It's amazing that politicians think it's normal that they
should not retire, while they think it's
normal to push scholars into retirement."

MARY K. MURPHY

# Selected Bibliography

## WORKS BY ALLAIS

*A la recherche d'une discipline économique.
Première partie: l'économie pure.*
Paris: Ateliers Industria, 1943.

*Economie et intérêt.* Paris: Imprimerie
Nationale, 1947.

"L'extension des théories de l'équilibrie
économique général et du rende-
ment social au cas du risque."
*Econometrica* 21 (1953): 269–90.

"Le comportement de l'homme rationnel devant le risque: critique des
postulats et axiomes de l'Ecole
Americaine." *Econometrica* 21
(October 1953) 503–46. Translated
in *Expected Utility Hypotheses
and the Allais Paradox.* edited
M. Allais and O. Hagen, Dordrecht:
Reidel, 1979.

"La psychologie de l'homme rationnel
devant le risque. La théorie et
l'expérience." *Journal de la Société
de Statistique de Paris* (January
1953): 47–72.

"Méthode d'évaluation des perspectives
économiques de la recherche minière
sur des grands espaces. Application
au Sahara Algerien." Paris: mimeo,
1954. Translated in *Management
Science* 3 (July 1957): 285–347.

"L'influence du coefficient capitalistique
sur le revenue réel par tête."
*International Statistical Institute
Bulletin* 38 (1960): 3–27.

"The Influence of the Capital-Output
Ratio on Real National Income."
*Econometrica* 30 (October 1962):
700–28.

"Reformulation de la théorie quantitative de la monnaie:" *Bulletin SED-
ELS* No. 928, Supplement, 1965a.

"The role of capital in economic development." In *The Economic Approach to Economic Development.*
Amsterdam: North-Holland, 1965b.

"A Restatement of the Quantity Theory
of Money." *American Economic
Review* 56 (December 1966): 1123–
57.

"Some Analytical and Practical Aspects
of the Theory of Capital." In
*Activity Analysis in the Theory of
Growth and Planning.* Edited by
E. Malinvaud and M. Bacharach.
London: Macmillan, 1967.

"Growth and Inflation." *Journal of
Money, Credit and Banking* 1 August (1969): 355–426.

"Les théories de l'équilibre économique
général et de l'efficacité économique.
Impasses récentes et nouvelles perspectives." *Revue d'Economie
Politique* (May 1971). Translated
in *Equilibrium and Disequilibrium
in Economic Theory,* edited
G. Schviodiauer. Dordrecht: Reidel,
1971.

"The Psychological Rate of Interest."
*Journal of Money, Credit and Bank-
ing* 6 (August 1974): 285–331.

*L'impôt sur le capital et la réforme
monétaire.* Paris: Hermann, 1977.

*Contributions à la science économique.
Vue d'ensemble 1943–1978.* Paris:
Centre d'Analyse Economique,
1978.

*Principaux ouvrages et mémoires 1943–
1978.* Paris: Centre d'Analyse Economique, 1978.

"The So-called Allais Paradox and Rational Decisions under Uncertainty." In *Expected Utility Hypotheses and the Allais Paradox.* edited M. Allais and T. Hagen. Dordrecht: Reidel, 1979.

"La théorie générale des surplus." Vol. I, Economie et sociétés. *Cahiers de l'ISMEA*, Series EM No. 8; Vol. II, Modèle Illustratit, économie et sociétés. *Cahiers de l'ISMEA*, Series EM No. 9, 1981.

OTHER WORKS

Bernoulli, D. "Specimen theoriae novae de mensura sortis." 1938. Translated as "Exposition of a New Theory on the Measurement of Risk." *Econometrica* 22 (1954): 23–36.

Cagan, Phillip. "The Monetary Dynamics of Hyperinflation." In *Studies in the Quantity Theory of Money.* Edited by Milton Friedman. Chicago: The University of Chicago Press, 1956.

Negishi, T. and E. H. Hahn. "A Theorem on Non-Tâtonnement". *Econometrica* 30 (July 1962):463–69.

Negishi, T. "The Stability of a Competitive Economy: A Survey Article." *Econometrica* 30 (October 1962): 635–669.

Neumann, J. Von and D. Morgenstern. *Theory of Games and Economic Behavior* 2nd. ed. Princeton: Princeton University Press, 1947.

# KENNETH J. ARROW 1972

Kenneth Joseph Arrow, now the Joan Kenney Professor of Economics and Professor of Operations Research at Stanford University, shared with Professor Sir John Hicks of Oxford the 1972 Nobel Prize for Economic Sciences. Arrow's award recognized primarily his contributions to general-equilibrium theory and welfare theory. These theories provided the basis for the direct application of economics to questions of both optimal resource allocation and the role of the competitive hypothesis in this allocation.

We may debate whether economics is an art or science. Arrow's research, however, has always been based on rigorous mathematical analysis. Indeed, one of this continuing contributions over the the past forty years has been to show how economic analysis naturally lends itself to the methods of mathematics, set theory, and symbolic logic.

## Life and Career

George Feiwel (1987) recounts a story about an economics student from Yugoslavia who, after meeting the great Arrow, declared what an incredible pleasure it was to meet such a famous, genuine American Indian. However, despite his name, Kenneth Arrow has a more down-to-earth background. He was born August 23, 1921, in New York City to a middle-class family of Rumanian Jewish origin. As a child, he was surrounded by many books and encouraged by supportive parents. His father, Harry, was from a poor immigrant family yet managed to attain a degree from New York University's business school. Following in his father's footsteps, Arrow was educated in the city's public schools, attending Townsend Harris High School. Needless to say, he was not the ordinary kid on the block. His parents fretted that he read too much; they wanted him to go out and play football with the other neighborhood kids. Feiwel writes that:

as a child he suffered a number of ailments which fostered sedentary habits and developed an introspective attitude. The enforced leisure was conducive to evolving a lifelong propensity for avid and voluminous reading. His sister Anita remembers the quandary their mother faced when she wanted to punish Kenneth for some misbehavior or other. At first, she would send him to his room, but soon realized that nothing suited Kenneth better. He would trudge away with a volume of the encyclopedia under his arm and enjoy himself immensely. She then reversed the procedure: Kenneth's punishment was to be sent out to play. (1987, p. 3-4)

Arrow pursued his undergraduate studies at the City College of New York (CCNY), where he discovered books on a new field, mathematical statistics, while browsing in the library. He graduated with a bachelor's degree in 1940 with the Gold

Pell Medal, awarded for achieving the highest grades in the graduating class.

By this time, Arrow's political leanings were already formed; as with many thinkers of the period, they were influenced by firsthand observations of the impact of the Great Depression. In the days before anyone had heard of John Maynard Keynes's General Theory, Arrow remembers that the idea that people were unemployed because they were lazy or incompetent struck him as ludicrous. He continues to make the cogent argument today that political freedom is largely meaningless without economic freedom, which in turn is contingent on greater income equality. For Arrow, a commitment to democratic values implies a redistribution of income and wealth toward greater equality.

Upon graduation from CCNY, Arrow discovered there were no jobs available in high-school teaching, so he enrolled at Columbia University to study at the feet of the renowned statistician Harold Hotelling, who had also written some seminal articles in economic theory. After he received his master's degree in mathematics in 1941, Arrow's graduate training was interrupted by World War II. It was in conjunction with his service as a captain in the Weather Division of the Army Air Corps that he wrote his first scientific research paper, "On the Use of Winds in Flight Planning (1949)."

With the war over, Arrow returned to Columbia in 1946 to complete a doctorate. Arrow had borrowed the money to cover his first year's tuition at Columbia, but Hotelling used a fellowship offer to "bribe" Arrow into enrolling in economics rather than mathematics. After only one year of course work, he completed the written Ph.D. examinations in economics. We might regard this as genius in action; Arrow on the other hand attributes it to the low standards then prevailing in the department, which was largely institutionalist or empirical and antitheory.

Was he stimulated by great teachers? Evidently, other than Hotelling, the professorial landscape was pretty barren, and he was to a large extent self-educated in these years. He enrolled in a rather boring course on business cycles given by Arthur Burns ("The readings in the course were trash"), and took History of Economic Thought from Wesley Clair Mitchell himself ("Quite one of the worst teachers I have had in my life . . . he was just abysmal").

There was a close call. After he joined the Cowles Commission at the University of Chicago (under the direction of Jacob Marschak) in 1947, Arrow was having second thoughts about an academic research career, even though his environment at Cowles was the epicenter of mathematical economics and econometrics in America, with such productive minds as Tjalling Koopmans, Lawrence Klein, Leonid Hurwicz, and Marschak in residence. Arrow had been an excellent student, yet the world seemed to be expecting too much of him in light of his record as a prodigy. He was

advised merely to write a craftsman-like dissertation and get on with other matters like getting a teaching post. Unsure of these matters and his vocation, Arrow considered the possibility of a career in insurance. While he was doing graduate work at Columbia, he took the Actuarial Society of America examinations and eventually passed three.

Arrow recounts how he changed his mind after Tjalling Koopmans pointed out that actuarial statistics were unchallenging, saying with characteristic reticence, "There is no music in it." History will no doubt record the vast loss to the insurance industry—and the corresponding bonanza to economic science.

Arrow married Selma Schweitzer, then a graduate student in economics at the University of Chicago, in 1947. (They have two sons, David and Andrew.) A year later, he was recruited by the newly formed think tank, RAND Corporation in Santa Monica, California. RAND was an exciting place to be in those days. It was at the forefront of pure research in rapidly developing areas of linear programming, mathematical economics, and game theory, with the famous John von Neumann dropping in from time to time to talk shop. Arrow was invited back to RAND for several subsequent summers, and he completed some unusual technical papers—at least two of which were coauthored with his wife—dealing with cost analysis of bomber-frame construction.

After a brief appointment at the University of Chicago (1948–49), Arrow accepted an offer of acting assistant professor of economics and statistics at Stanford University in 1949–1950, where, in the summers of 1950 and 1951, he began a very fruitful collaboration with Leonid Hurwicz.

In 1951, Arrow was finally awarded his doctorate after submitting a dissertation so genuinely original that it was immediately published as *Social Choice and Individual Values*. Arrow was promoted rapidly at Stanford. Hired to strengthen the economics department's offerings in pure theory, he did so at a furious pace. Between 1951 and 1954, two of his most important contributions appeared: "An Extension of the Basic Theorems of Classical Welfare Economics" (1951) was developed for the Second Berkeley Symposium on Mathematical Statistics and Probability, and "Existence of Equilibrium for a Competitive Economy" was written with Gerard Debreu (1954).

Arrow's breakthrough in the theory of social choice, which started at RAND, was addressing a new research area where virtually no previous analysis had taken place. He has always had a knack for surveying an existing body of literature and then reformulating it to furnish fresh insight on old problems and for discovering propositions which were beyond the comprehension of previous economists. But social-choice theory was different: he was almost completely the creator of the questions as well as their answers.

Based on this track record, Stanford advanced Arrow to associate professor and then to professor of economics, statistics, and operations research in 1953. Between 1953 and

1956, he served as executive head of the Department of Economics. In the fall of 1956, Arrow was visiting professor at the Massachusetts Institute of Technology. He was a fellow of Churchill College, Cambridge University, in England in 1963–64, 1970, and 1973.

Except for a traditional course in public finance, most of his classes were small seminars accessible only to a select few students with solid mathematical aptitude. These sessions were a bit forbidding as were his writings, in pure theory.

I can recall the stories about Arrow circulating on the Stanford campus when I was there in the early and mid 1960s. I had attended an Arrow talk; his overall appearance was striking and awe-inspiring. The suits he wore seemed relics of a prewar era. Our public finance class had heard the rumor that Arrow always destroyed his lecture notes at the end of each semester to avoid the trap of repetitive, rote presentations of his ideas. Some doubted this story—and stated flatly that Arrow already had all the facts and equations in his head and had no need at all for lecture notes, whether yellowed with age or freshly minted. And, they claimed that Arrow did not have a comparative advantage in anything, but rather an *absolute advantage in everything*.

On the other hand, Arrow's reputation was often the source of mirth, and one could poke fun at pure theory without fear, since he was and is a good sport. When Arrow received the highest award the U.S. profession offers, the John Bates Clark Award of the American

Economic Association, in 1957, introductory remarks were provided by George Stigler, who advised Arrow, in a low stage whisper, "You should probably just say, 'Symbols fail me.'"

Arrow temporarily abandoned Stanford in 1968, when Harvard made him an offer he couldn't refuse (or, perhaps more to the point, that Stanford was too slow to match). From 1968 to 1974 he was professor of economics there, and from 1974 to 1979 he was James Bryant Conant University Professor. His years at Harvard were mostly productive, although considerable internal departmental bickering evidently was going on at the time, with at least one retention decision proving divisive among the senior colleagues.

In 1979, Stanford came to its senses and lured Arrow back to the place he and his family regard as "home." He has been on the faculty there continually since then, holding a specially created chair. In 1981, Arrow was appointed a senior fellow by courtesy to the Hoover Institution, a research-promoting organization on the Stanford campus.

What about Kenneth Arrow as a person? Everyone who knows him intimately speaks in glowing terms of his humility, acute sense of social responsibility, compassion for his fellow human beings, and willingness to walk the extra mile to help others, particularly his students. Three of his now-famous former students, Walter Heller, Ross Starr, and David Starrett write:

Arrow is personally accessible and unpretentious, addressed as Ken by students, colleagues, and staff. The student, however junior, who steels his nerve to talk with the distinguished professor discovers that he has Arrow's undivided attention. To devoted students and colleagues, Arrow is a legendary figure, larger than life. Stories abound, highlighting his abilities:

• Arrow thinks faster than he—or anyone else—can talk. Hence conversation tends to take place at an extremely rapid pace; no sentence is ever actually completed.

• The breadth of Arrow's knowledge is repeatedly a surprise, even to his friends. By the end of an evening's dinner party whose guests included a professor of art specializing in the art of China, it seemed clear to the host that Arrow was as well versed as the specialist in his subject.

• Arrow can quote passages of Shakespeare and facts of English history accurately and at length.

• Arrow's presence in seminars is legendary. He may open his (abundant) mail, juggle a pencil, or give every evidence of inattention. He will then make a comment demonstrating that he is several steps ahead of the speaker. (1986, pp. xvi–xvii)

# The Paradox of Voting: Arrow's Impossibility Theorem

Kenneth Arrow's first major, and perhaps most notable, accomplishment was to create, in *Social Choice and Individual Values*, a formal theory of social choice, which studies the relation between individuals and society. Although the origins of social-choice theory go back to the the Frenchman Condorcet in 1785, Arrow independently formalized the theory with a rigorous and innovative application of the tools of symbolic logic. In presenting his "impossibility theorem," he provided the foundations for modern social-choice theory.

Arrow derived the impossibility theorem (also known as the "General Possibility Theorem") from the theory of binary relations. He was fascinated with mathematical logic as early as his high school days, primarily through an exposure to the works of the great philosopher Bertrand Russell. There, and in more advanced treatises, he discovered concepts pertaining to such relations as transitivity and orderings.

While at City College, Arrow took a course in the calculus of relations from a world-famous mathematician, Alfred Tarski. Clearly an inspiration in Arrow's early years, Tarski was there by chance: it seems that the vacancy for a visiting professorship had been created by a New York court which had blocked the appointment of Russell on the grounds that he was immoral.

Arrow began by assuming that each decision maker or agent is able to select between any two social alternatives, and hence between all social alternatives, in a consistent manner. In a capitalist democracy, there are two basic ways social choices are made: by voting, which yields "political" decisions, and through the competitive-market mechanism, used to make "economic" decisions. Arrow then asked if there is, for each set of individual

orderings, a corresponding social ordering that satisfies some plausible acceptability criteria so that social choices reflect individual preferences. Thus, the paramount problem of social choice is the aggregation of the multiplicity and divergence of individual preference scales about attainable alternative social actions.

For Arrow, a welfare judgment or evaluation is identical to a constitution, which is a process of social decision making. Arrow wanted to provide a way to counsel ethically neutral public officials whose only aims are to implement the values of citizens as directed by a known, objective rule of collective decision making. To form public values, one needs a nonarbitrary constitution constructed with reasonable conditions which must be obeyed. The Arrovian constitution is merely a rule which assigns to any set of individual preference orderings a rule for making society's choices among alternative social actions in any possible environment.

Arrow established four axioms or minimal conditions in *Social Choice and Individual Values*:

(C) COLLECTIVE RATIONALITY. For any given set of orderings, the social-choice function is derivable from an ordering. The social-choice system mirrors the individual value systems. The mechanism must work for all logically possible individual-preference orderings.
(P) PARETO PRINCIPLE. If alternative A is preferred to alternative B by every single individual according to his ordering, then the social order-

ing also ranks A to B. If everyone prefers A to B, the society must also prefer A to B.

(I) INDEPENDENCE OF IRRELEVANT ALTERNATIVES. The social choice made from any environment depends only on the orderings of individuals with respect to the alternatives in that environment and not on irrelevant alternatives.

Arrow explains the last condition with an extreme case: suppose the voters in the nine-county San Francisco Bay Area were asked for their preferences for solving the traffic congestion problem. The alternatives presented are another bridge, more diamond lanes (limited to car poolers), additional buses, encouragement of van pooling, casual car pooling, or additional rapid transit cars. The voters develop their preference systems for this scenario, and the constitution generates the choice. Later, someone objects that to rank preferences, officials should also consider "instantaneous transportation by dissolving the individual into molecules in a ray gun and reforming him elsewhere in the city as desired." Everyone knows this is not a feasible alternative. Arrow's assumption is that preferences for nonavailable alternatives should have no influence on actual social choices made.

(D) NONDICTATORSHIP. There is no individual whose preferences are automatically society's preferences independent of the preferences of all other individuals. Group decisions must not be dictated by anyone in or outside the community.

Given these rather innocuous criteria, one version of the impossibility theorem establishes a negative and embarrassing result: that the social ordering determined by majority voting rule is inconsistent, even though every individual voter has consistent preferences. In technical terms, if the set of voters is finite and the number of distinct social states is at least three, there is no social-welfare function (constitution) satisfying criteria (C), (P), (I), and (D).

Arrow's major discovery was that not only does the majority decision fail these acceptability conditions, but so must any known or conceivable method of social choice. It is impossible to find a majority-voting scheme which simultaneously reflects the personal preferences of voters, ensures maximum welfare, and does not depend on the order that the issues are voted upon. There cannot possibly be found an ideal voting scheme or perfect democracy. Nor does the market mechanism create a rational social choice.

As we have seen, Arrow regards voting as a method to combine individuals' preferences or choices for candidates or legislative proposals to make a proper social choice. The puzzle originally occurred to Arrow in the context of corporate ownership and control:

I had observed that large corporations were not individuals but were supposed (in theory, at least) to reflect the will of their many stockholders. To be sure, they had a common aim, to maximize profits. But profits depend on the future, and the stockholders might well have different expectations as to future conditions. Suppose the corporation has to choose among alternative directions for investment. Each stockholder orders the different investment policies by the profit he or she expects. But because different stockholders have different expectations, they may well have different orderings of investment policies. My first thought was the obvious one suggested by the formal rules of corporate voting. If there are two investment policies, call them A and B, the one chosen is the one that commands a majority of the shares.

But in almost any real case, there are many more than two possible investment policies. For simplicity, suppose there are three, A, B, and C. The idea that seemed natural to me was to choose the one that would get a majority over each of the other two. To put it another way, since the policy is that of the corporation, we might want to say that the corporation can order all investment policies and choose the best. But since the corporation merely reflects its stockholders, the ordering by the corporation should be constructed from the orderings of the individual stockholders. We might say that the corporation prefers one policy to another if a majority of the shares are voted for the first as against the second.

But now I found an unpleasant surprise. It was perfectly possible that A has a majority against B, and B against C, but that C has a majority against A, not A against C. In other words, majority voting does not always have the property I have just called transitivity. (Arrow [1986], p. 48)

Arrow's theorem implies that a theory of social choice must go beyond pure theories, such as those in microeconomics, that are based on individual choice. Free markets do make individual decisions coherent and can guarantee Pareto optimality, but that result has no moral force. No economic theory has been discovered that can offer rules for moving to a socially "better" allocation of goods and services.

In technical jargon, the voting paradox happens when voters' preferences are not "single peaked," a common situation in the actual economy, as the example below illustrates. Consider a vote on educational expenditures in your community. Suppose you are rich and your child attends a private school that has better teachers and curriculum than public school. The community contains three groups: yuppie, blue collar, and poor. There are three alternative levels of state expenditures on public schools: High (H), Medium (M), and Low (L). All voters are subject to taxes no matter which school their children attend. The yuppies, of course, prefer (L) over (M) and (M) over (H), because they always opt for private schools. More government spending on public schools merely increases their taxes with no direct benefit to their households. The blue-collar group will choose private schools only when spending on public schools is low or medium but will switch to public schools when per-pupil expenditure is high, their overall preferred position. The poor, in contrast, never choose to use private schools in this example, and their ranking is as-

TABLE 1

ARROW'S VOTING PARADOX

| Alternative Levels of Public Education Expenditure | Voters' Ranking | | |
|---|---|---|---|
| | Yuppie | Blue Collar | Poor |
| L (Low) | #1 | #2 | #3 |
| M (Medium) | #2 | #3 | #1 |
| H (High) | #3 | #1 | #2 |

sumed to be medium (M) preferred to high (H) and high (H) to low (L). Table 1 summarizes our assumptions; these are also illustrated in Table 2 below.

From these tables, it can be demonstrated that there is no determinate outcome to a democratic majority vote. It all depends, unfortunately, on the order or sequence of voting between (H), (M), and (L).

This is shown in Table 3 below. In a vote between low expenditures versus medium, low wins (preferred by yuppie and blue-collar voters); in a vote of low versus high, high wins (preferred by the blue-collar and poor voters); and, in a vote of high versus medium expenditures, medium wins (preferred by yuppies and poor).

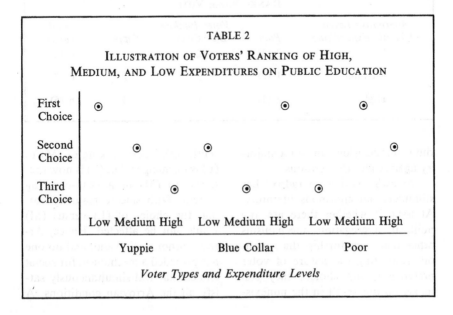

TABLE 2

ILLUSTRATION OF VOTERS' RANKING OF HIGH, MEDIUM, AND LOW EXPENDITURES ON PUBLIC EDUCATION

*Voter Types and Expenditure Levels*

TABLE 3

VOTE OUTCOMES AND RANKING

| Election | Winner | Votes |
|---|---|---|
| L vs. M | L | 2-1 |
| M vs. H | M | 2-1 |
| H vs. L | H | 2-1 |

This example demonstrates "cycling" or "nontransitivities": the social ordering revealed is a violation of the transitivity or consistency requirement. Low (L) is preferred to medium (M) and medium (M) is preferred to high (H), yet high (H) is preferred to low (L). There is obviously no majority voting equilib-

tence-of-equilibrium problem. In the tables above, majority voting satisfies (P), (I), and (D) of Arrow's criteria but violates condition (C).

Objectors to the above education-expenditure voting example may say: Why not use some reasonable alternative, for example, rank-order voting? In fact, that procedure yields a determinate equilibrium:

Whatever the voting order, the result is now a tie. Note, however, that the Arrovian condition (I) is violated: that is, suppose we look at the vote between low and medium educational expenditures, ranked equally, given the preferences indicated; then assume that poor voters reconsider and prefer high to medium (new rank order shown in pa-

TABLE 4

RANK-ORDER VOTE

| Alternative Levels of Public Expenditure | Poor | Voter Ranking Blue Collar | Yuppie | Total Ranks |
|---|---|---|---|---|
| Low | 3 (3) | 2 | 1 | 6 (6) |
| Medium | 1 (2) | 3 | 2 | 6 (7) |
| High | 2 (1) | 1 | 3 | 6 (5) |

rium—no decision can win a majority against all other options.

Arrow's voting paradox has stimulated an enormous literature. At issue is whether there are any political aggregation mechanisms other than dictatorship that, without restricting the nature of voter preferences and choices they can make, do not result in the nonexis-

rentheses). Their ranking of (M) to (L) is unchanged, but (L) is now preferred to (M) in a rank-ordering system. With sincere majority voting, the choice of (L) versus (M) would not be affected. Hence, Arrow's proof is still valid, and no one has provided a mechanism for social choice that will simultaneously satisfy all the Arrovian conditions. A perfect democracy is impossible, and we must settle for second or third best.

# General-Equilibrium Theory

The lifelong focus of Arrow's labors goes to the heart of economic science. Almost forty years ago, Arrow proved a number of important theorems involving social optimality. In a so-called Pareto optimal allocation, any reallocation of resources that makes one individual better off will make someone else worse off. At issue was whether such an allocation is analogous to an equilibrium in a competitive-market system.

What is a competitive-market equilibrium? It may be regarded as a solution to an appropriately designed general-equilibrium model of an actual economy. General-equilibrium theory is a rigorous approach to the basic law of universal mutual interdependence: in an economic system, everything depends upon everything else. Arrow provides a simple example:

The price of oil became very low in the 1930s because of discoveries in Texas and the Persian Gulf area. Homeowners shifted in great numbers from coal to oil for home heating, thereby decreasing the demand for coal and employment in the coal mines. Refineries expanded, so more workers were employed there. There was as well a demand for refinery equipment, a complicated example of chemical processes. This in turn induced demands for skilled chemical engineers and for more steel. Gasoline was cheaper, so that more automobiles were bought and used. Tourist areas accessible by road but not by railroad began to flourish, while railroads decayed. Each of these changes in turn induced other changes, and some of these in turn reacted on the demand for and supply of oil. (Arrow, [1986], p. 51)

The moral of the story is that the demand for a commodity depends upon the prices of all other commodities, including the prices of both labor and capital services (wages and profits). On the other hand, the supply of any product or of capital and labor will in turn depend on the prices of all commodities. What determines the eventual prevailing prices? The usual neoclassical economic answer is that of "equilibrium." Equilibrium prices are those that "clear" all markets, that is, the set of relative prices that causes the quantity demanded to equal the quantity supplied in every market. General-equilibrium theory goes back to the rather turgid writings of the French economist, Leon Walras, who grappled with the mathematics of general equilibrium in 1874. John R. Hicks, with whom Arrow shared the Nobel Prize, tried his hand at developing mathematical tools to apply to the problem in the 1930s.

There was always a nagging problem to perplex the theoretician, and Abraham Wald attacked this analytic issue in Germany in the 1930s. As Arrow states:

General equilibrium theory asserts that the prices of all commodities are determined as the solution of a large number of equations, those that state the equality of supply and demand on each market. Did these equations necessarily have a solution at all? If not, the general equilibrium theory could not always be true. (Arrow [1986], p. 52)

Some amazing turns of events contributed to a pending theoretical breakthrough. Simultaneously, on both the east and west coasts of the United States, in August 1950, Gerard Debreu and Arrow developed models of a competitive economy and an existence proof. Arrow and Debreu began applying S. Kakutani's fixed-point theorem to the problem of existence, and they exchanged manuscripts in time to benefit from common research efforts and realize the need to relax an overly severe assumption that both had made. Both of their studies relied on the seminal work of Koopmans [1951], which analyzed production in terms of activity analysis. They independently showed that all competitive equilibria for these models are Pareto-efficient; further, Pareto-efficient allocations can be attained by a price system such that the allocation is a competitive equilibrium. Hence, every Pareto optimal allocation can be achieved by the equilibrium state of a competitive mechanism if parameters are chosen appropriately.

To most professional economists, Arrow's most important contribution has been to hard-core economics—his work in general equilibrium and welfare economics rather than the voting paradox and

social choice. As codiscoverer of the existence proof, he employed new mathematical techniques and simpler and more general proofs. In his 1951 Berkeley Symposium paper, he used the theory of convex sets to formulate a rigorous, precise meaning for the general efficiency of competitive economics, an idea going back at least to Adam Smith in 1776. Arrow proved in the most general terms at that time the first and second theorems of welfare economics: all competitive equilibria are optimal, and all optimal states can be achieved via the competitive-market process.

The method of analysis is straightforward set theory. The collection of all feasible alternatives is treated as a set, and one can examine the relationships between the set of consumer alternatives and the set of producer alternatives. Using set-theoretic tools such as closure, boundedness, continuity, and convexity provided essential insight. The traditional classical approach relied on differential calculus and hence concealed the pivotal role of convexity and related assumptions. The techniques developed in this pathbreaking research having become standard among economic theorists and have been used by many others to explore the effects of uncertainty, externalities, and various market structures on the original theorems.

Arrow's summary of the Berkeley Symposium paper states:

The classical theorem of welfare economics on the relation between the price system and the achievement of optimal economic welfare is reviewed from the viewpoint of convex set theory. It is found that the theorem can be extended to cover the cases where the social optima are of the nature of corner maxima, and also where there are points of saturation in the preference fields of the members of society. (Arrow, [1951c], p. 507)

Arrow applied an alternative methodology, convex sets, in place of the traditional marginal-analysis approach to equilibrium and Pareto efficiency. He was concerned that in the accepted calculus formulation, there was no mathematical guarantee of nonnegative solution prices or the necessary production of every product by every firm in the model. In order to obtain his result, Arrow worked with distributions representing the amount of each commodity to be given to each individual. He assumed that the quantities consumed are nonnegative and that individual preferences are "selfish" and strictly convex.

In a retrospective *International Encyclopedia of the Social Sciences* article 1968 on economic equilibrium, Arrow makes an extremely important observation that the usual atomistic-competition assumptions of textbooks on microeconomics covering individual households and firms are not sufficient to establish the existence of equilibrium. Instead, two "global" assumptions are required. This limits the simplification tendency implicit in price theory, especially its mathematical versions, to deduce all the properties of aggregate economic behavior from mere assumptions about individual economic agents.

Convexity plays a pivotal role, eliminating the possibility of economies of large-scale production. A set is convex if it contains every point on the line joining any two points in the set. "Nonconvexities" in production is the general-equilibrium theory technical term for economies of large scale, and in consumption it excludes indivisibilities. In production, nonconvexities may lead to monopoly pricemaking behavior in concentrated industries, which invalidates the perfectly-competitive hypothesis. The economy may not be large enough to provide "numerosity" of traders; with a small number of sellers, it may be unfeasible to hold incentives toward imperfect competition in check. Government procompetitive intervention is then called for. Arrow notes that the hypothesis of convexity both in household preferences and in production are the most "vulnerable" parts of the above sets of assumptions. In production, convexity precludes indivisibilities or economies of scale. The consumption case is also important; here, convexity eliminates instances where mixed bundles are inferior to extremes. For instance, Arrow argues that in the very short run, a mixture of whiskey and gin is regarded by many to be inferior to either alone, or that living part time in each of two distant cities may be inferior to living in either alone. Arrow is not sure how far these assumptions may be relaxed.

The major result of Arrow-Debreu general-equilibrium theory was the discovery that the conditions for existence of equilibrium are highly restrictive. The central role of convexity was first indicated in their research, and yet "convexity" is rarely found in the real-world firm's technology of production. Hence, the workability of competitive systems is highly dependent on a large number of economic agents.

Arrow's original general-equilibrium findings have endured: The existence of a competitive multimarket equilibrium under conditions of perfect competition requires "forward markets" in all goods and services. The layman only thinks of today's markets, or "spot" markets, in which goods and services or securities are traded at market-clearing prices in the current time period. Forward markets are those in which we can pay today to obtain delivery in the future, or accept delivery today for the promise of payment tomorrow.

Arrow's original proof cast doubt on the practical importance of general-equilibrium theory, given the lack of complete markets, and much of Arrow's subsequent research was determined to show that general-equilibrium theory remains robust even in actual markets. This is the thrust of a comprehensive 1971 work coauthored with Cambridge University economist Frank Hahn.

# The Case of the Missing Markets

Arrow has always loved puzzles and has worked continually to explore the idea that "missing mar-

kets" were at the foundation of market failure in perfectly competitive economies. This observation stimulated quite a stir in the profession.

Economic theorists, long enamored of the competitive hypothesis, have nonetheless faced the fact that free-market efficiency frequently breaks down. A Pareto model posits that private costs and benefits equal social costs and benefits. Yet, every freshman knows that one person's consumption, or one firm's production, will affect others via spillover effects (externalities such as pollution). The prohibitive expense of establishing markets, the free-rider problem, etc., implies that market failures will continue to be common. Arrow's research theme has drawn important attention to a more important cause of market failure, namely, "missing markets."

Most general-equilibrium models which establish Pareto optimality depend on the assumption that markets are complete. More than internalizing externalities, the theory must include the far-fetched assumption that there are relative prices or terms of exchange for every pair of goods that an individual might want to exchange. Arrow realized that the real-world markets for future goods, risky goods (services), and information itself are constrained by such things as moral hazard and adverse selection. Also perfect competitive equilibrium will be efficient only if all buyers face the same set of prices, which follows from the assumptions of perfect knowledge. Yet, different prices may exist for identical commodities; information is costly to obtain, and the very definition of a "good" presents problems.

The issue is of practical importance in discussing such issues as whether the world will ever run out of oil—that is, will the price mechanism efficiently allocate the increasingly scarce world oil reserves? Can markets allocate oil to competing uses now and at every point in the future in an efficient manner? It is not trivial to prove that we are not pumping out more oil today than we should relative to tomorrow. We need an Arrow-Debreu framework to analyze a commodity as a spatial-temporal object. Does there exist an intertemporal competitive-equilibrium set of prices?

This is not easy to approach. What is the rigorous economic meaning of a "good"? An ice cream cone in Berkeley in January's rain and cold is not the same as one in my home town of El Centro when summer temperatures hit 120°. Competitive theory requires that the description of an economic good include not only the time it is available in the market but its physical location and the prevailing "state of nature"—even, for example, who is president of the United States.

Given uncertainty in the world, markets are required to meet people's changing needs to shift risks or shift funds over time. Consider two physical goods each available at a given location and date but with ten different "states of nature" possibly prevailing. This is an indicator of our uncertainty. Competitive theory requires twenty distinct markets to handle this problem. These will al-

most never exist in the actual world. One cannot calculate a price quote for an ice cream cone in El Centro two years from now, or the value of a bomb shelter in the event of nuclear war.

We can boil the problem down to fewer markets than the twenty in the above example. With "Arrow securities," an economy could attain the same outcome with twelve markets instead of twenty. There would still be two spot markets for the physical goods, with ten more for securities. Each of these traded securities would pay off if one state of the world prevailed, but not in the remaining nine states. Arrow thus proved that we can be equally well off with a smaller number of markets.

This provided an important result to finance students. The incentives to create new and different securities in the actual economy would end only when the number of different securities equaled the number of possible alternative economic outcomes or states of nature. By "different securities," Arrow meant that each security must offer a set of future payoffs that is not duplicable by purchasing existing securities or any combination of securities. "States of nature" means the virtually infinite number of configurations of economic events which could occur at any given future date.

Arrow's suggestion proved prophetic. In the last few years, a vast number of financial innovations in the securities market have emerged—exchange-traded stock options, futures markets in U.S. Treasury securities and in stock market indices, zero-coupon corporate bonds, options markets on futures contracts, options on residential real estate, variable interest-rate debt instruments, and money-market mutual funds, to name but a few examples. However, in the actual world, with millions of states of nature, only a miniscule fraction of the markets required for the competitive hypothesis to be valid actually exist.

Arrow's *Econometrie* article (originally written in French), "The Role of Securities in the Optimal Allocation of Risk-Bearing" (1953, 1964) established that "weak-convexity" of preferences implies risk aversion; Debreu independently arrived at similar findings. After teaming for joint research, Arrow and Debreu provided the basis for incorporating risk and time preference into general-equilibrium theory; thus, by extending general-equilibrium theory to uncertain outcomes, they furnished the foundation for modern neoclassical capital theory.

One principal theme runs throughout Arrow's professional work in applied policy: namely, the cause of market failure is not that markets are inadequate—that is, that spillover effects or externalities drive a wedge between social and private costs, thereby inducing overproduction and misallocation of resources. Instead, market failure arises primarily because markets do not exist—the problem of missing markets.

Markets can of course fail to attain the theoretically virtuous Pareto optimality because of monopoly power, or taxes placed on

goods, or because of asymmetric information (buyers lacking the information they need). Arrow found that asset markets are incomplete. If contingent commodity markets existed in a competitive economy, then it would be possible to allocate risk efficiently. However, the set of markets for trading goods contingent on all states of nature would be incredibly large. Given this intractable requirement, Arrow asked what minimum set of financial assets would be needed that, when combined with existing spot markets, would provide a best allocation. The minimum set he distilled has come to be called "Arrow securities." When actual asset markets are incomplete, they offer fewer risk-sharing opportunities than Arrow securities.

Information problems pose a unique opportunity for a breakdown of competitive markets. Attempts to transfer technology by market contracts can break down because of Arrow's "paradox of information." The information-asymmetry problem is immense, and the buyer (usually the less-informed agent) must be suspicious of any opportunistic claims made by the seller. One example is the used car as a probable "lemon." If the seller lowers the price, and the price is the only information available to the buyer, this action may fail to clear the market, since the buyer perceives any price-reduction behavior as a sure signal that the car is in fact a "lemon." The fundamental paradox of information states that "its value for the purchaser is not known until he has the information, but then he has in effect acquired it without cost" (1971, p. 152).

# Economics of Uncertainty and Information

By introducing contingent contracts, which provide delivery of goods or money contingent on any possible state of the world, Arrow was essentially postulating insurance against all conceivable risks. This was a model against which the methods of risk bearing and risk shifting in the actual economy might be compared in order to gauge inefficiency or set policy. Arrow is justifiably proud of the remarkable insights he was able to provide to this problem. He is yet prouder since the Ford Foundation has funded his further research on a pure theorist approach to the economics of medical care. Arrow's theoretical perspective in "Uncertainty and the Welfare Economics of Medical Care" (1963) concluded that there was inadequate insurance to protect against exceptionally large financial risks. He inquired as to the reasons for obstacles to full insurance coverage for health costs. The answer turned out to be that insurance creates incentives to spend more freely on health than is optimal.

This early work is an example of the blending of theoretical structure, logic, practical applications, and ideas for further empirical research. Arrow derived the original concept of "incentive compatibility" and called for establishing codes of trust and ethical relationships in businesses where there exists unequal information and where government regulation and legal liability are inadequate so that market failure persists.

Thus, an important policy form of risk control is quality certification by government. We can hardly imagine the medical-care profession without some form of medical-board certification and licensing; otherwise, any quack could simply open an office and begin to perform surgery on unsuspecting patients. In such a world, the cost of information would be high; the average person does not have the technical expertise to test a physician's competence. And the price paid for a mistake could be high—potentially death or permanent disability.

Arrow considers the entry and licensing requirements, which require a demonstration of some medical training (imposed on the medical profession by society) as one way to mitigate uncertainty. Still, some uncertainty about the quality of care received remains. At issue is whether licensing requirements have social benefits greater than their social costs. Milton Friedman characteristically says no—the requirements are inefficient. Instead, they merely create barriers to entry, which gives to suppliers of medical services monopoly power and unconscionable profits. Fees are higher and the availability of care lower than in an unregulated market. Market forces would drive out the least competent suppliers: news of unsuccessful brain surgery spreads quickly in the community, leaving only competent doctors left to see patients seeking treatment.

Arrow's conclusions are in sharp contrast to Friedman's view. The uncertainty costs of an unregulated regime will be too great. Consumers traditionally learn about quality by trial and error. Infrequent and specialized as our needs for care often are, decisions to see a doctor would resemble Russian roulette. The commodity sold by the medical profession is, first and foremost, information, but the asymmetry of information between doctor and patient is pronounced.

Arrow concludes that the "welfare case for insurance is overwhelming. It follows that the government should undertake insurance in those cases where this market for whatever reason, has failed to emerge" (1963, p. 961).

The asymmetry of information concerning production, whereby the producer of the commodity almost always knows more than the consumer, can be generalized for other economic decisions. Nevertheless, an insured person knows more about his or her actual state of health than does the insurer. Arrow's observation that people have informational differences is a key facet of all economic systems, not merely health care or health insurance.

One danger of limiting the efficiency of insurance is "moral hazard," the notion that issuing insurance policies to individuals induces them to alter their behavior in ways that increase the risks against which the insurance is written. For example, once your car is insured, you may carelessly leave it parked at night in a high crime area. Health insurance, once taken out, is in ef-

fect a reduction in the price of care, and a rational person will increase the amount consumed, which prompts higher insurance payments, ultimately leading to higher premiums. This is an "externality"—a social cost—because an increase in my use of medical care increases everyone's premium and makes them worse off.

Any policy that insures economic-decision units against adverse outcomes tends to modify their behavior in the direction of taking less care to avoid risks. This disincentive effect reduces sound decision making. Arrow's analysis has generated a significant secondary literature, particularly examining ideal insurance schemes. And his formulation of the phenomenon of asymetric information has fundamentally changed the way economists model the world.

The informational imbalances which pervade any economy result in three classes of outcomes: (1) inefficiencies, (2) overt contractual arrangements, (3) informal arrangements. The goal is to protect the less-informed individuals in society or in a particular type of transaction. In a world of costless information, the problems of adverse selection and moral hazard would vanish. If information were free, the insurer would merely specify the actions to be taken by the insured; monitoring would pose no problem, since it would be a free good.

A further word about Arrow's analysis of "incentive incompatibility" is in order. Arrow provides an elementary example taken from tenant farming:

If the landlord hired someone to work his or her farm, the farm worker would have limited incentives to work to full capacity, since the worker's income is assured. The owner could indeed direct the worker if fully informed about what the worker was doing. But his information can be obtained only by costly supervision. In its absence, the two parties will have different information, and production will be inefficient. The other extreme alternative is to rent the farm at a fixed fee. Then indeed incentives to the worker (or, in this case, tenant) are very strong. But farming is a risky business, and poor farmers at least may not be able to bear the uncertainty. Hence, the compromise of sharecropping arose. It dulls incentives, but not completely, and it shares risks, but not completely. (Arrow, [1986], p. 56)

Many economic institutions have evolved to provide better incentive compatibility. The coinsurance feature of health insurance is a risk-sharing device that makes the insured's incentives compatible with those of the insurance company—namely to economize.

# Other Contributions

Throughout his research, Arrow dissects the successes and failures of the price system as one of several ways of organizing society to mediate competition. In his book *The Limits of Organization* (1974), he explores alternative modes of attaining an efficient allocation of scarce resources, for example, government, the internal organization of firms,

and certain "invisible institutions" of ethical and moral principles. These various systems create channels to effective decision making in the face of needs for information that is costly to acquire. Arrow stresses the need for rigorous study of information costs and the ways they are measured. Many of the problems encountered in understanding the nature, structure, and operation of large organizations can only be handled by introducing information and communication channels more directly into the agenda of economic analyses. The formal boundaries between market and internal resource allocation must be analyzed in these terms. He defines an organization as a means of handling social functions where the price system fails.

Arrow develops his model of organizations into a rich theme that all authority must be accountable for achieving the explicit or implicit goals of the organization (firm, party, university, or government). Irresponsible authority corrupts those with power and those subject to that authority. Unnecessary errors result from failure to provide information or failure to use it. The system can also be swamped with excess information; the resulting tendency is to "filter information in accordance with one's preconceptions." Review groups could be formed to handle charges of errors and ways devised to ensure findings are not disregarded. The review group must be charged with some real authority. Often there are no penalties for government agencies which perpetuate policy errors or consistently fail to deliver on a public mandate or their own enunciated operating rules. There is no way to generate information and effectively disseminate it back to the organization and to the public. Arrow argues that authority "is undoubtedly a necessity for successful achievement of an organization's goals, but it will have to be responsible either to some form of constitutional planned review and exposure or to irregular and fluctuating tides of disobedience" (1974b, p. 79).

In a 1973 article, Arrow attempts to use the powers of his analytical model to explain the unexplained persistence of wage and income gaps between advantaged and disadvantaged groups in the labor market. Discrimination exists when employers use criteria unrelated to productivity in their decisions to hire or in determining rates of remuneration. Arrow considers discrimination only as it appears on the market, and this means that such characteristics as race or sex, which are unrelated to productivity, will affect labor values. Arrow argues that discrimination imposes higher costs on the firm which has a taste for discrimination. Competition tends, in the long run, to reduce the degree of discrimination in the market, especially as capital flows to the more profitable, nondiscriminatory firms. In the short or intermediate run, adjustment costs of search and hiring explain some of the income gaps between, for example, white and black workers.

Arrow's major contribution is his deduction that imperfect information tends to reinforce or perpetuate discriminatory tendencies. If em-

ployers prejudge women or ethnic minorities to have lower productivity, they will only hire them at lower wages. This then becomes a self-perpetuating vicious circle, as victims of discrimination are discouraged from developing nonapparent attributes of high productivity.

Arrow was also the pioneer in developing and applying a new conceptualization of uncertainty and risk to economic analysis. He explained his ideas in academic seminars in 1963, and in subsequent articles applied these architectonic concepts to medical-care insurance, organizational control, public investment, the role of information costs in market failure, and the formation of expectations—a glaring omission from formal theory at the time Arrow addressed the topic. It is critically important that the lack of information among economic decision makers is a source of uncertainty and risk. The recognition of this fact enabled Arrow to study how economic information is defused and why some markets have emerged to reduce this risk while others have not. In the presidential address to the 1973 American Economic Association meetings, Arrow continued to press his theme, declaring, "the uncertainties about economics are rooted in our need for a better understanding of the economics of uncertainty; our lack of economic knowledge is, in good part, our difficulty in modeling the ignorance of the economic agent" (1974a, p. 1).

Arrow was ahead of his time in seeking rigorous microfoundations for the major questions arising in macroeconomics. In a 1959 price-adjustment paper, he pointed out that when markets are in disequilibrium, agents are in a position to affect their own terms of trade. For instance, wages are sticky downward in periods of unemployment and excess supply of labor. One explanation is that a given firm may decide not to lower wages in the presence of some unemployment because to do so involves a perceived risk of losing its workers to a competitor firm on the chance that there is in fact full employment. This explanation anticipated the "island economy" models of the rational expectations theorists as well as the literature on efficiency wages.

C. DANIEL VENCILL

# Selected Bibliography

## WORKS BY ARROW

"On the Use of Winds and Flight Planning." *Journal of Meteorology* 6 (1949): 150–59.

"An Extension of the Basic Theorems of Classical Welfare Economics." In *Proceedings of the Second Berkeley Symposium on Mathematical Statistics and Probability*, edited by J. Neyman, pp. 507–32. Berkeley: University of California Press, 1951. Reprinted as Cowles Commission Paper, New Series, No. 54, and in Arrow, *Collected Papers* (1983), vol. 2, pp. 13–45.

*Social Choice and Individual Values*, New Haven, Ct.: Yale University Press, 1951, 2d. ed., 1963.

"Le role des valeurs boursieres pour la repartition la meilleure des riskes." *Econometrie*, 11 (1953): 41–47 Translated as "The Role of Securities in the Optimal Allocation of Risk-Bearing." *Review of Economic Studies* 31 (1964): 91–96.

"Toward a Theory of Price Adjustment." In *The Allocation of Economic Resources*, edited by Moses Abramowitz, *et al.* Stanford, Ca.: Stanford University Press, 1959.

"Economic Welfare and the Allocation of Resources for Invention." In National Bureau of Economic Research, *The Rate and Direction of Inventive Activity: Economic and Social Factors*, pp. 609–25. Princeton, N.J.: Princeton University Press, 1962.

"Uncertainty and the Welfare Economics of Medical Care." *American Economic Review* 53 (1963): 941–69. Reprinted in Arrow, *Collected Papers* (1985), Volume 3, pp. 15–50.

"The Organization of Economic Activity: Issues Pertinent to the Choice of Market vs. Non-Market Allocation." In Joint Economic Committee, *The Analysis of Public Expenditure: The PPB System*. Vol. 1, pp. 47–64. Washington, D.C.: Government Printing Office, 1965. Reprinted in Arrow, *Collected Papers* (1983), vol. 2, pp. 133–55.

"Economic Equilibrium." In *International Encyclopedia of the Social Sciences*, edited by David Sells. vol. 4, pp. 376–86. New York: Crowell Collier and Macmillan, 1968. Reprinted in Arrow, *Collected Papers* (1983), vol. 2, pp. 107–32.

*Essays in the Theory of Risk Bearing*, Chicago: Markham, 1971.

"The Theory of Discrimination." In *Discrimination in Labor Markets*, edited by Orley Ashenfelter and Albert Rees, pp. 3–33. Princeton, N.J.: Princeton University Press, 1973a. Reprinted in Arrow, *Collected Papers* (1985), vol. 6, pp. 143–64.

"General Economic Equilibrium: Purpose, Analytic Techniques, Collective Choice." In *Les Prix Nobel en 1972*. Stockholm: The Nobel Foundation, pp. 206–31. Reprinted in *American Economic Review* 64 (1973b): 253–72.

"Limited Knowledge and Economic Analysis." *American Economic Review*, 64 (1974a), 1–10. Reprinted in Arrow, *Collected Papers* (1984), vol. 4, pp. 153–66.

*The Limits of Organization.* New York: W. W. Norton, 1974b.

*Collected Papers of Kenneth J. Arrow.* 6 vols. Cambridge, Ma.: Harvard University Press, 1983–85.

"Kenneth J. Arrow." In *Lives of the Laureates* edited by William Breit and Roger W. Spencer, pp. 43–58. Cambridge, Ma.: MIT Press, 1986.

Arrow, Kenneth J., and Debreu, Gerard. "Existence of an Equilibrium for a Competitive Economy." *Econometrica* 20 (1954), 265–90.

Arrow, Kenneth J., and Hahn, Frank H. *General Competitive Analysis.* San Francisco: Holden-Day, 1971.

## OTHER WORKS

Debreu, Gerard. "The Coefficient of Resource Utilization." *Econometrica* 19 (1951), 273–92.

Feiwel, George R., ed. *Arrow and the Foundations of the Theory of Economic Policy.* London: Macmillan, 1987.

Heller, Walter P., Starr, Ross M., and Starrett, David A. *Social Choice and Public Decision Making: Essays in Honor of Kenneth J. Arrow.* 3 vols. New York: Cambridge University Press, 1986.

Koopmans, T. C. "Analysis of Production as an Efficient Combination of Activities." In *Activity Analysis of Allocation and Production*, edited by T. C. Koopmans, ch. 3., New York: Wiley, 1951.

# JAMES MCGILL BUCHANAN  1986

The Royal Swedish Academy of Sciences cited James McGill Buchanan's "development of the contractual and constitutional bases for the theory of economic and political decision-making" in awarding him the 1986 Nobel Memorial Prize in Economic Sciences. In so doing, the academy recognized an expanding interdisciplinary school of thought known as "public-choice theory." An integration of economics and political science, the theory ascribes to the public sector the basic economic axiom which economists have traditionally used to describe the private sector—the self-interest of the individual decision maker. However, while private individuals acting in their own self-interest are assumed to promote a greater good, the same motivation on the part of elected officials and bureaucrats is assumed to generate harmful societal effects. Thus, in order to improve the functioning of government, Buchanan has further developed a theory of constitutions which emphasizes the importance of rules in generating desirable or undesirable economic policy choices.

# Evolution of a Conservative

Born in 1919, the grandson of a populist governor of Tennessee, James Buchanan graduated from Middle Tennessee State Teachers' College and completed a year of graduate work at the University of Tennessee. He would have studied statistics at Columbia University had he not been drafted into the Navy in 1941. At officer training school in New York, he sensed the eastern establishment's discrimination against outsiders and, following his discharge in 1945, shunned Columbia, opting instead for the University of Chicago, where he received his Ph.D. in 1948.

As described in his autobiographical work, "Better Than Plowing" (*Banca Nazionale del Lavoro Quarterly Review*, 1986), Buchanan was quickly converted from "libertarian socialist" to "zealous advocate of the market" upon his enroll-

ment at Chicago in Frank Knight's course in price theory. An appreciation of the work of Knut Wicksell was the result of casual perusal of the stacks of Harper Library, which occurred coincidentally just after he had completed his German-language examination. In a dissertation Buchanan was later partly to translate from German to English as "A New Principle of Just Taxation" (in *Classics in the Theory of Public Finance*, 1958), Wicksell in 1896 had argued for the rule of unanimity in public expenditure and taxation decisions as the only means of acknowledging individual preferences and for the need to proscribe the behavior of public officials, who do not act as "benevolent despots," through rule changes.

Knight and Wicksell are the acknowledged intellectual forebears of Buchanan, and the portraits of both hang in his office. Knight provided the ideological framework and Wicksell the specific ideas for much of Buchanan's work. Research during a year in Italy on a Fulbright grant in 1955–56 further cemented his notion of government as a less than ideal institution.

With ideas hammered out during the Italian year from reading the works of Maffeo Pantaleoni, Antonio de Viti de Marco, and others, Buchanan began work on his first singly authored book, *Public Principles of Public Debt* (1958). The book generated considerable controversy, as it attacked what Buchanan labeled the "new orthodoxy" in favor of "vulgar theory." The issue concerned who holds the primary burden of an internally held public debt. While the new orthodoxy maintains that the creation of internally held public debt does not constitute a burden to future generations but rather that the repayment of debt is simply a transfer from taxpayers to bondholders, the vulgar opinion, which Buchanan upholds, is that future taxpayers do bear a burden which is not offset by the interest payments to government bondholders. Buchanan succinctly defended his position in 1986, arguing that "National economies, as such, cannot enjoy gains or suffer losses. The fact that making guns 'uses up' resources in years of war tells us nothing about *who* must pay for those guns, and *when*. The whole macroaggregation exercise that had captured the attention of post-Keynesian economists was called into question." Indeed, Buchanan's insistence on the individual (the *who*) as the basis of any analysis has become the hallmark of his work.

## Public-Choice Theory

The seminal work in public-choice theory was *The Calculus of Consent: Logical Foundations of Constitutional Democracy* (1962), coauthored with Gordon Tullock. The purpose of the book was to set out a theory of collective choice based on rational, individual, informed, utility-maximizing behavior—an approach described by the authors as methodologically individualistic—that would generate a set of predictions concerning the structural characteristics of group decisions. The basic question they

sought to answer was how an individual chooses among rules of governance (this stage is referred to as the constitutional stage) given that he or she does not know whether certain decisions or policies of the government once in place will promote or reduce personal welfare. In deciding upon which rule to favor, the individual weighs the costs of having an action pass that would lower individual utility against the costs of decision making. The costs of the former are assumed to decrease as the number of votes required for passage increases, while the costs of the latter are assumed to increase with the number of votes required for approval. The costs of decision making include the opportunity cost of a preferred action failing. Each individual will favor the voting rule that minimizes the sum of these costs. Since, at the constitutional stage, each individual operates under a "veil of uncertainty," agreement on a voting rule is possible.

Several interesting implications arise from this model. First of all, the analysis implies that having constitutions is rational. Secondly, a simple majority rule is but one of many possible rules, and this rule may not be optimal for the individual. Thirdly, different decision-making rules may be adopted for different kinds of government activities. According to the authors:

In our construction, therefore, there is no necessary inconsistency implied in the adoption of, say, simple majority rule for the making of certain everyday decisions for the group with respect to those activities that have been explicitly collectivized, and the insistence on unanimity of consensus on changes in the fundamental organization rules. The organizing principle or theme of our whole construction is the concentration on the individual calculus, and it is easy to see that both the unanimity rule at the constitutional level and other less-than-unanimity rules at the operational level of decisions may be based directly on this calculus. (*The Calculus of Consent*, 1962, pp. 251–52)

In general, the greater the economic importance of collective action and the higher the potential costs to the individual, the more restrictive the appropriate voting rule. Finally, it is argued that support for public versus private-sector activities rests on whether or not the voting rule which exists is such that the expected cost of collective action is less than the cost of private action.

The model predicts that societies will operate under more restrictive voting rules for constitutional changes than for daily operational decisions. In this context, the authors argue, the American system of checks and balances appears quite reasonable, since it may be seen as a proxy for a restrictive voting rule. The model also predicts advocacy of special-interest legislation by groups of individuals who will benefit from that legislation. Taken in its entirety, the book becomes a call to reexamine basic political and governmental decision-making processes and rules.

These ideas evolved further in *The Limits of Liberty: Between*

*Anarchy and Leviathan* (1975) and in *The Reason of Rules: Constitution Political Economy* (1985), coauthored with Geoffrey Brennan. *The Limits to Liberty* reflected Buchanan's growing pessimism in the 1960s concerning the ability of government to implement the preferences of individuals. As he later explained:

> I lost my 'faith' in the effectiveness of government as I observed the explosive take-off in spending rates and new programs, engineered by self-interested political agents and seemingly divorced from the interests of citizens. At the same time, I observed what seemed to me to be a failure of the institutional structure, at all levels, to respond effectively to mounting behavioral disorder. The United States government seemed to take on aspects of an agent-driven Leviathan simultaneously with the emergence of anarchy in civil society. ("*Better Than Plowing,*" p. 369).

The same pessimism is also reflected in *Academia in Anarchy: An Economic Diagnosis* (1970), coauthored with Nicos E. Devletoglou. The authors argued that the anarchy (that is, campus unrest) of the universities in the late 1960s was the result of an institutional establishment in which the students (consumers) do not buy, the faculty (producers) do not sell, and the owners (taxpayers) do not control.

*The Limits of Liberty* (1975) is concerned with the construction of a contractarian theory of the state and with forces which tend to make the state grow beyond its legitimate bounds. In Buchanan's view, the role of the state is to enforce rights which were mutually agreed upon by free persons in a state of nature, that is, of anarchy. Political institutions protect the contractual agreement and provide the public goods that individuals want. However, these institutions operate through real people who, acting in their own self-interest, will try to go beyond original intent in providing public goods. Politicians, as well as employees of the government, that is, bureaucrats, will favor government expansion. In essence, these individuals begin to violate the intent of the social contract.

*The Reason of Rules* (1985) is a detailed analysis of rules. It provides a defense of a constitutional or rules-oriented approach to promote justice, defined to be nonviolation of agreed-on rules. The book addresses the question of whether or not constitutional changes are possible in a democracy, since some individuals stand to lose from any rule change. The conclusion that change is possible rests on Buchanan's ever-present distinction between in-period, or postconstitutional, choice, which occurs under an existing set of rules, and constitutional choice, which refers to the setting up of the rules themselves. Constitutional choice has been likened to choosing the rules for playing a game, while post-constitutional choice involves choosing a strategy for playing a game under a given set of rules. To the extent that one's position in postconstitutional society is uncertain, thereby lowering the individual's assessment of the cost of collective action, and to the extent that

there exists a set of accepted norms of the community, agreement on changing the rules, they argue, may be possible.

*Democracy in Deficit: The Political Legacy of Lord Keynes* (1978), coauthored with Richard E. Wagner, provides an example of how public-choice theory can be applied. The authors argue that in the pre-Keynesian era, the analogy between public and private finance was widely accepted, and thus the notion that public spending was to be accompanied by taxation served as an effective fiscal constitution to restrain the natural spending proclivities of elected officials concerned about reelection. This essentially moral restraint ended with the acceptance of Keynesian ideas, and its absence ushered in a prolonged period of public deficits. In this work, he argues that "Keynesian economics has turned the politicians loose; it has destroyed the effective constraint on politicians' ordinary appetites. Armed with the Keynesian message, politicians can spend and spend without the apparent necessity to tax" (p. 4).

Thus, a balanced-budget amendment is necessary to provide an effective constraint on budgetary excesses. It is only through a change in the constitutional framework, and the more stringent voting rule for repeal that is required, that fiscal responsibility and long-term economic health can be restored:

We do not suggest that we relinquish political and public control of our affairs, but only that politicians be placed once again in an effective constitutional framework in which budgetary manipulation for purposes of enhancing short-run political survival is more tightly restrained, thereby giving fuller scope to the working of the long-term forces that are so necessary for the smooth functioning of our economic order. Just as an alcoholic might embrace Alcoholics Anonymous, so might a nation drunk on deficits and gorged with government embrace a balanced budget and monetary stability. (p. 159)

Buchanan has also sought empirical evidence to support his theories. In "The Expanding Public Sector: Wagner Squared," in *Public Choice* (1977) written with Gordon Tullock, he maintained that the data suggest a public sector which is out of control in the literal sense of the term. They argued that the rise in salary of government employees as compared to nongovernment employees could only be explained by the political power of bureaucrats who exert pressure and ultimately vote according to their own self-interest.

Buchanan's alarm about the post-World War II growth of the public sector was further elaborated on in "Why Does Government Grow?" In this introductory essay to an edited volume entitled *Budgets and Bureaucrats* (1977), by Thomas E. Borcherding, he cites empirical evidence, based primarily on Borcherding's "The Sources of Growth of Public Expenditures in the United States, 1902–1970" (*Budgets and Bureaucrats*), to show that government growth has been far in excess, perhaps by one-third, of what

can be considered to be the natural result of changes in such factors as prices, income, and population.

The remaining growth in government spending, he argues, must be the result of what he calls a nondemocratic model of politics, that is, a model in which decisions made by the government do not correspond to those desired by the citizens for whom spending programs are allegedly undertaken. Some of the excess is attributed to fiscal illusion, an inaccurate perception of the amount of taxes paid and the cost of government services received. However, the main culprits are the self-interested politicians and bureaucrats and the processes that they have created to obscure their actual activities. For example, the cost of displacement of political incumbents is high. Moreover, those who benefit from spending programs tend to be identifiable groups, whereas those who would benefit from less government spending are more amorphous. A particular group of voters who stand to gain from public spending are bureaucrats themselves. These governmental employees recognize that they are more likely to receive higher salaries and more frequent promotions in a growing government as compared to a stagnant or shrinking one. Again, Buchanan's solution to lessening the power of entrenched bureaucracy is to seek reform at the constitutional level.

*Toward a Theory of the Rent-Seeking Society* (1980), coedited with Robert D. Tollison and Gordon Tullock, suggests yet another source of wasteful expenditure that arises when governments can grant favors to special interests. While the economic waste of government-granted monopoly, tariffs, and the like has been widely recognized and addressed by others, the papers in this volume refer to the waste of resources by those seeking favors from the government. That is, in trying to influence government decisions in their favor, private individuals and firms must reallocate resources away from productive activities and towards lobbying government officials. This type of behavior grows along with the growth of government itself, since greater government budgets imply greater potential gains. In *The Power to Tax: Analytical Foundations of a Fiscal Constitution* (1980), coauthored with Geoffrey Brennan, government is described as a "revenue-maximising Leviathan."

Recognition by individual citizens of the need to change the rules so as to reduce the role of government was evidenced, Buchanan argued in a speech following the announcement of the Nobel Prize, by the election of Ronald Reagan. However, the focus of his administration on specific agenda items, rather than on structural reform of political institutions—that is, on changing the rules of the political game—severely curtailed any long-term impact on society.

## Career and Critics

In addition to research related directly to public-choice theory, Buchanan has also researched areas more traditionally covered in public finance. Frequently cited are his paper with W. C. Stubblebine "Externality" (1962) and his paper "An Economic Theory of Clubs" (1965). Singly authored books include *The Demand and Supply of Public Goods* (1968) and *Cost and Choice: An Inquiry in Economic Theory* (1969). In all, Buchanan has authored more than 20 books and 300 articles.

Most of Buchanan's career has been spent at three universities in Virginia. Following brief stints at the University of Tennessee from 1948–51 and at Florida State University from 1951–56, Buchanan spent twelve years at the University of Virginia. There he established, with Warren Nutter, and directed from 1958–69, the Thomas Jefferson Center for Political Economy. In 1963, he and Gordon Tullock founded the Public Choice Society, which has over 1,500 members today. From 1969–83, Buchanan was the University Distinguished Professor at Virginia Polytechnic Institute. There, he, along with Tullock and Charles Goetz, founded the Center for Study of Public Choice that he says "became, for a period in the 1970's and early 1980's, an international haven for research scholars who sought some exposure to the blossoming new subdiscipline of public choice" (*"Better Than Plowing,"* 1986, p. 373). In 1983, the center moved to George Mason University. Buchanan is currently the general director of the center and holds the title of Holbert L. Harris University Professor.

Buchanan has received two honorary doctorates, from the University of Giessen in 1982 and from the University of Zurich in 1984. He has been both an adjunct scholar of the American Enterprise Institute and a fellow of the American Academy of Arts and Sciences since 1976. Since 1983 he has been a distinguished fellow of the American Economic Association. He served as president of the Southern Economic Association in 1963, of the Western Economic Association during 1983–84, and of the Mt. Pelerin Society from 1984–86. He was also vice-president of the American Economic Association in 1971.

Just as Buchanan's works are controversial, so is opinion divided concerning the man himself. Married and childless, Buchanan is described by some colleagues as austere and cold. They say that he is intimidating to students and that he seems driven to prove that he belongs on the academic forefront. Others argue that he is an inspiration—a person of unbounding energy who encourages critical thinking and raises the performance level of those around him.

By his own admission, Buchanan has always been somewhat of an outsider in the economics profession. "I have faced a sometimes lonely and mostly losing battle of ideas for some thirty years now in efforts to bring academic economists' opinions into line with those of the man of the street, and economists are an intellectually stubborn lot," he told the *New York Times* (October 17, 1986).

His selection as Nobel Prize winner, while praised by many, did generate considerable controversy. His writings provide the intellectual underpinnings for the conservative movement in its efforts to reduce the size and scope of government activities. His critics question the precision of his polemically argued analysis. One newspaper columnist likened his writings to those of political columnists rather than academicians.

At a more academic level, Scott Gordon, in reviewing *The Limits of Liberty* (1976), has argued that according to Buchanan's model of how a new social contract is renegotiated, the changes in social and political mores of the 1960's could be viewed as legitimate attempts to revise the social contract by individuals who were not involved in its initial formation. Moreover, response by those in power to appease the reformers could also be viewed as rational and not as feeding violence with concessions, as Buchanan argued in *Academia in Anarchy* (1970). Why then, Gordon asks, does Buchanan view such events as wholly bad? Why are they seen as only the embodiment of a decline in respect for legitimate practice and a dissipation of the law? It would appear that Buchanan must have in mind a preferred type of social contract.

Similarly, D. E. Moggridge, in his review of *Democracy in Deficit*, responded to Buchanan's call for two constitutional amendments—one to balance the federal budget except in times of national emergency and the other to impose a monetary rule on the Federal Reserve Bank. He argued that it did not seem clear to him why the dynamics or logic of the theory of choice used would lead voters or politicians willingly to choose the constraints implied by the constitutional proposals, even if they understood and accepted the economic doctrines implied, such as the natural-rate hypothesis, monetarism, and other parts of the authors' package of reform. Moreover, the actions would be especially difficult to accomplish given the very arduous transition period, a point accepted by the authors. Thus, he queried, is not the authors' reform program just another proposal from wise men that they would decry if derived by so-called Keynesians? And why is the authors' program the only one open to democrats?

In addition, fellow conservative Nobel Prize winner George J. Stigler in a review of *The Theory of Public Choice: Political Applications of Economics* (1972), a collection of essays edited by Buchanan and Robert Tollison, has criticized the failure of the public-choice school to search for empirical tests of its theories. A similar comment was made by Richard Zeckhauser in his review of *Toward a Theory of the Rent-Seeking Society* (1981). Zeckhauser argued that instead of empirical work to test the assumption that rents are wasted, the book is instead a collection of papers that produce results by invoking the assumption.

Nonetheless, Buchanan can claim many loyal followers, and his ideas have had impact on both academic and political circles. Economists must now take into account whether market failures can be cured by an imperfect government and whether politicians and bureaucrats will be motivated to respond productively. Will the "cure" by government be worse than the disease? Political scientists are increasingly using the approach of public-choice theory to explain the behavior of government officials. At the political level, the movements towards deregulation and towards balancing the budget can at least in part be traced to the tireless efforts of James McGill Buchanan.

LIBBY RITTENBERG

# Selected Bibliography

## WORKS BY BUCHANAN

*Public Principles of Public Debt.* Homewood, Il: Richard D. Irwin, 1958.

"A New Principle of Just Taxation" (translation of Knut Wicksell, *Finanztheoretische Untersuchungen*). In *Classics in the Theory of Public Finance*, edited by R. S. Musgrave and A. T. Peacock, pp. 72–118. London: Macmillan, 1958.

"An Economic Theory of Clubs." *Economica* 32 (1965): 1–14.

*Demand and Supply of Public Goods.* Chicago: Rand McNally, 1968.

*Cost and Choice: An Inquiry in Economic Theory.* Chicago: Markham, 1969.

*The Limits of Liberty: Between Anarchy and Leviathan.* Chicago: University of Chicago Press, 1975.

"Why Does Government Grow?" In *Budgets and Bureaucrats: The Sources of Government Growth*, edited by Thomas E. Borcherding, pp. 3–18. Durham, N. C.: Duke University Press, 1977.

"Quest for a Tempered Utopia." *Wall Street Journal* (November 14, 1986), p. 26.

"Better Than Plowing." *Banca Nazionale del Lavoro Quarterly Review* 159 (1986), 359–75.

Buchanan, James McGill, and Brennan, Geoffrey. *The Power to Tax: Analytical Foundations of a Fiscal Constitution.* New York: Cambridge University Press, 1980.

———. *The Reason of Rules.* Cambridge, England: Cambridge University Press, 1985.

Buchanan, James McGill, and Devletoglou, Nicos E. *Academia in Anarchy: An Economic Diagnosis.* New York: Basic Books, 1970.

Buchanan, James McGill, and Stubblebine, W. C. "Externality." *Economica* 29 (1962), 371–84.

Buchanan, James McGill, and Tollison, Robert, eds. *Theory of Public Choice: Political Applications of Economics.* Ann Arbor: University of Michigan Press, 1972.

Buchanan, James McGill, Tollison, Robert, and Tullock, Gordon, eds. *Toward a Theory of the Rent-Seeking Society.* College Station: Texas A&M University Press, 1980.

Buchanan, James McGill, and Tullock, Gordon. *The Calculus of Consent: Logical Foundations of Constitutional Democracy.* Ann Arbor: University of Michigan Press, 1962.

———. "The Expanding Public Sector: Wagner Squared." *Public Choice* 31 (Fall 1977), 147–50.

Buchanan, James McGill, and Wagner, Richard E. *Democracy in Deficit: The Political Legacy of Lord Keynes.* New York: Academic Press, 1978.

## OTHER WORKS

Borcherding, Thomas E. "The Sources of Growth of Public Expenditures in the United States, 1902–70." In *Budgets and Bureaucrats: The Sources of Government Growth,* Thomas E. Borcherding, pp. 45–70. Durham, N.C.: Duke University Press, 1977.

Gordon, Scott. "The New Contractarians." *Journal of Political Economy* 84 (June 1976): 573–89.

Hershey, Robert D., Jr. "An Austere Scholar: James McGill Buchanan." *New York Times* (October 17, 1986), p. D1.

Moggridge, D. E. "Review of *Democracy in Deficit: The Political Legacy of Lord Keynes.*" *Journal of Economic Literature* 16 (March 1978): 106–07.

Rowen, Hobart. "Discreetly Lifted Eyebrows over Buchanan's Nobel Prize." *Washington Post* (October 26, 1986), p. D1.

Stigler, George J. "Proof of the Pudding?" *National Review* 24 (November 10, 1972): 1257–58.

Zeckhauser, Richard. "Review of *Toward a Theory of The Rent-Seeking Society.*" *Journal of Political Economy* 90 (December 1982): 1303–06.

# GERARD DEBREU *1983*

Gerard Debreu became the twenty-first scholar to receive the Nobel Prize in Economic Sciences in 1983 for the introduction of new analytical methods in economic theory and for a thorough reformulation of the general economic equilibrium.

## Background and Career

He was born in Calais, France, on July 4, 1921. His father, Camille Debreu, was a partner with his father-in-law in the business of lace manufacturing, which at the time was of great importance in Calais. The crash of 1929 and a revolution in feminine fashion, particularly a new preference for shorter and more simple dresses, created difficulties for lace manufacturers. His mother, Fernande (née Decharne), was a housewife. His paternal grandfather, who died in the early 1940s, had created a manufacturing plant in the small town of Marquise between Calais and Boulogne. Debreu's parents died when he was fairly young, leaving him free to decide his course of study in high school and later in college.

Debreu did all of his elementary and high school studies in Calais College. In France, college is a pre-university establishment which prepares students for entrance to the universities. Influenced by his excellent high school physics teacher, Debreu considered becoming a physicist. In 1939, he had completed his secondary studies and had gone through the French baccalauréate while preparing for the entrance examination to one of the Grandes Écoles in Paris. In the summer of that year, however the Second World War began, and instead of going to Paris, as originally planned, he studied mathematics at Ambert and Grenoble.

In the summer of 1941 he was admitted to the prestigious École Normale Supérieure, where he was a student until 1944. In an interview with this author he describes his experience there as follows:

Those three years were an extraordinary experience in many ways. The small size of each entering class (about twenty in the sciences, and thirty in the humanities at the time) and the strict admission procedures helped to create a superheated intellectual atmosphere. The dark outside world of Paris under German occupation also exerted a strong containing pressure. . . . Of all the teachers I had during that period, Cartan was the most influential. Indirectly, N. Bourbaki also fashioned my mathematical taste.

Debreu was about to graduate from the École Normale Supérieure by taking the Agrégation de Mathématiques in the spring of 1944, but D-Day intervened, and the examination was postponed until the end of 1945. Meanwhile, he enlisted in the French Army and was sent to Cherchell, Algeria, to attend officers' school. Later he served in the French occupational forces in Germany until the end of July 1945. Eventually, at the end of 1945 and the beginning of 1946 he took his degree and began graduate studies in Paris. But, although he admired the Bourbaki version of mathematics, which had become dominant in France, he was not willing to devote his entire professional life to such an extremely abstract form of study. His search for an intellectually appealing field in which he could do applied work led him to economics. He had become interested in the mathematical theory of general economic equilibrium when he read _La recherche d'une discipline économique_, by Maurice Allais, in 1943. His passion for economics was further enhanced by a feeling that economics could play an important role in the reconstruction of Europe after World War II. Debreu's work in economics is considered to be highly abstract and mathematical by many nonmathematical economists. Yet, Debreu considers himself an economist. Although he has used advanced mathematics in his economic work, all of the mathematical problems he has solved have been motivated by economics. Many mathematicians consider him one of their own. In fact, he has a joint appointment in the mathematics and economics departments at the University of California at Berkeley, where he currently teaches.

Debreu joined the Centre National de la Recherche Scientifique as a researcher, staying for two-and-one-half years. In 1948 he attended the Salzburg Seminar in American Studies under the instruction of such figures in economics as Wassily Leontief. In the same year he was nominated by Allais for a scholarship from the Rockefeller Foundation. (Marcel Boiteux, who later became the director of Electricité de France, lost this nomination to Debreu through a coin toss.) The Rockefeller Fellowship gave him the opportunity to spend the period 1948–50 in the United States, Norway, and Sweden, visiting Harvard University, the University of California at Berkeley, the University of Chicago, Columbia University, the University of Oslo in Norway, and the University of Uppsala in Sweden. At the time, Ragnar Frisch was the most prominent economic theorist in Scandinavia, and the Stockholm school had a high reputation in Sweden. It was there that Debreu met several prominent figures in economics such as Erik Lindahl and Erik Lundberg. These visits and contacts brought him completely up to date with new frontiers in economics.

During Debreu's visit to the University of Chicago, the Cowles Commission offered him a position as an economics research associate. He considered the offer very attractive, as it provided him with the opportunity to pursue his interest in mathematical economics, something that was not easily attainable in France at the time. A professor in a French department of law and economics needed a degree in economics, yet Debreu's degree was in mathematics. The Cowles Commission was just the right vehicle for him to devote his time and exceptional talent

to research in mathematical economics. As he described it to this
author:

> The Cowles Commission in the early
> fifties proved itself to be more than I
> had hoped for. It seemed to be a focal
> point for mathematical economics
> where every recent development was
> discussed. The small research staff in-
> teracted in weekly meetings, in bi-
> weekly seminars, and in numerous
> conversations. In that exceptionally
> supportive environment, in which al-
> most all my time was devoted to re-
> search, my work on Pareto optima,
> on the existence of a general econom-
> ics equilibrium, and on utility theory
> made quick progress.

While with the Cowles Commission, he was introduced to Kenneth
J. Arrow by Tjalling Koopmans,
who was the director of research.
Arrow was at Stanford University at
the time and, like Debreu, was
working on the problem of the existence of a general economic equilibrium. The Debreu and Arrow association worked extremely well and
resulted in many joint publications,
such as the one on the existence
problem, published in 1954.

In the summer and the fall of
1953, during Debreu's last year at
Chicago, he took a six-month leave,
which he spent in France at the Electricité de France. There he studied a
problem of uncertainty involving
the amount of water in the utility's
hydroelectric-plant reservoirs. Influenced by his experience in Paris, and
by an article on contingent commodities written by Arrow, he set
the groundwork for the chapter on
economic uncertainty in his classic

work, *Theory of Value: An Axiomatic Analysis of Economic Equilibrium* (1959). At this time Debreu
was seriously thinking about going
back to France. His sensitive, peace-
loving nature was deeply disturbed
by the social events in the United
States during the McCarthy era. But
his devotion to pure scientific research and his fascination with the
intellectual community which existed at the Cowles Commission
overwhelmed his disappointment at
the state of democracy in the United
States at the time. He decided to
stay in the United States and moved
to Yale University in 1955 with the
Cowles Commission, which became
The Cowles Foundation. While at
Yale, he completed *Theory of Value*,
which presented an axiomatic analysis of the theory of a general economic equilibrium. The first version
of this classic work was presented as
his doctoral dissertation at the University of Paris in 1956.

The thrill of scientific insight and
discovery always motivated Debreu
to move from one environment to
another. He left his native country
in pursuit of his interest in mathematical economics, and he was able
to use his exceptional talent most
fruitfully in different scientific com-
munities in the United States. He is
very conscious of the value of these
opportunities, as expressed in his
statement to the Committee on
Science and Technology of the U.S.
House of Representatives on March
8, 1984:

> The environment provided for scien-
> tific work by our universities, private
> foundations, corporations, govern-

ment agencies, and especially the National Science Foundation, has been superb during the greater part of the last half-century. And I vividly recall the deep impression that it made on me at the time I discovered it in 1949 as a Rockefeller Fellow making a one-year visit to the United States.

He stayed at Yale until 1960, investigating several problems on the theory of cardinal utility. The following year was spent at the Center for Advanced Study in the Behavioral Sciences in Stanford, California, where his entire time was devoted to a complex proof of a general theorem on the existence problem. That is, whether there exists a unique set of prices which clear all markets simultaneously. While he was at the center, Berkeley offered him an attractive job, which led to his resignation from Yale. The combination of Arrow, Herbert Scarf, and many other prominent figures at nearby Stanford as well as the scientifically strong opportunity presented by Berkeley was an offer he could not refuse.

Debreu spent his last semester at Yale in the fall of 1961 working on the core of an economy, which later resulted in a joint paper with Scarf in 1963. In January, 1962, he became a professor of economics at Berkeley, where he has remained ever since, and also was made a professor of mathematics in July 1975. Beginning in the fall of 1968 he took several long leaves, which were spent lecturing and conducting research at many distinguished foreign and domestic universities and research centers. He also received

many honorary doctoral degrees and participated in several prestigious professional organizations and journals as a distinguished member, fellow, officer, and member of editorial boards. To mention only a few of his honors, he was a member of Econometric Society (1964–72) and later a member of its executive committee (1969–72, 1980–82) as well as its vice president and its president (1969–71). He became a member of the National Academy of Sciences in 1977, and during the period from 1982 to 1985 he was the chairman of its section of economic sciences. He has been a fellow of the American Economic Association since 1982, and a fellow of the American Association for the Advancement of Science since 1984. In 1970 he became a fellow of the American Academy of Arts and Sciences. In addition to the Nobel Memorial Prize in Economics, which was awarded to him in 1983, he received the Senior U.S. Scientist Award of the Alexander Von Humboldt Foundation, The University of Bonn (1977), and was made a chevalier of the Legion of Honor in 1976. In addition to the latter award, his native country demonstrated its high regard for this scholar by honoring him as foreign associate of the French Academy of Sciences and commander of the National Order of Merit in 1984. Debreu has also served as a member of the editorial boards of the *Journal of Economic Theory* (since 1972) and the *SIAM Journal on Applied Mathematics* (1976–79), and as a member of advisory board of the *Journal of Mathematical Economics* (since 1974). He has received honorary degrees in science from universities such as the University of Bonn (1977), The University of Lausanne (1980), Northwestern University (1981), and the University of Social Sciences of Toulouse (1983). His trips abroad include visits to the Center for Operations Research and Econometrics at the University of Louvain as a Guggenheim fellow and visiting professor (1968–69, 1971–72); as an overseas fellow, Churchill College, Cambridge University, (1972); as visiting professor, University of Canterbury, Christchurch, New Zealand (1973, 1987); and research associate, CEPREMSP, Paris (1980).

# Main Contributions to Economics

Perhaps Debreu's major professional achievement is his contribution to the theory of general economic equilibrium. A full appreciation of his contribution requires a brief historical review of the general equilibrium literature, which is at the heart of issues raised in political economy.

The founding father of this literature was the eighteenth-century classical economist Adam Smith. The central issue is whether a decentralized market economy without any formal or comprehensive economic planning can achieve equilibrium—that is, achieve balance of all forces, especially supply and demand. The economic state of a capitalist economy at any moment is determined by the interaction of millions of agents (actors) in the market. These agents are drawn from two distinct groups, house-

holds (consumers) and firms (producers). Motivated by self-interest, consumers decide how many units of different goods and services to demand and how many units of labor to supply. Similarly, producers make production decisions based on profit maximization.

At first it may seem that such an economic system is doomed to face chaos and an eventual decay and demise. The radical social scientists have argued that in the absence of central planning, capitalism lacks the harmony needed for its growth and survival. But Adam Smith, in his pioneering, work, *The Wealth of Nations* (1776), argued quite delicately that all of these decentralized decisions will reach a state of equilibrium through the so-called "invisible hand," which, according to Smith, allows persons, while seeking their self-interest, to achieve good for all. This great insight convinced him and many others of the existence of an equilibrium without using any mathematical tools. However, Smith's explanation lacked any mechanism as to how the theory could actually work.

The first mathematical formulation of the theory of a general economic equilibrium was by Léon Walras in 1874. In *The Elements of Pure Political Economics*, Walras presents a system of simultaneous equations that consists of many nonlinear equations, each representing either supply or demand for each commodity in the economy. Economic decision making requires choosing different quantities of each product, either as a supplier or as a demander, based on relative prices.

In the Walras exposition, the existence of an equilibrium is assumed, based on the belief that the equality of the number of equations and unknowns guarantees a solution to the simultaneous-equation problem. The nonlinearity of the system and the possibility of its yielding meaningless negative prices led Walras to develop a process of successive approximations in search of relative prices at equilibrium. Later Francis Y. Edgeworth and Vilfredo Pareto showed the connection between competitive equilibrium and optimal allocation of resources. The existence problem was followed by the question of the uniqueness of a competitive equilibrium, for example, whether the competitive system achieves a unique set of equilibrium prices or if there are multiple equilibria. A simplified version of the Walras system was discussed by Gustav Cassel in 1924, but, similar to the previous work, it suffers from a naive way of counting the number of equations and unknowns.

Abraham Wald in 1934 and 1935 demonstrated the existence of a competitive equilibrium in alternative models. The rigorous, complex, and sophisticated nature of his mathematical paper discouraged further research in that area until John Von Neumann's theory of games came to the rescue. Mathematical tools used in his games theory were applied to the area of general equilibrium. Specifically, Von Neumann showed the existence of equilibrium in two-person zero-sum games, using L.E.G. Brouwer's fixed-point theorem in topology. All of these developments in the literature were praised for their novel and elegant use of sophisticated mathematical tools, but they lacked simplicity and generality. For example, in the games-theory models, the competitive equilibrium was included as a special case under varying notions of equilibrium.

In 1953, Debreu presented a paper, "A Social Equilibrium Existence Theorem," which utilized some of the most general applications of the fixed-point theorem in addressing the existence problem. His generalization of the concept of Nash equilibrium and his classification of the conditions needed to achieve social equilibrium was a major step toward his subsequent work with Arrow in 1954, which provided the existence proof for a competitive economy.

Debreu's reformulation of the general economic equilibrium is regarded as a highly abstract exposition of the problem by traditional economists, but economists with some training in modern mathematics find it the most general, simple, and honest way of stating his assumptions in the model. This is due to his approach, which is the axiomatization of economic theory. The axiomatic method was applied to economic problems by authors such as Wald, Von Neumann, and many others, but no one had used it as systematically and forcefully as Debreu did in *Theory of Value*. He describes the axiomatization of economic theory in his November 1986, article in *Econometrica* in these words:

An axiomatized theory first selects its primitive concepts and represents each one of them by a mathematical object. For instance the consumption of a consumer, his set of possible consumptions, and his preferences are represented by a point in the commodity space, a subset of the commodity space, and a binary relation in that subset. Next assumptions on the objects representing the primitive concepts are "specified," and consequences are mathematically derived from them. The economic interpretation of the theorems so obtained is the last step of the analysis. According to this schema, an axiomatized theory has a mathematical form that is completely separated from its economic content. If one removes the economic interpretation of the primitive concepts, of the assumptions, and of the conclusions of the model, its bare mathematical structure must still stand. (p. 1265)

Debreu's insistence on the use of an axiomatic approach stems from the fact that it permits him to pursue his scientific inquiry into economic problems by way of the purely objective laws of mathematics. This approach completely divorces the scientifically derived results and conclusions from the economic interpretations. Critics of this method assert that the modern economic theorists do not address the problems of the real world and are preoccupied with problems of limited technical nature. Debreu is well aware of these criticisms and admits that modern theorists only take small steps, one at a time, as part of a scientific work which would ultimately lead the way to finding solutions to the more pressing issues of the time.

Regardless of these criticisms, the benefits of the axiomatization of economic theory reach far beyond its disadvantages. For one, it is ideologically neutral, in the sense that once mathematical conclusions are reached, one can try to find the relevance of the assumptions in different social, economic, and political environments. It also enables other researchers to build upon the explicit assumptions and conclusions of a particular model with no confusion about the applicability of assumptions of one model to another. For instance, in Debreu's *Theory of Value*, a commodity is a primitive concept that includes its physical characteristics and location in space and time. The generality and simplicity of this concept permit one to cover phenomena such as risk, transportation, and interest. In fact, Arrow's idea of contingent commodities is simply a new interpretation of the concept of commodity as selected by Debreu. Werner Hildenbrand, in his excellent introduction to *Mathematical Economics: Twenty Papers of Gerard Debreu* (1983) highlights the importance of Debreu's concept of a commodity. He writes:

The analysis of efficient allocation of economic resources would be of little relevance to the actual world if it were not applicable to situations where the commodities are sharply defined, that is to say, in which a commodity is defined by its physical characteristics as well as by the time, location, and possibly by the state of the world of its availability. (p. 12)

Debreu became interested in the problem of the existence of a general economic equilibrium in the 1940s, when he read the works of Allais and Walras. He became aware of Von Neumann's model of growth, J. F. Nash's paper of 1950, and Shizuo Kakutani's fixed-point theorem while he was at the Cowles Foundation in 1950. He learned of Konel McKenzie's trade model of general equilibrium at the 1952 meeting of the American Economic Association in Chicago. He describes the work of Von Neumann, which resulted in Kakutani's fixed-point theorem, as crucial for the proof of existence.

The fixed-point theorem argues that any continuous mapping of a closed, bounded, and convex set in euclidean space maps at least one point into itself. A simple way of explaining this important concept from topology seems an awkward task. A set is closed if it contains its boundaries, and it is bounded if it has finite dimensions. Convexity means that there are no holes in the set. For example, any line drawn between two points in the set contains points which are also in the set. In a two-dimensional euclidean space, any bounded, closed, and convex set will cross the diagonal at at least one point. This fixed point proves the existence of equilibrium in a market economy. The uniqueness of this equilibrium has been studied by Debreu, like many other mathematical economists. He introduced the techniques of differential topology into economics, which enables an economist to present the general conditions for global uniqueness.

Another important aspect of the competitive equilibrium analysis is the concept of the core of an exchange economy. The core of economy consists of allocations which do not provide any group in the economy with a possibility of trading among themselves and improving their utility. This part of the literature was originated by Edgeworth in the nineteenth century. He showed that in an exchange economy all efficient allocations of the existing goods belong to a curve that is called a contract curve. Points along the curve are Pareto-optimum, since moving from one allocation to another may improve one's situation at the expense of some one else's utility. Points off the curve are not efficient. The contract curve and the core were connected by M. Shubik in 1959 under the game theory. In 1962, Scarf presented a complicated analysis of the core and Walrasian equilibria for exchange economies. Basically, he indicated that for large economies the core allocation becomes the competitive allocation. A different and simpler proof of Scarf's results was presented by Debreu in a paper entitled "On a Theorem of Scarf" (1963). In the same year a rigorous, simple and elegant analysis of the core was presented by Debreu and Scarf in the paper "A Limit Theorem on the Core of an Economy." They showed that as the economy becomes infinitely large the core allocation and competitive equilibrium allocations coincide. In 1975, Debreu showed that the convergence takes place at a rate equal to the inverse of the number of agents in the economy.

Welfare economics has also benefited from Debreu's sophisticated contributions. Inspired by the state of France's postwar economy and its statewide planning programs, Debreu published a paper entitled "The Coefficient of Resource Utilization" (1951). In this paper he employed the separation theorem for convex sets and extended some of the propositions of classical welfare economics with regard to the optimality of the competitive equilibrium. Contrary to prior works, he did not use any marginal rates of substitution in his definition of the optimum. Rather, he used the convex set theory to show that in a competitive environment, any equilibrium is also Pareto-optimum. In 1954, he studied the welfare loss due to a tax or subsidy by applying his measure of the coefficient of resource utilization that he previously derived in his 1951 paper.

Debreu's *Theory of Value* deserves closer examination. This classic work presents an advanced exposition of the theory of a general economic equilibrium in seven succinct and precise chapters. Despite the concise nature of the book, each page provides a rich body of concepts and knowledge that have been used by many economic theorists as the main tools of general equilibrium analysis. The first chapter reviews the mathematical instruments used in the remainder of the book. His heroic and successful attempt to familiarize the reader with the essential mathematical tools needed in later chapters testifies to the clarity of the exposition. As Hal R. Varian (1984) points out, this chapter has been used by many generations of graduate students as an introduction

to mathematics for economics. Almost one-fourth of the monograph is devoted to this important mathematical review.

The dual notions of commodity and prices are presented in the second chapter. The simplicity, richness, and generality of the concept as presented in this chapter project a feeling of excitement and enjoyment to the reader. It sounds as if one is listening to a classical symphony played by a masterful orchestra. The next two chapters are devoted to a discussion of producers and consumers. After a careful specification of the properties of profit functions, supply correspondence, and consumer preferences, Debreu looks at profit maximization and consumer theory.

Chapter Five combines the previous discussions and provides a proof of existence and its required conditions. The following chapter extends the existence proof to the study of welfare economics. He provides the necessary and sufficient conditions for every competitive equilibrium to be Pareto efficient. The last chapter discusses economic uncertainty within the framework provided in the first five chapters of the book.

Despite its high reputation, Debreu's *Theory of Value* has been subject to some criticism. For example, it has been argued that there is no public good in the model and that the externalities in consumption and production are excluded. Also, it is assumed that the set of prices is "quoted" and considered as exogenously determined by all economic agents. This is similar to his definition of "perfect competition" in other papers of this area. But Debreu does not find it necessary to use the term "perfect competition" anywhere in the monograph. In fact, the conceptual contradiction between perfectly competitive economies and the assumption that there are only a given finite number of producers may have contributed to his reluctance to mention the term in his book. Debreu was once asked why he did not use the term "perfect competition" in the *Theory of Value*. He responded:

I did not find it necessary to use the expression. I assumed that the agents were price takers, that is, that they behaved as if prices were given. The behavior required explanation, and this was done by the theory of the core developed shortly afterward. It was necessary to go through the limit theorems and the measure theoretical approach to give a satisfactory account of what one meant by perfect competition, namely of the circumstances in which agents act as price takers. (Feiwel, 1987, p. 251)

In addition to the criticism above, the *Theory of Value* does not consider cases under any market imperfections, increasing returns to scale, fixed costs in production, or some other problems. And the theory of a general economic equilibrium has received some criticism by mainstream economists as well as by critics of the neoclassical theory of which Debreu's work is in the forefront. Stephen Resnick and Richard Wolff (1984) question the validity of the neoclassical theory because of its nonclass tradition. They argue that

Debreu's axiomatic mathematics are designed simply to establish neoclassical theory as the science of economics:

Debreu seems to want to cleanse neoclassical theory of what he considers to be vague word meanings as well as unwelcome moral, philosophical and political influences upon an otherwise "pure" science. He wants to establish the minimum and privileged set of logical, simple, and precise theoretical statements against which all other theoretical claims about economics should be judged. (1984, p. 38)

Other authors argue that Debreu's axiomatic approach is unconnected to the real world and uncompromisingly separates theory from any empirical verification. They generally acknowledge his important contribution to the theorem of the existence of a competitive equilibrium but believe that his efforts, like many others, have been thwarted by the poor results obtained in the area of global stability of competitive economic equilibrium.

Despite the arguments of Debreu's critics, the history of economic thought will remember Debreu's work as a classic which has revealed the weaknesses, strengths, and limitations of the general economic equilibrium theory. He has certainly provided a new foundation for future research and development in this area.

## Private Life

Debreu is punctilious, displaying an obvious desire for accuracy, a characteristic which stems partially from the mathematical nature of his work, and partially from his remarkable quest for excellence and correctness. He presents his scientific findings to the public only after a long process of careful examination and evaluation. He admits that his practice has sometimes resulted in not publishing what he could have published had he not been so demanding in terms of accuracy. The fruit of his discreteness is a distinguished record of publication, with few errors of findings or exposition.

On June 14, 1945 Debreu married Françoise Bled, a French woman who enjoys singing and belongs to the University Choir at the University of California at Berkeley. Her husband tries to attend all her concerts. Her love and understanding have provided Debreu with a peaceful and supportive environment that has enabled him to achieve the greatest success in his profession. Their two daughters, Chantal (Mrs. Paul Teller) and Florence (Mrs. Daniel Hanen), were born in 1946 and 1950, respectively.

Debreu has always maintained a regular schedule. He begins to work early in the morning and continues until six o'clock at night with a break for lunch that he often spends swimming. Unlike many of his colleagues, Debreu seldom works late into the night. His study room is very well organized and attractive. It contains only a small collection of books. He does not decorate his house with long rows of books shelved in dusty bookcases. Instead, he cherishes only those with special value.

Debreu is a nonreligious, apolitical person with superior scientific insights that have helped him to find felicity through the thrill of scientific discovery. But despite his aversion to politics he is deeply concerned about the survival of mankind and the dangers of nuclear warfare. He believes as well that an aggressive search for solutions to population explosion, pollution, and exhaustion of natural resources is among the most pressing issues of our time.

John Stuart Mill once wrote, "Genius can only breath freely in an atmosphere of freedom." Debreu's life is an excellent manifestation of this phrase. Shortly after he arrived in Chicago in 1950, he contemplated applying for American citizenship, but the political events of the McCarthy era were disturbing enough to him to delay that action until 1975. Crucial to his decision to become a U.S. citizen was the Watergate episode, which demonstrated to him democracy in action. He finally came to the conclusion that he prefers the decentralized system of democracy in the United States to the highly centralized democratic society in France.

Debreu is very concerned about human rights violations in the Soviet Union and some Third World countries. He was a member of a delegation that was sent to Chile by the Committee on Human Rights of the National Academy of Sciences in March 1985. He is convinced that a case-by-case study of the issue is the most politically practical approach to the problem of human rights.

Debreu continues to teach in the French tradition. According to his former students, he is a well organized and precise teacher. In the words of Varian, "Each lecture was carefully prepared and delivered; and each lecture was characterized by the elegance of presentation." Although he enjoys teaching both undergraduate and graduate classes, each offers separate satisfaction. The former provides him with fresh, intellectual minds, and the latter with sophisticated professionals who can challenge him with their mature questions.

In conversation with Debreu, he clearly emphasized the importance of excellence in teaching and research at both the graduate and undergraduate level, although he admitted that occasionally an institution of higher education must accept a brilliant scientist who is not a talented teacher. Debreu is concerned about the state of education in the United States, particularly at the high school level, yet he has great faith in the ability of American colleges and universities to train well-educated scientists and scholars. He has been a strong advocate of a more liberal policy for research funding at universities.

In economics, Debreu firmly believes in the division of labor and law of comparative advantage among nations. But he refuses to comment on contemporary economic problems such as unemployment, inflation, and economic development in the Third World countries. Rather he leaves these questions to the experts in those fields. He is a private man who shares his wisdom and vision of the world with us through his elegant

manuscripts. As the Nobel Prize committee stated, Debreu will be remembered by many generations of economists for having incorporated new analytical methods into economic theory and for his rigorous reformulation of the theory of general equilibrium.

SIAMACK SHOJAI

# Selected Bibliography

Allais, Maurice, *A la Recherche d'une discipline économique*, Tome I, Paris: Ateliers Industria, 1943, Chapter IV, Section E.

Arrow, Kenneth J., and Debreu, Gerard. "Existence of Equilibrium for a Competitive Economy." *Econometrica* 22 (1954): 265–90

Cassel, Gustav. *The Theory of Social Economy.* New York: Harcourt, Brace, 1942.

Debreu, Gerard. "The Coefficient of Resource Utilization." *Econometrica* 19 (1951): 273–92.

———. "A Social Equilibrium Existence Theorem." *Proceedings of the National Academy of Sciences* 38 (1953): 597–607.

———. "A Classical Tax-Subsidy Problem." *Econometrica* 22 (1954): 14–22.

———. *Theory of Value.* New York: John Wiley and Sons, 1959.

———. "On a Theorem of Scarf." *Review of Economic Studies* 30 (1963): 177–80.

———. "A Limit Theorem on the Core of an Economy," (with H. Scarf). *International Economic Review*, 4 (1963): 235–46.

———. "The Rate of Convergence of the Core of an Economy." *Journal of Mathematical Economics* 2 (1975): 1–7.

———. "Theoretic Models: Mathematical Form and Economic Content." *Econometrica* 54 (1986): 1259–70.

Feiwel, George R., ed. "Oral History II: An Interview with Gerard Debreu." In *Arrow and the Ascent of Modern Economic Theory*, pp. 243–57. London: Macmillan, 1987.

Hildenbrand, Werner. Introduction to Gerard Debreu, *Mathematical Economics: Twenty Papers of Gerard Debreu*. Cambridge: Cambridge University Press, 1983.

Ingrao, Bruna and Israel, Giorgio. "General Economic Equilibrium Theory. A History of Ineffectual Paradigmatic Shifts." *Fundamenta Scientiae* 6 (1985): 1–45.

Kakutani, Shizuo. "A Generalization of Brouwer's Fixed Point Theorem." *Duke Mathematical Journal* 8 (1941): 457–59.

McKenzie, Lionel W. "On Equilibrium in Graham's Model of World Trade and Other Competitive Systems." *Econometrica* 22 (1954): 147–61.

———. "On Existence of General Equilibrium for a Competitive Market." *Econometrica* 27 1959: 54–71.

Nash, J. F., Jr. "Equilibrium in N-person Games." *Proceedings of the National Academy of Sciences* 36 (1950): 54–71.

Neumann, John von. "Über ein ökonomisches Gleichungssystem und eine Verallgemeinerung des Brouwerschen Fixpunktsatzes." *Ergebnisse eines mathematischen Kolloquiums* 8 (1937): 73–83.

Resnick, Stephen A. and Wolff, Richard D. "The 1983 Nobel Prize in Economics: Neoclassical Economics and Marxism." *Monthly Review* 36 (1984): 29–46.

Varian, Hal R. "Gerard Debreu's Contributions to Economics." *Scandinavian Journal of Economics* 86 (1984): 4–14.

Wald, Abraham. "Über die eindeutige positive Lösbarkeit der neuen Produktions-gleichungen." *Ergebnisse eines mathematischen Kolloquiums* 6 (1933–34): 12–20.

———. "Über die Produktionsgleichungen der ökonomische Wertlehre," *Ergebnisse eines mathematischen Kolloquiums* 7 (1934–35): 1–6.

Walras, Léon. *Eléments d'économie politique pure*. Lausanne: L. Corbaz, 1874–77. Translation of the definitive edition by William Jaffé as *Elements of Pure Economics*. London: Allen and Unwin, 1954.

# MILTON FRIEDMAN   *1976*

Few twentieth century economists are as well known as Milton Friedman. A man of diminutive physical stature, Friedman is considered a giant by the economics profession, having altered the course of economic affairs not only through his own professional and popular writings but also by the influence he exerted on his students and their subsequent academic and nonacademic work. Even his severest critics recognize the significance of Friedman's contributions in the areas of empirical research, macroeconomic theory, monetary history, and public-policy analysis. Perhaps his most memorable additions to the professional economic literature are his development of the permanent-income theory, his restatement of the quantity theory of money, his monetary history, his formulation of the "natural rate of unemployment" hypothesis, and his work on stabilization policy. In 1976 he received the Nobel Prize in Economic Sciences for "his achievement in the fields of consumption analysis, monetary history and theory, and for his demonstration of the complexity of stabilization policy."

Milton Friedman was born on July 31, 1912, in Brooklyn, New York. His parents, Jeno Saul and Sarah Ethel (Landau), were immigrants from Ruthenia, formerly part of the Austro-Hungarian Empire. The family moved to Rahway, New Jersey, in 1913 and opened a small dry goods business, which Sarah

Friedman operated. Jeno Friedman died in 1927, when Milton was fifteen years old. That same year he graduated from Rahway High School and won a scholarship to attend Rutgers University. He received a B.A. degree from Rutgers in 1932 and a M.A. degree from the University of Chicago in 1933; however, it was not until 1946 that he received his Ph.D. from Columbia University. On June 25, 1938, Friedman married Rose Director; they have two children—Janet and David. Rose, herself an economist, has been a significant influence on Friedman's professional life, collaborating with him on two books and compiling several collections of his essays.

Friedman joined the faculty of the economics department at the University of Chicago in 1946; he became the Paul Snowden Russell Distinguished Service Professor of Economics at Chicago in 1962. He retired on January 1, 1977, to become senior research fellow at the Hoover Institute at Stanford University. His association with the National Bureau of Economic Research in New York spanned the years 1937–45 and 1948–81. He is the recipient of many honorary degrees and awards; most notably, he won the John Bates Clark Medal of the American Economics Association in 1951 and served as the association's president in 1967. At the time he received the Nobel Prize, the bibliography of Niels Thygesen's article, "The Scientific Contributions of

Milton Friedman," *Scandinavian Journal of Economics* 79 (1977), listed 245 Friedman publications, including 26 books. Friedman has lectured all over North America, in Europe, in Asia, and in Latin America. From 1966–84 he was a columnist for *Newsweek*. In 1984–85 he served as President of the Western Economic Association.

While his recognition by the Nobel Committee was a result of these and other substantive contributions, his recognition by persons outside of the economics profession is due largely to his ability to translate these ideas into lay terms and to present them effectively to the public via books, lectures, debates, articles in the popular press, and on radio and television broadcasts. His adroit arguments about such controversial issues as individual freedom and its relation to capitalism, his distaste for big government and big business, his faith in the power of the marketplace, and his policy suggestions for the management of the political economy were introduced to the public as early as 1956 in a series of lectures which were later compiled as a book entitled *Capitalism and Freedom* (1962).

Friedman has become an important spokesperson for the libertarian view, that is, for the nineteenth-century liberal who celebrates the free-market process and distrusts the discretionary power of government. Views that were considered liberal in the nineteenth century have been redefined as conservative in the twentieth. Friedman's "conservative" ideas concerning the importance of allowing the marketplace

rather than the government to resolve economic problems encouraged presidential hopeful Barry Goldwater, U.S. Presidents Richard Nixon and Ronald Reagan, and British Prime Minister Margaret Thatcher to seek his advice.

# Early Professional Years

Friedman graduated from Rutgers with a double major in economics and mathematics in 1932. The general economic conditions could not have been worse, as the United States was in the depths of the Great Depression. The country was turning to the federal government for solutions to economic and social problems that American capitalism seemed no longer able to provide. A desire to understand the economic factors contributing to the depression, coupled with a scholarship from Chicago, were undoubtedly factors in Friedman's decision to pursue additional study in economics. At Rutgers he had met two young academics: Arthur Burns, who was finishing his Ph.D. at Columbia University and the National Bureau of Economic Research (NBER), and Homer Jones, who was completing his degree at the University of Chicago. In the early 1930s Columbia and Chicago represented two competing emphases in economics: Columbia and its close affiliate, the NBER, both emphasized scientific empiricism and value-free statistical research, whereas, Chicago was considered the bastion of classical economic theorists. Friedman's decision to study at Chicago introduced him to several of these luminaries. He studied with Frank Knight and Henry Simons, who transmitted their skepticism about any form of government intervention in the economy; with Jacob Viner, who taught him classical economic theory; and with Henry Schultz, who encouraged his interest in mathematics and statistics and their application to economics.

Adverse financial circumstances forced Friedman to leave Chicago after one year; however, a substantial scholarship allowed him to continue his studies at Columbia and NBER. There he met Harold Hotelling, who fortified his interest in mathematics and economics, and Wesley Mitchell, who taught him the importance of data and its interpretation within the institutional structure. In 1935 lack of funds again forced Friedman to interrupt his graduate studies. This time he left academics and took a job with the National Resources Committee in Washington; ironically, this action made him a part of Roosevelt's New Deal administration. His assignment was to provide statistics about the consumption aspects of the economy and to evaluate various proposals for economic recovery and expansion. In 1937 he returned to NBER to work with Simon Kuznets on a study of independent professional practice in the United States. This study which was eventually to become his Ph.D. dissertation, began one year following the publication of John Maynard Keynes's *General Theory of Employment, Interest and Money*

(1936). Mainstream economic theory was about to take a decisive turn.

Friedman was invited to be a visiting professor at the University of Wisconsin at Madison for the 1940–41 academic year. Unfortunately he became caught in the middle of an ugly departmental realignment struggle and decided to return to NBER the following year. He finished his dissertation, but his finding that doctors earned significantly higher salaries than other professionals and his suggestion that the higher compensation was due to barriers to entry in the medical profession proved to be too controversial for NBER. The study's publication and Friedman's degree were delayed.

In 1941 the country was experiencing a period of rapidly rising prices. An explanation based on the work of Keynes suggested that federal spending to support World War II was the cause. This "new economics" view was at odds with contentions of the classical school which assumed that market forces would create downward pressure on prices to clear the market to the full-employment level. The events of the depression had convinced Keynes and his followers that such flexibility in prices was not possible in a complex economy. Friedman was certainly familiar with Keynes's discussion on market failure and his multiplier theory of the relationship between changes in initial expenditures and ultimate income. Friedman undertook a project, commissioned initially by the Carnegie Foundation, to study inflation and how to tax to prevent it. This assignment took him back to Washington and to a post as principal economist for the Division of Tax Research. His investigation led him to recommend a spending tax to curb inflation rather than the establishment of wage and price controls. While his policy suggestion implied a Keynesian demand-management strategy, his recommendation was for the type of policy that later became his trademark: minimal government intervention. His two assignments in Washington apparently left Friedman as skeptical of the government's ability to manage the macroeconomy as had been his mentors, Knight and Simons.

Friedman returned again to New York in 1943 and spent the next two years as the associate director at the Division of War Research at Columbia University. His position there was noneconomic, as he worked as a mathematician and statistician. Following the war, Friedman spent one year as a visiting professor at the University of Minnesota. Then, having finally overcome the objections at NBER to publishing his dissertation, he received his Ph.D. in 1946 and joined the faculty at the University of Chicago. Friedman's path to Chicago had been rather circuitous. During the previous thirteen years he had been exposed to scholars at Chicago, Columbia, and NBER, to teaching via his visiting faculty posts, to government bureaucracy, and to rigorous statistical analysis. This varied experience provided the foundation for the remainder of

Friedman's extraordinary career. In 1951, only five years after achieving faculty status at Chicago, the significance of his contribution to economic theory was acknowledged by the American Economic Association when he was honored with the John Bates Clark Medal for his distinguished scholarship.

## Friedman's Methodology

Friedman always endeavors to apply the value-free methods of objective scientific inquiry. He describes his methodological approach to economics in an essay, "The Methodology of Positive Economics," which was the first in a collection of articles entitled *Essays in Positive Economics* (1953). In the essay Friedman contrasts normative and positive economics. Normative economics concerns itself with "what ought to be", whereas, positive economics examines the facts of a situation to determine "what is." Friedman favors an emphasis on positive economics, with its ability to predict consequences, rather than the normative approach, which reduces opponents to arguing about the advisability of those consequences. In fact, Friedman believes that the free market helps to reconcile normative conflicts over values, that is, over what "ought to be," and provides society with the necessary stability inherent in a common set of shared principles, for example, political freedom, economic efficiency, and equality of economic power. He asserts that most policy disagreements are a result of competing predictions as to the effects of policies—"what is"—rather than differing common values. Thus for Friedman testable hypotheses arise in the area of positive rather than normative economics.

Because Friedman sees economics as a positive science, he asserts in his essay on methodology that the task of economics is "to provide a system of generalizations that can be used to make correct predictions about the consequences of any change in circumstances" (1953, p. 4). Because the world is so complex, Friedman believes that it is not possible to construct a model incorporating total reality. Therefore, models must be simple and yield predictions that can be empirically tested. A model is then judged by how accurately it forecasts economic phenomena rather than by the realism of its initial assumptions. "A hypothesis is important if it 'explains' much by little" (p. 14). Hypotheses can be about past historical periods or be predictions for future periods.

Friedman's definition of the methodology of economics has been the source of much criticism and controversy in the professional literature. His insistence on simplicity has made him a target for those researchers who employ general-equilibrium models and those who employ deductive reasoning and therefore insist on realistic assumptions. His detractors call his position backward-looking and reactionary and challenge him on both philosophical and empirical grounds.

# The Permanent-Income Hypothesis

In 1957 Friedman published his *Theory of the Consumption Function* (1957). As he states in the preface, he had done no empirical work in this area since 1935–37, when he was in Washington studying consumer purchases. However, his wife Rose and her friend Dorothy Brady continued their interest in household consumption. They, along with Margaret Reid and Friedman, worked out the central hypothesis to be tested. Friedman wrote the underlying theory and supervised the statistical work. The resulting study represents an enormous theoretical and econometric achievement.

Ever since Keynes's publication of the *General Theory*, researchers had been studying his representation of the consumption function. Keynes postulated that current consumption expenditure has a stable relation to current income and that a greater proportion of income is saved as real income rises. Friedman and others, in an attempt to verify Keynes's theory, were puzzled by two apparently contradictory empirical facts: (1) time-series data from World War II forward and cross-section data from surveys of individuals and families during the prior 150 years confirmed that current consumption was highly correlated with income and that the percentage of income saved increased with rising income; and (2) the ratio of savings to income in the United States since 1899 had been relatively constant despite a substantial rise in real income. Friedman's model helps to resolve this apparent conflict.

In a simple Keynesian model, consumption in the current period is a function of income in that period. Friedman revises this assumption to say that individuals consume with an eye to their expected or permanent lifetime income, not just their income of the current period. Friedman, who calls his theory the Permanent-Income Hypothesis (PIH), had used the idea of permanent income in his dissertation study of the differences in professional incomes. If in any period income rises or falls above this permanent amount, a person considers the increase or decrease to be only temporary or, in Friedman's terminology, "transitory." Because all consumption is geared to permanent income, any transitory increases flow mainly into savings rather than being consumed. Any transitory decreases cause people to use their savings to keep their consumption at some constant level. Therefore, those with higher incomes, of which some part is assumed transitory, are observed to save a greater amount than those with lower incomes, who are assumed to have negative transitory incomes. In both cases, however, the individuals are observed to consume a constant amount. Thus, Friedman's model has the ability to resolve the empirical controversy posed. It also provides some testable hypotheses regarding policy prescriptions, such as: Will permanent changes in taxes have the same effect on consumption as temporary changes—for example, tax rebates? The answer, according to the PIH, is

no. Permanent changes affect permanent income; temporary changes affect only transitory income and therefore do not affect consumption. Empirical data in the United States and Europe have shown this to be the case; temporary increases in income are consumed at a lower level than are permanent changes in income.

Certainly Friedman's model can be criticized by saying that he neglects both the effects of interest rates and financial wealth on consumption and the relation between saving and wealth. Nevertheless, for Friedman his theory passes the test of positive economics: it is a simple model with predictive power and a testable hypothesis.

# The Quantity Theory of Money

Friedman is most closely identified with his work in the area of monetary theory and money supply. As early as 1947 Friedman turned his attention to monetary affairs and stabilization issues in his essay "A Monetary and Fiscal Framework for Economic Stability" (1948). Consistent with his view of the positive role of economics, Friedman encourages government policies that are simple in design and noninterventionist. "Government must provide a monetary framework for a competitive order . . . this monetary framework should operate under the 'rule of law' rather than under the discretionary authority of administrators" (p. 246). Friedman calls for various reforms, including: limiting the powers of the Federal Reserve System over the money supply, reducing the ability of the government to attempt countercyclical fiscal policies by varying the levels of government spending, financing all government expenditures via taxes or the sale of noninterest-bearing government securities to banks, and allowing the money supply to change only in response to changes in the federal deficit. These measures, he believed, would help to create stability and to prevent inflation in the macroeconomy.

Friedman's view that the supply of money provides the dominant influence on economic activity and price levels was an obvious challenge to Keynesian followers. Friedman's insistence of the central role of money in economic stability was not new. Known as the quantity theory of money, it had been the dominant view until the late 1930s and continued to be the one held by Knight, Simons, Viner, and others at Chicago. Keynes had dismissed the quantity theory by asserting that the supply of money is less important than the spending of money. For Keynes monetary policy, that is, making changes in the supply of money, is less important than fiscal policy, making changes in taxes and federal spending. Thus, Keynesian policy to control inflation calls for countercyclical activism: increasing taxes in inflationary times and reducing taxes or increasing government spending in recessionary periods.

Friedman attempts in his *Studies in the Quantity Theory of Money* (1956) to reestablish what has come to be known as the monetarist view that money and monetary policy play a significant role in determining output and prices. The simple quantity theory of money states that the amount of currency and checking-account balances multiplied by the number of times they are exchanged is equal to the price level times real income. Written as an equation, the relationship is:

$$Mv = Py$$

where:

M is the money supply consisting of currency, coins, and checking-account balances
v is the average number of times the money is exchanged during a given accounting period
P is the price level
y is real income

Classical theorists believed that the velocity of money was largely institutionally determined and very stable. They, therefore, interpreted the theory to say that the price level is proportional to the stock of money. The idea that any change in the money supply generates a change in the price level, while leaving other macro variables unchanged, is called the neutrality of money. Thus, the simple quantity theory is a theory of inflation in which the money supply has the sole control.

The quantity equation can also be rewritten and interpreted to say that money supply equals money demand. Because the simple theory implies that the demand for money is not influenced by interest rates but rather only by velocity and by income, it is considered to be deficient even by those who favor the position that money is the key variable in the macroeconomy. In his restatement of the theory, Friedman assumes the demand formulation but adds that, while the demand for money is a function of income and velocity, velocity is itself a function of several additional factors: yield on bonds, yield on stocks, interest rate on physical capital, rate of return of human capital, and the expected rate of inflation. The demand for money, therefore, is defined as a function of income and the cost of holding money.

Friedman and his students studied this relation and found that interest rates do affect the demand for money, but not by very much. Once again, using the concept of permanent income, Friedman is able to resolve an apparent empirical contradiction: over time, as real income rises the velocity of money (measured as the ratio of actual income to the stock of money) declines; however, during short periods of expansion, velocity rises, and during contractions velocity falls. Friedman asserts that people make their money-demand decisions based on their permanent income rather than on their actual measured income. In the long run, both velocity and the demand for money are stable functions of this permanent income. As permanent income rises, the demand for money increases, causing the velocity of money to decrease. In contrast, in the short run the reported velocity of money rises during periods of high output because actual income is greater than permanent income and falls during

periods of contraction, when actual income is less than permanent income. The empirical difference generated between the long run and the short run is a result of using *actual* rather than *permanent* income in calculating the short-run measure of velocity.

In the long run, as income rises and demand for money increases, expanding the money supply allows the price level to remain stable. Thus, Friedman predicts the neutrality of money in the long run, while acknowledging that changes in the money supply can have short-run effects on income, employment, and interest rates. His findings have resulted in the central monetarist policy suggestion: because the money supply is the key factor in ensuring economic prosperity and stability, the government should establish a constant rate of growth of the money supply approximately equal to the desired rate of growth of real output and then leave it alone. Such a policy excludes the use of any monetary activism or fiscal discretion in attempting to stabilize the price level.

In 1959, while testifying before the Joint Congressional Economic Committee, Friedman warned that the government was preoccupying itself with fiscal policy while ignoring monetary policy. The Federal Reserve policy makers appeared to have embarked on a policy of reacting to economic conditions by contracting the money supply in periods of strong aggregate demand and then expanding it in recessionary periods. The problem with this strategy, according to Friedman, was the time lags that occur between policy implementation and policy effectiveness. Therefore, Friedman repeated his advice of set rules governing the money supply. In subsequent years most have come to agree with Friedman about the lags in macro policy; however, many continue to see a role for an activist monetary policy.

Friedman continued to work with colleagues and students at Chicago on monetary topics. In a controversial work with David Meiselman published in *Stabilization Policies* (1963), Friedman argues that monetary velocity is more stable than the Keynesian investment multiplier. Using time series data from 1897–1958, they compute the correlation between consumption spending and the money stock and the correlation between consumption spending and investment spending. Their finding that the correlation is stronger between consumption and money allows them to assert that money is a better and more stable predictor of income than is investment. These findings did not go unchallenged by others in the profession. *The American Economic Review* (September 1965) printed an extended debate between Friedman and Meiselman and their critics.

## Monetary History

Certainly one of Friedman's most scholarly works is *A Monetary History of the United States 1867–1960* (1963), coauthored with Anna Schwartz. The work was sponsored by NBER and was to have been a part of a series of five volumes on the cyclical behavior of monetary factors. In fact, only four were com-

pleted, with the most recent being *Monetary Trends in the United States and the United Kingdom* (1982). The first of the series examines the fluctuations in the money supply and relates these changes to economic events. For Friedman and Schwartz, the key to understanding the way the economy works is to be found in examining the historical record. Their work uncovers two historical generalizations: (1) all periods of severe economic instability have been accompanied by an equal instability in the money supply; and (2) the chain of causality in economic events generally leads from changes in the quantity of money to changes in business conditions rather than the other way around.

Perhaps the most significant period covered in the study is between 1929–33. For Keynesian followers the depression was proof that interventionist policies by the government were essential for economic stability. Both the stock market crash and the crisis in the banking system were interpreted by Keynesians as a condemnation of laissez-faire economics. Friedman and Schwartz carefully document in impressive statistical detail the activities of the Federal Reserve System during the Depression period. The Fed's contraction of the money supply following the stock market crash in 1929 and during the early 1930s, when many banks were failing, is interpreted to have had enormous consequences. Friedman and Schwartz maintain that, if the Federal Reserve had expanded the money supply during this period, the Depression would have been no more than a recession and the massive bank failures would have been avoided. Friedman and Schwartz see the consequences of the actions of the Federal Reserve as evidence of the power of monetary policy rather than its impotency. For Friedman and Schwartz, data in their monetary history bolster their contention that money is the most significant economic factor and that monetary policy inappropriately administered is disastrous. The events of the Depression years only confirm the monetarist preference for fixed rules governing monetary policy.

## Inflation and Unemployment

In 1967 Friedman was elected president of the American Economic Association. His presidential address, "The Role of Monetary Policy" (*American Economic Review*, 1968), is a discussion of the role of money in creating inflation. Friedman asserts that monetary policy can neither peg interest rates nor unemployment rates for more than short periods of time. In making his case for these two assertions, he discusses the importance of price expectations in inflation theory and introduces the concept of the natural rate of unemployment. This latter idea is presented in contrast to the Keynesian notion, based on the Phillips curve, of a trade-off between unemployment and inflation. The Phillips curve is a graphical display of the empirical relationship between the unemployment rate and the rate of inflation. The curve implies that low rates of

unemployment can be achieved by having higher rates of inflation and vice versa.

Friedman's natural-rate theory asserts that there is some rate of equilibrium unemployment consistent with the market structure of the economy. Any attempt to reduce unemployment below this level will lead to ever-escalating inflation. For Friedman there is no long run trade-off that can be made between inflation and unemployment; however, short-run trade-offs are possible, due to workers' inaccurate assessments of the actual rate of inflation. Friedman pictures the following scenario: suppose the monetary authority wishes to push the rate of unemployment below the natural rate. It does so by expanding the money supply in order to lower interest rates, thereby stimulating aggregate demand. Firms respond to the increase in demand by increasing output, which requires the hiring of more workers, so employment expands. Supply may not initially be able to keep up with the increase in demand, so prices respond by rising. In the short run workers are induced to provide more labor services at a particular money wage, but once they realize that prices have risen their expectations about prices and future price increases are altered. Workers demand higher wages to offset the increased prices, but at the higher wages employment drops. In the end there is an increase in the price level with no long-run increase in the number of people employed. Unemployment, reduced in the short run, returns to the natural rate.

Friedman's distinction between real and anticipated variables and his theory about the natural rate of unemployment have become so widely accepted that virtually all intermediate-theory texts include them as essential to the understanding of modern macroeconomics. In addition, Friedman's initial research has stimulated further work, resulting in an enormous literature on the influence of expectations on the macroeconomy and the importance of the natural rate of key macro variables.

Friedman was awarded the Nobel Prize in Economics in 1976. Perhaps he would have received the award even sooner had his free-market approach been one shared by the Swedish government. When it was announced that he would receive the prize, there were a number of angry demonstrations against the decision, because people objected to Friedman's having recently given economic advice to the oppressive Pinochet government in Chile.

Friedman uses his "Nobel Lecture: Inflation and Unemployment" (*Journal of Political Economy*, 1977), to defend and illustrate his method of social-science analysis. He believes that his methodology reflects the same level of objective science as natural-science investigation. He demonstrates the methods of economic empiricism by subjecting his natural-rate hypothesis to the test of recent data. He describes how his theory is consistent with "stagflation"—that is, the co-existence of high inflation and unemployment. Friedman blames unanticipated changes in demand and prices for the higher levels of inflation existing temporarily with levels of unemployment above the natural rate. Then he turns to a discussion of a new phenomenon, "stumpflation"—simultaneously escalating inflation and unemployment that persist over a longer period. He acknowledges that the natural-rate hypothesis alone cannot explain this new macro problem, suggesting that supply-side shocks like increases in energy prices may be responsible but also blaming the interventionist policies of government in combination with a changing monetary environment. His analysis demonstrates the evolution of the theory associated with the trade-off between unemployment and inflation as it is brought into conformity with existing data. In the end, for Friedman and those who practice positive science, only data can prove the correctness of a hypothesis.

# Friedman's Public-Policy Agenda

In 1956 Friedman gave a series of lectures at Wabash College dealing with applied economics. The essence of the lectures was published under the title, *Capitalism and Freedom* (1962) which became the first in a series of books written on policy issues for the general public. Over the years additional volumes joined the first: *Dollars and Deficits* (1968), *Bright Promises, Dismal Performance* (1972) containing essays extracted from his *Newsweek* columns, and *Free to Choose* (1980), coauthored with Rose Friedman and based on a series of television documentaries which the Friedmans made for public television. All of these works are attempts to bring to the public's attention the same issues that Friedman had been writing about in his scholarly papers.

In *Capitalism and Freedom*, Friedman makes policy suggestions on a wide range of topics. Similar ideas echo throughout his subsequent books. First, he calls for the government to discontinue the following: price supports for agriculture, tariffs and quotas on imports, rent control, minimum wages, regulation of industries by government agencies, compulsory old-age retirement programs, licensing of professions or occupations, public housing, military conscription, national parks, the prohibition on carrying first-class mail for profit, and publicly operated toll roads. In addition, he proposes a steady rate of growth of the money supply; the demonetization of gold and freely floating exchange rates to solve balance of payments problems; that taxes must equal government expenditures and that the government be restrained from employing countercyclical fiscal policy because it is destabilizing; the creation of a voucher system for education whereby the government would give money to families for education and the families could purchase whatever type—private, public, or parochial—they prefer; the elimination of the corporate tax and the imposition of a flat-rate personal income tax that eliminates all loopholes; and the establishment of a "negative income tax" to help the poor by giving them cash payments from the government, which they can spend as they see fit. Many of these suggestions were instituted in the following years.

There was never any doubt that Milton Friedman would at some point receive the Nobel Prize in Economics. It is difficult to think of others who have contributed and are still contributing so much in so many different areas. Certainly his work in the areas of consumption, monetary theory and history, inflation, and public policy has provided others with research agendas to last into the twenty-first century.

Perhaps the essence of Friedman is best captured by his colleague, collaborator, and friend, Anna Schwartz who when asked to describe him wrote:

A small man with a giant intellect, free of complexes, whether Napoleonic or of any other kind. A scholar and scientist, whose impact on the economics profession has been profound. A persuasive proponent of private rather than government provision of goods and services and of individual freedom from government compulsion. (*Challenge* 22 [May–June 1979]:67)

NANCY M. THORNBORROW

# Selected Bibliography

## WORKS BY FRIEDMAN

"A Monetary and Fiscal Framework for Economic Stability." *American Economic Review* 38: (1948), 245–64.

*Essays in Positive Economics.* Chicago: University of Chicago Press, 1953.

*Studies in the Quantity Theory of Money*. Chicago: University of Chicago Press, 1956.

*Theory of the Consumption Function*. Princeton, N.J.: Princeton University Press, 1957.

*Capitalism and Freedom*. Chicago: University of Chicago Press, 1962.

*A Monetary History of the United States 1867–1960* (with Anna Schwartz). Princeton, N.J.: Princeton University Press, 1963.

and Meiselman, D. "The Relative Stability of Monetary Velocity and the Investment Multiplier in the United States, 1897–1958." In *Stabilization Policy*. Englewood Cliffs: Prentice-Hall, 1963.

and Meiselman, D. "Reply to Ando and Modigliani and to DePrano and Mayer." *American Economic Review* 55 (1965): 753–83.

"The Role of Monetary Policy." *American Economic Review* 58 (1968): 4–17.

*Dollars and Deficits*. New York: Prentice-Hall, 1968.

*Bright Promises, Dismal Performance*. New York: Harcourt Brace Jovanovich, 1972.

"Nobel Lecture: Inflation and Unemployment." *Journal of Political Economy* 85 (1977): 451–72.

*Free to Choose* (with Rose Friedman). New York: Harcourt Brace Jovanovich, 1980.

*Monetary Trends in the United States and the United Kingdom* (with Anna Schwartz). Chicago: University of Chicago Press, 1982.

## OTHER WORKS

Burton, John. "Positively Milton Friedman." In *Twelve Contemporary Economists*, J. R. Shackleton and G. Locksley, eds. New York: Wiley, 1981.

Finn, Daniel R. "Objectivity in Economics: On the Choice of a Scientific Method." *Review of Social Economy* 37 (April 1979): 37–61.

Frazer, W. J. and Boland, L. A. "An Essay on the Foundations of Friedman's Methodology." *The American Economic Review* 73 (March 1983): 129–44.

Mason, Will E. "Some Negative Thoughts on Friedman's Positive Economics." *Journal of Post Keynesian Economics* 3 (Winter 1980–81): 235–55.

Schwartz, Anna J. "Portrait—Milton Friedman." *Challenge* 22 (May–June 1979): 67–69.

Silk, Leonard. "Milton Friedman." In Silk, *The Economists*. New York: Basic Books, 1976.

Sobel, Robert. "Milton Friedman." In Sobel, *The Worldly Economists*. New York: The Free Press, 1980.

Thygesen, Niels. "The Scientific Contributions of Milton Friedman." *Scandinavian Journal of Economics* 79 (1977): 56–98.

Wible, James R. "Friedman's Positive Economics and Philosophy of Science." *Southern Economic Journal* 49 (October 1982): 350–60.

# RAGNAR ANTON KITTIL FRISCH
*1969*

Ragnar Anton Kittil Frisch was born in Oslo, Norway, on March 3, 1895. He graduated from Oslo University in 1919 and was awarded his doctorate there in 1926. He was made an assistant professor at Oslo in 1925, associate professor in 1928, full professor of the university from 1931 until 1965, and director of research at the Oslo University Institute of Economics. He was one of the founders and the first president of the Econometric Society and editor of *Econometrica* from 1933 to 1955.

Frisch shared the first Nobel Prize in Economic Sciences with Jan Tinbergen in 1969. They were awarded the prize for having developed and applied dynamic models for the analysis of economic processes. The Nobel Committee considered that "The most salient feature in the development of the economic sciences in recent decades is the emphasis on mathematical and statistical descriptions of precision of the processes involved," and that, "Frisch has for a long time been the leading pioneer in the realm of theory and method development."

## Formative Influences and Career

Ragnar Anton Kittil Frisch was the son of Anton Frisch, a gold and silver merchant in the family firm, and Ragna Fredrikke (née Kittilsen) Frisch. His mother clearly had a most important influence on his choice of career. It was, in his words, "more or less taken for granted that [he] should follow the gold and silver tradition," and accordingly he assumed an apprenticeship in one of the main Oslo firms. His mother felt, however, that in the long run the gold and silver trade would not be enough for Frisch, and she persuaded him to follow university study at the same time as his apprenticeship. In his words,

> We perused the catalogue of Oslo University and found that economics was the *shortest* and *easiest* study. So therefore economics it became; that is the way it happened. Later on the study of economics in Oslo University. . . . [became]. . . . more advanced and time-consuming. (Some people seem to think that somehow I have been instrumental in this development.)

After completing his degree, Frisch traveled abroad to study economics and mathematics in France (particularly in Paris), in the United States, where he lectured at various universities, including Yale and Minnesota, and also in Germany, Great Britain, and Italy. In 1930 he was invited as a visiting professor to Yale, through Irving Fisher's initiative. They collaborated on early attempts to measure utility functions, which was an issue that had interested Frisch since 1923. He was also a visiting professor at the Sorbonne in 1933, and a Rockefeller Fellow from 1926 to 1928.

By the late 1920s it was apparent to several members of the Norwegian Parliament and others in Norway that it would be a tragedy if someone of Frisch's talent was lost to the country. Accordingly, to persuade him to stay in Oslo, a special chair was created for him at Oslo University in 1931. While he continued to travel extensively, Frisch's base remained in Oslo for the rest of his life. Indeed, this is of some importance in explaining Frisch's highly original approach to econometrics and his reluctance to be swept along by developments in the subject with which he did not agree.

Alfred Cowles has written that, "Ragnar Frisch, more than any other one man, took the initiative in founding, and in establishing the broadly international character of, the Econometric Society and. . . . *Econometrica*." He was the first president of the Econometric Society, and editor of *Econometrica* from 1933 to 1955. Tinbergen has written of Frisch's passionate commitment to the early econometric study meetings, calling him the "soul of the group," and describing his extraordinary energy for study. The meetings were so exhausting, apparently, that Tinbergen, "for one, always needed a rest, back home." Frisch was also the chairman of the first session of the Economic and Employment Commission of the United Nations.

Frisch was a member, honorary member, or fellow of many of the most distinguished learned societies, including the American Academy of Arts and Sciences, the American Philosophical Society, the Academy of Human Rights, the American Economics Association, the Institute of Mathematical Statistics (USA), the International Statistical Institute, the British Academy, the Royal Economic Society of Great Britain, the Royal Statistical Society of Great Britain, the Norske Videnskapsakademi i Oslo (Norwegian Academy of Science and Letters), the Kungliga Humanistika Vetenskapssamfundet i Lund (Royal Society of The Humanities at Uppsala [Lund] in Sweden), and the Kungliga Svenska Vetenskapsakademi (Royal Swedish Academy of Sciences). He won the Schumpeter Prize at Harvard University in 1955 and the Antonio Feltrinelli Prize of the Accademia Nazionale dei Lincei (National Academy of the Lincei, Rome). The latter was particularly important to him, as an honor from the society of which Galileo Galilei was an early member. He was awarded honorary doctorates by Handelshögskolan i Stockholm (Stockholm School of Economics), and the universities of Copenhagen, Stockholm, Cambridge, and Birmingham.

It has been suggested that a number of the most eminent economists were surprised to hear that Frisch had become jointly the first recipient of the award. In his introduction to Frisch's collection of essays, *Economic Planning Studies* (1976), Frank Long suggested that, "For many he was an unfamiliar dark horse, enough so to be a source of mystery." This was probably more true in North America than in Europe. It may also reflect the fact that, while Frisch wrote a great deal, he did not often refine his manuscripts to make them accessible to a wide audience. It could be said, indeed, that such was his enthusiasm to advance his own understanding that others would just have to do their best to keep up.

Frisch was married twice: first, in 1920, to Marie Smedal, who died in 1952, and in 1953 to Astrid Johannesen, whom he had known from childhood. Frisch died on January 31, 1973, in Oslo. In the last years of his life, he was active in campaigning against Norway's (and indeed Iceland's) entry to the European Economic Community (EEC), and he lived to see the 1972 referendum that resulted in the Norwegian government withdrawing its application to join the EEC. Tinbergen has suggested that this position reflected Frisch's strongly held belief that Norway could better remain an example of democracy and social justice by remaining independent of the EEC.

Frisch described his hobbies as outdoor life, including mountain climbing on "a modest scale," but above all beekeeping, which occupied him for some fifty-seven years. His particular interest was in bee eugenics, and indeed he published a paper on his studies in a journal of beekeeping. This hobby had a curious hold on him, as he reveals in his own biographical notes that prefaced his Nobel Prize address: "If someone asked me if I find this occupation pleasant and entertaining, I'm not sure that I could honestly say yes. It is more in the nature of an obsession that I shall never be able to get rid of."

# Research and Ideas

Frisch is best known as a (if not *the*) pioneer of the "three triads" of econometrics: economic theory, mathematical method, and statistical techniques as applied to the analysis of practical economic problems. Econometrics, indeed, was a word coined by Frisch himself. Frisch's influence is to be found in many areas of economics, but Leif Johansen considered that perhaps the three most important themes were the effort to make economics a quantitative science, making economics an aid in the formulation of rational economic policy, and the development of a dynamic analysis of economics.

## *Utility, Demand Analysis, Index Numbers, and Production Theory*

Some of Frisch's earliest work was on the foundations of utility theory and the theory of index numbers. He was one of the first to write down an axiomatic foundation for consumer choice, in a paper titled "Sur une problème d'économie pure" (1926). He assumed an ordering over commodity bundles, and over movements from one bundle to another. From this he derives a utility function which is unique up to an increasing linear transformation. Using this work on utility functions, he also undertook pioneering work on the measurement of marginal utility, following collaboration with Irving Fisher. This is described in his *New Methods of Measuring Marginal Utility* (1932). Subsequently, ordinal approaches to utility were preferred by economists to the cardinal utility functions of Frisch.

In a famous survey paper of 1936, "Annual Survey of General Economic Theory: The Problem of Index Numbers," Frisch further developed the idea—due to Alexander Könus and others—that a price index could be defined as the ratio of costs to reach a particular utility level in two different situations. This built on some of his earlier work on index numbers: in particular, his analysis in a 1930 article of whether and when index numbers could meet Fisher's criteria. Indeed, he had shown that some of Fisher's criteria were inconsistent. There were two particular directions in which Frisch took this work. First, he studied the issue of placing bounds on true price indices. Second, he introduced what he termed the "double expenditure" method into the study of indices based on quadratic approximations to the utility function.

Other important early work by Frisch on the traditional core of microeconomics was in the area of production theory. This research led him towards what was later to be known as mathematical programming—that is, optimization subject to minimum (or maximum) constraints that are not necessarily binding.

At a relatively late stage in his career, Frisch returned to the analysis of demand, and in a 1959 paper proposed "A Complete Scheme for Computing All Direct and Cross Demand Elasticities in a Model with Many Sectors." The marginal utility of money in this formulation may depend on all prices, there are simple relationships between elasticities of demand and money flexibility (elasticity of the marginal utility of money). With today's taste for flexible functional forms, this proposed system may be rather restrictive, but it should be seen in the context of Frisch's belief, stemming from his work on econometrics that only equations of low cardinality could be identified.

## Economic Dynamics

The Nobel Prize citation for Frisch and Tinbergen made particular reference to their work on economic dynamics. This was an area that Frisch came into via his concern with the economic explanation of business cycles. His early work in this area had recognized that the acceleration principle alone did not explain the upper turning point of a business cycle, and that the empirical comparison of turning points in different economic cycles could not be interpreted in terms of one dynamic relation alone but needed to be interpreted in terms of a complete dynamic system.

His classic contribution was the 1933 paper "Propagation Problems and Impulse Problems in Dynamic Economics." This work set out a model of economic cycles which did, however, show a tendency towards damping. Frisch felt that the continuation of business cycles would be explained within such a model by the persistent occurrence of random shocks, which he suggested could well be of a Schumpeterian kind. This model shows some similarity to Keynesian analysis of business cycles and macrodynamics, and is described in more detail later.

Another important innovation in this area was his 1936 paper "On the Notion of Equilibrium and Disequilibrium," which contributed much to later methodology and terminology in dynamic economics. Subsequent work on economic dynamics included a paper on the technical matters of solving mixed difference and differential equations as they occur in economics (1935), a method for countercyclical regulation of banking activity (1936), analysis of the phase diagrams for two economic variates (1937), a general analysis of the elements of business-cycle theory (1947), and a review of repercussion studies at Oslo (1948) that drew out the practical relevance of these studies of economic dynamics.

## Planning and Programming Studies

After the Second World War, much of Frisch's work was on the problems of economic planning. His contributions in this area can be summarized in terms of three themes, the first of which involves developing and using tractable planning models. An early contribution from Frisch was his 1948 article "Repercussion Studies at Oslo," which brought out the practical relevance of his earlier work on dynamics. This work provided the founda-

tion for his studies for the United Nations Subcommission on Employment and Economic Stability. These models could be used in a dynamic fashion by making various assumptions about relative growth rates, allowing the user to tackle the question of long-run optimization.

A second (and to him very important) theme on which Frisch was working was the issue of calibrating a social preference function. In his paper "Numerical Determination of a Quadratic Preference Function for Use in Macroeconomic Programming" (1963), Frisch proposed to calibrate the parameters of a quadratic function by questionnaires put to policy makers. He had by this time expressed severe doubts about the scope for calibrating such functions by indirect inference (that is, standard regression methods).

The third theme was to develop techniques for optimizing planning models in the light of the preference functions that he calibrated. To some degree this theme had been anticipated in his early paper "Circulation Planning" (1934), which anticipated several other themes in modern planning theory. Because Frisch's quadratic preference functions exhibited separability of a particularly convenient form, the maximization problem was one of piecewise linear programming. Frisch sought alternatives to the simplex method of solving these linear programming problems, which would be faster for large problems. The techniques were to some degree informal and required judgement on the part of the researcher. For this reason, and given the (at that time unforeseen) subsequent growth in computing technology, it is not perhaps surprising that these maximization techniques were abandoned in favor of more easily formalized and more easily programmed techniques.

Much of Frisch's work on planning models and methods was never published, but the collection of his papers titled *Economic Planning Studies* (1976), edited by Long, gives an important selection of his work in this area.

## Econometric Methodology

From an early stage, and indeed throughout all his work, it is evident that Frisch was very interested in the choice of methods of estimating economic relationships. Frisch's concerns stemmed from his observation that economists usually had to work with "passive observations where the investigator is restricted to observing what happens when all equations in a large determinate system are actually fulfilled simultaneously."

This observation has two implications. First, whereas in statistical analysis of experimental data there would be a natural choice of dependent variable, this would not necessarily be so in economic relationships. As a consequence, the unique point estimators of classical regression analysis were no longer appropriate. Second, when all equations in the system are interrelated and fulfilled simultaneously, Frisch recognized that a relationship between k variables might lie in a restricted domain of variation—restricted not just to dimension k-1, but even less. This would mean that it is difficult to separate the influence of different variables in any economic relation.

Frisch addressed the first issue in his study of *Pitfalls in the Statistical Construction of Demand and Supply Curves* (1933), which built on the well-known work of E. J. Working. Here he was concerned with how a two-dimensional scatter diagram of prices and quantities should be interpreted—as demand curve, supply curve, or something in between? The second issue was addressed in his classic work *Statistical Confluence Analysis by Means of Complete Regression Systems* (1934) and developed further in some of his unpublished memoranda. This work was a vital precursor to the analysis of identification developed by Koopmans, and others. Confluence analysis is described in more detail below.

## Other Areas

Frisch made some very original contributions to the early analysis of oligopoly—"polypole" was his French word for this. His concern was primarily with dynamic issues in oligopoly, though these issues were to some degree lost after the development of the game theoretic approach to oligopoly. Frisch's solutions for the equilibrium of these dynamic games have much in common with the later equilibrium solutions of John Nash.

Frisch's early work was in mathematical statistics, and indeed his doctoral thesis was on the semi-invariants and moments used in the study of statistical distributions. He spent a fair proportion of his research energies during the 1920s and 1930s on challenging analytical and mathematical issues, though less so after World War II. He saw this research as an "indispensable preliminary step" for effective work on his empirical studies, including work on harmonics of time series, approximations to integrals, methods of decomposing time series into trend and cyclical components, analysis of difference and differential equations, and the famous Frisch-Waugh Theorem on partial regressions.

## The Unsung Contributions

Johansen has written of Frisch that "When he had clarified a problem for himself, he was more interested in taking up new problems than in preparing final versions of preliminary manuscripts." As a consequence, Frisch could justifiably be credited with some developments in the subject that have actually been attributed to others. Many of his most interesting papers were not published, or at least not until some time after they were written. He probably had almost as much influence as a result of his lectures, lecture notes, and memoranda as through his published papers. Finally of course, he tended to use his own terminology for economic analysis, which reflects the originality and pioneering nature of much of his work. It also meant that some of his work was very difficult to read, and that he tended to be sidetracked into technicalities. Yet he always

saw such diversions as "indispensable preliminary steps" for his empirical research projects.

For example, Johansen has suggested that Frisch may have been the first to draw an isoquant. Likewise, while the 'hedonic' regression—relating price to quality—is usually attributed to A. T. Court in 1939, Frisch's book *Statistical Confluence Analysis* (1934) contains what amounts to an hedonic analysis of vegetable prices. Frisch's interview techniques were not regarded very seriously by fellow econometricians but now occupy an important role in some of the other social sciences.

# Two Most Important Contributions

Two of Frisch's most important contributions were published within a year of each other, and at a time when Frisch was publishing a very large number of other equally significant contributions. The first contribution, on economic dynamics, is very probably one that the Nobel Committee had in mind when it cited Frisch's contribution to the development of dynamic economic models. The second, on the other hand, is not one referred to in the Nobel citation, and indeed for all its influence on subsequent developments in econometrics, was generally reckoned to have been superseded by these later developments—though Frisch himself did not believe so. Nevertheless recent work in econometrics suggests that the full implications of confluence analysis have not yet been appreciated by econometricians.

## *"Propagation Problems and Impulse Problems in Dynamic Economics"*

Kenneth Arrow (1960) considers this work as "almost certainly the first careful study of a complete dynamic system." By "propagation," Frisch meant analyzing how the structural properties of a dynamic system influence the cyclical behavior of that system when it is started from some particular state. By "impulse," he meant the random shocks (and even endogenously generated shocks) that hit the dynamic system from time to time.

Frisch's model had three key elements: an accelerator effect, relating capital starting to the growth in consumption; a gestation period between capital starting and the completion of capital goods; and a relationship between consumption and the scarcity of cash balances. From these three elements, Frisch was able to construct a dynamic model of business cycles. This model consisted of a mixed difference-differential equation, which was more difficult to solve than the pure difference or pure differential equations that became the norm in later dynamic models. Typically of Frisch, however, he did not seek to avoid such technical difficulties, but tackled them head-on.

Each of the three elements plays a critical role in the model. For example, Frisch noted that if there were no gestation period for capital-

goods production, then the system would reduce to a first-order differential equation and so would not be capable of cyclical behavior. With such a gestation period, however, the mixed differential-difference equation has an infinite number of roots (including complex ones). Frisch conducted a large number of simulation experiments with this model and found that, with plausible parameter values, the model generated a variety of cycles with lengths of a few years. Moreover, he showed that the length of the cycles depended primarily on the length of the gestation period.

The cycles were almost invariably damped, however, so that they tended to collapse, and as Frisch observed, this did not square with the undamped cycles observed in reality. Nevertheless, he considered that this model provided a good explanation of the "propagation" problem (the structural properties of the swinging system), but did not explain the "impulse" problem (the source of shocks to the system). To explain the existence of persistent cycles, Frisch stressed the importance of random disturbances in economic relations, as had been suggested by Kurt Wicksell, Eugen Slutsky, Udner Yule, and Joseph Schumpeter. Indeed, he saw his analysis relating in a particularly important way to Schumpeter's analysis of innovations, which stressed that the oscillatory system itself generated the seeds of shocks to that system.

It is useful to place this study of Frisch's in the broader context of business-cycle research in the 1930s.

As J. C. Andvig (1981) shows, early business-cycle research had separated into two camps: the institutionalist-empirical school of Wesley C. Mitchell and others, and the theoretical school of Dennis Robertson, John Maynard Keynes and others. Frisch's work in the early 1930s really constituted a different research program. He was unhappy with the purely theoretical approaches to the problem, which did not seek to confront their theories with statistical observation, but at the same time felt frustrated with the institutionalist-empirical work, which "tells us nothing if not illuminated by theoretical analysis."

This in a nutshell is an example of Frisch's econometric approach to economic analysis. The impulse to study this topic was driven by his concern at the extent and likely duration of recession, and he sought to bring together careful economic, mathematical and statistical analysis to illuminate the problem. Frisch's paper on propagation and impulse problems gained a wide respect even among nonmathematical economists and proponents of the established schools of business-cycle research.

## Statistical Confluence Analysis by Means of Complete Regression Systems

A number of observers have not been able to understand why Frisch, with all his enthusiasm for regression at an early stage, should have counseled resort to interview techniques for the calculation of government preference functions in his planning studies. The beginnings of an answer can be found in his extraordinary book on confluence analysis, which contains many new ideas on the use of regression analysis in economics but makes for very difficult reading. Indeed, one of Frisch's successors as president of the Econometric Society described it as "very hard to read and understand, even with hindsight." The conclusions of the book are somewhat pessimistic, and this goes some way towards explaining why Frisch later came to the view that something beyond pure regression method would be required for the calibration of economic relationships.

As noted above, Frisch recognized that the application of statistical techniques to economic data was complicated by the fact that economists had to work with passive observations, where all equations in a large determinate system are fulfilled simultaneously. This leads to difficulties over the choice of a natural endogenous variable in any equation and also raised the possibility that it might not be possible to calibrate all equations in the system from these passive observations. The earliest regression studies of Christian Gauss had used time as the regressor, so that there was no ambiguity about the direction of minimization in regression. Work by Corrado Gini had established that the appropriate direction of minimization would depend on the distribution of errors from the regression and how these errors were correlated with regressor and regressand.

In this book, Frisch argued that in most economic applications of regression analysis, errors were unlikely to be independent of *any* of the variables under analysis, so that there was no natural direction of minimization. Accordingly, he extended Gini's result to the multidimensional case, which would make it possible to put bounds on the uncertainty in regression estimates due to uncertainty about the nature of errors in the model. This technique was one of Frisch's major contributions to the analysis of econometric estimation, and he named it "bunchmap." (The bounds described by these bunch maps are not to be confused with the confidence intervals which summarize uncertainty due to sampling uncertainty.)

While *Confluence Analysis* was a vital foundation for the later development of econometrics, the bunch-map technique fell into disuse after important developments in identification at the Cowles Commission and elsewhere in the 1940s and 1950s. Indeed, a common view was that they had been superseded by these developments, though Frisch himself did not accept this. While he clearly accepted one conclusion of later work on identification, namely that *within the errors in equations approach* instrumental variables play a central role in identification, nevertheless he remained skeptical for two reasons: first, because there was still the practical problem of knowing whether regressors used in practice were truly instrumental variables, and second, because the errors in equations approach did not attack the problem

of errors in variables (or measurement errors).

In short, Frisch did not believe that the Cowles Commission approach to identification had actually reduced the fundamental uncertainties arising from the use of regression techniques with economic data. He does not seem to have changed his mind on this point. In his 1963 paper, "Numerical Determination of a Quadratic Preference Function," Frisch commented on the "errors in equations" approach:

> There exists nothing in the problem which permits us to single out one of the variables from the others and treat this one differently from the others. . . . The "error in the equation" approach is therefore only a concealed and unfounded form of polarisation. . . . It is my conviction that much of the current practice of equation fitting . . . is off the mark because too much emphasis is put on an exact derivation of stochastic conclusions from given assumptions and too little is put on the nature of the mechanism that has produced the observed phenomenon.

One reason why Frisch's bunch-map technique has not seen widespread use is that the bunch maps for many of the examples that Frisch and his followers had studies were wide open—that is to say, the different regression estimates obtained from minimizing sums of squares in the direction of each regressor were widely different. This essentially negative result may explain why economists seeking more positive conclusions from econometric studies had to find a way around this problem. Frisch himself was clearly disappointed by this tendency in estimated bunch maps and concluded in writings in the late 1940s that:

> It is very seldom indeed that we have a clear case where statistical data can actually determine numerically an autonomous structural equation. . . . We must look for some other means of getting information about the numerical character of our structural equations. The only possible way seems to be to utilise to a much greater extent than we have done so far the interview method.

Recent work by Edward Leamer, among others, has revived Frisch's confluence analysis and given it a more formal foundation. The whole matter of measurement error in econometrics is now being taken much more seriously, and Frisch's pioneering work of the 1930s is enjoying something of a revival.

It is interesting to note the implications of these views of Frisch on his subsequent approach to empirical work. Although at an early stage Frisch was insistent about the need for a wide range of regression studies, he himself did less work of this sort than might have been expected. His concern about the inherent difficulty of making inferences from passive observations is undoubtedly an important reason for this apparent anomaly. Likewise, his enthusiasm for interview techniques in his planning studies probably stems from this concern over regression methods.

# Influence on Economics and Public Policy

Many of Frisch's most important papers and books are classics in their field. The development of empirical demand systems, the use of convenient parameterizations to yield insights into price and income responses, the axiomatic derivation of preference functions, and the measurement of index numbers and appreciation of their properties are all areas where Frisch's work has provided the foundation for later research.

By distinguishing between propagation and impulse, and by generating a rigorous model of economic cycles, Frisch laid the foundation for much of the subsequent work in economic dynamics. Moreover, his contributions in the area really constituted a new research program and research methodology. His pioneering work on planning models has had a pervasive influence on subsequent efforts at building planning models, calibrating social-preference functions, and devising appropriate optimization techniques with which to design appropriate policy measures. Tinbergen himself acknowledged in the preface of his book *On the Theory of Economic Policy* (1952) that "the core of the theory presented is nothing but an application of the notion of decision models as introduced by Ragnar Frisch." And as noted above, Frisch's study of confluence analysis provided the foundation for important subsequent work on identification by Haavelmo, Reirsøl, Koopmans, Anderson, Rubin, and other researchers at the Cowles Commission in the 1940s and 1950s.

Yet Frisch's influence can be felt equally, if not more so, through his activities as a pioneer in the econometric method and as a founding father of the Econometric Society. Before the 1920s there were a few other pioneers who made use of mathematics and statistics to illuminate economic analysis; Frisch himself was clearly a great admirer of the Norwegian quantitative economist Einar Einarsen. But more perhaps than anyone else, Frisch was responsible for the spread of the econometric method throughout the economics profession.

His exhortations and advice have been enormously influential. Noted earlier were Tinbergen's remarks about Frisch's unbounded energy in Econometric Society meetings. Frisch himself tells of how, at their first meeting, the enthusiasm and optimism of the participants meant that discussion continued throughout dinner, with the tablecloth being used as a blackboard—to the evident concern of the waiters. Earlier editions of *Econometrica* contained enthusiastically worded editorials about the agenda for the new science.

Not all economists, of course, were enthusiastic about the impending econometric revolution. Keynes, for one, was lukewarm and told Frisch that if econometricians did not have something to show at the end of their elaborate calculations then the econometric method was in

danger of falling into disrepute. In the late 1930s, Keynes made his famous critique of the multiple-regression techniques employed by Tinbergen in his study of business cycles. Some of the criticisms Keynes raised were issues that probably concerned Frisch too, but Frisch was resolute in defending the aim of subjecting theoretical work to statistical test.

Yet he was always ready to temper his enthusiasm with necessary caution. In an editorial published shortly after the end of World War II, Frisch wrote of the responsibility of the econometrician. He was beginning to recognize that econometrics could become a pursuit in its own right, and one that could provide deceptively persuasive conclusions. He warned that econometrics is a powerful tool but a dangerous one.

Indeed, this was a theme that recurs throughout his subsequent writings. In September 1955, at the Kiel meeting of the Econometric Society, Frisch again emphasized that econometrics should be the application of statistics and mathematics to the problems of economics, with an equal emphasis on each element. He saw no purpose in cultivating any of these elements on its own. Yet, while Frisch was enormously encouraged by the progress in economic theory and econometric method, he was disappointed by what he saw as a distortion in research activity, declaring, "time and time again it has turned out that it is much easier to sit down and develop refined abstract schemes than to bring numerical data into such a shape as really to make them fit our theories."

At this same meeting, he exhorted fellow economists not to become too enamored of theories and data that would only explain the economic happenings of the past, which he saw as "belated economics." Speaking in paraphrase, he argued that, "The next war will. . . . be decided by an entirely new kind of weapon."

Ten years later, at the First World Congress of the Econometric Society in Rome, Frisch again returned to the matter of social and scientific responsibility and coined the word 'playometrics'—which obviously needs no translation—to summarize his frustration with some developments in the subject. Nevertheless, he suggested in his Nobel Prize speech of June 1970, that the sheer difficulty of economic problems was the reason that econometricians had not yet managed to use the "three triads" of econometrics to full effect.

Frisch was an adviser to the Norwegian Labour government from 1935 onwards. In the later part of his life, his stance on domestic public-policy issues was a radical one. He argued strongly against Norway joining the European Economic Community and lived to see the decision of the 1972 referendum, as a result of which Norway withdrew her application to join the EEC.

After the Second World War, during which he was interned in a Nazi concentration camp, Frisch became very concerned about the planning problems of developing countries, and much of his effort in the postwar period was directed at advising the governments of developing countries. In his Nobel Prize lecture, Frisch tells of an occasion when the Indian ambassador to Norway remarked to him: "Understanding is not enough, you must have compassion." This was a remark that clearly had a profound influence on Frisch. He believed that his "economy-wide" planning models could make a valuable contribution to economic planning and development in those countries.

At the 1955 Kiel meeting of the Econometric Society, Frisch reported that a Norwegian newspaper had been less than flattering about a proposal to send a Norwegian econometrician to India. The newspaper considered that "Norway could have done India a much better service by sending her one more. . . . Norwegian fishing boat." Frisch took this remark in good humor, but the observation betrays his sadness at what he felt was a distortion of priorities within the economics profession.

At his Nobel Prize speech he expressed his pleasure that politicians in a number of countries did find econometric work useful. Frisch said that "it warmed my heart" when a Norwegian politician opened the annual debate on financial matters in November 1969 (a fortnight after the announcement of Frisch's award) with a brief eulogy of the econometrician and a tribute to how much politicians owe to the efforts of econometricians. Frisch felt that Norway was probably (in the late 1960s) the country where the policy application of econometric models had been taken the furthest, and this is a great tribute to Frisch's ability to persuade governments that the economist has a vital role to play in policy discussion.

G. M. PETER SWANN

# Selected Bibliography

The range of Frisch's contributions to economics is enormous, and some of the greatest economists have written excellent essays on his work and fascinating biographical sketches. The following books and articles are among the most important. Arrow (1960) contains a complete list of Frisch's published work to 1960 (prepared by Haavelmo and others at the Oslo University Institute of Economics), and Johansen (1969), updates this to 1969.

## WORKS BY FRISCH

"Sur une problème d'économie pure." *Norsk Matematisk Forenings Skrifter Senes I* 16 (1926): 1–40.

*New Methods of Measuring Marginal Utility.* Tübingen: Verlag van J. C. B. Mohr, 1932.

*Pitfalls in the Statistical Construction of Demand and Supply Curves.* Leipzig: H. Buske, 1933.

"Propagation Problems and Impulse Problems in Dynamic Economics." In *Essays in Honour of Gustav Cassel*, pp. 171–205. London: Allen and Unwin, 1933. Reprinted in Robert A. Gordon and Lawrence R. Klein, *Readings in Business Cycles*, pp.

155–85. Homewood, Il.: Irwin, 1965.

"Circulation Planning," Parts 1, 2. *Econometrica* 2 (1934): 258–336; 422–35.

*Statistical Confluence Analysis by Means of Complete Regression Systems.* Oslo: University Institute of Economics, 1934.

"Annual Survey of General Economic Theory: The Problem of Index Numbers." *Econometrica* 4 (1936): 1–38.

"On the Notion of Equilibrium and Disequilibrium." *Review of Economic Studies* 3 (1936): 100–05.

"Repercussion Studies in Oslo." *American Economic Review.* 38 (1948): 367–372.

"A Complete Scheme for Computing All Direct and Cross Demand Elasticities in a Model with Many Sectors." *Econometrica* 27 (1959): 177–96.

"Numerical Determination of a Quadratic Preference Function for Use in Macroeconomic Planning." In *Studi di Economia, Finanza e Statistica in Onore di Gustavo del Vecchio.* Padua: Edizione CEDAM, 1963.

*Economic Planning Studies: A Collection of Essays.* Edited by Frank Long. Dordrecht, the Netherlands: D. Reidel, 1976.

"From Utopian Theory to Practical Applications: The Case of Econometrics" (Nobel Prize lecture). *American Economic Review* 71:6 (1981): 1–16.

## OTHER WORKS

Andvig, J. C. "Ragnar Frisch and Business Cycle Research During the Interwar Years." *History of Political Economy* 13 (1981): 695–725.

Arrow, Kenneth J. "The Work of Ragnar Frisch, Econometrician." *Econometrica* 28 (1960): 175–92.

Johansen, Leif. "Ragnar Frisch's Scientific Contribution to Economics." *Swedish Journal of Economics*, 71 (1969) 302–24. Reprinted in H. W.

Spiegel and W. J. Samuels, eds., *Contemporary Economics in Perspective*. Greenwich, Ct.: JAI Press, 1984.

Tinbergen, Jan. "Ragnar Frisch's Role in Econometrics: A Sketch." *European Economic Review* 5 (1974): 3–6.

# FRIEDRICH AUGUST VON HAYEK
## *1974*

In 1974 the Royal Swedish Academy of Sciences awarded the Nobel Prize in Economic Sciences jointly to the Swedish social theorist Gunnar Myrdal and the Austrian monetarist and political economist Friedrich August von Hayek (born in Vienna, May 8, 1899). In announcing the award, the two were cited for discovering original and striking ways to "put forward new ideas on causes and politics, a characteristic that often makes them somewhat controversial. . . . This is only natural when the field of research is extended to include factors and linkages which economists usually take for granted or neglect."

## Life and Career

Hayek, scion of a cosmopolitan and scholarly family (he is a peripheral relative of Ludwig Wittgenstein), was raised in an atmosphere permeated by scientific and intellectual curiosity. His maternal grandfather, Franz von Juraschek, a professor of constitutional law, later became a statistician and eventually attained the post of president of the K.u.K. Statistische Zentralkommission (National Statistical Office of Imperial Austria). His father, trained as a medical doctor, later pursued research and taught botany at the University of Vienna. Friedrich's younger brothers became, respectively, professor of anatomy at the University of Vienna and professor of chemistry at the University of Innsbruck.

During World War I, Hayek served as an artillery officer in the Austrian Army on the Italian front (March 1917-November 1918). After the armistice, he enrolled at the University of Vienna, where he studied law and political science, earning doctorates in both fields—in 1921 and 1923, respectively. It was during his years at the University of Vienna that he came under the influence of the Austrian School of Economics—Carl Menger, Friedrich von Wieser, Eugen von Böhm-Bawerk, and Ludwig von Mises.

At the completion of his law degree in 1921, Hayek took a position with the Österreichische Abrechnungsamt (the Austrian bureau for the settlement of prewar debts), directed by Mises. It was during this period as well that Hayek became a member of the famous Mises-Privatseminar, which met at the latter's office at the Vienna Chamber of Commerce. After a brief period (March 1923-May 1924) of study of monetary policy in the United States (Columbia and New York University), Hayek returned to Vienna and became cofounder (with Mises) of the Austrian Institute for Business Cycle Research (1927). While director of this institute (until 1932), he became the first scholar (February 1929) to predict the imminent collapse of the U.S. economy. In 1931, Hayek accepted an appointment to the faculty of the London School of Economics as Tooke Professor of Economic Science and as its first foreign professor. Hayek became a naturalized British citizen in 1938 and remained there until 1949, carrying on an intermittent intellectual and theoretical battle with John Maynard Keynes over what he considered the deleterious results of deficit spending and inflationary manipulation of money and credit by the government.

During the 1930s Hayek and Keynes were the poles around which economic debate revolved over which theoretical path would lead mankind most rapidly out of the slough of the Great Depression. Hayek also became a central figure in the reawakened controversy over the potential of socialism as a means to a more equitable economic order. Despite his flirtation with Fabian socialism in his youth, from the 1930s on he was an inveterate opponent of what he considered any centralized, collective economy's naive and noxious dogmas. Hayek considered himself a champion of classic individualist, free-market liberalism, and it was on his initiative that a conference of social scientists, politicians and media professionals was convened in Mont Pelerin, Switzerland, in 1947. This event led to the establishment of an informal, international think tank, the Mont Pelerin Society, dedicated to sustaining and enhancing the economic and philosophical superstructure of a free society. Under Hayek's leadership (as president until 1960 and since then as honorary president), the society has remained aggressively anti-Communist, and it has grown from its original thirty-nine members (all academics) to a diverse group of some 400 by 1984.

At the end of the fall semester 1949, Hayek resigned from the faculty of the London School of Economics and came to the United States. He spent a semester as visiting professor at the University of Arkansas, and in 1950 he accepted an appointment as professor of social and moral sciences at the University of Chicago and as a member of its Committee on Social Thought. This appointment was owing in part to the extraordinary American success of his *The Road to Serfdom* (1944), which had been published in the United States by the University of Chicago Press. He became associated with the highly traditionalist, liberal "Chicago School" of economics there, whose members included Aaron Director, Milton Friedman, and Frank Knight. He remained at Chicago until 1962, when he was forced into mandatory retirement at age sixty-three.

Almost immediately, Hayek accepted a chair in political economy at the University of Freiburg in West Germany, where he served until 1969. He then accepted a visiting professorship in Austria at the University of Salzburg (1969), returning to Freiburg once again in 1977.

Although not as consistently hectic and controversial as his academic and intellectual life, Hayek's personal life is not without interest. He was married in 1926 to a fellow Viennese, Hella Fritsch. They were divorced in 1949, and he remarried (Helene Bitterlich, also of Vienna) in 1950. His move from London to Chicago was partly due to the emotional strain of the separation and the financial drain of trying to maintain two separate households. The latter pressure perhaps also played a role in Hayek's decision to sell his unique personal library of some 7,000 volumes to the University of Salzburg in 1977.

Hayek has two children by his first marriage, Christine, a biologist at the British Museum, and Laurence, a pathologist. He has been described as a traditional moralist: "reserved," yet possessing an "Old World courtliness." It is a measure of the humane breadth of his interests that he has written not only on such rational ethics as those developed by Bernard de Mandeville,

David Hume, and John Stuart Mill but also has edited the love letters of Mill and Harriet Taylor.

Although perhaps most widely known through his World War II polemical work, *The Road to Serfdom* (1944), and his philosophical disquisitions on the nature of individual freedom—*The Consitution of Liberty* (1960), and *Law, Legislation and Liberty* (Vol. 1: *Rules and Order* [1973]; Vol. 2: *The Mirage of Social Justice* [1976]; and Vol. 3: *The Political Order of a Free People* [1979])—Friedrich von Hayek was a prolific writer not only in the field of economics but in a diverse range of social science disciplines. Fritz Machlup, in a bibliography of Hayek's works that was published in 1976 as a byproduct of his evaluation of the recent Nobel laureate's intellectual contribution and significance, listed fifteen books, ten edited collections of essays, and over 130 articles and shorter pieces. (Machlup's bibliography, impressive as it is, does not include translations and revised editions or any of Hayek's work published after 1976.)

Hayek is unusual in that his works, while appropriately scholarly (that is, reasonably detached and objectively argued), have been focal points of political controversy throughout his career. Clearly, he was aware of the effect his work had on current intellectual debates, for in his only openly tendentious work, *The Road to Serfdom* (1944), he warns the reader in the preface: "This is a political book. I do not wish to disguise this by describing it, as I might perhaps have done, by the more elegant and ambitious name of an essay in social philosophy" (p. ix). His most popular and most widely read book, it sets the tone for the measure of the man's work. It is a frank, open, and courageous book. As Hayek himself says in the preface, "I have every possible reason for *not* writing or publishing this book. It is certain to offend many people with whom I wish to live on friendly terms; . . . and above all, it is certain to prejudice the reception of the results of the more strictly academic work to which all my inclinations lead me" (p. ix–x).

Indeed, as Hayek suggests here, his intellectual development and the direction of his thought were molded in the cauldron of historical experience. Born at the onset of the twentieth century, his work bears the imprint of the crucial events of the modern era. For Hayek, World War I and the runaway inflation in Central Europe it spawned, the Great Depression and the rise of the welfare state, World War II and the threat of totalitarian fascism, and the cold war and the dangers of expansive Soviet-style (Marxist-Leninist) state socialism were the seminal events that directed his attention to particular aspects of sociopolitical experience.

# A Foe of Easy Money

In historical context, the development of Hayek's thought neatly parallels the course of historical events. In the 1920s he was involved in an official capacity with the Austrian attempt to fight free of the burden of wartime debt and inflation. In this period his primary concerns were monetary policy, business-cycle theory, and the control of inflation. Ignored as a prophet in his own country as elsewhere, Hayek went to the London School of Economics in the year the depression he had predicted struck the world economy. His first book, *Geldtheorie und Konjunkturtheorie* (1929), set the tone for his work in the 1930s. Later published in English under the title *Monetary Theory and the Trade Cycle* (1933), it was a direct challenge to those who sought to maintain a balanced economy through price stabilization. In fact, Hayek questioned the whole concept of "price level" as it was then understood. He denied any reciprocal relationship between prices and total volume of production.

For Hayek, it was the actual flow of money expenditure (through credit policy and banking decisions) that had the greatest influence on both prices and production. Thus, as he argued elsewhere, between 1927 and 1929 in the United States, when prices would naturally have fallen, bringing the artificial and frenetic economic boom of the late 1920s to a relatively smooth and gradual end, the U.S. government pursued an easy-money policy, thereby sparking overinvestment and prolonging the boom for two more years. Then, after the depression had begun, again the government pursued economic policies to sustain consumption, and thereby production, artificially. As a result, Hayek argued, what might have been a relatively mild depression will forever be known to history as the "Great" Depression (*Prices and Production* [1931], 161–62).

For the rest of the decade 1931–41, Hayek's work centered on purely economic issues, developing his general argument that inflationary monetary policies were irrational in that they misled investors, causing them to confuse artificially created demand with genuine market-generated demand. The result, he maintained, was a severely dislocated economy, the direct consequence of a concentration of capital and resources in less productive areas.

It was also in this period that Hayek began his fifty-year ongoing debate with the teachings of John Maynard Keynes. The first salvo in this intellectual battle over economic theory came with Hayek's review of Keynes's *Treatise on Money* (1930) in *Economica* (August 1931 and February 1932). Keynes's response was in the first instance a counter attack on Hayek's *Prices and Production* (1931), and in the second instance the assertion that he had changed his mind about the system outlined in the *Treatise*.

Thus, when Keynes published his *General Theory of Employment, Interest and Money* (1936), Hayek uncharacteristically did not respond. His stated reasons for not doing so are interesting and are very useful in helping us put Hayek's economic thought into perspective. In the first place, Hayek found the work vaguely meretricious. Quite naturally, he also felt that Keynes might well change his mind again, as he had earlier. Finally, and most sig-

nificantly, he found that his disagreement with Keynes was not merely over the details of implementation of the fiscal program but with the very essence of the analytical approach. It was the validity of macroeconomics that was at issue. Hayek later had cause sincerely to regret his decision not to address critically the *General Theory*, because it was that work more than any other that led to the ascendancy of macroeconomic analysis in the 1940s. The kind of microeconomic theory propounded by Hayek was eclipsed by the triumph of Keynesianism in the nearly four decades between 1936 and 1972.

Indeed, one of Hayek's students at the University of Chicago in the early 1950s described his circle as "a tiny minority of social outcasts denounced as a bunch of 'reactionaries.'" Chiaki Nishiyama went on to note that Hayek found himself almost an "untouchable" in academic circles who was routinely attacked by critics of a free-market economy. No doubt he exaggerates for effect when he describes Hayek's academic life as characterized by fierce integrity and tenacity that alone made it possible for him to endure "this intellectually almost unbearable life" (*Essence of Hayek*, p. lx), but it is no exaggeration to say that Hayek's economic theories were out of favor during the hegemony of Keynesianism. It was largely the accuracy of his predictions in the long term— that inflationary monetary policy would only lead to an accelerating spiral of inflation coupled with productive entropy and higher levels of unemployment (the phenomenon described as "stagflation" in the early 1970s)—that brought Hayek wider influence in theoretical economic circles and by the mid-1970s, a Nobel Prize.

## Free-Marker Theorist and Critic of Statism

In the mid-1940s Hayek turned his attention away from pure economic theory and began to investigate the links between the political order and economic organization. This inquiry was an immediate outgrowth of his more technical work, especially his vehement opposition to central economic planning and the emergent welfare states of the West. The most powerful and accessible statement of his ideas was *The Road to Serfdom* (1944). He followed this work with a collection of essays, *Individualism and Economic Order* (1948), a number of which address the thorny problems of socialist economic planning, especially the quest to unravel the gordian knot of effectively, efficiently, and equitably allocating resources through centralized economic direction. The other major theme addressed in both of these volumes is the symbiotic relationship between individual freedom and a spontaneous market economy.

*The Road to Serfdom* is a thoroughly inverted utopia for those who believe in the universal panacea of a centrally planned, rationally integrated, equitable social-welfare state. Yet even here Hayek's approach is not a simple mechanistic laissez-faire one. He does not set an anarchistic free market against an ordered, planned one but establishes an antithesis between "planning" and the "rule of law." In a democratic polity, the irony of planning to enhance egalitarianism is that it undermines individual responsibility and fosters a hypertrophied statism. The end result of a planned or mixed economy (just as of a pure socialistic one) is an insinuating totalitarianism and the death of freedom. Two years before George Orwell's *Animal Farm* and five years before Orwell's classic depiction of a bleak future devoid of personal choice and identity, Hayek had warned of the dangers of "1984" inherent in the utopic ignis fatuus of a planned economy.

In the end, Hayek argues, belief that a planned economy can provide greater security for all society's members is little more than an act of faith. What has made it such a prepotent creed is its presumed rationalism, but that rationalism is itself, he tells us, incomplete and erroneous.

Hayek also anticipated the onset of the cold war in *The Road to Serfdom*. He explicitly rejected the idea of a "Third Way" of socioeconomic organization. Mankind was at a cross-roads and must choose between two systems, "two irreconcilable types of social organization." One he characterized as "commercial," the other as "military." Control equals security at the cost of regimentation; openness equals danger with the cost of responsibility. Hayek summarizes the two alternatives in an epigram borrowed from Wilhelm Roepke: "The last resort of a competitive economy is the bailiff; the ultimate sanction of a planned economy is the hangman" (*The Road to Serfdom*, p. 126).

Hayek intended *The Road to Serfdom* to be read not as predictive but as premonitory; it was a kind of cautionary tale or theoretical morality play. Like Scrooge, we had been shown the shadows of things that *might* be; if we mended our ways we could still alter the shape of the future. Nor did Hayek believe that economic justice was absolutely inconsistent with an economy in which the market rather than men determined the boundaries of economic choice.

## Philosophical Idealism

As a mature scholar in the 1950s, Hayek turned his attention to the evolutionary process alluded to in his analysis of the postwar world, concerning himself both with the evolution of mental order and socioeconomic institutions. In *The Sensory Order* (1952), his primary interests revolved around epistemological questions, particularly the psychology of the process of knowing. Although his argument is seemingly adventitious, a brief survey amply repays the reader through a deepened understanding of the conceptual notions that underlie the abstract entity of the market and the interaction of individual human beings with the economic system associated with market dynamics. Briefly, for Hayek, our knowledge of the external world is not mediated through a series of discrete,

isolated facts; rather we perceive the world as a set of general systems of classifications. This series of "orders," is not derived from the qualities of objects themselves but is imposed on reality by the mental processes of the mind itself. The sensory realm is a unitary, orderly one; the empirical details of sensory data have meaning only within the scope of the overarching mental order that perceives, arranges, and encompasses them into an integrated system of knowledge. The function of the mind is to classify sensory perceptions, to create an order out of subjective experience.

Hayek's philosophical position here is a form of idealism, or perhaps more accurately, subjectivism, in that it denies that thought and the mind can be explained by reference to objective empirical phenomena. Experimental science, which concerns itself with measurable, physical phenomena, cannot understand either sensory perception or the interaction of mind and matter. The external world is to be understood through the mental process of categorization, through the generation of classifications of objects and theories about their operation and interaction. Finally, given the complexities of the perceived world, Hayek insists on the ineluctable limitations on human knowledge. This absolute limitation on man's understanding he grounds in a logical extension of the Cartesian anthropological or a posteriori argument for the existence of God. Any agent or apparatus of classification can only comprehend entities and systems less complex than itself. Any system provides sufficient structure to understand the elements of which it is comprised, but it cannot fully encompass the totality of its own system.

In the light of this somewhat technical philosophical discussion, it is easier to see why Hayek believes that systemic, centralized economic planning can never work. The economy is a vast and complex system of the natural world, a structure of groups; as such it is beyond the capacity of any single mind or any set of minds to fully comprehend. Policies based on partial knowledge of the economic order (a subcategory of the general sensory order) cannot but fail; control and order of the economic realm require a transcendently complex agent of perception. Man is not that agent. We can, however, come to know (to the extent of our capacities) the theory of that portion of the economic order we come into direct contact with, and we can base our economic decisions in our limited spheres on that understanding.

Hayek developed this line of thinking in his other major work from this period, *The Counter-Revolution of Science* (1952). Especially in the essay "Scientism and the Study of Society," he attacked the then-current dominance of scientific methodology in the social sciences. Pure science relies on simple models of empirically verifiable phenomena; a social science like economics involves a psychological dimension, an interiority, that renders it essentially praxeological. Given the complexity of the economic order, the essentially behavioralist nature of the data about the interrelationship between individuals and economic processes, and the kind of laws sought by science—those that yield predictability—the scientific model is inadequate for the social sciences.

We must be careful not to conclude from this quick summary of some of the more abstruse aspects of Hayek's thought that he was an irrationalist (or, as some have more generously put it, an intuitionist for whom the objective world was subjectively realized), or a dogmatist. Like David Hume, he employed the sword of reason to question the apotheosis of Reason, but he certainly did not advocate irrational approaches to problems. As a rough tool, reason works well enough for the individual mind; only when its grasp outreaches its ken, as when it seeks to plan the economic order of an entire society, does reason become unreason. Nor is Hayek dogmatic. He shares the Aristotelian sense of becoming, that the world is constantly in a state of change. As he maintained in his introduction to *Capitalism and the Historians* (1954), the "facts" of the objective world are considered such only within the perceptual paradigms we bring to our understanding of them. We develop hypotheses about reality based on those facts, but if they do not correspond to our altered perceptions of that reality, we develop a new paradigm and discard "'facts which everybody knows' have long been proved not to have been facts at all" (*The Essence of Hayek*, p. 162).

Inherent in Hayek's thinking is a theory of the autonomous-spontaneous evolution of social institutions. It owes much to Bernard de Mandeville, Adam Smith, David Hume, and Adam Ferguson, who all questioned a socioeconomic order grounded in intentional design serving as the basis for the anthropormorphic projections of deism's deity—the great designer or cosmic watchmaker. Social evolution, for Hayek, proceeds through "group selection"; it is the result of the actions and activities of numerous individuals, which may be intentional on a personal level, but the collective results of which transcend individual or even particular group intentionality. As Hayek expressed it, evolution constituted a process whereby "practices which had first been adopted for other reasons, or even purely accidentally, were preserved because they enabled the group in which they had arisen to prevail over others" (*Law, Legislation and Liberty*, Vol. 1: *Rules and Order*, p. 9).

# Reevaluating the Liberal Tradition

In the 1960s and 1970s, Hayek turned his scholarly attention to a major project in political philosophy—the reevaluation of the classic English liberal tradition. That task was initiated in *The Constitution of Liberty* (1960), a massive volume that reformulated classical liberal doctrine in modern terms and began to expand its philosophical bases. It provides a unique argument for the necessity of individual freedom: it is precisely man's mental limitations that make individual freedom im-

perative. Taking a cue from Michael Polanyi's concept of "tacit knowing," Hayek argues that the relativity of human knowledge is such that not only is our knowledge extremely limited, but we are not conscious of all the knowledge we do have. A centralized governmental system would be able to exploit only our explicit or conscious knowledge and would thus provide society access only to that part of social knowledge that can be expressed in logical propositions. Hayek also introduces the concept of the rule of law in this work, so it might best be considered an extended prolegomenon to his central opus, *Law, Legislation and Liberty*.

In the first volume of this latter work, *Rules and Order* (1973), Hayek lays out the fundamental socal/philosophical insights that inform it. He makes a careful distinction between a "spontaneous order," by which he means to imply what Adam Smith meant by "the Great Society" (but certainly *not* what Lyndon Baines Johnson meant by the same term!), and an "organization." An "organization" is a group of individuals who come together for a particular purpose, and it is governed by "construction" or intentionality. The Great Society, on the other hand (the invisible one!), is the product of social evolution. These two social entities are governed by different kinds of rules or laws.

In contradistinction to the "organization" order of modern pluralistic democracies, Hayek sets a spontaneous, "grown" order that simultaneously expands and limits our powers of control over our social environment. This spontaneous order is perceived as organic in nature, since it "results from the individual elements adapting themselves to circumstances which directly affect only some of them, and which in their totality need not be known to anyone, [and] it may extend to circumstances so complex that no mind can comprehend them all" (*Rules and Order*, p. 41).

The bulk of this first volume of *Law, Legislation and Liberty* is taken up with a consideration of the social evolution of law. The main argument here is that law precedes legislation and probably even language. The second stage of evolution is what Hayek calls "nomos: the law of liberty." This constitutes judicial law, established to regulate interpersonal conduct. It is part of a system of interrelated laws designed to define the boundaries of personal liberty and to be applicable to an unforeseeable set of similar incidents in the future. The final evolution of law is the legislative or nomothetic stage, or what Hayek calls "thesis." Here we move from the realm of universal rules of just conduct (nomos) to those rules necessary for governmental organization (more commonly the distinction is described as private versus public law). Over the last century, as public law has come to predominate in Western societies, Hayek contends that "the principle that in a free society coercion is permissible only to secure obedience to universal rules of conduct has been abandoned . . . mainly in the service of what were called 'social' aims." Thus, Hayek

confronts us with yet another of the ironies characteristic of his vision of the operation of the social order: the expansion of the realm of law has resulted in less rather than more protection of the rights and freedoms of the individual.

*The Mirage of Social Justice* (1976), the second volume of the series, extends the critique of statist legalism made in the first volume and contends that "in a free society the general good consists principally in the facilitation of the pursuit of unknown individual purposes" (p. 1). The rules (laws) of a free society thus facilitate rather than legislate the general welfare of its citizens.

Social or distributive justice, from Hayek's perspective, is the attempt to force society rather than individuals to behave justly. But society is an impersonal entity; it is incapable of acting for a specific purpose. Only individuals, if they organize themselves, have the power to assign particular shares of goods and services to various individuals and groups. In order to accomplish this purpose, though, society must displace justice from the realm of individual responsibility and place it increasingly in the hands of authorities who have the power to command obedience. In other words, distributive justice can only be achieved at the price of individual freedom.

For Hayek, "society" is an abstraction; it is "not an acting person but an orderly structure of actions resulting from the observation of certain abstract rules by its members." "We all owe the benefits we receive from the operation of this structure," he concludes;

> not to anyone's intention to confer them on us, but to the members of society generally obeying certain rules in the pursuit of their interests, rules which include the rule that nobody is to coerce others in order to secure for himself (or for third persons) a particular income. This imposes upon us the obligation to abide by the results of the market [that is, the structure of interdependent rules] also when it turns against us. (*Mirage*, p. 95)

But Hayek does not consistently and remorselessly maintain the absolute impersonality of the market and the effects of its rules on individuals. He concedes that a free society may provide protection against extreme deprivation in the form of a guaranteed minimum income. Such a program, apart from moral considerations, may well be in the interests of all and can most importantly be accomplished without interfering with the general structure of complexly interdependent rules that constitutes the market. On the other hand, he opposes such interventions in the market as agricultural price supports pursuant to a parity farm program and the existence of labor unions, since both are "organizations" that seek to realize a schedule of limited benefits through intentionality and thereby violate the delicate systemic balance of the intricate and highly interdependent structure of autonomous law that is the market. To fully grasp the theoretical bases of Hayek's argument here, we must keep in mind that he has a very specific definition of "market"—or in broader terms, "economy"—in mind here.

Hayek has coined the term *catallaxy* "to describe the order brought about by the mutual adjustment of many individual economies in a market. A *catallaxy* is thus the special kind of spontaneous order produced by the market through people [as individuals] acting within the rules of the law of property, tort, and contract" (*Mirage*, pp. 108–09).

It is the *catallaxy* that for Hayek provides the basis for a free society, without which free will is impossible. "Men can be allowed to act," Hayek asserts,

> on their own knowledge and for their own purposes only if the reward they obtain is dependent in part on circumstances which they can neither control nor foresee. And if they are to be allowed to be guided in their actions by their own moral beliefs, it cannot also be morally required that the aggregate effects of their respective actions on the different people should correspond to some ideals of distributive justice. In this sense, freedom is inseparable from rewards which often have no connection with merit and are therefore felt to be unjust. (*Mirage*, p. 120)

In the third volume of the series, *The Political Order of a Free People* (1979), Hayek addresses the political dimensions of a free society made possible by *catallaxy*. His basic tenets of belief again tend toward the libertarian. He fears what John C. Calhoun, the great political pundit of antebellum Southern separatism, called "the tyranny of the majority." That coercion, he maintains, while necessary in any state, "should be allowed only for the purpose of ensuring obedience to rules of just conduct approved by most, or at least by a majority, seems to be the essential condition for the absence of arbitrary power and therefore of freedom" (p. 5). He deplores the devolution of democracy and in fact suggests that "demarchy" (which implies popular government by rules) or "isonomy" (the rule of equal law for all) would be preferable political ideals.

In sum, the guardians of freedom must insure that the powers of government politically and economically (as the public sector) are strictly delimited to protect individuals against arbitrary and excessive taxation, expropriation, and invasion of privacy. Hayek makes the interdependence of the economic and political spheres clear when he asserts that the public sector "should not be conceived of as a range of purposes for the pursuit of which government is asked to meet so long as and in so far as they cannot be met in better ways" (p. 49).

# Hayek's Intellectual Legacy

Throughout a long and extraordinarily productive career, Friedrich von Hayek has been a consistent champion of the rights of the individual, the benefits of a free economy, and an open, democratic society. Long considered a reactionary because of his outspoken opposition to the Keynesian hegemony, he has lived to see many of his predictions

relating to the inherent tendency of an expansionist monetary policy to produce not a stable economy but accelerating inflation fulfilled in the long term. His contention that the therapeutics of Keynesian economics treated the symptoms but only exacerbated the disease seems to have been accurate. His critique of political economy in the broadest sense served as the philosophical basis for the resurgent fiscal conservatism of the 1970s that swept Ronald Reagan into office in 1980.

Some of the specific practical remedies Hayek suggested, like smaller government, an end to arbitrary taxation (translated into political terms as lower taxes), and more significantly, the end of reliance on "social engineering" and the dismantling of "welfare statism," have become the ideological shibboleths of a resurgent Right that has employed them in a cynically amoral and antiintellectual way that betrays the spirit of Hayek's work. He has often erroneously been considered, for example, both by opponents and epigones, an ardent advocate of laissezfaire economics. In reality, Hayek has consistently maintained that in a genuinely free society order emerges spontaneously through the systemic rules developed by nonteleological individual choices and actions. Laissez-faire doctrine routinely seeks freedom through elimination of rules. This doctrine Hayek considers a prescription not for a better society but for anarchy.

On the other hand, Hayek's concept of an omnificent, transcendent, and autonomous market has provided the intellectual respectability for current doctrines that assert an omnipresent market which subsumes all human activity. In this view, all areas of human endeavor are and always should be controlled by the conditions of the market (in Hayek's terms, by the "economies," which are the limited portion of the total universe in which they subsist). Any distinction between more strictly quantitative kinds of endeavor and qualitative and aesthetic ones is lost. Given the realities of competition, this aspect of Hayek's legacy can only be seen as a further and perhaps catastrophic detriment for those areas of the *catallaxy*, like education and social services, that have traditionally experienced devaluation.

Hayek's thought is not only extensive in depth but nearly universal in scope. He has analyzed political-economy and political philosophy from the perspective of numerous disciplines, among the most prominent being philosophy, economics, jurisprudence, political science, psychology, anthropology, biology, and history. His ideas are complex and subtle; his conclusions emphasize the limitations on human capacity and the ironies of free will and human intentionality. Indeed, the rhetorical device most characteristic of his work is paradox. It is not surprising that he has frequently been misunderstood and his ideas perverted to baser purposes by meanspirited politicians.

While it is difficult to agree wholeheartedly with Hayek's economic theories, especially in light of practical malapplications, his significance as a philosophical thinker will undoubtedly be the core of his

enduring intellectual legacy. His achievement in that area is easy to underestimate, and the esoteric nature of some of his ideas again has led to misunderstanding. He has been considered by some an old-fashioned Burkean conservative and by others a utopian radical. Yet, no doubt he has sought to stand with a general humanity between the political extremes. Like Goethe in 1774 (*Dichtung und Wahrheit*), he saw "Prophete Rechts, Prophete Links, Das Weltkind in der Mitten" (Prophets on the right and left, mankind in the middle).

What Hayek attempted to do was nothing less than to drag rationalism, classical liberalism, and traditional individualist democratic theory as a viable body of thought into the twentieth century, against the stream of irrationalism, statism, and collectivism that has characterized modern sensibility. He has been condemned as a reactionary because he considered our era "an age of superstition, chiefly connected with the names of Karl Marx and Sigmund Freud" (*The Political Order of a Free People*, pp. 175–76). Yet, with characteristic irony, he emphasized that those "superstitions" and a concomitant "tribal ethics" were largely the inheritance of the Age of Reason that so deplored ignorant credulity. He fervently believed that if Western Civilization were to survive it would need to renounce the errors of superstition. Rationalism provided the last best hope for mankind, but only a rationalism suited to modern sensibilities. His great accomplishment was to provide the link between the great English tradition of rationalism associated with Adam Smith, John Locke, Bernard de Mandeville, and David Hume, and the body of modern scientific and social scientific thought. This critical rationalism, or "methodological individualism," as one critic called it, is the very essence of his thought. (*Essence of Hayek*, p. liv).

In *The Fatal Conceit* (1988), Hayek again turns his attention to a refutation of socialism as an egalitarian "superstition." Consistently, throughout his career, he has warned a society that values individualism and deplores coercion that "freedom means that in some measure we entrust our fate to forces we do not control; and this seems intolerable to those constructivists who believe that man can master his fate—as if civilization and reason itself were of his making" (*The Mirage of Social Justice*, p. 30). Only when we fully understand and willingly accept the limitations of our freedom will we be truly and finally free. This is the ultimate challenge for a democratic society as we, like Yeats's "rough beast," slouch toward the twenty-first century.

LOUIS KERN

# Selected Bibliography

## WORKS BY HAYEK

*Prices and Production*. London: Routledge, 1931.

*Monetary Theory and the Trade Cycle*. London: Jonathan Cape, 1933.

*Profits, Interest and Investment and Other Essays on The Theory of Industrial Fluctuations*. London: Routledge & Kegan Paul, 1939.

*The Pure Theory of Capital*. London: Routledge & Kegan Paul, 1941.

*The Road to Serfdom*. Chicago: University of Chicago Press, 1944.

*Individualism and Economic Order*. Chicago: University of Chicago Press, 1948.

*The Sensory Order*. Chicago: University of Chicago Press, 1952.

*The Counter-revolution of Science: Studies on the Abuse of Reason*. Glencoe, Il.: Free Press, 1952. 2d ed. Indianapolis: Liberty Press, 1979.

*The Constitution of Liberty*. Chicago: University of Chicago Press, 1960.

*Studies in Philosophy, Politics and Economics*. Chicago: University of Chicago Press, 1967.

*Law, Legislation and Liberty: A New Statement of the Liberal Principles of Justice and Political Economy*. Vol. I, *Rules and Order*. Vol. 2, *The Mirage of Social Justice*. Vol. 3, *The Political Order of a Free People*. Chicago: University of Chicago Press, 1973, 1976, 1979.

*New Studies in Philosophy, Politics, Economics and the History of Ideas*. Chicago: University of Chicago Press, 1978.

*The Fatal Conceit*, W. W. Bartley, ed. London: Routledge, 1988.

Hayek, Friedrich von, ed. *Capitalism and the Historians*. Chicago: University of Chicago Press, 1954.

## OTHER WORKS

Barry, Norman P. *Hayek's Social and Economic Philosophy*. London: Macmillan Press, 1979.

Nishiyama, Chiaki, and Leube, Kurt R. *The Essence of Hayek*. Stanford, Ca.: Hoover Institution Press, 1984.

# JOHN RICHARD HICKS   *1972*

John Richard Hicks was born in 1904 in Leamington Spa in the English Midlands. He went to school at Clifton College and to university at Balliol College, Oxford, where he studied politics, philosophy and economics (1922–25). A year's research led to a teaching post at the London School of Economics (1926–35). In 1935 he married the economist Ursula Kathleen Webb (1896–1985). After an interval at Cambridge (1935–38), Hicks was appointed to the Jevons Chair at Manchester University (1938–46).

In 1946 he accepted a fellowship at Nuffield College, Oxford, and in 1952, the Drummond Professorship at Oxford University. After retiring in 1965 he continued to work at Oxford, where he is a Fellow of All Souls College. In 1964 he was knighted for services to economic science. This résumé, together with a small library of publications, public service on government commissions in Great Britain and abroad, and a lifetime of university teaching and administration, is a bare outline of Sir John's academic career. Its distinction was acknowledged by the award (jointly with Kenneth Arrow) of the 1972 Nobel Prize.

The official announcement of the Royal Swedish Academy of Sciences cited Hicks's and Arrow's "pioneering contributions to general equilibrium theory and welfare theory." The Prize was also seen as a lifetime achievement award, since each made fundamental advances in many areas.

The pairing of Hicks and Arrow was not inappropriate. Hicks's *Value and Capital* (1939) was the starting point for Arrow's general-equilibrium theory in the 1950s, and they have several academic interests in common. They are, however, of different generations and did not work together. In retrospect, it seems slightly unfortunate that the prize committee gave the appearance of being in a hurry to reduce the backlog of eminent contenders by awarding jointly a prize which both Hicks and Arrow richly deserved to win outright.

The historian who attempts to describe the achievement and influence of Sir John Hicks will be faced by a formidable amount of information. His writing spans nearly sixty years, from "Wage Fixing in the Building Industry" (*Economica*, 1928), to *Methods of Economic Dynamics* (1985). The flow of books, articles, and reviews has been continuous. Scarcely any of these contributions are ephemeral, some have been reprinted many times, and others are so fully incorporated into the main body of economics as to make it difficult sometimes to appreciate how much was novel at the time. Other work is on the frontiers of the subject and remains to be assessed fully.

Fortunately we have the best possible guide to Hicksian economics in Sir John himself; frequently, he has returned to earlier themes with comments, explanations, and revisions. A personal account of his career and intellectual development is contained in "The Formation of an Economist" (*Banca Nazionale Del Lavoro*, 1979), and he has edited his *Collected Essays* (3 vols., 1981–83). If Hicks is a less than perfect guide to his own work, it is because, often, he has been his own sharpest critic. This endearing trait is rare in academics. Other economists have been anything but reticent in acknowledging Hicks's importance. William Baumol wrote a comprehensive appreciation (*Swedish Journal of Economics*, 1972), and a volume of essays was presented to Sir John on the occasion of his retirement (*Value, Capital and Growth*, J. N. Wolfe, ed., 1968). Another distinguished group contributed to *Economic Theory and Hicksian Themes* (D. A. Collard, et al., 1984), to mark his eightieth birthday.

What then are Hicks's achievements? He supposed that he got the Nobel Prize for *Value and Capital* and for a series of papers which came to be known as Kaldor-Hicks welfare economics. Probably this supposition was correct, but two diagrammatic devices make an indelible impression on economists at the undergraduate level. In microeconomics, whenever economists face a problem which involves choice, be it a consumer choosing baskets of goods, an investor selecting a portfolio of shares, or a burglar weighing the profits of crime against the cost of being caught, instinctively they conjure up a picture of an indifference curve. Similarly, in macroeconomics, when some change in the

system is contemplated, as a first approximation at least, it is impossible to avoid a mental picture of schedules labelled IS and LM. Hicks invented IS-LM and is responsible for the pervasive influence of the indifference curve.

If we add to these the concepts of the elasticity of substitution (for production and utility functions) and post-Marshallian refinements of the notion of consumer surplus, it becomes apparent that Hicks is responsible for a large part of the average economist's tool kit and for a lot of examination questions. As an overview, this summary places too much weight on Hicks as a toolmaker and too little on his later work. In what follows, some attempt will be made to correct the balance but, in Hicks's opinion, much of his best work was complete by the time he left the London School of Economics in 1935.

## The LSE Years

According to his own account, Hicks's economics education consisted mainly of "on the job training" at the London School of Economics (LSE). Although he says he left Oxford with no useful economics, he had a good education in philosophy and politics, was well trained in mathematics, and acquired a reading knowledge of Italian, French, and (later) German. Probably it is also important to remember that boys of his generation who were educated at good public schools (which in Britain means private schools), were thoroughly grounded in the classics. The cleverest products of this system acquired a disciplined sensitivity to the precise use of language that is basic to clear thinking and the ability to multiply intellectual distinctions. This ability is a feature of Hicks's economics and is perhaps fundamental to progress in many areas of scientific enquiry.

Hicks was determined on an academic career and says, "I was advised that economics was an expanding industry, so I would have a better chance of employment if I went that way. So I did." At the LSE he was a member of an exceptionally talented group, which included Lionel Robbins, Roy Allen, Friedrich von Hayek, Richard Sayers, Abba Lerner, and Nicolas Kaldor. The LSE was regarded popularly as a hotbed of socialism, but the Economics Department had a free-market tradition which was continued by Robbins when he became head of the department in 1929. Although Hicks, Kaldor, and others were to depart from it in later years, the general view of the LSE economists in the 1930s was that the market system, if left to itself, was capable of dealing with the unemployment problem.

However, another feature of the LSE Economic Department was of greater importance in Hicks's intellectual development. Much more than any other university in Britain, the LSE was international in its outlook. It attracted many distinguished foreign visitors, and young lecturers were encouraged to take an interest in the European schools. A colleague, Hugh Dalton (chancellor of the exchequer, 1945–47), first suggested that Hicks should read

Vilfredo Pareto. Later he became familiar with the Austrian school and the work of Knut Wicksell and Gunnar Myrdal. Intellectually, the LSE was nearer to Vienna and Lausanne than it was to Cambridge, which was about to embark on the Keynesian revolution. Though the economics of John Maynard Keynes came to preoccupy Hicks, as it did most economists of his generation, he learned much of his economics from the Europeans. Their influence on his work was always strong and become even more evident in his later years.

Hicks's first major work was *The Theory of Wages* (1932). It was published when Hicks was still primarily a labor economist and content to go along with the LSE free-market consensus. The book treated the major topics of labor economics in the marginal-productivity framework and seemed to stress the neoclassical view that interference with market mechanisms (such as trade unions and minimum-wage laws) that raised wages above their equilibrium level would cause unemployment.

The publication of *The Theory of Wages* was untimely. It coincided with the worst year of the Depression, when Keynes and others were becoming convinced of the inadequacy of neoclassical theory for explaining widespread long-term unemployment. Hicks rapidly repudiated parts of it, and today *The Theory of Wages* is best remembered for its technical accomplishments in production and distribution theory. It introduced the concept of the elasticity of substitution as a measure of the curvature of an isoquant (the locus of all labor-capital quantities that generate a particular output), and investigated its importance for the effect of biased technical change on factor shares. An appendix contained a demonstration of the conditions in which the sum of the marginal products will, in pure competition add up to the value of the total product. These innovations led to a large literature on biased technical progress and relative factor shares, although Hicks played little part in it.

## Demand Theory

Hicks's reputation as a theorist was established by a pair of articles written with Roy Allen, entitled "A Reconsideration of the Theory of Value" (*Economica*, 1934). These articles contain the basic elements of modern demand theory. They also introduced the indifference curve into the everyday thinking of economists. The main force of Hicks's and Allen's analysis was to free demand theory from its dependence on a notion of utility which could be quantified on a cardinal scale. Using indifference curves and budget lines, Hicks and Allen derived the same results as those based on cardinal utility theory with fewer assumptions and greater clarity. Their method, which is described fully in all textbooks, had the additional advantage of allowing income and substitution effects to be decomposed diagrammatically and mathematically.

It is possible to question both the importance and the novelty of the Hicks-Allen approach to demand theory. Hicks has doubted whether the ordinal approach was so great an advance over Marshall's method and has denied similar claims for the superiority of Paul Samuelson's revealed-preference theory. We also know that a Russian economist, Eugen Slutsky, anticipated Hicks and Allen and that the indifference curve was introduced into economics by F. Y. Edgeworth in 1883 and had been used in demand theory by Pareto. But these are minor qualifications.

Hicks and Allen have dominated the way in which demand theory has been taught for fifty years, and their approach is a masterpiece of theorizing from minimal assumptions to interesting hypotheses. Above all, they designed a powerful analytic apparatus. G. L. S. Shackle has called the indifference curve "the most efficient visualizer that economists possess." Hicks and Allen grasped its importance and are responsible for its pervasive influence, which can be seen in countless applications in many areas of economics.

## Money and Keynes

Hicks has said that in 1929, he "knew nothing at all about money; so when I read of the stock market crash I had no idea what it meant." In those days monetary economics was concerned largely with banking theory and was scarcely integrated with the rest of economics. At the LSE, the classical dichotomy between money and the "real" world was actually institutionalized, since monetary economics was taught in a separate department. Hicks was aware of the inadequacy of the monetary component of *The Theory of Wages* and, after his work with Allen, was struck by the applicability of their methods to the demand for money. The result was "A Suggestion for Simplifying the Theory of Money" (*Economica*, 1935), which remains one of his best regarded and most frequently cited articles.

The article might have been described as a generalization rather than a simplification. Hicks already thought of liquidity as a concept ranging over the whole spectrum of assets and proposed that "we ought to regard every individual in the community as being, on a small scale, a bank." Individuals, like banks, hold portfolios of real and financial assets which include money, and to a value theorist it seemed obvious that the choice between these assets ought to depend on their value at the margin. Hicks defined the central problem as the need to explain why individuals and institutions sacrifice income by holding money.

He first discusses "frictions" such as transactions costs and then turns to a world of imperfect knowledge, where portfolio selection depends on the mean and variance of probability distributions of expected yields. He goes on to argue that the demand-for-money function may not be stable and speculates about the connection between wealth and the demand for money. Here, in outline, was an agenda for research into the portfolio approach to the demand for money which lay dormant for more than twenty years, until it was taken up by James Tobin and others.

This article marked the beginning of Hicks's transition to the Keynesian way of thinking. Earlier he had written about risk and liquidity. Gradually he came to believe that "the use of money is enough in itself to make a free-market system unstable." At the time, he was not aware of the similarities between his article and Keynes's theory of liquidity preference, though Keynes was. By this time Hicks had moved to Cambridge, but he was not close to Keynes or his junior colleagues and was relatively aloof from the bitter fighting between Keynesians and anti-Keynesians. In 1936, Keynes, who edited the *Economic Journal*, asked Hicks to review *The General Theory of Employment, Interest and Money*, presumably because he thought that Hicks would be an independent but sympathetic reviewer.

# Keynes and the Classics

Throughout his career, Hicks has assessed and reassessed the *General Theory*, but his second attempt, "Mr. Keynes and the 'Classics'" (*Econometrica*, 1937), remains the best known. The entertainment value of the *General Theory* was enhanced, as Hicks observed, by the invention of "the classical economist" who was dim enough to be swept aside by the brilliance of Keynes's insights but sufficiently clever to have understood A. C. Pigou's *The Theory of Employment*, which was "a fairly new, and an exceedingly difficult book." This literary fiction was offensive to many who might otherwise have learned more from Keynes more quickly.

Hicks, with a head cooler than most, constructed a less contentious classical model and, as a means of spotlighting the issues at stake, compared it with his own understanding of Keynes's innovations. For purposes of exposition, Hicks presented the Keynesian model in two reduced-form equations, which represented equilibrium in the goods and the money markets. In graphical form, they were labelled IS and LL, but this did not catch on, so eventually Hicks, like everyone else, called them IS and LM. He then showed that differences in Keynesian and classical policy prescriptions could be explained by different assumptions about the slopes and positions of the schedules.

In his later years Hicks has seemed almost embarrassed by the success of IS-LM, and in 1975 he wrote that the diagram was "much less popular with me than I think it still is with many other people." Prominent among those other people was Robert Solow, who, in the first annual Hicks lecture (in *Economic Theory and Hicksian Themes*) found much to say to Hicks the Elder in defense of Hicks the Younger. There have been at least two strands to the long debate about the demerits of IS-LM. Some have asked whether it is a faithful representation of the economics of Keynes; others, seeming almost to overlook its origins as an expository device, have criticized it as a model in its own right.

It is undoubtedly true that IS-LM does not capture all of the *General Theory*. Some Keynesians have argued that its core is in Chapter 12, which deals with expectations and uncertainty. They never liked IS-LM. On the other hand, Keynes seemed to approve. In a letter to Hicks, he wrote, "I found it very interesting and have next to nothing to say by way of criticism."

The other line of attack, which seemed to treat IS-LM as a model in its own right was, on the face of it, unreasonable, but it had a certain logic, since IS-LM came to have a life of its own. Like the indifference curve, IS-LM was a brilliant visual device, and probably this accounted for its popularity. Hicks had by no means exhausted its possibilities in the 1937 article. It was a simple matter to incorporate rudimentary government and foreign-trade sectors so that a wide variety of effects could be analyzed. The differential impact of monetary and fiscal policy with fixed and flexible exchange rates was one. Alternative specifications of the investment and consumption functions were tried out, and there was speculation about the possibility of an upwards sloping IS function (which Hicks considered but dismissed as improbable). In these and many other ways, IS-LM proved to be a wonderfully flexible way of presenting "Keynes-type" economics so that even fairly recent debates between Keynesians and monetarists have been conducted within its framework. Most importantly, almost all textbooks made use of it.

One of the first texts was Alvin Hansen's *Guide to Keynes* (1953), which was a chapter-by-chapter explanation of the *General Theory*. Hansen made frequent use of IS-LM and, in the United States, it became known as the Hicks-Hansen diagram. This work, and many less good texts, were the staple fare of undergraduate courses, so that, for many students, IS-LM and Keynesian economics became synonymous. Then, from the late 1960s, courses became concerned with what was wrong with IS-LM, so that one way or another, for forty years, IS-LM has dominated what most students have learned about macroeconomics.

As a teaching aid IS-LM remains unsurpassed, but scarcely anyone ever thought that it represented all of macroeconomics. The reservations of Hicks and others relate to IS-LM as a vehicle for making progress in economic theory. It would be a serious charge if IS-LM could be said to have retarded creative thinking in macroeconomics, but this seems unlikely to have been the case. While IS-LM crystallized the issues raised by the *General Theory*, its limitations stimulated research in many areas. One of the first was the investigation of the long-run properties of the Keynesian system by Roy Harrod, Evsey Domar, Hicks, and others. This was the point from which modern growth theory started. Similarly, dissatisfaction with the modeling of the labor market, stocks and flows, and expectations has generated large literatures and innovations throughout macroeconomics.

# Value and Capital

Keynesian economics was, at first, a distraction from Hicks's main work. At Cambridge between 1935 and 1938 he was working on *Value and Capital* (1963), which is commonly held to be his masterpiece. Keynes is discussed towards the end of the book, but in spirit and content it is a product of the LSE years.

*Value and Capital* described the working of a whole economy. Its objectives were not dissimilar to those of Keynes, but the method differed. Keynesian economics proceeded by "heroic aggregation." Theories were proposed concerning the behavior of large aggregates, such as investment and consumption, but their macroeconomic underpinnings were specified less than fastidiously. Hicks's method was general-equilibrium (GE) analysis in the tradition of Pareto and Léon Walras. GE analysis works from the bottom upwards. It specifies rigorous theories about the behavior of individuals acting in firms and households and proceeds to examine their implications for the whole economy.

The tools which Hicks had invented or sharpened were put to work in a restatement of the Hicks-Allen contribution to demand theory and a parallel analysis of equilibrium in the production sector. Important and innovative though these were, Hicks's aim was to free GE theory from "the reproof of sterility" by making it more dynamic. Time entered the Hicksian framework in markets for money, securities, and captial goods. These markets trade in stores of values and depend for their existence on the willingness of people to forego present consumption in return for assets that are a claim on production in an uncertain future. Thus time and expectations have to be modeled explicitly.

The problem was to focus on dynamic aspects of the economy while retaining the maximizing principles which underpinned the essentially static theories of consumption and production. Hicks's solution was to regard time as a stream of short periods called "weeks," during which agents went about their maximizing activities saddled with expectations formed on "Mondays." The economy would then work to a temporary equilibrium during the "week." On the following "Monday" expectations would again be revised, and the economy jerked forward to a new temporary equilibrium.

Although it was an artificial device (and criticized as such by Hicks), the temporary-equilibrium method allowed price expectations to influence current and future prices and raised the issue of the instability of the economic system. Hicks showed that if expectations were elastic with respect to price changes, the system was prone to fluctuations. Thus, like Keynes, he was skeptical of the economic system as a self-righting mechanism. There were special reasons which gave it "a sufficient amount of stability to enable it to carry on . . . , but it is not inherently and necessarily stable." The "special reasons" included long-term contracts, sticky prices, and unemployed labor. "Un-

employment," he noted wryly, "is the best [price] stabiliser we have yet found."

When Hicks visited America for the first time in 1946, he met Paul Samuelson, Kenneth Arrow, Milton Friedman, and Don Patinkin, and he found that they regarded *Value and Capital* as the beginning of their own work, but "only the beginning, for they and their contemporaries, with far more skill in mathematics than my own, were sharpening the analysis I had merely roughed out." In truth, some parts of Hicks's work were sharpened; others were blunted. Samuelson, Arrow, Gerard Debreu, and others working in the 1940s and 1950s concentrated on the problems of stability and existence of equilibrium in economic systems. Their works are landmarks in mathematical economics but, because the problems were intrinsically difficult to formalize, the complications which interested Keynes and Hicks were commonly excluded by assumption. Hicks admired the mathematical virtuosity involved but regarded subsequent developments as overly mechanical and remote from real problems.

*Value and Capital* did more than redirect GE theory. It bristled with new concepts such as the elasticity of expectations and decisive comment on controversies such as the loanable-funds versus liquidity-preference debate. Suggestions abounded for further investigation, including an embryonic theory of the term structure of interest rates. It remains a classic of economic theory. Robert Solow, in 1984, spoke for more than one generation of economists when he recalled that, "in 1945 Wassily Leontief gave us *Value and Capital* to read. All of a sudden economics seemed to be a subject worth studying for its own sake. . . . *Value and Capital*, the *General Theory* and Paul Samuelson's *Foundations of Economic Analysis* were the books that formed the way my friends and I thought about economics."

## Welfare Economics

Hicks's only textbook was *The Social Framework* (1942). It ran to four editions in the United Kingdom, was translated into six foreign languages, and special editions were prepared for the United States (1945) and Japan (1974). Designed for introductory teaching, its novelty lay in the use of national-income data and concepts which at the time were not widely understood. The statistical material has passed into economic history; otherwise it is still a good first book for economists and is a model of descriptive economics.

Careful concern for definitions, facts, and measurement is a hallmark of Hicks's work and is a particular feature of *The Social Framework* and his welfare economics, which was the other major accomplishment of his time at Manchester University (1938–46). It was a natural extension to consider the circumstances in which a change in the economy could be described unambiguously as a improvement in productive efficiency. This problem was addressed in his "The Foundations of Welfare Economics" (*Economic Journal*, 1939). It drew on contri-

butions by Harrod, Kaldor, and Harold Hotelling to place the "new welfare economics" within a Paretian framework. Having established the marginal conditions for optimal welfare, it went on to extend Pareto's scheme by considering changes in the system which involved redistribution. Most reforms benefit some people and, by reducing their consumer surpluses, disadvantage others. Hicks argued that measures of this sort need not be dismissed from an unwillingness to make interpersonal utility comparisons, since, if rational compensation criteria could be devised, it would be within the government's power to compensate the losers.

At about the same time, Hicks and Kaldor reached the conclusion that compensation criteria could be based on measurements of the loss of consumer surplus. Dissatisfaction had long existed with the "Marshallian triangle" as a measure of welfare loss, but Hicks showed the circumstances in which it could be used with reasonable confidence. He devised the compensated-demand curve ("a fiddling business, fortunately not likely to be of much importance"), which adjusted for income effects of price changes, and showed that there were four measures of consumer surplus which were closely related to Paasche and Laspeyres index numbers. There is a true index which requires a knowledge of the unobservable compensated-demand curve, but Hicks, sensitive as usual to operational practicality, showed that the four measures converge as long as income effects are not large. In these circumstances, the Marshallian measure is a reasonable approximation to the ideal index.

These concepts, which became known as the Kaldor-Hicks welfare criteria, gave rise to much discussion and criticism. Much of this criticism is now accepted, but a hard core of the Kaldor-Hicks approach remains in the theory of cost-benefit analysis. In thousands of applications, cost-benefit analysis, using the rough and ready data which are available, tries to decide what would be a fair compensation for those damaged by an alteration in the economic system. Although cost-benefit analysis was scarcely invented at the time, Kaldor and Hicks established a large part of its theoretical foundations.

Looking back, Hicks saw a gap in his theoretical work between *A Contribution to the Theory of the Trade Cycle* (1950) and his later work, which began in earnest in about 1960. It was perhaps more of a traverse than a gap, because although he was heavily involved in university work at Oxford, the flow of articles and reviews continued unabated. However there was a switch from high theory to applied economics. Throughout the 1940s Hicks coauthored books and articles with his wife, who was an authority on local-government finance. In the 1950s they turned to practicalities and traveled widely in Africa, Asia, and the Caribbean to advise governments on fiscal matters.

## A "New Start"

Hicks prepared for a "new start" in economics by brushing up his mathematics and finding out what the Americans were up to. The first fruit was "Linear Theory: A Survey" (*Economic Journal*, 1960), which reviewed developments in linear programming, input-output analysis, and game theory. This was followed by an explanation of the Samuelson-Solow Turnpike Theorem. Parts of the next major work, *Capital and Growth* (1965) continued in this vein, which was expository, critical, and useful, since it made Frank Ramsey, John von Neumann and the literature on optimal growth more accessible to the "not-so-very mathematical" economist.

*Capital and Growth* was by no means pure exposition. It contained the flex/fix price distinction, and introduced the theory of the "traverse." The traverse was Hicks's term for the route between two balanced-growth paths and was another example of his happy knack of coining memorable labels. Nevertheless, the novelty of *Capital and Growth* was not widely appreciated, and Hicks's own dissatisfaction led him to revise Part I in *Methods of Economic Dynamics* (1985).

In 1965 Hicks retired from his professorship. He might have used the extra leisure to indulge the enthusiasm for gardening which he shared with his wife, but there was to be no respite for his bibliographers. If anything, his academic output increased.

Time, capital, and growth are themes closely interwoven in the "post-retirement" period. All were present in *Capital and Growth* and earlier work, but it was uncharacteristic of Hicks that, having drawn alongside the latest research, he did not press ahead in equilibrium growth theory. His aim was to write economics "in historical time." Equilibrium growth theory is about the passage of time, but it relates to a world which would find little employment for historians, since each period is much like another. To be "in time," a theory has to explain the processes by which an economy moves from a known past to an unknown future. To be in historical time, a theory must admit the possibility of surprise, regret, and not only growth but also change.

The survey of equilibrium growth theory was productive in a negative way. It convinced Hicks that the sort of problems which interested him could not be analyzed by these means. The search for alternative means led to the invention of new concepts. Three of these—the flex/fix price distinction, liquidity, and the impulse—encapsulate much of what is distinctive in later Hicksian economics.

# Flex/Fix Price Markets

The temporary-equilibrium method of *Value and Capital* does not explain the processes by which prices are established within the Hicksian week. To do so, a theory of markets is required. Hicks suggests that there are two types of market: flexprice markets in which prices adjust fast enough for equilibrium to be reached in a "week," and fixprice markets, which are highly organized and administered, so that prices are relatively sticky. In a fixprice world only partial equilibrium is established in the short period, and the

economy moves forward with stocks which are greater or lesser than those which are desired.

Hicks contends that Marshall and earlier writers thought in terms of a flexprice system in which adjustments take place through price changes. Keynes, it is claimed, understood implicitly the tendency of modern economies towards fixprice structures, so that in the *General Theory* adjustment works through quantities (except in the bond market, which is flexprice). The upshot is that, in the Keynesian system, an increase in investment will impact first on output and employment rather than on prices and wages. Hicks comments that, "when one thinks it through, [that] was perhaps the main thing that had to be said."

The flex/fix price distinction is used again in *The Crisis in Keynesian Economics* (1974), to show the importance of stocks for an understanding of Keynes's multiplier process, and it also is featured in *A Theory of Economic History* (1969), which explains the assertion that fixprice markets have tended to replace the flexprice sort. The story is told in terms of the rise of the merchant. The merchant buys in order to resell, and his profit is a reward for intermediation. In the emergence of markets from barter systems, intermediation was crucial. The merchant made the market by adjusting prices to market conditions. By contrast, in fixprice markets, the role of the intermediary is reduced. Economies of scale and product standardization give more power in price fixing to large modern firms, so that in organized markets, with high transactions costs, prices tend to be sticky.

In this way history is made to serve theory, but *A Theory of Economic History* contains much more. It discusses the growth of economic activities and institutions over the whole sphere of history from the Neolithic era, through classical and medieval cultures, to the beginnings of modern times. Along the way are fascinating insights on currency, inflation, public finance, and the decline of the slave trade. Perhaps no other work conveys so strong an impression of Sir John's wide reading and broad human sympathies.

# Money and Liquidity

A sense of history is also apparent in Hicks's monetary economics, in which he sees a long continuity in controversy between those who seek an automatically functioning monetary system and those who would attempt to manage it. These issues, which divided the currency and banking schools in the 1840s, have much in common with modern debates between Keynesians and monetarists (*Critical Essays in Monetary Theory*, 1967).

*Critical Essays* also contains "The Two Triads," in which Hicks sets out to revise the monetary parts of the *General Theory* along the lines of his "simplifying" paper of 1935. Here, and in several later essays, the key concept is liquidity. Keynes's liquidity-preference theory operated over a simplified monetary sector which admitted choice be-

tween money and only one asset— bonds. Hicks attempts to complete the theory with a full model of financial markets.

The portfolio approach to the demand for money, associated with Tobin and others, is set in a similarly broad context, but Hicks demurs from it in two main respects. First, he denies that the transactions demand for money is a matter of choice; instead he prefers to regard it as the amount of money needed to finance a certain volume of transactions. Second, in Hicks's view, the portfolio approach is, like Keynes's theory, not sufficiently concerned with the relation between liquidity and time. "Liquidity is not a matter of a single choice; it is a matter of a sequence of choices, a related sequence. It is concerned with the passage from the unknown to the known—with the knowledge that if we wait we can have more knowledge" (*The Crisis in Keynesian Economics*, 1974).

Thus, liquidity buys flexibility. By holding money, an economic agent foregoes income but acquires freedom to choose over a broader range of future opportunities. The decision to hold fewer liquid assets narrows the range of responses to unexpected options. The force of this proposition is seen in the industrial sector, where assets are highly illiquid and past decisions to commit resources to fixed capital and equipment reduce seriously the ability of firms to respond quickly to changes in technology and market conditions. The liquidity concept, as it applies to the industrial sector, is an important link between Hicks's monetary theory and the impulse theory of growth, which Hicks regards as the third major invention of his later work.

# Capital, Growth, and the Impulse Theory

Dynamic methods, capital, and growth are constant themes that come together in *Capital and Time* (1973). This work is subtitled "A Neo-Austrian Theory" and reflects a long-standing appreciation of the Austrian school. Hicks claims to be only an "irregular and imperfect" Austrian, but he shares their view of the importance of time in economics and has contributed to a revival of interest in the Austrian School (see *Collected Essays*, Vol. 2).

The first part of *Capital and Time* sets up an Austrian-style steady-state model, in which growth processes are analyzed sequentially. This is a starting point for an extended theory of the traverse, which analyzes ways in which an economy might react to a major disturbance. Here the need for a sequential approach becomes apparent because, out of equilibrium, time periods are no longer alike. Economies may or may not move smoothly and rapidly between equilibria. In this difficult area Hicks is on, or over, the edge of a theoretical frontier. The problem of the traverse is of great practical concern. The economy is required frequently to make more than minor adjustments. Whether these are accompanied by unemployment and whether they are completed in three

months or forty years is a matter of importance to the car workers of Detroit, as it was, in the nineteenth century, to the handloom weavers.

The impulse theory of growth, introduced in "Industrialism" (*Economic Perspectives*, 1977), draws on the distinction between autonomous and induced investment which Hicks first made in the 1930s. An impulse is a major event, such as an invention or the opening of new markets, which creates profit opportunities and has multiple impacts on the economy. In the sector most immediately affected, there is a demand for new capital stock. This is autonomous investment. The initial impact causes shortages and price adjustments elsewhere in the economy, and these induce additional investment. Thus the impulse is an event which puts the economy on a traverse, and along that path monetary factors are an important determinant of the pace at which adjustment can take place. A highly liquid economy can respond quickly; an illiquid economy will be less flexible.

"Industrialism" can also be read as a final chapter to *A Theory of Economic History* (1969), which stopped short of the modern industrial phase. Hicks suggests that modern economic growth proceeded in a series of impulses generated mainly by science-based technological improvements. He denies any attempt to construct a grand scheme of history and theory, but the impulse idea draws money, capital, and growth theory into a distinctive body of thought which is unified by its emphasis on the importance of time. It is difficult to assess Hicks's later work because, unlike many of his earlier contributions, it has not been incorporated readily into economic orthodoxy. No future historian of economic thought will doubt that Hicks was still wrestling with issues of importance, but only time will tell whether his later work will remain interestingly heterodox or whether it will chart new directions in economic theorizing.

# A Humane Economist

Hicks's contributions are many and various, but in a scholar of the first rank one expects not only ideas of importance and originality but also style and a distinctive view of the subject. Hicks has both.

As long ago as 1939, Harrod announced that Hicks had joined the select band of economists whose style is distinctive and distinguished. One distinctive feature is the imagery of journey and exploration which abounds in Hicks's writing. Mountaineering is the theme for an extended metaphor which David Collard has used to interpret Hicks's work. As Collard puts it, "we come across surfaces, slopes, frontiers, balanced growth paths, full employment paths, dismal paths, ups, downs, peaks, traverses, profiles and perspectives. We frequently deliberate about the route, assess the state of the terrain, and consider the view from the point now reached. . . . Hicks is explorer, mountaineer and guide" (*Economic Theory and Hicksian Themes*, 1984).

The style contrasts sharply with much of modern economics writing, which seems to take the scientific paper as its model. Hicks's method owes more to the techniques of public speaking. It is plain, sometimes almost conversational, though never anecdotal, and usually confidential. He flatters by seeming to engage the reader in his own intellectual processes. It is as if Hicks and the reader are engaged in a joint enterprise. The reader is addressed not quite as an equal but as a junior officer, about as clever as Hicks but lacking slightly in experience. Of course, this is an expository trick, but through it Hicks seems to convey a genuine desire to avoid didacticism and to persuade rather than impress.

The question of style also involves the choice of analytical techniques. When Hicks started in economics, many colleagues and more students had scarcely any mathematics. A few had more than a competence but, like Marshall, regarded mathematical economics as a slightly unhealthy pursuit. Hicks has retained something of this old view while making several significant contributions to mathematical economics. In his early work, the main weight of exposition was carried by prose and diagrams, with mathematics confined largely to appendices. Later Hicks allowed more mathematics into the text and has confessed to mild bouts of self-indulgence, during which he pursued mathematical puzzles rather than economics. He still works things out in mathematics but sticks mainly to literary explanations as a matter of choice. As he puts it, "though I have dabbled in mathematics, my spiritual home is in the Humanities. It is because I want to make economics more human that I want to make it more time conscious; and since I am approaching the task from that end I am content with a more earthy way of going about it" ("Time and Economics," *Collected Essays*, Vol. 2).

In several matters of methodology and philosophy Hicks stands aside from the body of opinion in mainstream economics. In "The Formation of an Economist," he makes plain his lack of sympathy with theory for its own sake and his lack of faith in econometrics as a means of making contact with reality. The reservations about econometrics, explained in *Causality in Economics* (1979), derive from doubts about the use of probability concepts better suited to the natural sciences. He is also skeptical about positivism and the scientific status of economics. His own view is summarized in the title of an essay, "A Discipline Not a Science" (*Collected Essays*, Vol. 3).

Hicks has, with justice, been termed a "high theorist," but even in GE theory, which is about the most rarified sort of economics, he is never content with a generalization or an assumption not rooted in human behavior, and he declines steadfastly to define economic problems to suit mathematical convenience. Almost always, his concern is with real economic problems. "A Reconsideration of the Theory of Value" was, in part, a response to an econometric problem, and the IS-LM article was designed to explain Keynes to econometrists (Hicks never calls them econometricians). Elsewhere, papers which are theoretical in character start with questions such as, "what is capital?" and "how can it be measured?" Usually it turns out that there are several answers and that theoretical insights emerge from the multiplication of these distinctions.

As Hicks makes plain, this consistent concern for operational usefulness is a product of his own view of the subject and the influence of his wife. Lady Hicks will be remembered for contributions to the theory of public finance and as a founder of the *Review of Economic Studies*, which, under her coeditorship, gained an international reputation in mathematical economics. The preface to *Value and Capital* contains a tribute which goes beyond normal matrimonial requirements. Hicks wrote, "There is no part of this book which has not profited from the constant reminder which I have had from her work, that the place of economic theory is to be the servant of applied economics."

To aspire to serve applied economics is not a modest ambition for a theorist, but this and more can be claimed for Hicks. He has been acclaimed as a great toolmaker, a lucid expositor, and a supreme theoretician whose work has influenced profoundly at least two generations of economists. In addition, he is an outstanding representative of a rare breed—the humane and philosophical economist.

RICHARD STEVENSON

## Selected Bibliography

### WORKS BY HICKS

"Wage Fixing in the Building Industry." *Economica* 8 (1928): 159–67.

and Allen, R. G. D. "A Reconsideration of the Theory of Value." *Economica* n.s. 1 (1934): 52–76.

"A Suggestion for Simplifying the Theory of Money." *Economica* n.s. 2: (1935): 1–19.

"Mr. Keynes and the 'Classics.'" *Econometrica* 5 (1937): 147–59.

"The Foundations of Welfare Economics." *Economic Journal* 49 (1939): 696–712.

*The Social Framework.* Oxford: Clarendon Press, 1942.

*A Contribution to the Theory of the Trade Cycle.* Oxford: Clarendon Press, 1950.

*Value and Capital.* 2d ed. London: Oxford University Press, 1963.

*The Theory of Economic History.* Oxford: Clarendon Press, 1967.

*A Theory of Economic History.* Oxford: Clarendon Press, 1969.

*The Crisis in Keynesian Economics.* New York: Basic Books, 1974.

*Economic Perspectives.* Oxford: Clarendon Press, 1977.

*Causality in Economics.* Oxford: Basil Blackwell, 1979.

"The Formation of an Economist." Banca Nazionale del Lavoro 130 (1979): 195–204.

*Collected Essays.* 3 vols. Oxford: Basil Blackwell, 1981–83.

*Methods of Economic Dynamics.* Oxford: Oxford University Press, 1985.

### OTHER WORKS

Baumol, William. "John R. Hicks' Contribution to Economics." *Swedish Journal of Economics* 74 (1972): 503–27.

Collard, David A., et. al., eds. *Economic Theory and Hicksian Themes.* Oxford: Clarendon Press, 1984.

Helm, Dieter, ed. *The Economics of John Hicks.* Oxford: Basil Blackwell, 1984.

Wolfe, J. N., ed. *Value, Capital and Growth.* Chicago: Aldine Press, 1968.

# LEONID KANTOROVICH    *1975*

Leonid Vitalevich Kantorovich (1912–86), joint winner of the Nobel Prize in Economic Sciences with Tjalling Koopmans in 1975, is not only the sole winner to date from either the Soviet Union or Eastern Europe but also probably the most distinguished mathematician amongst the economics laureates. He also had to practice his economics in (for a time) the least favorable political circumstances of any laureate, since his active life as an economist from the mid-1930s onwards coincided with unusually turbulent periods in both the Soviet economy and in Soviet economics. As a result, his contribution—though intensely individual and original—is probably more closely bound up with the status and development of his discipline than that of any other economist discussed in this volume.

Kantorovich was born in 1912 in St. Petersburg (later Leningrad) to the family of a doctor. Few details are known of his early life, which was dominated, we may assume, by his precocious mathematical gifts. He entered Leningrad University at the age of fourteen and wrote his first mathematical papers at fifteen. Upon graduation in 1930 he joined the faculty of his university, being made a professor in 1934. In 1935 he was awarded a doctorate in physical and mathematical sciences. In the Soviet Union such degrees correspond not to British or American Ph.D.'s but to the Doctor of Science degrees normally awarded to distinguished scholars at the middle or towards the end of their careers. To attain the degree at the age of twenty-three is unusual, even in mathematics, where youthful achievement is not uncommon. Moreover, Kantorovich had the honor of not being required formally to defend his thesis.

Thus far, Kantorovich's career had developed as that of an exceptionally gifted mathematician—a discipline in which Russia and the Soviet Union was (and still is) preeminent. Indeed his mathematical career continued until his death, with major contributions to a number of fields of both pure and applied mathematics, including ap-

proximation theory, computational mathematics, and functional analysis. In the last field, Kantorovich developed the theory of semiordered vector spaces, which are called in his honor K-spaces. It is notable that his mathematical interests covered the range from the abstract to the applied, and that he was awarded a number of distinguished mathematical prizes. This mathematical background—and the applied "problem solving" approach that he also exhibited—contributed fundamentally to his work in economics. But his contribution to economics was also profoundly influenced by the political and economic context in which he lived and worked.

# The Discovery of Linear Programming

In the 1920s Soviet economics—like other cultural and intellectual activities—was flourishing. The economy, recovering from the ravages of the First World War and the civil war (1917–20), was run on fairly liberal lines. Private enterprise was tolerated, and central direction was weak. Political and economic debates within the Communist party, and to a lesser extent outside it, were comparatively free. The period saw innovative contributions to economics, many of them involving policy issues concerning the rate and direction of Soviet industrialization. In a sense, many of the twentieth-century debates on "development economics," subsequently contributed to by such Nobel laureates as Simon Kuznets and W. Arthur

Lewis, began in the Soviet Union in the 1920s. Moreover, much of the work, including some by younger scholars who were to become influential later, was mathematical in character. In this respect they were drawing on contributions made by prerevolutionary economists such as V. K. Dmitriev, E. E. Slutsky, and M. I. Tugan-Baranovsky.

At the end of the 1920s, the situation changed radically. The first Soviet five-year plan (approved in 1928) adopted a policy of crash industrialization concentrating on heavy industry; the accompanying collectivization of agriculture revolutionized the countryside. At the political level, Stalin strengthened his hold on the party and the government, and in the 1930s the purges began. Intellectual debate was subordinated to the effort to attain ambitious (and probably unfeasible) growth targets.

Economics suffered particularly harshly in this process—probably as harshly as any discipline except biology. This development arose from its closeness to the crucial policy issues. With the economic line decided by the party, economics was reduced at best to developing a "political economy of socialism," at worst to the collection and organization of relevant quotations from Marx, Engels, Lenin, and Stalin. Stalin himself expounded the subordinate position of the discipline in one of his last works (*Economic Problems of Socialism in the USSR*, 1952), in which he wrote, in a passage ominously entitled "Other Errors of Comrade Yaroshenko," that "the rational organization of productive forces, economic planning, etc., are not problems of political economy, but problems of the economic policy of the directing bodies. . . . To foist upon political economy problems of economic policy is to kill it as a science."

This formulation excluded economists from most of the interesting policy questions. But it did leave one small loophole through which a form of economic analysis could squeeze. If it could show itself to be useful to plan fulfillment at a very detailed level, it might have a role. It was in performing a task of this kind that Kantorovich embarked on what was to be his decisive contribution to economics, and to Soviet economics in particular.

The circumstances could hardly be more prosaic. A plywood factory in Leningrad was having difficulty in finding an efficient means of meeting its output targets. It had to work out a way of scheduling the production of five types of plywood from eight lathes, in such a way as to produce final output in given proportions. The problem was passed to Kantorovich at Leningrad University. He not only solved the particular problem but in doing so formulated and developed a solution procedure for the general class of problems of which this is an example. In addition, he gave a crucial economic interpretation to one key element in the solution procedure and showed how the method could be applied to a whole range of related microeconomic problems.

The mathematical problem Kantorovich faced was one of maximization subject to constraints. The objective function was maximization of the output of sets of plywood products (in given proportions). Each lathe had the capacity to produce varying quantities of the different kinds of output in the course of an hour. There were also other constraints, on electricity consumption for example. The trick was to assign the right product or products to the right machine.

Problems of this general kind were familiar to mathematicians, but solution mechanisms available (mostly using the technique of Lagrange multipliers) were incapable of solving large problems. Kantorovich developed a solution procedure which exploited the fact that the relationships involved were linear (which means in this instance that the input and output mix was given—no substitution between inputs or outputs was permitted—and that production took place with constant returns to scale, so that doubling all inputs also doubled all outputs). By exploiting this feature, Kantorovich overcame the problem of scale.

Kantorovich at once recognized the wide range of possible applications of his procedure. As a result, his monograph, entitled *Mathematical Methods of Production Planning and Organisation* (1939), not only discussed the production scheduling model outlined above, but a whole range of further problems with the same essential mathematical structure. These included the optimal use of machinery, the rational use of fuel, the best use of building materials, the most favora-

ble distribution of crops, and the best plan of transportation. For example, Kantorovich's crop distribution problem maximizes output of different grains from a given area, taking account both of the suitability of different soils and climatic conditions and of the effects of crop rotation. In this example, Kantorovich contrasted his proposed optimal procedure with current administrative practice, as reported by a delegate to the Nineteenth Party Congress of the CPSU (1936): "According to him, in the northern districts of his county the best crop is barley, whereas in the southern districts wheat grows best. Yet the County Agricultural Department automatically divides the plan for all districts according to the total areas for all cultures; it does not matter that barley would not grow in a certain district—you still have to sow barley." (1964, p. 241). The theme of faulty administrative procedures getting in the way of rational economic solutions would recur throughout Kantorovich's writing.

Through a process of independent discovery which is as familiar in economics as in other disciplines, a group of American researchers working on logistical and other problems in the Second World War encountered problems akin to those identified by Kantorovich. One of them, George Dantzig, formulated the problem in a way similar to Kantorovich and developed an alternative solution procedure. Dantzig gave a name to the new technique—linear programming. (His work was published in 1951 in an influential volume edited by Koopmans.) A number of special formulations of the problem were identified, and solutions found for them. Koopmans, and others, defined a class of linear programs with a special structure, known as transportation problems. The problem is that of getting shipments of goods in given quantities from specified supply points to specified demand points at minimum cost using a range of alternative routes, each with given costs (and sometimes with a given capacity). This was the final problem identified by Kantorovich in his 1939 monograph. He went back to it subsequently in an article entitled "On the Translocation of Masses," published in 1958.

There is no doubt either about the independence of the Soviet and the American work or about the priority of Kantorovich's results. There has, however, been some debate about whether Kantorovich's formulations are as general as the subsequent work of Dantzig. The view taken by Koopmans is that the two formulations are equivalent in the class of linear programming problems that possess an optimal solution. From a computational standpoint the Dantzig solution procedure—the simplex method—came to dominate Kantorovich's proposal, because it is more general and more easily programmed for computers.

The reader may at this stage be wondering how Kantorovich's major discovery—that of linear programming—qualified him for a Nobel Prize in economics rather than an award in what would now be called operations research or management science. The reason is that Kantorovich recognized and exploited a fundamental interpretation of his method that goes to the heart of modern economics—the notion of duality between an allocation formulated or guided in terms of quantities and one formulated or guided in terms of prices.

The notion of the price system as an "invisible hand" guiding the economy towards a distribution of factors of production, goods, and services that is in some sense optimal goes back to Adam Smith and even earlier. Much of Western microeconomic theory of the 1930s and 1940s was devoted to establishing conditions for the existence and optimality of such a general or multimarket equilibrium. Amongst Nobel laureates in economics, major contributors to this work include Kenneth Arrow, Hicks, Koopmans and Paul Samuelson.

Within the framework of a linear programming model, the duality between prices and quantities can be formulated most simply as follows. Consider the problem of maximizing the value of output of two goods, each with a given price or social valuation. Production of each good requires inputs in given proportions of two factors of production, where each factor is in given supply. This problem can be formulated as a linear program that yields the optimal (positive) quantity produced of each good as its solution. Economists call it the "primal" problem and assume it has a solution.

Now consider a related problem, the "dual." Suppose we wish to find input prices that minimize the total cost of hiring the factors of production in the primal problem. At the same time the input prices cannot be arbitrarily small, because the cost of producing a unit of output with a given technology may not be less than its price, or otherwise it would be profitable to make output indefinitely large. This too is a linear program, and we assume it has a solution.

The essence of duality theory is the relations between the primal and the dual solutions, in particular the fact that they lead to an identical configuration of output. This result can be interpreted as meaning that we can either solve the primal problem and impose the optimal solution administratively by quantity targets, or alternatively we can solve the dual problem, identify the optimal valuations of inputs, and instruct firms to produce output subject to those input prices in such a way as to avoid making losses in production. The model thus suggests that an appropriate price system can "sustain" the optimal composition of output.

Duality theory can be interpreted in another way, which invokes the useful concept of shadow prices. Suppose we solve our primal problem twice, in the second case increasing the availability of one factor of production by a single unit. The value of goods produced will normally go up in the second case: call this increase the "shadow price" of the input, or the increase in value of output made possible by having an additional unit of that input.

That shadow price is also the optimal valuation of the same input in the dual problem.

The full significance of duality theory was only appreciated in the West in the late 1940s. Yet shadow prices were used to solve linear programming problems and interpreted as implying a possible decentralized economic mechanism in works published or drafted by Kantorovich in 1939 or the early 1940s.

Shadow prices appear in Kantorovich's 1939 solution method in the guise of "resolving multipliers." His procedure involved a step-by-step technique in which multipliers (or dual variables) were estimated and revised at successive iterations. When a set of multipliers is found such that all constraints specified in physical units are satisfied in the primal problem, the procedure comes to an end. Thus far the multipliers simply play a role in the algorithm. Yet it is clear that Kantorovich realized in 1939 that they had a broader significance: "not only do they produce the result of a problem, but they also provide a series of important characteristics of this result." He then goes on to point out that they are capable of the shadow price interpretation noted above. This is not to claim, of course, that in 1939 he had fully developed linear duality theory; but clearly he had grasped the conceptual significance of the "resolving multipliers." His next scientific achievement, which went unpublished for nearly twenty years, was to offer an interpretation of shadow prices as the possible basis of a full-blown price-guided economic system.

# The Influence of Kantorovich's Ideas

Following publication of his 1939 monograph, Kantorovich began work on a generalization of the results. By some accounts, he had drafted his next major work in economics in the first half of the 1940s, but it was not published in the USSR until 1959 (and in English translation until 1965).

This work, *The Best Use of Economic Resources*, is a remarkable achievement of analysis and advocacy. Kantorovich extends the application of his linear programming framework to the level of the economy as a whole. The notion of shadow prices is applied to all inputs into the production process, including rentals for capital equipment and rent for land and natural resources. He also points out that the shadow prices can be used to evaluate small adjustments to the plan in the neighborhood of the optimal solution, thus making possible quick comparison of alternatives. His analysis amounts to a proposal for a new type of producer price in the USSR, though he correctly points out that consumer prices may differ from producer prices and reflect social goals other than efficiency.

It is quite clear that Kantorovich's ideas trespassed far beyond what Stalin considered the proper territory for economics. Not only did they seek to intervene in the planning process by proposing alternative plan targets, but they even advanced new conceptions of plan evaluation and implementation

which implied use of what were effectively prices, even though the author thinly disguised their true nature with the phrase "objectively determined valuations." A major change in attitude was required before Kantorovich's ideas became acceptable.

The circumstances in which the Soviet political economy of the Stalin period was displaced by new ideas have been described in an exceptional recent book by the Finnish economist Pekka Sutela. Even in the 1940s and 1950s, Kantorovich was not wholly isolated in his detachment from the orthodox position. His distinguished Leningrad colleague V. V. Novozhilov was occupied at that time with fundamental researches into investment efficiency and choice of technique, which were at odds with the mainstream discussion (though not, interestingly enough, with the views of practitioners facing these issues in sectors such as transport or energy). Other economists, including survivors from the 1920s, were devoting themselves to related issues. Nonetheless Kantorovich's work went virtually unnoticed in the official economics literature until the late 1950s.

When the climate changed, it did so fairly rapidly. Following the liberalization introduced by Khruschev at the Twentieth Party Congress in 1956, the traditional economists initially sought to limit the role of the new mathematical economics to that of a mere tool for investigating problems at the quantitative level. But this wholly unsatisfactory proposal soon foundered as the mathematical economists won official publication and institutional position. The year 1959 saw not only the publication of Kantorovich's major work but also the first in a series of volumes entitled *The Use of Mathematics in Economics*. The first issue contained a book-length study by Novozhilov, a reprint of Kantorovich's 1939 study, a further paper by Kantorovich, and additional articles by other Soviet economists. It was edited by V.S. Nemchinov, a statistician and agricultural economist who was to play a major role in the development of Soviet economics and in the acceptance of the ideas of innovators like Kantorovich.

In 1958 small laboratories concerned with mathematical economics were set up in Moscow (headed by Nemchinov) and Leningrad (headed by Kantorovich). In 1960 Kantorovich took his unit to the Siberian Division of the USSR Academy of Sciences, based at Academgorodok (Academic City) near Novosibirsk. The Moscow unit later became the Central Mathematical Economics Institute (TsEMI), the major research center in the field. Kantorovich was elected a corresponding member of the USSR Academy of Sciences in 1958 and a full member in 1964. Perhaps even more significantly, in 1965 he, Nemchinov, and Novozhilov were jointly awarded a Lenin prize, a major official recognition of their new status. The award was condemned by some of their conservative opponents.

Welcome as this recognition must have been, it did not mean that the ideas of the group, by then called the "optimal planners," won acceptance at the practical level. Nevertheless, the climate of Soviet economic administration in the early 1960s was fairly favorable to reform (more favorable than it was to be at any time until the start of the Gorbachev era in the mid-1980s). The traditional centralized economic mechanism, in which a large bureaucracy issued enterprises with detailed quantitative instructions, was increasingly recognized as being inefficient and unable to meet the needs of an age in which technical change and consumer satisfaction were becoming ever more important. Kantorovich himself estimated at this time that the economy was producing substantially (he estimated 30–50%) below capacity as a result of planning inefficiency.

By this time Kantorovich had fully developed what was effectively a static (one-period) linear programming model and had applied it both to local production problems and to the national economy. He had also made considerable progress in understanding and expounding duality theory and its interpretation as a potential means of decentralized management. The leap from micro to macro was a major one, as was the jump from control by quantity to control by price. At the level of an individual enterprise, embedded in a planned economy, there is not too much argument about what should be maximized or minimized. Yet formulating an objective function for the economy as a whole is much more problematic, and some Soviet economists have argued that it is inappropriate in theory, as well as being impossible in practice.

Equally, within a small organization the problem of control of and incentives for subordinate units is less severe, as direct monitoring is sometimes feasible. At the national level the problems of coordinating the interests of major sectors or regions are much more severe. From this perspective, Kantorovich's proposals seemed to be technocratic and to ignore social reality. (Indeed he was criticized on this score in 1960 by A. G. Aganbegyan, who in the mid-1980s was to become one of Gorbachev's most "reformist" advisers.)

The inadequacy of programming solutions without incentive reforms is shown by a case which was widely cited in both Soviet and Western literature: transport organizations in the USSR have the task of shipping goods from suppliers to customers, subject to the planned output of the former and the planned demand of the latter. This is precisely the "transportation problem" formulated by Kantorovich in 1939 and 1942, and by the early 1960s it was quite capable of solution on available Soviet computers. Yet it was found that optimal transport plans were always ignored by the relevant organizations. The answer was not hard to seek. The transport bodies themselves had plan targets, formulated in ton-kilometers. By using optimal solutions they would shorten their routes and thus run the risk of losing their bonuses by not meeting the ton-kilometer quota.

Kantorovich himself had a fairly sophisticated sense of the centralization/decentralization issue

and of the role of incentives. At the same time, his basic results were always capable of interpretation in two ways, either as a blueprint for an "efficient" highly centralized system, or (in the "dual" version) as a formula for decentralization. In the first half of the 1960s it seemed possible that the second interpretation might take hold, but after the very modest Soviet reforms of 1965, and especially after 1968, which marked the start of the highly conservative Brezhnev era, reformist ideas fell into the background for fifteen years, although they continued to be developed by academic economists.

At the technical level, Kantorovich was quite closely involved with attempts to improve economic planning. In 1971 he returned to Moscow to join the Institute of Management Problems of the USSR State Committee on Science and Technology, an organization heavily involved in training senior managers, as well as in research and consultancy. (He left in 1976 to join a more research-oriented institute and to specialize on questions of technical progress.) Always keen on applications, he was a member of major government committees on pricing, transport problems, science and technology, and supply.

One piece of consultant work undertaken by Kantorovich in the early 1970s illustrates both the author's technical skill and the problems facing applications of his ideas in the context of the Soviet economy. At that time the Soviet government, following a decision of the 1971 party congress, was pursuing an ambitious plan to computerize economic planning and management on a large scale. The aim was to construct a "statewide automated system" of information processing centers, each serving an administrative agency (such as the State Planning Commission or the State Supply System), a ministry, or an enterprise. This objective was seen at the time as a means of bringing the economic system into the computer age, yet at the same time preserving many of its centralized features.

Kantorovich became involved in the design and implementation of one particular system, dealing with the manufacture and distribution of steel. The system involved forecasting demand for steel products on a disaggregated basis and allocating the orders to various steel plants in a way intended to minimize costs. The main features of the problem were its size and complexity. Planning is done at a variety of different hierarchical levels, and there were acute problems of ensuring consistent aggregation and disaggregation. At the same time the work involved cooperation among different jurisdictions—the ministry responsible for the steel plants, the supply system, which has the responsibility of assigning suppliers to customers, and the transport organizations that shift the finished products.

Kantorovich was chief mathematician on the project. He was able to formulate the basic model as a linear program in a fairly straightforward way. The constraints were the need to satisfy demand at various points, the production capaci-

ties of the various steel mills, and (in some variants) the capacity of the transport system. The objective function was a variant of minimizing the total costs of producing and transporting steel products. In principle this was little more than an amalgamation of two of his 1939 applications. In practice the model was enormous, with 40,000 customers and 250,000 varieties of rolled and calibrated steel. Even after aggregation the model for plate mills included 7,000 variables and 2,000 equations.

The model naturally raised questions about the accuracy of the underlying data, especially since customers had an incentive to exaggerate their requirements in order to get a guaranteed supply. As a result, some demands could not be met, and a priority system, which could not be formulated mathematically, had to be introduced. There were also problems in providing incentives for officials working in the supply system to use the optimal solution. Apparently even when the system had been introduced, work continued in the old way and the computer printouts detailing the optimal solutions were ignored. The results of this system, as of others in the computerization drive, were disappointing.

At a purely formal level there is no special difficulty in transforming a static programming model into a dynamic one. It is simply necessary to distinguish products by the date at which they are produced or used and to incorporate additional constraints reflecting additions to the capital stock through investment and storage activities. There are difficulties in fixing end-state constraints in finite models or coping with the problem of an infinite horizon, but these are not insoluble. Some of Kantorovich's early work on dynamics expounded this generalization, identifying in particular the various 'discount factors' which can be derived by looking at the ratio of successive 'dated' shadow prices.

However, Kantorovich, soon began to work with more aggregated models incorporating substitution possibilities between capital and labor. Much of this work was done using the so-called Cobb-Douglas production function, a specification of the technology widely used by Western economists in the 1960s but now regarded as not very satisfactory. Using this (and other) functions, he made estimates in 1965 of the marginal productivity of capital on various assumptions.

These issues had direct policy relevance. Before 1960 opposition to interest or profit as an income category appropriate to a socialist society had prevented the use of discount rates in appraising investment projects. When a crude system of appraisal was finally introduced, the required rate of return was set at a different level for different branches. As well as arguing for a uniform rate, Kantorovich proposed that it should be raised to reflect his estimation of the rate of return on capital at the margin. Although he was probably right, it is questionable whether, given the arbitrary level of Soviet prices in general, any uniform rate would generate an efficient investment allocation.

Theoretically more interesting are Kantorovich's attempts to incorporate other features into the growth model, such as nonlinearities, probabilistic elements, and technical progress. In an article published after Kantorovich's death, V. L. Makarov, his collaborator on growth models for over twenty years, noted that "over this period the feeling never left me that he had in his head a much more complete dynamic model of the economy than those set out in his publications. This model was not, of course, so formalized as his published models and took account of new knowledge and new problems arising in economic practice. It often occurred to me that Kantorovich was verifying the solution of any practical problem on his model. Perhaps for this reason he was always so logical and consistent."

According to Makarov, Kantorovich viewed this model "primarily as theoretical, as an instrument of analysis, a sui generis framework for ordering a fairly wide range of economic phenomena." We can deduce from his published writings that it incorporated some quite sophisticated notions both of probability and of technical progress. In the latter connection he was interested in the impact of technical change on depreciation profiles and in the question of appropriation of the benefits of technical advances. In his view, revolutionary technological developments led to structural changes that took a long time to work through; they also had a "public good" property. Due to the first of these factors, models of smooth, continuous adjustment are not appropriate. Because of both factors, there is a case for subsidizing innovation in its early stages. As a member of the USSR State Committee on Science and Technology, Kantorovich was able to advance his policy prescriptions at a high level.

## Honors and Legacy

Towards the end of his life, Kantorovich was showered with honors both at home and abroad. The Soviet government awarded him a second Order of Lenin—an unusual honor. He received honorary degrees from a number of universities in Europe and America. He continued to write papers on mathematics, programming, economic theory, and economic policy right to his death on April 6, 1986. An obituary in the leading Soviet journal on mathematical economics noted, "Kantorovich exhibited a deep sense of democracy, a broad education, and gentleness and simplicity of conduct. However, this did not prevent him from showing inflexible strength of character in scientific debates of principle, and in the struggle to bring progressive scientific ideas to life." (1987, p. 93)

There is no reason to doubt that Kantorovich's courageous and determined development of his ideas in the difficult period before 1959 earned him the respect of his colleagues, as much as did his intellectual brilliance. His life as an economist was so profoundly and directly affected by developments in the social and economic system of the USSR. At the same time he and his colleagues have had an influence upon the operation of the Soviet economic system.

Kantorovich's discovery of linear programming, coupled with his recognition of its potential application in a range of detailed production activities, was a remarkable achievement. But even more remarkable was his realization that the discovery had such fundamental implications through the shadow prices for understanding the operation of the economy. The same discovery was made at about the same time in the West, notably by Koopmans, and it is entirely appropriate that they should be joint winners of the Nobel Prize. Both combined remarkable mathematical skill with outstanding economic intuition.

Kantorovich's early work on generalizing his discovery was done unofficially, almost in secret. For about twenty years, knowledge of it was confined to a small circle of colleagues. When finally it was published it had an immediate impact on the way economics was understood and practiced in the USSR. In Kantorovich's view, mathematics could lay bare previously unknown laws. Although critical of earlier Soviet economics, he believed that his ideas could be reconciled with Marxist ideas such as the labor theory of value, though to do so would require adaptation in the latter. He thus combined a commitment to socialist values with an openness to the implications of rigorous economic logic.

As noted above, Kantorovich is the only Nobel laureate in economics whose work was done within the

USSR. The Russian and Soviet commitment to mathematics assisted him, just as the intellectual atmosphere of the 1940s and 1950s delayed his work. At present there is no obvious candidate to be a second Soviet prizewinner (although Eastern Europe has a number of distinguished economists). In this respect Kantorovich occupies a unique position. At the same time his pathbreaking discoveries have acted as a powerful stimulus to economists everywhere, but especially in the USSR.

MARTIN CAVE

# Selected Bibliography

Cave, Martin. *Computers and Economic Planning*. Cambridge: Cambridge University Press, 1980.

Johansen, Leif. "L. V. Kantorovich's Contribution to Economics." *Scandinavian Journal of Economics* 78 (1976): 61–80.

Kantorovich, Leonid. "On the Translocation of Masses." *Management Science* 5 (1958); 1–4.

———. "Mathematical Methods of Production and Planning and Organisation." *Management Science* 6 (1960); 366–422. Reprinted in Alec Nove, ed., *The Use of Mathematics in Economics*. Edinburgh: Oliver and Boyd, 1964, pp. 225–79.

———. *The Best Use of Economic Resources*. London: Pergamon Press, 1965.

———. *Essays in Optimal Planning*. Oxford: Basil Blackwell, 1977.

Kantorovich, Leonid and Akilov, G. P., *Functional Analysis in Normed Spaces*. Oxford: Pergamon Press, 1954.

Kantorovich, Leonid and Krylov, V. I., *Approximate Methods of Higher Analysis*. New York: Interscience Publishers, 1958.

Kantorovich, L. V.; Bogachev, V. N.; Makarov, V. L. "Estimating the Effectiveness of Capital Expenditures" *Matekon* 8(1) (1971): 25–52.

Kantorovich, L. V., et al. "On the Use of Optimization Methods in Automated Management Systems for Economic Ministries" *Matekon* 15(4) (1979): 42–66.

Katsenelinboigen, Aron "L. V. Kantorovich: The Political Dilemma in Scientific Creativity" *Journal of Post Keynesian Economics* 1(2) (1978–79): 129–47.

Koopmans, Tjalling C., ed. *Activity Analysis of Production and Allocation*. New York: John Wiley and Sons, 1951.

Makarov, V. L. "On Dynamic Models of the Economy and the Development of L. V. Kantorovich's Ideas." *Matekon* 23 (1987): 50–74.

———. L. V. Kantorovich: an Obituary." *Matekon* 23 (1987): 84–93

Sutela, Pekka, *Socialism, Planning and Optimality: A Study in Soviet Economic Thought*. Helsinki: Societas Scientiarum Fennica, 1984.

# LAWRENCE R. KLEIN    *1980*

Lawrence R. Klein was born in 1920 in Omaha, Nebraska. He earned a B.A. degree in 1942 from the University of California, Berkeley, and a Ph.D. in 1944 from the Massachusetts Institute of Technology. Klein, who has four children, is widely regarded as the father of econometric model building for the U.S. economy and was awarded the Alfred Nobel Memorial Prize in Economic Sciences in 1980 for his contribution to the discipline.

Professor Klein has been an achiever throughout his life and maintains a level of activity that even leaves the observer gasping for breath. As a student, Lawrence Klein was among the best, winning a Phi Beta Kappa key and highest academic honors as an undergraduate and subsequently earning his Ph.D. in a record two years. He has been active in many organizations and has served as president of the Econometric Society, the American Economic Association, and the Eastern Economic Association. Other organizations for which Klein has served include the National Association of Business Economists, the National Academy of Sciences, the Institute for International Economics, the Social Science Research Council, the Brookings Institution, the American Philosophical Society, the National Economists Club, and the Institute for Advanced Studies, just to name a few.

Fortunately, Klein has also found time to serve various government agencies in advisory and other capacities. These agencies and organizations include the Federal Reserve Board, the Congressional Budget Office, and the Economic Advisory Committee of the State of Pennsylvania. Professor Klein has served as consultant to international organizations, including UNCTAD and UNIDO.

Given all of these affiliations, it is incredible that Klein has also found the time to publish over 250 articles and 26 books, many of which are classics in the field of economics. He is truly a prolific writer and, not surprisingly, has served on the editorial board or as editor of *Econometrica,* the *International Economic Review, Empirical Economics*, and *Comparative Strategy*.

Professionally, Klein began his career after graduate school as a research associate of the Cowles Commission at the University of Chicago (1944–47) and subsequently became a research associate with the National Bureau of Economic Research (1948–50). His first teaching position was as lecturer in economics at the University of Michigan from 1950 to 1954. Upon leaving Michigan, Klein worked for the Oxford University Institute of Statistics in England as both a senior research officer and reader in econometrics.

He returned to the United States in 1958, becoming professor of economics at the University of Pennsylvania. This university has been his home ever since, although he has accepted visiting positions at Osaka University in Japan, the University of Colorado, the City University of New York, Hebrew University in Jerusalem, the University of California at Berkeley, Princeton University, and Stanford University, as well as other institutions.

At the University of Pennsylvania, Klein has been closely associated with Wharton Econometric Forecasting Associates, having served as chairman from 1969–80 and currently serving as chairman of its professional board. Although Klein's interest in econometric model building precedes his association with the Wharton School, it is Wharton Econometrics that, at least partly, provided Klein the vehicle to make his Nobel Prize winning contributions to the discipline.

# The Formative Years

It is well known that a number of great economists have been deeply and profoundly affected by the events and circumstances of their lives and that these experiences provided a starting point and a perspective for their view of the economy. John Maynard Keynes was so deeply affected by the Great Depression of the 1930s that he rejected his classical underpinnings in favor of a fundamentally new model of the macroeconomy. Although Lawrence Klein was only a boy during the Great Depression, he too was touched by this experience. In Klein's own words:

I entered economics because, as a youth of the depression, I wanted in-

tensely to have some understanding of what was going on around me. It was psychologically difficult to grow up during the depression. It was easy to become discouraged about economic life and did not give one, at eighteen or twenty years, the feeling that there were boundless opportunities just waiting for exploitation. (1986, pp. 21–22)

Klein was also very interested in mathematics as well as economics. As an undergraduate, Klein took all the mathematics he could, although he received no encouragement from the economics faculty to develop these skills. The young Lawrence Klein was simply operating on a personal belief that mathematics and mathematical statistics could provide powerful and important tools for economic analysis. Armed with a personal interest in economics and a penchant for mathematics, it is not surprising that Lawrence Klein developed an appreciation for the work of Paul Samuelson. This respect and admiration ultimately led Klein to attend graduate school at the Massachusetts Institute of Technology, where Samuelson taught. As a graduate student, Klein worked closely with Samuelson, which further nurtured and honed his interest in statistics and in the Keynesian approach to macroeconomic analysis. While at MIT, Klein worked hard to formalize and mathematize Keynes' views. This effort resulted in a seminal book, *The Keynesian Revolution* in 1947.

After graduate school, Klein's first professional position was with the Cowles Commission at the University of Chicago, where he worked with a talented group of researchers who have since won an incredible four Nobel Prizes in economics. It was here that Klein began his legendary career as a model builder, attempting to integrate his mathematical and statistical tools with the Keynesian view of the macroeconomy. At the Cowles Commission, Klein and his colleagues developed statistical methods and systems that have become part of the basic training for contemporary economists.

Klein left the Cowles Commission in 1947, but his interest in model building continued. The summer of that year was spent constructing a model of the Canadian economy. Klein subsequently went to Europe where he met many "true" Keynesian economists, including Piero Sraffa, Kahn, and Joan Robinson. While in Europe Klein also worked with and studied under the great Ragnar Frisch.

When Lawrence Klein returned to the United States in 1948, he accepted a position with the National Bureau of Economic Research under the direction of Arthur Burns. Klein shortly went to work for the University of Michigan's Survey Research Center, where he learned about techniques for measuring household behavior. At Michigan, Klein received funding from the Ford Foundation to begin the Research Seminar in Quantitative Economics. As a result of this endeavor, Klein became associated with Arthur Goldberger (a graduate student at that time) and with him developed what became known as the Klein-Goldberger model of the U.S.

economy. This model was essentially an extension of the work begun at the Cowles Commission.

In 1954, Klein went to the Institute of Statistics at Oxford, where he continued his model building efforts. In 1958, he returned to the United States, becoming full professor of economics at the University of Pennsylvania's Wharton School. Klein's passion remained model building, and he immediately resumed his work on modeling the U.S. economy. These early efforts at Pennsylvania represent the birth of the now-famous Wharton econometric model.

Lawrence Klein's work and reputation grew rapidly. In 1959, he was asked by the Social Science Research Council to serve as a principal investigator for its Committee on Economic Stability. Klein's particular charge was to develop a short-run forecasting model for the U.S. economy. A major innovation of the resulting model was the inclusion of a detailed monetary sector which was not included in the ancestral Klein-Goldberger model. This model, constructed for the Social Science Research Council, was ultimately co-opted by the Brookings Institution, thereby becoming the "Brookings model."

In the early 1960s several large corporations became enamored with the new, high-powered econometric models pioneered by Klein and solicited his help for their own commercial purposes. With temporary funding from the Ford Foundation and the National Science Foundation running out, Klein proposed that these corporations jointly support the University of Pennsylvania's econometric programs so that the Wharton School might develop a common model to be used by all the subscribing firms. In 1963, Michael Evans (who had just graduated from Brown University) joined Klein at the Wharton School and was instrumental in advancing this commercial version of the basic Wharton model.

From this initial venture the industry of commercial forecasting was born. The Wharton Econometric Forecasting Unit grew rapidly, becoming a nonprofit corporation in 1969. In 1980, it was sold by the University of Pennsylvania to outside interests.

From the very beginning Lawrence Klein has been an ardent follower of John Maynard Keynes. He is a strong advocate of activist fiscal policies and in the efficacy of fiscal-policy multipliers. But it is interesting and revealing that Klein has never been ideological in his approach to economics. In an early article (1947), Klein compared the classical and Keynesian models of the economy. He expresses a preference for the Keynesian model because he finds some empirical evidence to support it. Yet there are no ideological overtones to Klein's analysis and he is zealous only in the pursuit of truth. This debate is not a holy war but simply an effort to discover how the world actually works.

In fact, Klein has been quick to recognize Keynes' shortcomings:

The Keynesian theory of employment provides us with the starting point for macroeconomic analysis, but its use now is primarily as a pedagogical device. If one is to try to apply this theory for problems of scientific prediction—the necessary test for any good theory—he finds that he must build on the original formulation. The simple Keynesian theory is static and involves too few variables to be useful in direct application to problems of prediction. (1951, p. 449)

Klein further comments that "Keynes failed to make the *General Theory* clear and that it was never fully understood until mathematically inclined economists formulated it in unambiguous, precise models" (p. 450). Even at a relatively young age, Klein exhibited a judicial temperament, with an ability to separate the good from the bad. And, demonstrating the courage of his convictions, he was willing to criticize Keynes even in the direct glow of the Keynesian revolution.

The young Klein was confident and relentless in his commitment to careful and thorough analysis. In a 1950 article, he is emphatic that "in analyzing from theoretical models the analyst must, among other things, define terms carefully, reveal the substance behind the relationships used, and tie the argument together with no loose ends." (p. 605) This commitment to thoroughness and objectivity would become a hallmark of Klein's unique career.

Further, Klein argues that good models must accurately represent and describe the economic behavior of people:

One cannot simply build tricky models that have solutions in some mathematical sense and then claim automatically to have a representation of economic behavior. Each equation must be capable of being derived from some set of first principles and identified with the economic behavior of units that make up the system. Models built on the basis of anonymous relations or contradictory relations are thoroughly unacceptable (p. 606)

These sentences reveal a philosophy and a set of principles which would guide Klein in his future work. They reveal much about the man and his quest for excellence. It is this commitment to excellence that enabled Klein to achieve such stardom among his fellow scholars.

## The Monetarist-Keynesian Debate

Professor Klein has been a principal player in the Monetarist-Keynesian debate in the modern era. With reference to the fundamental monetarist tenet that the dominant determinant of both nominal gross national product (GNP) and the inflation rate is the growth rate in the money supply, Klein responds that:

This is an imputation of remarkable power to money. If the economy is at full capacity or full employment real GNP and if it is asserted that money determines the price level, then it is trivial to say it also determines nominal GNP. If the economy is not necessarily at full employment equilibrium, then it is remarkable indeed that money is such an important variable that it is predominant in the determination of both nominal GNP and the price level. I don't believe a word of it. (1973, p. 10)

Klein also dismisses the monetarist assumption that the velocity of money is constant, pointing out that "it is not difficult to find contradictory evidence on this proposition." (May 1983, p. 252) Similarly, he rejects the monetarists' "quantity theory of money"—the hypothesis that there is an exactly proportional relationship between the supply of money and nominal GNP.

In spite of his skepticism about the powers of money, Klein rejects the view that "money doesn't matter." Early in his career, with the Cowles Commission, Klein spent significant time and effort studying the "real balance effect"—the view that changes in the amount of purchasing power resulting from a change in the price level would affect the level of consumer spending. The original version of the Klein-Goldberger model included the real balance effect.

According to Klein, "we recognized the effects of monetary factors from the start, but not along the lines pursued by the Monetarist school" (1973, p. 10). As with most Keynesian economists, Klein's view is that the transmission mechanism for monetary policy is more complicated than the monetarists believe and that the effect of money on the economy is primarily felt through interest rates. More specifically, changes in interest rates are viewed as affecting the demand for housing, durable goods, and investment. As an important component of production costs, the interest rate is also viewed as affecting the supply of goods. Ultimately, changes in the prices of goods affect the balance of trade and international capital flows.

The recession of 1981–82 highlights Klein's differences with the monetarists. The monetary view is that the reduction in the inflation rate was caused by a restrictive monetary policy. The reduced inflation lowered expectations of future inflation, thereby permitting a broad based decline in interest rates. Klein's view is that the lower inflation largely resulted from lower oil prices, food prices, and primary-product prices. At the same time, a restrictive monetary policy collided with a large fiscal deficit to drive up interest rates. Near-record interest rates reduced the demand for housing, durable goods, and investment. The resulting unemployment reduced wage demands, causing a further moderation of inflation.

With characteristic candor, Professor Klein admits that econometric model builders are paying more attention to the monetary sector today than in the past. But the primary reason for this is not a change of heart but the fact that more and better data are available today, compared to the period immediately following World War II, and that interest rates have become much more volatile. In Klein's view, the inclusion of a more detailed monetary sector is simply part of a natural evolution:

Over the years, money has played an increasingly important role in successive generations of Wharton models. Interest rate levels and swings, deregulation, introduction of new credit instruments, and similar develop-ments have made money markets interesting from the viewpoint of economic analysis. They have also made credit market changes more influential; therefore, it is no surprise that the monetary sectors are growing in importance and demanding more attention of model builders. (May 1983, p. 238)

As part of this evolution, in 1977 the Wharton model included a complete flow-of-funds sector for the first time. The role of money acquired increasing significance when in October 1979, the Federal Reserve system announced a change in its operating strategy by placing greater emphasis on achieving announced monetary targets (designated growth rates for the various monetary aggregates) while simultaneously downplaying the goal of interest-rate stabilization.

Regarding the Fed's record in achieving these monetary targets, Klein agrees that the average growth rate of the monetary aggregates has been reduced. But he finds irony in the fact that the money supply has at the same time become more variable, leading to wide swings in the Treasury bill rate as well as other interest rates. Klein thinks that the pursuit of monetary targets may have actually destabilized monetary growth.

In response to the monetarists' allegation that the traditional Keynesian demand-management policies are destabilizing and foster an inflationary bias, Klein points to most of the post-World War II record, which indicates that "Keynesian economic policy of demand management was very successful in contributing to excellent domestic economic performance in one country after another ... with very modest inflation" (1983, p. 92). However, Klein does give "some recognition" to early critics of Keynes who believed that inflation would ultimately become a problem. In Klein's view, prolonged periods of full employment made possible by Keynes' contributions generated large inflationary pressure. Aggravating these inflationary pressures were new and largely unpredictable disturbances, including major crop failures throughout the world, OPEC oil boycotts, and the fall of the shah of Iran and the ensuing Iran-Iraq war.

Yet Klein is not willing to make any major concessions to the monetarists. The inflation experienced in the 1970s "confirms to my mind that Keynesian economics was not enough, *not* that Keynesian economics was misleading or incorrect" (1983, p. 93). The Nobel Prize winning economist is insistent that the appropriate analytical framework for dealing with inflation is not a fundamentally new approach, as suggested by the monetarists and others, but rather a greater emphasis on structural issues (for example, energy and productivity) within the framework of the traditional Keynesian model:

Every decade will have its disturbances, but those of the 1970s were unusually severe. I do not think, however, that they were severe enough to compromise the structure of the economy for modeling purposes. They did not invalidate the structures of the ... Keynesian model. (1983, p. 94)

Furthermore, Klein bristles at the allegation that the Keynesian model is incapable of explaining the simultaneous existence of inflation and recession ("stagflation") which characterized the U.S. economy in the 1970s, pointing out that in simulations of the Keynesian-inspired Wharton model, "I have no trouble at all in generating responses to external shocks of high grain or fuel prices that show positive association between unemployment and inflation" (1983, p. 94).

Professor Klein also challenges the notion that the Keynesian school views the economy as inherently unstable. He agrees that the economy is subject to fluctuations, possibly around an underemployment equilibrium, but this is not to say that the economy is unstable. In fact, Klein has subjected both the Wharton model and the Klein-Goldberger model to repeated shocks which reveal that the underlying economic system is stable.

Whatever his differences with the monetarists, Dr. Klein steadfastly stresses that the debate cannot ever be settled by argumentation:

Careful statistical study of the evidence following best econometric practice can probably do much to settle some of the debatable issues. It is extremely healthy and welcome to see the debate shift from speculative theorizing, casual empirical referencing, and unsupported asserting, to serious work in applied econometrics. We may not resolve matters, but we shall learn more about the crucial issues and know where each side stands. We shall probably find out what would be needed in order to convince both sides of the correctness or incorrectness of their positions. (1973, p. 12)

As always, Professor Klein is pragmatic and scientific and is willing to let the facts speak for themselves. These are the qualities of a Nobel laureate.

Related to monetarism is the emerging rational-expectations model of the macroeconomy. The essence of the rational-expectations approach is the view that if people are informed and if they fully understand the operation of the macroeconomy, monetary and fiscal policy actions of the government will be discounted by people as affecting only the price level and hence have no effect on output or employment. Like monetarism, the rational-expectations model argues against the use of activist and discretionary demand-management policies.

Regarding the use of expectational variables in economic models, Klein notes that Keynesian and other models have included expected values of economic variables for at least forty years. These expectations have been approximated by using various lag structures of historic data. In addition, surveys of investment expectations of firms and price and spending expectations of households have frequently been employed. However, the rational-expectations approach has a more exacting view of the role of expectations, arguing that ordinary consumers have in their possession all of the information and data used by professional economists and model builders and that they ultimately

form the same expectations of future economic events. Klein finds this notion quite incredible:

> It makes sense to assume that people make use of many information sources, maybe even as many as are available, but to assume, whether implicitly or explicitly, that they use them in the same way as do professionals is wholly unwarranted or implausible. I cannot imagine the ordinary citizen coming to my own conclusions, even indirectly, let alone following the same steps in reasoning that I follow. (1983, p. 99)

Overall, Professor Klein is unimpressed with the potential contribution of rational expectations, confidently predicting that rational expectations will simply not provide a breakthrough.

# Supply-Side Economics

Professor Klein generally agrees with "the basic characterization of contemporary macroeconomics as demand analysis" (1978, p. 2). He also feels that the traditional demand-management policies (both monetary and fiscal) served the United States well from the advent of Keynesian economics in the 1930s to the mid-1960s. With the exception of World War II and the Korean War, the primary economic problems of this era were rooted in a lack of effective demand.

However, beginning in 1965, the nature of the economy began to change. America's involvement in the War in Vietnam expanded, at least temporarily eliminating any

problems related to deficient demand. The late 1960s and early 1970s
witnessed the breakdown of the Bretton Woods fixed exchange-rate
system, which eliminated an external
constraint on the ability of central
banks to pursue expansionary policies. As a result of these and other
events the U.S. economy became increasingly volatile, with inflation becoming a more acute and serious
concern. Shortages and resource
constraints became commonplace.
In addition, according to Klein,
"there were new demographic issues,
the Iranian revolution, the decline of
productivity growth, and other new
conditions that surfaced, calling for
a fresh approach in both analytical
modeling and the formation of adequate policies" (1983, p. 4).

Klein is not arguing that the traditional demand-management policies employed were misguided or ineffective. To the contrary, he feels
that to some extent their success
made them obsolete. But the fundamentally new economic problems of
the modern era call for new approaches and policies. These new
approaches and policies "do not
necessarily call for a complete upheaval in economic analysis, but
rather solutions can be found within
the framework of existing theoretical knowledge that requires building
an appropriate full supply side on to
prevailing systems of demand orien-
tation" (1983, p. 5).

According to Klein, theoreticians and model builders must now
pay more attention to the supply
side of the economy, including input
supplies and prices, training of the
labor force, bottlenecks, and pro-

duction relationships in general. He
feels that monetary and fiscal policies have been overworked, with expectations of results that are not justified.

In order to understand Klein's
position, it is critical to realize that
this recent emphasis on the supply
of goods and services bears little re-
semblance to the popular version of
"supply-side economics," namely,
the relationship between marginal
tax rates and output which underlies
the Laffer curve and the Kemp-Roth
tax cut of 1981. Regarding the popular notion that tax rate reductions
will induce people to work harder,
thereby increasing productivity,
Klein observes that "it is not a question of saying straightaway that this
populist proposition is wrong; it is
simply that such a reaction pattern
has not been established . . . there is
every reason to doubt that the response (of increased work effort)
will be as fast or as large as they
anticipate" (1983, p. 11).

Klein's interest in the supply
side is with nascent structural problems. Specifically, his principal concerns relate to demography, energy,
food, the environment, regulation,
and competitiveness and productivity. To convey the nature of his analysis, consider the issue of demography. According to Klein, the
preeminent demographic problem
of the 1980s is for the work force to
absorb the "baby boom" generation.
Decades earlier, an associated problem had been to expand educational
facilities to handle the influx of students from an earlier baby boom.

In addition to the problems
created by the baby boom, the in-

creased percentage of working women has created strains on the job market that require creative solutions. Moreover, the migration of Americans from north to south and from east to west has spawned new economic problems for all regions. Klein asserts that these demographic problems are real and of significance, but they argue for specific tailored policies and not macropolicies. In Klein's view, some options to deal with these problems include reducing the minimum wage, selective industry or regional subsidies, and job training programs.

Along these lines, in his 1978 presidential address to the American Economic Association, Klein advocated a job training program for a million long-term and chronically unemployed. This would not be a typical demand-management (macroeconomic) policy but rather one designed to train highly motivated individuals for productive, private-sector jobs with upward mobility.

Klein's concern with the environment is also on his list of priorities. Just as with demography, environmental problems are resistant to traditional macroeconomic policies. Success in managing the environment will, he believes, require specific regulations, specific taxes, and specific subsidies.

It is an interesting point that the supply-side issues discussed by Klein are frequently interrelated and overlapping. For example, problems associated with the environment may result from the quest for additional energy supplies. In the search for new oil reserves, the oceans may be despoiled, while at the same time the

strip mining and use of coal may damage land and air. Both energy and environmental issues overlap with regulatory efforts to promote the health, safety, and general welfare of the society.

All of the supply-side issues important to Lawrence Klein relate ultimately to the overall problem of productivity. According to Klein, "Faltering productivity growth, even declining at times, appears to be at the heart of the issue. Vigorous productivity growth is needed if we are to be able to pass steadily improving economic life on to our children" (1983, p. 7).

With reference to economic policy, Professor Klein is adamant that the solutions to contemporary supply-oriented problems require industry-specific programs, not broad macropolicies. These programs should serve to encourage scientific research, train workers for existing and future job opportunities, enhance incentives to save and invest, protect the environment, and conserve scarce energy resources.

However, the implementation of such policies may meet with public resistance, since they will be industry-specific, with obvious winners and losers in the short run:

If supply side economics is understood in the sense in which I have been using the term, the associated structural policies will rarely have easy acceptance by the public at large. That is because some group is usually favored at the expense of others or is hurt either absolutely or relatively to others. Nonetheless, these impacts are only temporary. The policies are implemented in order to improve the overall function of the economy in the medium term. (1983, p. 23)

An example of this problem relates to the foreign sector of the U.S. economy. Professor Klein supports supply-side policies to reduce the importation of oil as well as to expand the level of exports. Such policies would improve the trade balance, and with a stronger dollar domestic inflation would be damped. But over the short run, clear winners and losers would emerge (at least in the relative sense), and advocacy of such policies would meet significant opposition. Similarly, Klein is supportive of an industrial policy which would establish an American trading company, patterned after the seemingly successful ventures in Japan. In Klein's view, an industrial policy would refurbish U.S. industries that have slipped and help others in which the United States has a comparative advantage.

Of course, the supply-side issues identified by Professor Klein have implications for the large-scale econometric models for which he is so well known. With characteristic completeness and balance, Klein advocates the inclusion of the supply side of the economy, along with the traditional demand side and the financial sector, in one fully specified and integrated representation of the economy.

Klein warns that this approach will inevitably lead to models that are large and detailed. In his view, the analytical processes have moved from the single-equation monetarist position and the two-equation Keynesian position to the thousand-or-more-equation position of modern supply-demand analysis. But this complexity is the price we must pay to develop a true understanding of a modern, industrial economy. He has argued that simple macro-rules of the abbreviated Keynesian or monetarist system are no longer very useful. The issue is to construct the theory and the model adequate to the task.

# The International Dimension

Klein is well known as the quintessential builder of U.S. econometric models. It is less well known, but not surprising, that he is also the premier modeler of the international economy. From the beginning of his professional career, Lawrence Klein had a deep interest in international economics. This interest was in part due to the time he spent in England and continental Europe, where the subject of international economics is of immediate importance. In addition, Klein had visited Japan many times and modeled the Japanese economy. In a joint venture between the University of Pennsylvania and Osaka University, Klein played a key role in founding the *International Economic Review*.

Klein also became involved in modeling the economies of less developed countries (LDCs), including Mexico, Brazil, and Argentina. This experience created opportunities for him to construct models for other countries, in the Far East, the Near East, and even Africa. In the 1960s, Klein consulted with the United Nations Conference on Trade and Development (UNCTAD) to estimate capital requirements in various Third World countries around the globe. As if these efforts were not enough, Professor Klein has also been active in constructing models for several socialist economies. A capstone of this effort was a model of the Soviet economy designed by Klein, in conjunction with Soviet scholars.

In the late 1960s, Lawrence Klein perceived the need to model the international economy as a whole. With financial support from the International Monetary Fund and the National Science Foundation, Klein spearheaded a drive to bring together model builders from the major OECD countries to develop a consistent set of equations across countries to analyze the interactions and linkages between national economies. This effort, formally begun in 1968, resulted in Project LINK (The International Linkage of National Economic Models).

Lawrence Klein has given much time and effort to LINK, which today includes both LDCs and planned economies, in addition to the Organization of Economic Cooperation and Development (OECD) countries. After twenty years of existence, LINK is still a vital and productive project. It is constantly growing, changing and adapting to new situations. Klein himself has characterized LINK as an

on going, live research activity in which the underlying system is constantly changing. New country or area models are regularly being added; existing models are being revised; series are being updated; and new economic processes are steadily being added. (1974, p. 617)

Indeed, the LINK Project has lived through turbulent economic times, including Richard Nixon's New Economic Policy and the currency realignment of the early 1970s, the oil boycotts of the mid and late 1970s and the resulting worldwide inflation, and the rise of protectionism in the 1980s. The LINK system has been used to forecast the effects on the world economy of all these events. In addition, the system has been used to simulate and analyze "hypothetical scenarios" (including international-debt default) posing a significant threat to world economic stability. As with Klein's purely domestic models, the objective of the forecast is to provide accurate predictions useful to policymakers.

Project LINK will undoubtedly continue to make a major contribution to understanding of the international economy. With the emerging world debt crisis, the modeling of LDCs has become a top priority. Specifically, one issue of particular interest to Klein is the possible feedback effects on the developed economies of import restrictions imposed by LDCs who are heavily in debt. On another front, the LINK system is making progress in including the determination of exchange rates within the system.

From a purely mechanical

standpoint, LINK has made significant strides and is currently operated by remote computer terminals on an interactive basis. According to Klein, the LINK system is faster, cheaper, and easier to use than ever before. In addition, participating researchers worldwide now have available an audiovisual telecommunications system with a computer screen in full view to facilitate the analysis of simulations.

An important aspect of the LINK project has always been the involvement and input of local economists (that is, economists from the individual countries involved). LINK assumes they understand the operation of their own economies better than anyone else. This emphasis continues today for the less developed and centrally planned economies as well as the OECD countries. Chile, Nigeria, Venezuela, Taiwan, India, the Philippines, Poland, and Hungary, as well as other countries, will soon be maintaining on site their own models, operated by indigenous economists.

# An Economist's Economist

Lawrence R. Klein is truly an economist's economist. His keen mind, pragmatism, and professional standards are unsurpassed within the discipline. Klein is unwilling to accept hypotheses as a matter of faith and is skeptical of those who do. He is a true scientist, not prone to religiouslike zeal or hyperbole.

The history of economics will record Klein as the quintessential builder of econometric models, both domestic and international. More than anyone else, Klein has brought economics into the modern age of empiricism. From his early work with the Cowles Commission to his long association with Wharton Econometric Forecasting Associates, Klein has devoted his life to econometric modeling and forecasting. These efforts have included not just the industrialized countries, but also many LDCs and most recently the socialist bloc. Simply put, no one has made a greater contribution than Klein, and no one has had more success. It is for his unique contribution that he was awarded the Nobel Prize in 1980.

History will also record Klein as a man of extreme moderation and objectivity. Klein is by admission and practice a follower of John Maynard Keynes. Yet he recognizes Keynes's shortcomings and has spent significant time developing a fully specified "supply side" for inclusion in the traditional Keynesian model. Klein is a generous man who shares his specialized skills freely and is proud of the growing legion of students and colleagues throughout the world who employ his techniques.

Inevitably, Klein has defended his econometric models and their underlying assumptions from the challenges of the monetarists and others. In this debate, he is spirited but not argumentative, preferring to let his models speak for themselves. To Klein, economics is by nature a living and changing science:

Research is constantly underway to improve the explanation of economic phenomena already incorporated in the model and to elaborate and extend the analytical capabilities both for forecasting and for policy analysis. Any model is an approximation to the economy of the real world. Our best approximation always leaves room for improvement as new data, new thinking about the economy, new institutions . . . and experience guide us to the next effort. (1980, p. 44)

Klein is a seminal and prolific writer, with hundreds of journal articles and dozens of books to his credit. On a few occasions he has ventured outside the realm of academia to the political world and the mass media, writing columns for magazines and newspapers and serving as economic advisor to Jimmy Carter, both as presidential candidate and president. But these digressions have not distracted him from his true love and home—scholarly economic activity in an academic setting. His contribution to the discipline is indelible, and we are all richer for his efforts.

ROBERT C. WINDER

# Selected Bibliography

Breit, William, and Spencer, Roger W., eds. *Lives of the Laureates.* Cambridge, Ma.: MIT Press, 1986.

Klein, Lawrence R. *The Keynesian Revolution.* New York: Macmillan, 1947.

———. "Theories of Effective Demand and Employment." *The Journal of Political Economy* 55 (1947), 108–31.

———. "The Dynamics of Price Flexibility." *American Economic Review* 40 (1950), 605–09.

———. *Economic Fluctuations in the United States, 1921–1941.* New York: Wiley, 1950.

———. "The Life of John Maynard Keynes." *The Journal of Political Economy* 59 (1951); 443–51.

———. *An Essay on the Theory of Economic Prediction.* Chicago: Markham Publishing, 1970.

———. "The State of the Monetarist Debate." Federal Reserve Bank of St. Louis *Review* 55 (1973): 9–12.

———. "The Supply Side." *American Economic Review* 68 (1978): 2–7.

———. *Econometric Models as Guides for Decision-Making.* New York: Free Press, 1981.

———. *The Economics of Supply and Demand.* Oxford, England: Basil Blackwell, 1983.

———. "Money in the Wharton Quarterly Model." *Journal of Money, Credit and Banking* 15 (1983): 237–59.

Klein, Lawrence R., and Adams, Gerard, eds. *Industrial Policies for Growth and Competitiveness.* Lexington, Mass.: Lexington Books, c. 1983–1985.

Klein, Lawrence R., and Goldberger, Arthur S., An Econometric Model of the United States, 1929–1952. Amsterdam: North-Holland Publishing, c. 1955.

Klein, Lawrence R., and Johnson, Keith. "LINK Model Simulations of International Trade." *The Journal of Finance* 29 (1974): 617–30.

Klein, Lawrence R., and Young, Richard M. *An Introduction to Econometric Forecasting and Forecasting Models.* Toronto: D. C. Heath, 1980.

# TJALLING C. KOOPMANS  *1975*

Tjalling Charles Koopmans was internationally known for his work in economic theory, mathematical economics, and econometrics. He was awarded the Nobel Prize in Economic Sciences in 1975, along with Leonid V. Kantorovich of the Soviet Union. In awarding the Nobel Prize to the two men, who had conducted similar work largely independently of one another, the Royal Swedish Academy of Sciences recognized that their work had led to improved economic planning. Upon receiving the award, Koopmans expressed 'delight' at sharing the prize with Kantorovich, whose work paralleled his own and with whom he had corresponded for years.

## Life and Honors

Tjalling Charles Koopmans was born August 28, 1910, in Graveland, the Netherlands. He was the youngest son of Sjoerd Koopmans and Wijkje (Van der Zee) Koopmans. One older brother, Jan, became a minister, and the other Hendrijk, an engineer. Koopmans's education began at the school where his father was headmaster. After receiving his M.S. degree in physics and mathematics from the University of Utrecht in 1933, his interest was diverted to economics. As he stated at the news conference following the award of the Nobel Prize, "I first aspired to being a mathematician and then to being a theoretical physicist. . . . I was halfway with math and halfway with physics when I found economics more challeng-

ing." He received his Ph.D. in economics from the University of Leiden in 1936.

Koopmans was a lecturer at the Netherlands School of Economics and an economist with the financial section of the League of Nations before coming to the United States in 1940. After serving as a research associate at Princeton University and as a special lecturer at New York University, in 1942 he joined the Combined Shipping Adjustment Board in Washington, D.C. It was here that he planted the seeds of his Nobel-winning research. While with the board, he tackled the problem of finding the most cost-effective way to ship goods from a large number of sources to a large number of destinations. This work led to a lifelong interest in problems concerning the optimal allocation of resources.

Koopmans left the board in 1944 and joined the Cowles Commission for Research in Economics at the University of Chicago as a research associate and professor of economics. In 1955 the Cowles Commission was transferred to Yale University and renamed the Cowles Foundation for Research in Economics. Koopmans followed the body to Yale and continued his work, again as both research associate and professor of economics. In 1967, he was appointed the first incumbent of the Alfred Cowles Professorship of Economics, a highly prized chair established by Cowles, Yale Class of 1913, a Chicago investment counselor and founder of the Cowles Commission. He held this position for the duration of his career and until his death February 28, 1985.

Koopmans and his wife Truus were the parents of three children, Ann, Henry, and Helen. His hobbies included chess and playing the violin at home with his close friends. While at Yale, he taught classes at both the graduate and undergraduate level in addition to conducting his research. In interviews Koopmans readily stated that he liked to teach and although it competed for his time with his other love, research.

In addition to the award of the Nobel Memorial Prize in Economic Sciences, Koopmans received many other awards and honors. Among these were four honorary degrees, from the Netherlands School of Economics (1963), the Catholic University of Louvain (1967), Northwestern University (1975), and the University of Pennsylvania (1976). He served as the Frank W. Taussig Professor of Economics at Harvard University in 1960–61. He was a member of the National Academy of Sciences, a fellow of the American Statistical Association, a fellow of the American Academy of Arts and Sciences, and former president and vice president of both the American Economic Association and the American Econometric Society.

# Contributions to Economic Science

The importance of the contributions to economics made by Koopmans is extraordinary. These contributions can be broken down into three main areas of quantitative economics. The first is the statistical identification and estimation of parameters in econometric models. The second is activity analysis, of which what is popularly known as linear programming is one aspect. The third is intertemporal utility maximization and the optimum allocation of resources over time. As stated by the authors of the preface to his first book of collected works, "Most economists would be pleased to make seminal contributions in just one area as he has done in each."

## Econometric Analysis

Koopmans became interested in problems concerning statistical and econometric analysis very early in his career. Roy J. Epstein, (1987) in a careful and thorough account of the development of econometric analysis, states that early econometricians such as Henry Moore, Henry Schultz, Jan Tinbergen, and Ragnar Frisch had concentrated their efforts on demand, supply, and estimation of marketplace equilibria. Their initial use of regression analysis led them to ponder questions of model specification, identification, and estimation bias. Koopmans particularly became interested in Tinbergen's early model of a macroeconomic system, developed during the Great Depression. This model used linear differential and difference equations to formulate dynamic theories of investment and output. As Epstein states, "The econometricians expected that the use of multiple correlation analysis, or ordinary least squares [OLS], would revolutionize government response to economic fluctuations by indicating the precise quantitative responses needed to minimize cyclical variations around a basic trend of growth" (p. 48).

Criticisms quickly arose concerning the use of this model for policy analysis. Many economists questioned the specification of the model. It was stated that trial-and-error methods of selecting significant independent variables led to the reformulation of important economic data. Koopmans (Epstein, p. 54), argued that the problem confronts all inductive sciences and that the only solution is to supplement data with "a priori information," or premises that help to limit the number of hypotheses being considered. Economic data alone support too many plausible alternative hypotheses.

Koopmans further defined specification procedures which helped to structure econometric analysis. He supported Tinbergen's theory that the regression equations must be limited by a priori information, but he also encouraged the use of new or lagged variables when results are inconclusive. He rejected the idea that econometrics could ever account for all variation in dependent variables. However, the hope is to include all significant independent variables and reduce error terms to only random noise. At this point, Koopmans believed that the more important questions revolved around the statistical problems of estimation. He was "mainly concerned with reforming the usual estimation procedures

by explicitly adapting the maximum likelihood approach of R. A. Fisher (1925), which was rapidly becoming a standard for workers in other fields of experimental science" (Epstein, p. 55). That is, Koopmans felt that the information contained in sampling error was important and could not be ignored when differentiating between alternative structural hypotheses.

After joining the Cowles Commission in 1944, Koopmans became heavily involved in debates central to the development of standard econometric analysis. Throughout the 1930s, the Cowles Commission had become increasingly well known as a center for mathematical economic research. (At this point in time, mathematical economics was not widely accepted and was studied at only a few universities.) The commission had been founded in 1932 by Alfred Cowles in the hope that the application of mathematical methods to the study of economic issues would lead to better predictions of stock market behavior. By 1944, when Koopmans joined the group, it included an outstanding staff of researchers including Jacob Marschak, Leonid Hurwicz, Lawrence Klein, and T. W. Anderson. Although they were very young, ranging from twenty-four to thirty-five years in age, their group would develop the bulk of the theoretical core of econometric analysis.

The first long paper summarizing the work of the commission was presented in 1945. In this work and in the following eighteen months, the group addressed the overidentification problem and found that it could produce OLS estimators that are biased downwards by as much as 25 percent. They were able to derive a method of indirect least squares which would allow experimenters to ignore overidentification restrictions. "The idea was to sacrifice some efficiency in order to reduce the computational burden of full-information maximum likelihood estimation while preserving consistent estimation of the structure" (Epstein, p. 62). This led to the formulation of the limited-information maximum-likelihood estimator. Also, they laid the foundation for the difference-equation model, which could eventually be converted into a model formulated in continuous time. Revised versions of these papers were published in 1950 and formed the base of many advances in the field of economic statistics and econometrics through the 1950s and 1960s.

## Activity Analysis

The second area in which Koopmans made a significant contribution to economic science is activity analysis. As explained by Herbert Scarf, a colleague of Koopmans at Yale, "Activity analysis is used by economists and operations researchers to select the optimum production techniques when several competing techniques are available" (*The New York Times*, p. 26). This analysis can be applied equally well at the corporate level in a capitalist system or at the national level in a centrally planned economy. It is this research which instigated his life-long interest in problems of resource allocation.

As stated earlier, Koopmans began his work on the allocation of resources during World War II. "It all started," he stated upon receiving the Nobel Prize, "with an assignment during World War II and I was in the humble role of statistician for the British Merchant Mission in Washington" (*Times, ibid*). While in Washington, he kept detailed records of ship deliveries and losses. For the British mission, as well as the Combined Shipping Adjustment Board, he eventually worked out a formula to route empty ships to their next and most efficient destination.

To do this, Koopmans employed a system of analysis referred to as linear programming, or more generally, activity analysis. This can be summarized in the context of the firm's problem as follows: A firm's production process can be defined by a production relation, which associates levels of input usage to output produced. Activity analysis divides the technology available to a firm, reflected in this complex production relation, into a finite number of processes. Each of these processes can be operated at many different activity levels, which define the number of units of output that are produced with the process. For example, a process might be defined as a worker using a loom to weave cloth out of string. If 200 yards of cloth are produced with the worker/loom/string combination, its activity level is 200. Thus in considering a firm with a fixed quantity of resources, activity analysis can be used to determine the profit-maximizing usage of these resources. Each unit of output resulting from a particular process yields the firm a certain amount of profit. Knowing the profit to be made from a unit of output from each process and recognizing the limited amount of inputs at its disposal, the firm can determine the activity level at which each process should be operated to maximize profits.

More generally, we can define an allocation problem using a matrix, in which all of the processes available are represented by the vectors of the matrix. The coordinates of each vector represent both the inputs and outputs involved in a single process. It is assumed that each process is capable of being operated at an arbitrary nonnegative level. In most applications of activity analysis, the matrix will have many rows and columns, with many possibilities of substitution between processes and activity levels.

In the specific application introduced by Koopmans during World War II, the objective was to find the most efficient use of transportation facilities. The idea was to select shipping routes to deliver a group of commodities to specified destinations in order to minimize the total costs of shipping. In this setting, Koopmans defined a process as the selection of a particular shipping route.

To take a simple example, consider a homogeneous commodity available at each of two locations, I and II, and which is required in definite amounts at each of three destinations, A, B, and C. The possibilities of shipping may then be described by the following activity analysis model

| 1 | 1 | 1 | 0 | 0 | 0 | I |
|---|---|---|---|---|---|---|
| 0 | 0 | 0 | 1 | 1 | 1 | II |
| 1 | 0 | 0 | 1 | 0 | 0 | A |
| 0 | 1 | 0 | 0 | 1 | 0 | B |
| 0 | 0 | 1 | 0 | 0 | 1 | C |
| 5 | 3 | 7 | 10 | 20 | 8 | Cost |

in which the last row represents the cost of shipping a single unit from a given origin to a given destination. In defining a solution to general problems of this nature, Koopmans proposed that an efficient production plan would be associated with a vector of prices; these prices would meet the condition that each process in use would make a profit of zero. Any alternative process would make a profit less than or equal to zero. By imposing this rule, the selection of the processes to be used can be done in a decentralized fashion by managers interested in their own concept of profit maximization. Thus it became a very useful tool for managers operating in a capitalist firm, as well as for managers operating in a centrally planned economy.

Koopmans's contributions to activity analysis are important for many reasons. As the author once stated, "[Their] merit is the combination and merging of economic theory, mathematical modeling, data collection, and computational methods and algorithms made possible by the modern computer. A genuine amalgam of different professional contributions!" (*Scientific Papers*, Vol. 2, p. 196). These sentiments have been echoed by many economists over the years since their development.

## Growth Models

The third area in which Koopmans made a significant contribution to economic science is intertemporal utility maximization and the optimum allocation of resources over time. This field is often referred to as the theory of optimal economic growth. In a wonderful book titled *Three Essays on the State of Economic Science* (1957), Koopmans highlights the importance of this field:

> relevance to the problems of ensuring stability in the growth of the economy remains an important criterion in the allocation of research resources. . . . The problem of stability is essentially one of balance between many types of decisions. We therefore need to go on fitting together the best pieces of analysis we have, if we are to make good judgements as to which gaps in our knowledge most inhibit progress on the problem of steadying our rate of economic growth. (p. 211)

As explained in his Nobel address,

> In most studies of this kind made in the countries with market economies . . . there is not an obvious choice of objective function, such as cost minimization or profit maximization in the studies addressed to individual enterprises. The field has more of a speculative character. The models studied usually contain only a few highly aggregated variables. One con-

siders alternative objective functions that incorporate or emphasize various strands of ethical, political, or social thought. These objectives are then tried out to see what future paths of the economy they imply under equally simplified assumptions of technology or resource availability. (*Scientific Papers*, Vol. 2, p. 196)

In summarizing the structure of growth models, Koopmans explained that the starting point for the models involves defining what is meant by "optimal" or "best." Following the earliest definition, given by Frank Ramsey in 1928, the objective is to maximize the discounted sum of utility flows derived from future consumption. (A discount factor is used to diminish the weight given to utility received further in the future.) Hence the objective of these models is to allocate scarce resources so as to maximize the expected utility of a series of generations. In this framework, two extensions have been made beyond the activity analysis models of his early career: First, rather than confining himself to productive activities, Koopmans is now considering an optimal consumption path. Second, rather than confining himself to a relatively short planning horizon, he is now considering a long-term, multigenerational time period.

Using this paradigm, Koopmans as well as future authors were able to analyze problems facing modern economies, such as exhaustible resource usage, adjustment to technological change, and population control. Admittedly, these models have not led to great insights into practical decision-making processes. However Koopmans, as well as many other economists, remained hopeful. As discussed in his *Essays*, "We must face the fact that models using elaborate theoretical and statistical tools and concepts have not done decisively better, in the majority of available tests, than the most simple-minded and mechanical extrapolation formulae" (p. 212). He further quotes James Tobin, a colleague at Yale and himself a Nobel laureate, "The new tools have made it possible to recognize and incorporate more information in our models. But we have not yet learned how to do so to best effect. A further trying out of the new tools for this purpose seems as important as a further increase in our understanding of individual behavior."

In his introduction to the second volume of Koopmans's *Scientific Papers*, Herbert E. Scarf, a well-respected economist in his own right, stated,

I have been privileged to know Tjalling Koopmans as a close personal friend and professional colleague since 1957. . . . Few economists of his stature have consistently displayed such intellectual freshness, conceptual originality, and stylistic clarity over such an extended period of time. Koopmans has had many laurels bestowed on him and has frequently beckoned the profession of economics into new and fruitful areas of inquiry; nevertheless, his work continues to have the directions and simplicity customarily associated with a young researcher in the early stages of his professional journey. (p. xi)

In concluding this biography, one is left with strong feelings of respect and admiration for Tjalling Koopmans. Although not one of the best known of the laureates, he quietly and consistently made a series of contributions ranging from statistics and econometrics, to microanalysis of the firm, macroanalysis, and growth patterns. Using the common theme of resource allocation, he was able not only to add to the body of abstract mathematical theory but also to the economist's "tool kit"— that is, he was able to translate complex mathematics into useful decision-making rules and techniques, which can then be applied to many types of problems. This is a rare and highly valued talent.

KATHRYN A. NANTZ

# Selected Bibliography

## WORKS BY KOOPMANS

*Activity Analysis of Production and Allocation*. New York: Wiley, 1951.

*Three Essays on the State of Economic Science*. New York: McGraw-Hill, 1957.

"On the Concept of Optimal Economic Growth." *The Econometric Approach to Development Planning*. Amsterdam: North Holland, 1965.

"Objectives, Constraints, and Outcomes in Optimal Growth Models." *Econometrica* 35 (1967), 1–15.

*Scientific Papers of Tjalling C. Koopmans*. 2 vols. Amsterdam: Springer-Verlag, 1970 and 1985.

"Economic Growth and Exhaustible Resources." In H. C. Bas, H. Linneman, and P. deWolff, eds., *Economic Structure and Development. Essays in Honour of Jan Tinbergen*, pp. 239–255. Amsterdam: North Holland, 1973.

"Economics Among the Sciences." *American Economic Review* 69, No. 1, March 1979.

OTHER WORKS

Cattell, Jaques, ed. *American Men of Science*. Vol. 3. New York: R. R. Bowker, 1956.

Epstein, Roy Jacob. *A History of Econometrics*. Amsterdam: Elsevier, 1987.

*New York Times*, "Two Economists Win Nobel Prize," "Econometric Planners," and "Prize Cites Pioneering of Analysis." October 15, 1975.

Scarf, Herbert. "The 1975 Nobel Prize in Economics: Resource Allocation." *Science*, November 14, 1975, p. 649.

# SIMON KUZNETS *1971*

Simon Kuznets (1901–85), who was awarded the Nobel Memorial Prize in Economic Sciences in 1971, was the second American so honored. Born in Kharkov, Russia, he was serving as the administrator of a statistical office in the Ukraine when, in 1921, he and his brother emigrated to the United States, where they joined their father. After teaching himself English over one summer, Kuznets was admitted to Columbia University with advanced standing; he received a B.A. degree in 1923 and a Ph.D. in economics in 1926. In 1927, he joined the National Bureau of Economic Research (NBER) whose director and founder, Wesley Mitchell, had supervised his dissertation on cyclical fluctuations in retail and wholesale trade. Two years later he married Edith Handler, who was also asso-

ciated with the NBER. (Their son, Paul Kuznets, one of two children, is a professor of economics at the University of Indiana.) Except for two years service (1942–44) as associate director of the War Production Board, Kuznets taught at the University of Pennsylvania from 1930 to 1954. Subsequently he held faculty positions at The Johns Hopkins University, from 1954 to 1960, and at Harvard University, from 1960 until his retirement in 1971. The Nobel Prize was conferred a few months after Kuznets's retirement.

Cited in the Swedish Academy's statement for his empirical interpretations of economic growth leading to new insights into the economic and social structure and process of development, Kuznets is equally renowned for his work in the organization of a system of national-income accounts. In addition to being an original thinker and distinguished scholar, influential teacher, and dissertation supervisor, Kuznets was an active participant in professional activities, serving as president of the American Statistical Association in 1949 and the American Economic Association in 1953. He continued to write and lecture following his retirement. The American Economic Association awarded him the Francis A. Walker Medal, its highest distinction, in 1977. Simon Kuznets died at Cambridge, Massachusetts, on July 9, 1985.

## Emphasis on Empiricism

Over 200 titles would be listed in a bibliography of Kuznets's work, covering a period of more than fifty years. A systematic sequence of investigation is exhibited in the prodigious volume of published research. Beginning with the publication of his first book, *Cyclical Fluctuations; Retail and Wholesale Trade, United States, 1919–1925*, (1926), based on his dissertation on cyclical fluctuations in trade and his work at the NBER, Kuznets broadened his field of inquiry in order to study the business cycle. Reliable national-income estimates, which were not available, were required to investigate cyclical variability in time-series data. Kuznets, therefore, turned his attention to the collection, refinement, and systematic measurement of national income data in the 1930s and 1940s.

The focus of his post-World War II research, the culmination of his work, was a study of the economic growth of nations, a subject area in economics to which Kuznets was ineluctably led by comparisons of international and intranational income measurements over time. In the preface to *Economic Change* (1953), Kuznets states the sequence of his interests: business cycles, national income, and economic growth. Because an examination of the data revealed that the growth process was a complete transformation of many aspects of economic life, Kuznets included an analysis of the connections and interconnections in consumption, saving, capital formation, the size and spatial distribution of the population, migration, industrial structure, factor productivity, and income distribution, as well as the international flow of goods, people, capital, and knowledge.

The scope of this work was unified by the methodological and philosophical approach which Kuznets employed, undoubtedly influenced by his statistical training and his association with Wesley Mitchell, a pioneer in the measurement of economic data. Classifying the Nobel Prizes that have been awarded in economics, Assar Lindbeck, a Nobel Prize committee member, calls Kuznets's contribution almost pure empirical research. That is, the award to Kuznets was for inductive rather than deductive analysis, which was the methodological approach of the majority of the recipients. Although Kuznets was skeptical of the usefulness of formal mathematical and econometric models, he regarded economic theory as the foundation of economic science. But a theoretical framework in his view must be preceded by careful accumulation and arrangement of the evidence in order to identify all of the relevant factors involved.

Kuznets offers a clear statement on his approach to economic theory:

> By a theory we mean a statement of testable relations among empirically identifiable factors, such relations and factors having been found relatively invariant under diverse conditions in time and space. Such a theory of economic growth of nations may never be within our reach. Obviously we do not have it now, and what is more important, we are not yet ready for it. . . . Under the present circumstances, such a theory would be either an expression of dogmatic belief in some "self-evident" trait of human nature . . . or a formalistic model of the mechanism of economic growth, lacking assurance that it is complete, that the relations are correctly drawn, and that we can ever have the data required for the empirical constants in the formulas. . . . It seems preferable to limit ourselves to a less ambitious task: to draw some suggestions from the empirical record . . . as guides to the further study of the data and particularly to the directions in which testable theoretical analysis must be pursued. (1965, pp. 4–6)

Because quantitative measurements form the basis for understanding economic phenomena, a painstaking, systematic examination of the available data is the first step in the Kuznetsian methodology. Early data which Kuznets, a meticulous scholar, required in order to obtain the necessary perspective on the underlying economic institutions, as well as to be able to distinguish transient from long-term movements of the series, are often fragmentary. Data from disparate sources must be sorted, skillfully integrated, and the sources of error evaluated. The colorful metaphors employed by Richard Goodwin in a review article are appropriate. "Professor Kuznets sinks his piles deep in the spongy morass of economic fact; he weaves great rafts to float the massive abutments which he painstakingly builds up bit by bit" (1956, p. 508). The next step is taxonomic in nature; a creative process that Wesley Mitchell has termed "analytic description." To attempt to speculate on the associations between the variables represented by the data series, and to check on consistency and plausibility, the data are classified, arranged, and rearranged. Explanations are conjectural; judgmental elements are involved. Guided by the concepts of economic analysis, the scattered and incomplete data are transformed into measurements, complementary to the theoretical framework, that can ultimately be employed to test relationships among economic variables.

# The Kuznets Cycle

The discovery, testing, and explanations of business cycles was the initial focus of the research program of the NBER. Business cycles can be defined as recurring but not periodic fluctuations—expansions and contractions—occurring about the same time in many economic activities. Business cycles recur at intervals of five to six years but can be as long as ten to twelve years. Superimposed on the business cycle is a clearly defined secular trend which in the United States, for example, has moved upwards since the earliest nineteenth century estimates. Three additional cycles with average durations lying between the business cycle and secular trend have been identified, although controversy regarding their validity continues. The three intermediate cycles are: the Juglar, duration eight to eleven years; the Kondratieff, duration forty to sixty years; and an intermediate cycle lasting fifteen to twenty years. The intermediate cycle is usually referred to as the Kuznets cycle. In addition to primary sources, the discussion of the Kuznets cycle is drawn from two articles by Moses Abramovitz, a former student and close associate. Since cyclical movements imply self-generation, Abramovitz prefers to substitute "swings" or "waves," following Kuznets's practice.

After removing both trend and cyclical influences for thirty-five price and sixty-five product series for commodities produced in the United States and eight foreign countries, Kuznets found "secondary secular movements," persistent swings with an average duration of twenty-two years. In the appendix to *Secular Movements in Production and Prices* (1930), Kuznets reviewed the pioneering contributions identifying an intermediate cycle, beginning with W. S. Jevons in the late nineteenth century. The exist-

ence of intermediate cycles for aggregate economic activity was found in a study by Arthur F. Burns, confirming Kuznets's results for individual commodities. A major finding in Kuznets's monumental study of capital formation, *Capital in the American Economy* (1961) was evidence of a similar long swing for nonfarm residential construction and durable capital railroad investment. Labor resources as well as capital exhibited similar long swings. Kuznets has related waves in economic activity to corresponding waves of immigration, the rate of population growth, and growth of the labor force. In analyzing the relation between economic and demographic variables, Kuznets made a pioneering and significant contribution to economic science. Population is a major determinant of economic activity; economic activity can be shown to influence the growth of population. Economists generally, however, regard population as an exogenous (outside) variable as, for example, in specifying production as output per capita—that is, the data are adjusted for population. Even so, damped Kuznets cycles have been generated in simulation studies of the Klein-Goldberger econometric model.

That the cyclical and secondary cycles are related, as Kuznets insightfully recognizes, implies that the unemployment rate is the key element and the link between the intensity of resource allocation (demand side), which produces the business cycle, and resource capacity (supply side) which affects the secondary cycle. When aggregate demand decreases, the unemployment rate increases. In *Immigration and the Foreign Born* (1954), Kuznets and Ernest Rubin investigated the association between the unemployment rate and immigration. Although different economic conditions prevailed in the many countries of origin of immigrant groups, declines in the rate of immigration coincided with depressions in the United States, while peaks occurred at the end of periods of sustained economic activity. Both railroad capital expenditure and residential construction, which Kuznets included in "population sensitive" forms of investment, were linked to waves of immigration.

A substantial literature has developed from the pioneering work of Kuznets and others in tracing the interaction of labor and capital resources with swings in economic activity. Although Abramovitz asserts that Kuznets had characterized an era from 1840 to 1914 encompassing four Kuznets cycles in the United States, he argues that changes in the structure of the economy have altered the major forces that produced the cycle in the past. Changes in methods of transportation and the cessation (until recently) of immigration are obvious examples.

# National-Income Estimates

Until the 1920s economic science was confined to microeconomic analysis, the static-equilibrium determination of commodity and resource price and output. Three parallel developments have significantly expanded its scope in the last fifty years: macroeconomics, the determination of aggregate production and the level of prices; econometrics, a mathematical formulation and statistical testing of economic theory; and national-income estimates; the measurement of aggregate economic activity, indispensable to the testing of macroeconomic theory. National income has been estimated in Great Britain from time to time since the initial efforts of Gregory King and Sir William Petty at the end of the seventeenth century. The first estimates provided for the United States were made by the NBER in the 1920s. Kuznets was given the responsibility for the preparation of the first government estimates for 1929–32 by the Department of Commerce. A series of publications followed, including the over-900 page *National Income and Its Composition, 1919–1938* (1941) and other studies by Kuznets which provided estimates back to 1869. Under Kuznets's direction, progress in the development of national-income statistics in the United States, which had lagged behind the work being done in Great Britain, Germany, and Sweden, was advanced to a leadership position.

Many controversial conceptual and statistical problems were encountered. Kuznets brought to the task his meticulous methodological approach, giving careful attention to the clarification of the basic underlying assumptions. That the subjective elements in these measures were not always appreciated by the users of the data and that impressions of precision were conveyed which could be misleading were particular concerns of Kuznets. Discussions of the assumptions, definitions, and interpretations of the published data were included in Kuznets's books on the subject. Gross National Product (GNP), for example, is the most comprehensive measure of economic activity, the basis for business and government policy decisions. But some goods and services are excluded. Because they are not marketed, services produced in the household are not included. Illegal activities are excluded as well, as they are not regarded as productive. Kuznets explains:

> For example, "racketeering" services are obviously rendered in return for compensation, at prices determined by the balance of supply and demand on the market for such services. They are therefore part of our economic system: but to include them in the national product totals would make it impossible to interpret the latter as the contribution of the economic system that appears useful to society at large. Such a criterion of productivity is unavoidable if estimates of the national product are not to become purely superficial measures of one aspect of the market mechanism. (1937, p. 5)

(Although they are excluded from GNP estimations, the value of both of these omitted categories has been estimated.)

Issues of social philosophy which were debated at length both in national-income literature and the many national and international conferences on the subject, were also addressed by Kuznets. The dis-

tinction between both final and intermediate, and gross and net product offers good examples. To avoid double counting, only final goods are included in GNP, for example, the familiar exclusion of the value of the flour used in the production of the final good, bread. Applying the same reasoning, however, it could be argued that the worker's transportation costs, which are included as final goods, could be regarded as an intermediate cost of the goods and services produced by the worker. And, again, the national accounts include the value of the automobile produced and the value of the new machinery used to produce the automobile, including that part of the machinery that is depreciated through the manufacture of the automobile. The issue is not resolved by the estimation of Net National Product (GNP minus depreciation of capital stock), as it can be argued that labor resources also depreciate; a part of consumer goods are used to maintain the productive resource, labor. These issues can be resolved, Kuznets maintains, by agreement on the ultimate goal of economic activity. One set of definitions would obtain if society's ultimate goal was to increase the supply of resources; a different set if consumer satisfaction is regarded as the ultimate goal.

> . . . The one justification for formulating the national income concept in this way is the general notion that it should measure the positive contribution of the economic system to the satisfaction of present and future needs of the nation as a body of

ultimate consumers; and this notion of ultimate consumption is essentially derivable only from the point of view that goods exist for men, and not men for goods. (1941, p. 38)

Some of the other limitations of the data and estimating procedures which Kuznets considers are: inequalities in the distribution of income and the competitive structure of industry, which affect the market prices at which goods and services are valued; the compulsive aspect in the form of taxes of the valuation of government services; and the effect of different pricing systems on international comparisons of national income or in comparing different time periods in country studies. In order to provide comparable data in estimating the growth of U.S. national product from 1870 to 1950, Kuznets and Raymond Goldsmith, in *Income and Wealth of the U.S., Trends and Structure* (1952), increased the value of output for the later years in the series to compensate for the reduction in the hours of work required to produce the national product.

Work continues on the issues which Kuznets raised on the extension and modification of the definition of final goods and market-valued output. Robert S. Eisner and a group of associates are compiling estimates of a Total Income System of Accounts (TISA), following the concepts and insights of Kuznets. The framework provided by national-income statistics is indispensable to the operations of modern governments. This framework, a task of organization of awesome proportions, has been put into place throughout the world in the past five decades. Kuznets assisted several countries established after World War II in the preparation of their initial income estimates. And, national-income accounts are the source of the data on consumption, saving, investment, and other variables required to test the macroeconomic models prepared by economists in government and educational and research institutions. A major contribution to this area of economics and statistics was made by Kuznets.

# Economic Growth

As early as 1930, in *Secular Movements in Production and Prices*, Kuznets commented on the centrality of the long-term dynamic growth process in furthering the understanding of economic phenomena, as well as noting the lack of interest in the subject by economists. In doing so, he anticipated both his own contributions as well as the large amount of work that has been attempted since in this area of economics. Confining economic analysis to static-equilibrium theory impedes its theoretical development in Kuznets's view. Uncompromising in his insistence on the importance of a long-term perspective, Kuznets asks: "and how can our study even of the instantaneous, static reactions of demand and supply be complete, if we know neither the general course of the changes about which these reactions take place, nor the influence which the former may have exercised on the latter?" (1930, p. 3). The Kuznetsian approach is evident in the investigation of economic growth: quantitative comparisons of both the growth over time of an individual country or countries; cross-section data at a particular time of the characteristics of a number of countries at different stages of development; and the search for the associative factors and their interrelationships. Although Kuznets studied differences in regional growth patterns, he regarded the "nation-state" as the appropriate unit of study, principally because sovereign governments have the power to initiate policies that either encourage or impede growth.

The time period or, to use the term Kuznets employed, "economic epoch," covering modern economic growth, dates from the second half of the eighteenth century to the present. An economic epoch possesses distinctive characteristics. It is delimited by an "epochal innovation," for example, the historical period characterized by the making of stone instruments. The application of science to economic production is the epochal innovation of the modern period. Referring to this period as "the scientific epoch" is both more general and representative, as Kuznets points out, than the general use of either the term industrial period, which implies, inaccurately, that technology has been applied principally to manufacturing, or capitalism, which implies that the means of production are only privately owned.

In the lecture that he delivered in Stockholm in December 1971, as Nobel laureate, Kuznets listed six interrelated characteristics of modern economic growth. Foremost among them is the large percentage increase in both total production and population. Kuznets has estimated that the annual rate of increase in population over the modern growth period was one percent and that total product increased three percent, which resulted, therefore, in the unprecedented increase in annual per capita income of two percent. This suggests, as Kuznets has estimated it, a rate of growth of product per capita ten times that of the previous epoch—"merchant capitalism." The second most important characteristic is the rate of increase in productivity, defined as output per unit of input of productive resources, labor, and capital. A structural shift of the economy from predominantly agricultural production to manufacturing and services, together with the prevalence of large-scale production, which resulted in impersonal working conditions for labor, is the third characteristic. Fourth are changes in the structure of society and in ideology. Kuznets cited urbanization and secularization as concomitants of the modernizing process. International interdependence effected by communication and transportation technology is the fifth characteristic. The last characteristic is the dichotomy evident in the world's economies. One-fourth of the world's population reside in high-income countries; three-fourths live in countries unable to provide a minimum standard of living for the majority of their citizens.

# Population and Economic Growth

Although the demographic trends displayed by developed countries are well known—a decline in mortality and corresponding decrease in morbidity rates, and a subsequent decrease in fertility—the economic formulations which Kuznets provided offer new insights. Kuznets wrote extensively on population subjects and attended many population conferences. As he pointed out, the decline in death rates was primarily a decrease in the death rates of infants and children, which contributed to economic growth by reducing the loss to society for the care of children who do not live to become productive adults. The decline in mortality rates was relatively greater in the cities, reversing the earlier urban/rural death-rate ratio and providing, therefore, the necessary support for urbanization. The significant decrease in morbidity rates contributed to social stability and offered an incentive for material achievement.

Because many of the problems of developing countries can be traced to a high rate of population increase, demographic literature has emphasized the deleterious effects of population growth. To counter these arguments, Kuznets discusses the positive features. Since the beginning of the modern growth period, no country has experienced increased population and an associated reduction in per-capita product. "The evidence thus suggests that in modern times growth in popula-

tion has been accompanied by growth in aggregate output—for many countries so large that there was also a market secular rise in per capita product" (1965, p. 123). With reference to developed countries, Kuznets reminds us that population increases are reflected in increases in the labor force, that is, in productive workers. Not only are younger workers more mobile and willing to migrate to take advantage of economic opportunities, the increase in young scientists and technicians produces a more creative society as well. Larger populations require more consumer goods, encouraging entrepreneurial activity and the scale economies of larger production units. Although population growth in developing countries impedes capital formation, in developed countries, Kuznets argues, more children can provide an incentive to work and to save. In a growing population a larger proportion of the inhabitants are active and saving for their retirement. Or to turn the argument around, the pressure of population can provide the incentive to produce capital-saving inventions. Another factor to be considered is the evidence of a faith in the future that a growing population implies. Further economic growth is encouraged. He concluded that both the benefits and costs must be considered in the discussion of population issues.

Kuznets's views are not in agreement with the prevalent neo-Malthusian perspective of most economic demographers. Mark Perlman comments on the dismissal of Kuznets's "pro-natalist" stance in his review of the published papers from two population conferences:

> I wonder whether Kuznets's contributions to the 1978 conference will go similarly neglected. In the past economists have all but ignored his concern with groups in society receiving the first impact of reduced childhood mortality. . . . Bad enough they do not recognize a lead when it is offered; worse yet, they reject it when it is offered by an acknowledged leader, whose intellectual capacity has been repeatedly proven. (1981, p. 81)

# Resources, Productivity, and Technology

Having defined modern economic growth as a significant sustained increase in per capita product, Kuznets turned to the determination of the contributing factors and an assessment of their relative contribution. Growth is the result of either or both an increase in inputs (labor and capital) or the effectiveness with which inputs are employed (factor productivity). After Kuznets examined input data for a number of countries, he concluded that both labor and capital inputs have declined in relative terms over time; the combined inputs contribute only about 28 percent of the increase in the growth rate. The residual is the estimated growth in productivity. Modern economic growth is the result of an increase in scientific activities, in the "stock of useful knowledge" which has improved input quality. Attributing the entire residual to productivity may overstate its contribution, as Kuznets points out, since certain costs of economic growth are omitted. Education costs, for example, which are investments in the quality of the labor force, are not included in labor input. The additional sanitation costs that an industrial society requires is another example of omitted costs. Although estimation problems of almost insurmountable difficulty are encountered, adjusting estimates for these and other costs would reduce the productivity contribution from .72 to .56 (1971, p. 308).

In a number of papers, Kuznets devotes attention to the analysis of the contribution of technological innovation to economic growth. He points out that the effect of economic growth on technological development must also be analyzed. His careful studied approach is in evidence: terms are defined; innovations are classified, for example, demand-creating and cost-reducing technologies; the successions of phases from "pre-conception" through application and diffusion to obsolescence are detailed; and the complexity and unevenness of societal adjustments are examined.

In economic analysis technological change as well as population is generally taken as given. Here also, Kuznets is critical of economists' neglect. As a result, he argues, the data linking technology with input and output statistics are inadequate. "The possibility of distinguishing between total output, labor force, and capital of the country or of an industry, components associated with recent, not so recent, and much older technology, would add immensely to the quantitative base for the study of the interrelationships between technological development and modern economic growth" (1979, p. 98). Significant shifts in industrial structure are generated by technological change. Kuznets considers industrial structure a "key aspect" of growth. Although part of the reduction in the share of agriculture and increase in the shares of manufacturing and services can be traced to changes in consumer demand that result from increased income, a wider selection of consumer goods, and the low elasticity of demand for food, as well as in part to shifts in comparative advantage and subsequent increases in trade among countries, the most important determinant is the impact of technological change, which is selective and shifts over time. Patterns of work and the scale of production units change as well: conflicts among sectors are an inevitable consequence. The "sovereign state" adds more and varied functions.

Technological change is embodied in capital formation, which adds to the stock of capital, a major factor in economic growth. Kuznets claims that between nine and thirteen percent of net national product embodies technological change (1973, p. 27). Kuznets employs four ratios in his discussion: the increment to capital (capital formation), dk, where k denotes capital and d is the incremental change; the capital-formation ratio, $dK/Y$, where Y denotes aggregate product (income); the rate of growth of product (income), $dY/Y$; and the incremental capital-output ratio, $dk/dy$, which equals $(dk/y)/(dy/y)$. Capital formation is equal to savings minus net investment in foreign countries. The terms can be analyzed in either gross or net (minus depreciation) terms. In cross-sectional analysis, Kuznets found the expected positive association between income and savings (investment). Over the long period, however, the capital-formation proportion, $dk/dy$, has been fairly constant. Moreover, there is very little evidence for a positive association of investment with a high growth rate of income. Noting this, Kuznets is critical of W. W. Rostow's "stages" finding that increases in the growth rate were preceded by increases in the proportion of capital formation to income. This proportion, in net terms, was estimated by Kuznets to be less than 15 percent and, therefore, not requiring sacrifices in consumer goods. This conclusion suggested to him that some societal constraints on the savings ratio may be operating in capitalist countries. After speculating at length on the possible explanations for international differences in the incremental capital-output ratio, Kuznets concludes that reconciliation of cross-section and long-term ratios await more and better data. In addition, and importantly, Kuznets speculates that the capital-formation ratio may be positively related to the growth rate of product if the definition of capital is expanded to include education and other investments in workers that are regarded as consumer goods, for example, health expenditures or such governmental expenditures as those for environmental protection.

## United States Growth

The growth experience of the United States in the period from the American Revolution to the present was the subject of the Richard T. Ely lecture delivered by Kuznets at the 1976 meetings of the American Economic Association. The discussion begins with an analysis of the relation between population growth and economic growth. Both a higher birth rate (not a lower death rate) and a high net rate of immigration were the factors which gave the United States a higher rate of population growth than that experienced by older developed European countries. As in other discussions, Kuznets emphasizes the positive growth effects of immigration. Immigrants were primarily males, and primarily laborers and operatives of prime working age who settled in urban areas. But even more importantly, Kuznets points out that the stresses of assimilation on economic and social institutions assisted the development process. As a corollary, Kuznets suggests that the movement of blacks to the North was a response to the employment opportunities resulting from the drastic decline in immigrant labor.

Before the period of industrialization began in the United States, the Kuznets estimates indicate, although the usual difficulties with data were encountered, that the level of per capita income was close to that of Great Britain at a similar period and exceeded the level of per capita income of other European countries at the time their process of

development was initiated from 1840 on. Even so, the growth of the United States has been exceptional. From 1800 to 1970 Kuznets's estimates are an increase in population by a factor of over eighty-five, an increase in per capita income by a factor of eleven and one-half, and the implication of a growth factor of total production close to one thousand. Kuznets concludes that, after adjusting for a later date of entry into the industrial period—the "making-up effect"—the growth rate of the United States is equal to Sweden and exceeds that of other developed countries. The technical innovations giving impetus to growth require effective application. Economic and social adjustments must be made. Kuznets attributes the successful implementation of technology in the United States to a "series of growth-setting decisions" which include enlarging popular participation in political organization and a sustained commitment to public education.

Turning his attention to the inequality in the distribution of income attributable to economic growth, the effects of slavery and immigration in widening income disparities are discussed. But the upward mobility of immigrant workers resulted in a larger income differential for the children of immigrants than for two generations of native-born workers over the same period.

Kuznets is concerned about the effects on the United States of changes in the "international framework," in particular the costs imposed by the strains of the major wars and political unrest of the twentieth century. Although noting the continued growth of the last quarter century, a time of great political strain, Kuznets warns:

> The growth problems of a developed country can be viewed within the context of a combination of technological and economic power, present and prospective; of a variety of accepted goals, and hence of responsibilities; and of the dangers of unforeseen (some unforeseeable) errors and of unavoided (some unavoidable) failures. . . . The dangers of error and failure are formidable because the power of advanced technology makes errors potentially that much more costly; because so much of the rest of the world needs assistance in its efforts to bridge the gap between attainments and minimum aspirations; and because the destructive potentialities of modern technology are so much greater, particularly in a divided world. (1977, p. 14)

# Economic Growth and Developing Countries

Kuznets conducted a number of comparative empirical studies of the growth processes of less developed countries (LDCs) and more developed countries (MDCs). The difficulties facing most LDCs in their efforts to raise living standards are formidable. Kuznets points out, however, that United Nations estimates show an average annual per capita LDC growth rate (excluding the People's Republic of China) from 1950–72 of 2.53 percent, a rate that for developed countries over the longer period of their development has only been exceeded by Sweden and Japan. Part of the explanation is the initial low level of LDC income. In addition, the variability of LDC income is greater than that of the MDCs. The average obscures the very low growth rates, for example, of the sub-Saharan countries. Although rate of growth of total product was higher for LDCs than for MDCs (Kuznets estimates are 5.03 and 4.42, respectively), the higher rate of LDC population growth results in a lower per capita growth rate for 1950–72. Still, Kuznets argues persuasively that population growth is an inadequate explanation for a lower per capita growth rate. The high rate of population increase, primarily the effect of lower mortality and morbidity rates, is only a phenomenon of the past forty years. Furthermore, consequent growth of the labor force and, therefore, production should be a concomitant effect. And, in addition, for individual LDCs, population growth and economic growth were positively associated (primarily in Latin America). Kuznets concludes: "over recent decades other factors tend to outweigh the high rates of population growth, at least among the LDCs" (1979, p. 41).

High birth rates persist, however, and Kuznets searches for a conjectural hypothesis with a high explanatory force. After studying fertility differentials between LDCs and MDCs, he identifies the distinguishing characteristics of the high LDC fertility rates: an early marriage age for females; a large

156                                    SIMON KUZNETS

number of children per family; a
large proportion of children born to
women and, particularly, to men
over forty; and a high rural/urban
fertility ratio. The data suggest to
him that the fertility rate of LDCs
reflects a rational response to economic and social conditions. An investment in children yields workers,
a greater chance for benefits from
the genetic pool (a genius or,
Kuznets comments, a general), and
economic security in old age, the rational alternative to provision by
weak governments. "In short, while
there may be some validity to the
statement that LDCs are poor because they are prolific, it may be
said that they are prolific because
they are poor" (p. 255).

In contrast to the prevalent view
that capital shortages inhibit LDC
growth, Kuznets asserts that poor
countries are not constrained by an
inadequate savings ratio. "With
flexibility of factor proportions, fa-
cilitated by choices in the rate of
utilization of both capital and labor,
relatively low capital-output ratios
can be attained" (p. 46).

What is lacking, in Kuznets's
view, is the ability to adjust economic and social institutions in
order to channel economic growth
effectively. These adjustments are
also hampered by a vulnerability to
emergencies and calamities, and by
adopting the inappropriate nature
of the technology of MDCs, for example, stressing nuclear technology
instead of water pumps. And, to
some degree the growth rate among
LDCs is inhibited by the "international framework" in which their relationship with the rest of the world

is structured. The conclusions which
Kuznets draws are cautionary: the
inadequacies of economic-growth
theory, particularly in the measurement of the social costs of adjustments, and the difference between
LDCs and MDCs at the same stage
of development, which present
LDCs with greater obstacles to development.

# Economic Growth and Income Distribution

The relationship between per
capita income and income inequality has been the subject of a large
number of empirical studies since
the seminal discussion by Kuznets in
his 1954 presidential address to the
American Economic Association,
"Economic Growth and Income Inequality," which was subsequently
published in the *American Economic Review* (1955). Kuznets considers two major factors that operate to increase income inequality:
unequal asset holdings and savings
among socio-economic groups and
the transfer of production and employment from agriculture to manufacturing and services. Almost all of
the studies are tests of the latter factor. Referred to as the Kuznets (inverted) U-hypothesis, the formulation proposes an increasing inequality in income distribution in the
early stages of development, a level-
ing in intermediate stages, and eventually a movement toward the more-
equal distribution characteristic of
most developed countries as the present time. Kuznets traces the effects
for a hypothetical two-sector econ-

omy of a shift out of the agricultural sector (A) into the manufacturing sector (B), assuming that income in B is either more unequally distributed than in A or that mean income in B is higher or both. The results show "a marked increase in inequality in the countrywide income distribution" (1955, p. 14).

In considering the implications of the hypothesis both for the future progress of the LDCs and the growth pattern of the MDCs, Kuznets offers an intriguing speculation on the process of nineteenth century industrialization. The impoverishment of the working class, an indictment of the capitalist system and a tenet of Marxian analysis, may have only been a characteristic of a particular phase of development, and therefore "an overgeneralization of an imperfectly understood trend" (p. 27).

Because the high savings ratios of upper income groups would be expected to perpetuate unequal asset holdings, a major determinant of an unequal income distribution, Kuznets searches for the compensatory factors which have permitted the more equal distribution of MDCs. They are to be found in "the dynamism of a growing and free society." A new generation of entrepreneurs working in new industries is one of the factors Kuznets cites.

## Macroeconomic Variables

There are several aspects of Kuznets's work that can be included in the contributions to Keynesian economics. Of primary importance is that Keynesian theory can be related to the development of national-income accounting. The relationship among the major macrovariables—income, consumption, saving, and investment—were established by Kuznets and others in the system of national-income accounts. In addition, some of the investigations conducted by Kuznets anticipated the work of Keynes. In his early work Kuznets studied and empirically tested the consumption function. It is the opinion of Erik Lundberg that Kuznets "treated the relation between consumption expenditures and income in a way that foreshadowed Keynes and with a 'lead time' of ten years" (1971, p. 452). Lundberg, Victor Zarnowitz, and others have pointed to Kuznets's estimates indicating the long-term stability of the ratio of capital formation to production in the United States and other estimates showing a stable long-term consumption function as an initial focus for the "permanent income" hypothesis of Milton Friedman and others, a restatement of the Keynesian current-income relationship. In an early work, *Durable Goods and Capital Formation in the United States, 1919–1933* (1934), Kuznets studied the cyclical variation in inventory investment and offered an empirical test of the accelerator principle, a dynamic relationship between investment expenditures and changes in income originally formulated by J. M. Clark in 1917, that was later incorporated into Keynesian analysis. The contributions of Kuznets should be included with those of other economists who worked both before and after Keynes to advance understanding in macroeconomics.

## Achievements

The outline of Kuznets's contributions to three major fields of inquiry can only suggest the full intellectual sweep of his work. A complete bibliography has been compiled by Bert Hoselitz. It is the collected work of prodigious scholarship, characterized by both breadth of scope and detailed measurement. The insights gained from a study of history and the history of technology and social institutions are assimilated as Kuznets asks and seeks answers for the larger questions in economic science. "Do estimates of national income measure the net contributions of economic activity to its primary goal—provision of goods to individuals—without errors of commission and omission?" (1946, p. 121). "Why under the free conditions in the United States was relatively little original work done in the natural sciences at the theoretical level, and so much in the applied disciplines and practical invention?" (1965, p. 90). "How should we compare growth in population and in the labor force with growth in capital formation?" (1961, p. 63). "What are the implications of the wide contrasts among the world regions in per capita income and the possibly increased disparity since the end of the nineteenth century?" (1965, p. 69).

On the occasion, on December 29, 1977, of the presentation of the Francis A. Walker Award, Kuznets received the following citation:

Simon Kuznets: founder of modern national income and product measurement: designer of new systems of seasonal and cyclical measurement: discoverer of Kuznets cycles: frontiersman in economic demography: pioneer in quantitative studies of the economic growth of nations: explorer of income distribution. To few scholars is it given to make a fundamental difference to the development of his science. Kuznets has done so more than once. Economics, which is in his debt beyond its ability to acknowledge, hails him after fifty years of stunning achievement and prays only that its debt may continue to grow.

HARRIET HINCK

## Selected Bibliography

Abramovitz, Moses. "The Nature and Significance of the Kuznets Cycle." *Economic Development and Cultural Change* 9 (April 1961): 349–67.
———. "The Passing of the Kuznets Cycle." *Economica* 35 (November 1968): 349–67.
Easterlin, Richard A. "Simon Kuznets." In *The International Encyclopedia of the Social Sciences*, vol. 18, pp. 393–97. Edited by David Sills. New York: Macmillan and Free Press, 1979.
Goodwin, Richard. Review of *Economic Change; Selected Essays in Business Cycles, National Income, and Economic Growth*, by Simon Kuznets. *Economic Journal* (1956): 507–09.

Hoselitz, Bert. "Bibliography of Simon Kuznets." *Economic Development and Cultural Change* 31 (January 1983): 433–54.

Kuznets, Simon. *Cyclical Fluctuations; Retail and Wholesale Trade, United States 1919–1925*. New York: Adelphi. 1926.

———. *Secular Movements in Production and Prices*. Boston, Ma.: Houghton Mifflin, 1930.

———. *Durable Goods and Capital Formation in the United States, 1919–1933*. New York: National Bureau of Economic Research, 1934.

———. *National Income and Capital Formation, 1919–1935*. New York: National Bureau of Economic Research, 1937.

———. *National Income and Its Composition, 1919–1938*. Assisted by Lillian Epstein and Elizabeth Jenks. New York: National Bureau of Economic Research, 1941.

———. *Economic Change*. New York: Norton, 1953.

———. "Economic Growth and Income Inequality." *American Economic Review* 45 (March 1955): 1–28.

———. *Capital in the American Economy: Its Formation and Financing*. Assisted by Elizabeth Jenks. New York: National Bureau of Economic Research, 1961.

———. *Economic Growth and Structure; Selected Essays*. New York: W. W. Norton, 1965.

———. *Economic Growth of Nations*. Cambridge, Ma.: Harvard University Press, 1971.

———. *Population, Capital, and Growth; Selected Essays*. New York: W. W. Norton, 1973.

———. "Two Centuries of Economic Growth: Reflections on the U.S. Experience." *American Economic Review* 67 (February 1977): 1–26.

———. *Growth, Population, and Income Distribution: Selected Essays*. New York. W. W. Norton, 1979.

Kuznets, Simon, and Goldsmith, Raymond. *Income and Wealth of the U.S., Trends and Structure*. Cambridge, Ma.: Bowes and Bowes, 1952.

Kuznets, Simon, and Rubin, Ernest. *Immigration and the Foreign Born*. (Occasional paper 46.) New York: National Bureau of Economic Research, 1954.

Lundberg, Erik. "Simon Kuznets' Contribution to Economics." *Swedish Journal of Economics* 73 (December 1971): 444–61.

Perlman, Mark. "Population and Economic Change in Developing Countries: A Review Article." *Journal of Economic Literature* 19 (March, 1981): 74–82.

# WASSILY W. LEONTIEF *1973*

Wassily W. Leontief was awarded the Nobel Memorial Prize in Economic Sciences in 1973 for his development of input-output analysis. He was born on August 5, 1906, in St. Petersburg, the seat of power of czarist Russia, and was for over forty years on the economics faculty at Harvard University. Since his retirement from Harvard in 1975, Leontief has been at New York University, where he is currently University Professor of Economics. He and his wife, Estelle, are the parents of a daughter, Svetlana Alpers, a fine-arts professor at the University of California at Berkeley.

In announcing his Nobel award, the Royal Swedish Academy of Sciences called Leontief the "sole and unchallenged creator of the input-output technique"; in fact, his seminal contribution in this field virtually overshadows his other work in economics.

## Input-Output Analysis

Input-output analysis divides the total economy into sectors or industries in a way that permits the effect of a change in one sector to be traced throughout the entire economy. In its simplest form, input-output analysis entails the construction of three tables. In each table, every sector of the economy is represented in one column and one row of the table. For example, if the seventh row is labelled at the left as coal mining, the heading of the seventh column would also be labelled coal mining. The entries in each table for all sectors taken together form what is called a square matrix, a two-dimensional array of entries with an equal number of rows and columns.

The first table constructed for input-ouput analysis is the Interindustry Transactions Table (ITT). This table shows the intersectoral dollar flows that take place in an economy. Reading across a given row, the table entries indicate the manner in which the output of the sector at the left of the row is distributed to the various sectors, including its own, listed at the top of the table. The table entries are expressed in dollars, and so the dollar volume of sales from a given sector to the various sectors can be ascertained by reading a table row. The ITT can also be read down a given column, showing the dollar volume of purchases the sector at the top of the column has made from each sector indicated at the left of the table. This connection is obvious. In tracing intersectoral flows, the amount of output that Sector A sells to Sector B can also be viewed as the amount of input that Sector B purchased from Sector A.

A second table, called the Direct Requirements Table (DRT), can be generated using the entries of the ITT. Each of the entries down a given sectoral column of the ITT is divided by that sector's total gross outlays. A sector's total gross outlays are the sum of all its intra-sectoral and intersectoral purchases (the sum of the entries in its column of the ITT), plus the dollar amount of all other factors of production purchased by the sector (one important component being the wages paid for labor employed). This division generates the entries of the DRT. Read down a given sectoral column, these column entries give the dollar amount of input purchases that the sector at the top of the column must make from the sector shown at the left of the table in order for it to produce one dollar's worth of its own output. These input-output ratios are called technical coefficients.

The third table in the Leontief input-output model is called the Total Requirements Table (TRT). It is generated using the entries of the DRT, the technical coefficients governing production. These coefficients are used to specify a system of simultaneous equations, the solution to which provides the entries of the TRT. Since Leontief formulated this set of equations and provided its solution, the table of entries based on the solution, the TRT, has come to be known as the Leontief inversion. This table shows the effect of a one-dollar increase in final demand in a given sector on the sales of all sectors. Final demand is the demand for final goods and services, those goods and services which make up the various spending categories (consumer spending, capital spending, government spending, and net exports) comprising gross national product, or GNP.

The first two tables of the Leontief system, the ITT and the DRT,

capture the intersectoral linkages governing the sale of intermediate goods and services within and between sectors. The third table, the TRT, relates the various industrial sectors to the production and sale of goods and services intended to satisfy final demand. The ITT and DRT show how the output of one sector is distributed as input to its own sector and all other sectors. The TRT shows the intersectoral linkages for production intended to meet final demand, rather than the intermediate demand of industry for inputs. Each entry in a given row of the TRT shows the effect of a one-dollar increase in the final demand for the output of the sector at the top of the column on the sales of the sector shown at the left of the row. Reading down the column for a given sector shows the increased purchases it must make from each sector listed at the left in order to accommodate a one-dollar increase in final demand for its output.

It is important to realize that these table entries capture the increase in both the direct and indirect requirements for each sector. For example, if the final demand for steel were to increase, the demand for coal would rise as well, since coal is an input in the steelmaking process. Given that some of this coal is taken from open-pit mines, the demand for spare parts for heavy mining equipment will go up. To the extent such parts are made of steel, this will add to the initial increase in the demand for steel, cause the demand for coal to go up yet again, and so on, and so on, in a seemingly endless circle. The entries of the

TRT sum up all of these circular flows. The input-output system described above is known as the Open Leontief Model. It has been in use for many years and replaced a much earlier and less sophisticated closed version of the model, which did not distinguish between interindustry sales and sales of final output.

The important assumptions that underlie the Open Model should be mentioned. All sectors are treated as if they produce just one good; a given good is assumed to be produced by only one sector. Each sector is assumed to have unused capacity, eliminating the possibility of production bottlenecks arising as output expands. In reality, each sector of the economy is made up of many individual firms, differing widely in size and efficiency. But input-output analysis aggregates all firms into one sector, and the production methods represented in its tables are for the average firm.

Input-output relationships are taken to be fixed, that is, the state of technology is given, making the model a static one. With constant technical coefficients, a doubling of output would require a doubling of inputs, meaning the production process exhibits constant returns to scale. This assumption may be perfectly suitable for small changes in output, but less satisfactory for larger ones. Since the model does not permit input substitution, the composition of inputs cannot respond to changes in relative input prices. In other words, relative input prices are taken as fixed. Should there be technological advances in production or a substantial change

in relative input prices, the input-output tables would have to be revised. The data gathering task involved in the construction of the tables is enormous. Given the limited resources committed to the task, the Commerce Department makes revisions to the U.S. tables very infrequently, about every seven years.

Despite its methodological difficulties, input-output analysis has proven to be extremely useful and is widely applied. Input-output models have been developed for countries, regions, states, cities, and more recently, for the global economy. Analyses of the economic effects of disarmament and the impact of environmental pollution have been successful. Attempts to apply it to underdeveloped countries also have been made, but scanty data bases have made such applications difficult. Applications to questions of international trade have sometimes been problematic, since they violate the one-commodity, one-source assumption. In the original open model, input-output analysis focused on the effect of changes in the demand for final output on sectoral output. This basic model has been recast to show the effects on income and employment. Dynamic models, which allow for technological advance and changes in relative input prices, have also been developed.

Input-output analysis can be useful in both macroeconomics and microeconomics. Many econometric models contain elements of the input-output approach. The Leontief model is politically agnostic and can be used for planning purposes by policy makers in both socialist command economies and market-based mixed economies. The Soviet Union, with its very centrally controlled economy, makes use of input-output analysis, as does France with its noncoercive indicative planning. Target levels of final output are established, and the sectoral production needed to reach those levels is determined by input-output analysis. Output targets are set by more democratic means and production goals followed less rigidly in France than in the Soviet Union, but policy makers in both countries find input-output analysis helpful.

At the microeconomic level, firms are able to assess the impact of changes in final demand on their sector, and ultimately on their own enterprise. Forecasts of changes in final demand in the various sectors can be obtained by standard econometric techniques. These forecasts, together with the row from the TRT for a firm's sector, will show the change in output required of the firm's sector. A firm need only estimate its market share to determine the effect on its own output.

## Early Career

Leontief was himself the son of a university professor; his father taught the social sciences, including economics. His mother was an art historian. An only child, at the tender age of fifteen, he entered the major university of his native city, renamed the University of Leningrad after the Bolshevik Revolution. He studied there from 1921 to 1925, receiving the M.A. in Social Science with the title of "Learned Economist" at the age of eighteen. Throughout his early education, Leontief was given thorough training in mathematics; given the nature of his later work, this preparation was to serve him well. Some of his ideas on input-output analysis can be traced back to work he did while at the University of Leningrad. In an article written in 1925, he refers to some of the economic interrelationships which later formed the basis of his input-output model. Many years thereafter, when nations of all political persuasion found his work to be useful, the Soviet Union cited Leontief's early work to support their contention that, among other things, input-output analysis was yet another accomplishment of the Soviet socialist state.

Leontief was only eleven years of age at the time of the Bolshevik Revolution in 1917. It took the new regime several years to consolidate its power, and he by this time had become what can be described as a socialist with independent views. This independence of mind led him to argue too passionately with a tutor and earned him a brief stay in prison. In 1925, in the aftermath of a serious illness and as a result of the serious differences his family had with the Communist government, he fled his homeland with his parents.

Leontief made his way to Berlin to continue his study of economics at the University of Berlin from 1925–28, receiving the Ph.D. in economics in 1928 at the age of only twenty-two. He encountered two major German academicians while at Berlin: Werner Sombart, the noted economic historian and pamphleteer, and Ladislaus von Bortkiewicz, a pioneer in the application of mathematics and statistics in economics. Leontief was a seminar assistant to Professor Sombart, who was unable to supervise Leontief's Ph.D. thesis on general-equilibrium theory due to its strong mathematical content. That task fell to the capable von Bortkiewicz, the eminent mathematical statistician credited with the development of the "law of small numbers," and an early solution to the Marxian transformation problem, itself a kind of input-output analysis.

Leontief's interest in economic research grew during his time at Berlin, and a steady stream of new opportunities came his way. From 1927–28 he was a research associate at the renowned Institute of World Economics at the University of Kiel in Germany. In *Twelve Contemporary Economists* (1981), Martin Cave reports that Leontief traces the origins of his input-output analysis back to the supply and demand studies he worked on while at Kiel.

One of Leontief's greatest adventures resulted from a fortuitous encounter with a group of visiting Chinese at a sidewalk cafe in Kiel. Some friendly conversation eventually led to an offer of employment with the minister of railways in China to advise on the construction of a railroad system. Leontief accepted and in 1928 began work as consultant to the Chinese government at Nanking. Much of his time was spent traveling and gathering the economic data needed to assess the transportation needs of China.

This collection activity was to become routine later, when he began to construct input-output tables. Leontief left China in 1929 and returned to Europe for additional study.

In 1931 Leontief came to the United States at the invitation of the National Bureau of Economic Research, (NBER) to join them as a research associate. His tenure with the NBER was short and unhappy but did afford him the opportunity to complete the preliminary work on his first input-output tables. In late 1931, Harvard University offered Leontief an appointment as an instructor in economics. In a less than auspicious start, he submitted a research proposal on input-output analysis that did not impress the Harvard Committee on Research. The committee provided the financial support requested but made it clear his proposal was regarded as a hopeless muddle and that he would no doubt be very shortly reporting his research failure. Despite the unenthusiastic reception accorded his ideas, he nevertheless assumed his post at Harvard in 1932.

Contrary to the expectations of his new colleagues, Leontief made immediate progress. Building on work started during his brief stay at the NBER, he gathered information from the U.S. Census Bureau and used it to generate the first input-output tables for the U.S. economy. In 1933, Leontief was promoted to the rank of assistant professor. By the mid-1930s his input-output tables were becoming progressively more sophisticated. He published his first article on input-output analysis, "Quantitative Input and Output Relations in the Economic System of the United States," in the *Review of Economics and Statistics* (1936). More papers followed in 1937 and 1938, but his work went largely unnoticed in the wider community of academic economists.

One has to appreciate the enormous computational difficulties faced by Leontief in these early years, long before the advent of the high-speed digital computer. In "Wassily Leontief's Contribution to Economics," *Swedish Journal of Economics* (1973), Robert Dorfman notes that Leontief's first input-output solutions, obtained by an automatic computing machine, the primitive Harvard Mark II, required fifty-six hours for a forty-two-sector economy. Prior to the use of the Mark II, the calculations were performed on punchcard machines and were even more time-consuming.

In 1935, Leontief had as a graduate student at Harvard Paul A. Samuelson, who became the first American Nobel winner in economics in 1970. Robert M. Solow, one of Leontief's Harvard graduate students in the 1940s, won the 1987 prize in economics.

## Research and Honors

Leontief was promoted to associate professor in 1939 and attaining the rank of full professor in 1946. In the early 1940s he published his first important book, *The Structure of American Economy, 1919–1929: An Empirical Application of Equilibrium Analysis* (1941), an elaboration

on the rudiments of input-output analysis and the basis for his later and more sophisticated formulations. With the onset of World War II, Leontief's research slowed as he devoted more of his time to consulting activities for the federal government. From 1941 to 1947 he was a part-time consultant to the Department of Labor, and from 1943 to 1945 he was the chief of the Russian economic subdivision for the Office of Strategic Services, later to become the Central Intelligence Agency.

Leontief developed many important associations during these years. He worked with George Dantzig, whose simplex algorithm provided the first solution to the linear-programming problem. Dantzig, who spent much of his career at the RAND Corporation, later acknowledged Leontief's influence on his own thinking. At the Labor Department's Bureau of Labor Statistics, Leontief worked with W. Duane Evans and Marvin Hoffenberg in the application of input-output analysis to the problems of postwar reconversion. Together they constructed input-output tables for the American economy for 1939 and, by using them to project employment patterns through to 1950, were able to assess postwar manpower needs. The results of their study were reported in the February and March 1947 issues of the *Monthly Labor Review*.

At war's end Leontief was able to devote his full attention to the further development of input-output economics. In 1948 he organized and founded the Harvard Economic

Research Project and served as its director until it was disbanded in 1972. The project was exclusively devoted to input-output analysis and generated many new developments in the field. In 1950 the first international conference on input-output economics was held in the Netherlands and attracted only fifteen participants. This would change dramatically with the passage of time; by 1974 the sixth international conference, held in Vienna, had 320 participants, with interest no doubt stimulated by Leontief's receipt of the Nobel Prize the previous year.

The late 1940s and early 1950s were important and productive years for Leontief's research group at Harvard. A collaborative volume of the project's early work, *Studies in the Structure of the American Economy: Theoretical and Empirical Explorations in Input-Output Analysis* (1953), was coedited by Leontief, Hollis B. Chenery, and other project associates. By the mid-1950s, a substantial literature on input-output analysis had developed.

The importance of Leontief's work received growing recognition not only within the economics profession but from the wider academic community. Clearly established as a major economic thinker, Leontief was given the Henry Lee Chair of Economics at Harvard University in 1953, a position he would hold until his retirement from Harvard in 1975. He was honored again in 1953 with the Order of the Cherubim from the University of Pisa, an award that reflected the continued

development of his worldwide reputation. In 1956 his faculty colleagues at Harvard elected him to the Society of Fellows, an elite group of scholars drawn from across the many disciplines of the university. He remained in the society as a senior fellow from 1956 to 1975, serving as its chair from 1965 to 1975.

Although the federal government showed considerable interest in Leontief's input-output analysis from the mid to the late 1940s, his government work came to a halt in 1952, when the funding for Project Scoop, an input-output study of procurement bottlenecks under wartime conditions partly underwritten by the U.S. Air Force, was canceled. For the laissez-faire Eisenhower administration, input-output analysis was seen as too closely associated with economic planning. Despite the withdrawal of government support, progress on input-output economics continued under Leontief's direction at the Harvard Economic Research Project. Renewed interest on the part of government would require a change in administrations.

Leontief's role as government consultant resumed in the early 1960s. From 1961 to 1965 he advised the Department of Labor on manpower problems. Starting in 1966 he began to consult on a part-time basis for the Commerce Department on the construction of input-output tables for the U.S. economy, a relationship that was to continue until 1982. He was also a consultant to the United Nations during 1961–62, advising on issues ranging from the economic impact of world disarmament to the economic development of the newly independent nations. Around this time he was awarded the first of his two Guggenheim fellowships. In 1962 the University of Brussels awarded him his first honorary doctoral degree; by 1981, he had received ten more. In the academic year 1964–65, Leontief was a resident at the Center for Advanced Study in the Behavioral Sciences in Stanford, California.

The interest of government policy makers in input-output analysis has waxed and waned as control of the White House has changed from one political party to the other. By the late 1960s, no such ambivalence was shown by the business community. In 1967 the American Chemical Society sponsored the first conference on the commercial applications of input-output analysis. Conference topics ranged from the use of input-output analysis for internal controls to its application in the evaluation of new market opportunities. Corporate participants included Celanese, U.S. Steel, American Oil, and North American Aviation. The latter was to combine with Rockwell Manufacturing to form the North American-Rockwell Corporation, with the rationale for the move being the benefits to be achieved through diversification, based on a merger analysis which employed the input-output technique.

The hostility to his ideas shown by government in the 1950s came as no surprise to Leontief. The political tide had turned conservative, and the ideological imperative for government officials was to defend the sanctity of the free-enterprise system from the evil posed by national economic planning and the input-output tables that would make such planning possible. At the same time, Leontief saw no irony in the eventual adoption of his input-output approach by the corporate world; their enthusiasm simply confirmed the usefulness of his ideas. The public pose struck by officialdom in defense of the virtues of laissez-faire capitalism could be admired by corporate America but would not be allowed to prevent the use of any analytical technique that might benefit the firm.

By the late 1960s, Leontief was an economic thinker of international stature. At home and abroad, in government circles, in the business community, in the world of academe, his ideas were discussed and debated. With his reputation firmly established, he was increasingly honored for his contributions. In 1970 he was awarded the prestigious Bernhard-Harms Prize of the Institute of World Economics at the University of Kiel, a fitting tribute given that Leontief had begun his research career at the institute many years before.

Elected to serve as president of the American Economic Association for 1970, he used his term in office as an opportunity to challenge his colleagues in the form of his presidential address delivered on December 29, 1970, in Detroit at the association's annual meeting. His address, published as "Theoretical Assumptions and Nonobserved Facts," in the *American Economic Review* (1971), leveled a profound attack on the direction that mainstream, orthodox economics had taken. To him the profession had become enamored with building abstract theoretical models in which the use of sophisticated mathematics seemed almost an end in itself. His attack was not limited to the conduct of economic theorizing but included econometrics and the statistical methodology upon which it rested. Leontief had come to believe that economics had abandoned its empirical basis. He urged academic economists to pay greater attention to the validity of the assumptions implicit in their models and to expend more effort in the collection of economic data. Continued preoccupation with pure theory and statistical procedure, disconnected from a data base founded on observable reality, would make economics irrelevant to solving the problems of the day. Leontief's challenge still stands, and its themes are ones to which he has returned frequently over the years.

Consistent with his later claim to have moved leftward as he grew older, Leontief had become increasingly associated with liberal causes and ideas. In the aftermath of the student uprising at Harvard in 1969, he split with his senior faculty colleagues and joined a minority faction of younger economists. This dissident group advocated more hiring of radical economists and an expansion of the curriculum beyond the conventional focus of orthodox neoclassical economics.

Leontief has claimed not to be a proponent of socialism, much less Marxism. He has often expressed his admiration for the market system

that has brought such prosperity to America. But his feeling is that different cultures may be best served by different economic systems, meaning that the American system is not necessarily the model for all nations to emulate. Mindful of the imperfections inherent in a market-based economy, Leontief has been a longtime supporter of government intervention as a means by which to promote both social equity and economic welfare. So it was with spirit and conviction that he joined the presidential campaign of Democratic party candidate George McGovern in 1972, serving as economic adviser and playing a major role in the formulation of McGovern's income-redistribution proposals.

By the early 1970s, Leontief was at the height of his career. His advice was sought by politicians and governments around the world. Fellow economists held him in high esteem, and his input-output analysis was finding wider use in the business community. By 1973 only one honor still eluded him, the Nobel Prize in Economics, first awarded in 1969. Leontief was from the start high on the unofficial list of potential recipients. The foregone conclusion on the part of many that he would be an early laureate led to an amusing, though perhaps apocryphal, account of Leontief's reaction to the announcement of the 1971 award. A self-assured man known to be confident of the importance of his work, Leontief was in New York City on the day this award was announced. While in an elevator, he heard that a Russian-born economist from Harvard had been named and, sure that the prize was his, hurried to buy a newspaper to read the great news. Only then did he find out that his Harvard colleague and fellow Russian emigré, Simon Kuznets, had received the award.

Leontief's supreme moment came on October 18, 1973, when the Royal Swedish Academy of Sciences announced that he had been chosen to receive the Nobel Memorial Prize in Economic Sciences for, according to the citation, "the development of the input-output method and for its application to important economic problems." His candidacy was surely enhanced by the fact that his work combined theory and application. Not only did he develop the theoretical aspects of economy-wide inter-industrial analysis, but he also pioneered in the empirical work that made it operational. Contemporary economics increasingly abounds in novel and sophisticated quantitative techniques. As Leontief has complained, these techniques are all too often rich in technical complexity, but trivial in content. What set Leontief's achievement apart was its rich content and the new insights it provided.

The obligatory press conference was held the next day at his Harvard office. Leontief, bowing and gesticulating, voice high-pitched and heavily accented, held forth on a number of topics. In his engaging way, this small man with his craggy features, Old World demeanor, and didactic style, explained the intricacies and applications of input-output analysis; assessed the shortcomings of the economic policies of the Nixon administration; and offered an opinion on the prospects for development in the People's Republic of China.

In December 1973, Leontief traveled to Stockholm to receive his prize and deliver the customary Nobel lecture, his address, published as "Structure of the World Economy: Outline of a Simple Input-Output Formulation," in the *American Economic Review* (1974), was a sketch of the preliminary work he had done on his most ambitious input-output model ever, one describing the entire global economy. This study, done under the auspices of the United Nations, was designed to project the structure of the world economy to the year 2000 under several possible economic scenarios.

Leontief's last years at Harvard were not happy ones. In 1972, the Harvard Economic Research Project, which he had directed for twenty-five years, was discontinued. In early 1975, Leontief announced that he would retire from the Harvard faculty and accept a teaching position at New York University. He became Professor of Economics at New York University in the fall of 1975. In 1978, the university established the Institute for Economic Analysis, in effect created for Leontief to enable him to continue his input-output research. He became its first director. In 1983, Leontief was named a university professor at New York University. Two years later, he relinquished his post as director of the institute and was appointed senior scholar there.

A lack of funds nearly forced Leontief to close the institute before, in December 1980, a major research grant from the Control Data Corporation restored its financial health. Control Data's Service Bureau Company was planning to market a new business information service and contracted with Leontief's institute for the commercial rights to its input-output research. Leontief was free to decide what research to support with the funds and retained the right to publish his research findings. Control Data's vast computer network was also put at his disposal.

Since leaving Harvard, Leontief has continued to work as a consultant to many governmental and international bodies. Between 1975 and 1980, he advised the Environmental Protection Agency on matters relating to air and water pollution as a member of the executive board of its Science Advisory Council. He has continued his long-standing relationship with the United Nations, advising on a range of issues, including the economic gap between the developed and developing nations. Since 1980, Leontief has also advised the U.S. Office of Technology Assessment on the effects of new technology on the work force. Since 1984 he has been under contract to the Italian government, directing the preparation of a comprehensive transportation plan for Italy. In late 1987 he became a consultant to the Spanish government on the economic and environmental impact of the proposed bridge and tunnel across the Strait of Gibraltar.

## Other Contributions

Leontief's accomplishments in the input-output field tend to overshadow his other contributions in economics. As an early critic of Keynesian methodology, he complained in "Implicit Theorizing: A Methodological Criticism of the Neo-Cambridge School," *Quarterly Journal of Economics* (1937), that Keynesian analysis relies on definitions which preordain Keynesian conclusions. Addressing the question of the aggregation of variables in economic analysis, for example, whether is it possible to aggregate capital in its many forms into one variable for analytical purposes, he specified in "Introduction to a Theory of the Internal Structure of Functional Relationships," *Econometrica* (1947) the conditions under which it is appropriate to aggregate variables—the so-called Leontief condition. This is not the only term to bear his name. References to the Leontief system or model abound in the literature, a result of the widespread use of systems of linear equations in economic models.

Another term bearing his name grew out of an application of input-output analysis to the theory of international trade: Leontief's paradox. Whereas conventional trade theory indicates that the United States should export goods produced by capital-intensive means and import goods produced by labor-intensive means, Leontief showed the reverse to be true. In a series of papers, most notably "Domestic Production and Foreign Trade: The American Capital Position Re-Examined," *Proceedings of the American Philosophical Society* (1953) and "Factor Proportions and the Structure of American Trade:

Further Theoretical and Empirical Analysis," *Review of Economics and Statistics* (1956), he examined this question. His explanation for the paradox was that American labor was so productive that it was, in effect, capital starved, making labor the relatively abundant factor and labor-intensive goods exportable. Alternative explanations as well as debate about the very nature of the paradox continue to generate controversy in the literature, decades after Leontief first raised the issue.

The four articles just cited and Leontief's other major works are contained in three volumes. *Essays in Economics: Theories and Theorizing* (1966) and *Essays in Economics: Theories, Facts, and Policies* (1977) include works of both early and more-recent vintage, covering a wide range of topics. *Input-Output Economics* (1986) is a collection of articles devoted exclusively to his work in the input-output field.

Leontief has coauthored two major books in which his input-output model of the world economy, first mentioned in his Nobel lecture, has been used to examine an important economic issue: *The Future of the World Economy* (1977), and, *Military Spending: Facts and Figures, Worldwide Implications and Future Outlook* (1983). Leontief and coauthor Faye Duchin utilized a dynamic input-output model of the U.S. economy in *The Future Impact of Automation on Workers* (1986) to assess the effect of ongoing computer-based technological change on the American labor force.

Throughout his career, Leontief has attempted to make both his technical ideas and his public-policy views accessible to as wide an audience as possible. He has testified before the U.S. Congress on military spending, energy policy, and labor affairs, and he has granted lengthy interviews to numerous periodicals. Most important are the articles and essays Leontief has written for publications such as *The Atlantic, Challenge, Foreign Affairs, Harvard Business Review, The New York Review of Books, The New York Times, Science,* and *Scientific American.*

One long-standing passion about which Leontief has written frequently is national economic planning, an issue which brings together the many themes he has sounded over his career. In one of his more elegant and oft-repeated metaphors, he has likened the profit motive of a market economy to the sail of a ship and the policy powers of government to the ship's rudder. The sail (or profit motive) is the power source that drives the economy forward. The government uses its rudder (tax policy, spending, subsidies, and regulation) to keep the economy on course. Leontief claims that the American economy relies primarily, and during the Reagan years, almost exclusively, on the sail. The economies of the East-bloc socialist countries tend to rely on the heavy-handed rudder of centralized government planning. The United States could steer its economy better with greater use of the rudder; the socialist economies would benefit from a greater reliance on the propelling force of the sail. In discussions concerning the reforms of the Soviet economy during the Gorbachev era, Leontief has stated that the critics of the Soviet system have gone too far in blaming poor economic performance entirely on the elimination of the market mechanism. He hopes that Soviet reformers draw a lesson from America's excessive reliance on the marketplace and seek a better balance between the sail and the rudder.

Leontief's input-output analysis has had a substantial impact on economics. The theorist has seen life breathed into Walrasian general equilibrium. The empiricist has a framework through which to identify and measure important economic relationships. The policy maker has a valuable tool with which to assess the effect of alternative policies. Leontief's contribution is seen by some as nothing less than the single-handed creation of an entirely new and lasting discipline within economics. Only the passage of time will determine whether he deserves to join the likes of Adam Smith and John Maynard Keynes in the pantheon of great economic thinkers. What can be said is that Leontief has put economic analysis to use in the service of his fellow man and has been steadfast in communicating his ideas to those outside his profession. In so doing, he has set a worthy standard for his fellow economists.

JAMES N. MARSHALL

# Selected Bibliography

## WORKS BY LEONTIEF

"Quantitative Input and Output Relations in the Economic System of the United States." *Review of Economics and Statistics* (1936): 105–25

*Essays in Economics: Theories and Theorizing.* New York: Oxford University Press, 1966. Reprint as *Essays in Economics, Volume I: Theories and Theorizing.* White Plains, N.Y.: M. E. Sharpe, 1977.

*Essays in Economics, Volume II: Theories, Facts, and Policies.* White Plains, N.Y.: M. E. Sharpe, 1977.

*The Structure of American Economy, 1919–1929: An Empirical Application of Equilibrium Analysis.* Cambridge, Ma.: Harvard University Press, 1941. Enlarged and updated version published as *The Structure of American Economy, 1919–1939: An Empirical Application of Equilibrium Analysis,* 2d ed. New York: Oxford University Press, 1951. Reprint White Plains, N.Y.: M. E. Sharpe, 1977.

*Input-Output Economics.* 2d ed. New York: Oxford University Press, 1986.

Leontief, Wassily W., Carter, Anne P., and Petri, Peter. *The Future of the World Economy.* New York: Oxford University Press, 1977.

Leontief, Wassily W., Chenery, Hollis B., et al. *Studies in the Structure of the American Economy: Theoretical and Empirical Explorations in Input-Output Analysis.* New York: Oxford University Press,

1953. Reprint White Plains, N.Y.: M. E. Sharpe, 1977.

Leontief, Wassily W., and Duchin, Faye. *Military Spending: Facts and Figures, Worldwide Implications and Future Outlook.* New York: Oxford University Press, 1983.

Leontief, Wassily W., and Duchin, Faye. *The Future Impact of Automation on Workers.* New York: Oxford University Press, 1986.

OTHER WORKS

Cave, Martin. "Wassily Leontief: Input-Output and Economic Planning." In *Twelve Contemporary Economists*, edited by J. R. Shackleton and Gareth Locksley, pp. 160–82. New York: Wiley, 1981.

Dorfman, Robert. "Wassily Leontief's Contribution to Economics." *Swedish Journal of Economics* 75 (1973): 430–49.

# WILLIAM ARTHUR LEWIS  *1979*

From his modest background as the son of an immigrant teacher from the island of St. Lucia, West Indies, William Arthur Lewis has passed through a wide array of experiences. As a brilliant eighteen-year-old, he chose to study economics in 1932, even though neither he nor anyone known to him on his native island was knowledgeable in the subject. He suffered the generalized discourtesy and other inequities faced by black professionals in the immediate post-World War II era, which made his transition to preeminence a bit more difficult. A constant was his dedication to the problem of economic development and the achievement of a sustained increase in the per-capita incomes of people in underdeveloped economies as rapidly as feasible.

Much has been written of the intellectual and policy relevance of current mechanisms by which output in developing economies can be increased. What is frequently cited in these considerations includes the pathbreaking "Economic Development with Unlimited Supplies of Labor" (1954), a work which commanded close scrutiny in the postwar literature on economic development and later received a special citation when he was awarded the Nobel Prize in Economic Sciences (jointly with Theodore W. Schultz) in 1979.

William Arthur Lewis earned a bachelor's degree in economics at the London School of Economics (LSE) in 1937 and was awarded a scholarship to pursue his Ph.D. to completion in 1940. Since then, a self-conscious Lewis has worked hard to expound good sense about industrial organization theory, economic history, and the political economy of development. After teaching from 1938 to 1948 at the

London School of Economics (LSE), he moved on to Manchester to occupy the Stanley Jevons Chair of Political Economy in 1948, where his interest in anti-imperialism matured into formal, systematic discussions on economic development.

Lewis devoted the equivalent of ten years between 1951 and 1973 to the practical aspects of development through working as an administrator and consultant to governments: at the United Nations in New York as a member of the Group of Experts on Underdeveloped Countries (1951) and the Deputy Managing Director of the United Nations Special Fund (1959–60); as the advisor to the prime minister of Ghana (1957–59); as the vice chancellor of the University of the West Indies (UWI) from 1959 to 1963; and as the first president of the Caribbean Development Bank (1970–73).

A knighthood was conferred upon him for his pioneering work in economic development at the end of his tenure at the helm of UWI in 1963. Later that year, he accepted a position at Princeton University and in 1968 became the James Madison Professor of Political Economy at the Woodrow Wilson School of Public and International Affairs.

A prolific writer, Lewis has published twelve books, ten official papers, and more than seventy other pieces. Despite his work as a philosopher of capitalist development in the Third World and occasional contributions to the debate on the international economic order, he continues to espouse the use of more exact approaches to domestic policy planning. Fortunately, the constant flow of books, critical reviews, and essays in his honor provides a guide to his works. Lewis himself has frequently returned to earlier themes with revisions and rebuttals.

Arthur Lewis has, since 1986, retired to live on the beautiful island of Barbados and to reflect on the paradigms of economic development. His extensive travels in the Third World and devotion to scholarly pursuits after 1950 were made possible by the support provided by his 1947 marriage to Gladys Jacobs, a native of Grenada who concentrated on making a home for their two daughters.

Even in retirement, Lewis has been anything but reticent in presenting his vision of poverty eradication, increasing employment, and accelerated growth and development. From his retreat near the Cove Hill campus of the University of the West Indies, Lewis continues to advise scholars and to function as a consultant to governments.

# The Beginning Years

Although Arthur Lewis is noted today for his monumental works in economic development, he started his career as an expert on British industrial ogranization with an interest in world economic history. His first book, *Economic Problems of Today* (1940), contained the initial ingredients of his later treatise on the theory of economic growth. His second book, *Economic Survey, 1919–1939* (1949), published at the end of his LSE years, was an attempt, in the wake of the Keynesian revolution, to provide his interpretation of world economic history during the interwar years.

In the company of John Hicks, Roy Allen, Nicholas Kaldor, and Friedrich von Hayek, all fellows at the LSE in the early 1930s, Lewis found his niche in the forefront of the development, empirical testing, and refinements leading to the global expansion of the neoclassical theory of capital and growth. His expertise in industrial structure served his academic career well from 1937 to 1948. Lewis closed his LSE tenure with the publication of an updated version of his Ph.D. thesis under the title of *Overhead Costs* (1949), a series of essays dealing with theoretical refinements in the application of price theory to issues in industrial organization.

In one of his essays in *Overhead Costs*, Lewis provided early discussion on how to spread fixed costs among users. His model of competition in retail trade was the first to combine economies of scale and customer convenience in determining the optimal number of retail outlets. In another essay, Lewis deals with time, demand for the services of regulated public utilities, and overhead costs. By linking the railway principle of "charging what the traffic will bear" and the results of Joan Robinson's work on price-discrimination theory, Lewis prescribed the now-famous two-part tariff and time-of-day pricing approaches used by regulated public utilities. This background in industrial structure can be regarded as the preparation for his work on economic development.

Lewis has never claimed to be a laissez-faire economist. In a personal account of his life, he recalls being introduced at age seven to the views of Marcus Garvey on Western imperialism. His anti-imperialist sentiments drove him into fellowship with members of the Fabian Society—the scholarly wing of the British Labor Party—who were critical of British colonial policies at the time. His first two published monographs, *Labour in the West Indies*, (1939), and *Monopoly in British Industry*, (1945), as well as his fourth book, *Principles of Economic Planning* (1949) were written for the Fabian Society to explain the problems and pitfalls of administering a mixed economy.

# The Quest for Excellence

Lewis is quick to concede that he became an applied economist by default; he really wanted to be an engineer but neither the British government nor private employers in St. Lucia would hire a black engineer in the 1930's. He also became a teacher because there was nothing else to do with this training. He began to teach industrial organization because Professor Arnold Plant, his mentor at LSE, put him to it. But we can accept his dedication to the problems of economic development as the best act of fate.

By 1952, Lewis had established himself as an excellent economic scientist. However, his prescriptions for guiding the welfare of humanity were as unorthodox as those of John Maynard Keynes and courageously pragmatic for their era.

Keynes started a revolution by calling attention to the limitations of the automatic self-adjusting mechanisms of the free-market system and providing the logical mechanism for informed government modeling. In Lewis's own analysis of the interwar years, he inadvertently supported Keynes by his economic argument that, despite its virtues, the limitations of the price mechanism often necessitate positive, intelligent government action. Consequently, his policy prescriptions suggested that the great problem for his generation was to learn to make government action positive and intelligent.

The call started by Keynes, to reexamine the basic tenets of laissez-faire economics encouraged other renegade neoclassical economists to develop more pragmatic theories of growth and development to meet the policy needs of nations. This wave of positivism has dominated the systems of thought, structure, and logical procedures of postwar economic deductions. It was within this environment that Lewis came of age by his pragmatic extension of theory to explain differing social concerns.

According to Lewis's own account, the publication of *Economic Survey* still left two unanswered questions which later became the central focus of his research. Recognizing the interdependence of world economies and the vulnerability of developing economies similar to that of his home country, he began to ponder: (a) what are the causes of growth and fluctuations of national economies? and (b) what determines the terms of trade between industrial and primary products? In his meticulously positivist fashion, Lewis had first defined the goals and scope of his subsequent treatise on the political economy of development in his monograph *Labour in the West Indies* (1939). His two most celebrated works, "Economic Development with Unlimited Supplies of Labor" (1954), and *The Theory of Economic Growth* (1955) launched him to preeminence. The period from 1948 to 1958 was his most productive by far, but Lewis continued to expand his models on economic growth and development through a long list of articles, official papers and seminars.

# Unlimited Supply

Arthur Lewis's ingenious blend of cognitive analysis and interactive policy prescriptions led to what has come to be known as the "Lewis model" in the development literature. Despite thirty years of critical attack by classical as well as neo-Marxist scholars and practitioners of economic development, it has retained its resilience. (The model is more readily referenced as the "dual economy" model by students and regarded as a founding contribution by those working within it.)

Lewis was not content to be an expert on British industrial organization. He had a deep desire to contribute to the eradication of unemployment and poverty in St. Lucia and other developing economies. The opportunity to undertake extensive research in the economic problems of British colonies arrived with his appointment as secretary of the Economic Advisory Committee to the Colonial Office in 1943.

Lewis used this background and his expertise in capitalist industrial economies to arrive at his original proposition on the development process, which he forcefully argued in the 1954 article and elaborated in "Unlimited Labour: Further Notes" (1958). He deliberately reverted to the traditions of nineteenth-century neoclassical analysis to recapitulate the principal elements of development. In so doing, he first distinguished the Keynesian remedy for depressions as uniquely appropriate when national output is constrained by a lack of effective demand. However, he sharply criticized the neoclassical economists of the period, Joseph Schumpeter in particular, for what he perceived to be a distorted interpretation of the classical theory of development. Lewis courageously rejected the neoclassical paradigm, which precluded attention to the problem of labor in unlimited supply in the poor countries of Asia and Africa.

It is, indeed, a formidable task to attempt to summarize the amount of information contained in Lewis's theory of unlimited supply of labor here. However, the many attacks which have been made on it provide a possible guide for organizing these thoughts.

According to Lewis, he began to teach development economics systematically and with a heavy emphasis on policy in 1948. He acknowledges that his chief contribution to the subject was the two-sector model advanced in 1954. In so doing Lewis was inspired by the conclusion of John and Barbara Hammond that the Industrial Revolution had not raised urban wages.

Simply put, the answer to the mystery of why the standard of living of the masses in a number of developing countries has remained low, came by breaking an intellectual constraint. Lewis was aware of the general-equilibrium condition that when elasticity of supply of labor is zero, an increase in investment is accompanied by an increase in demand for labor and rising real wages. However by expressing the supply elasticity of labor to be infinite, real wages can be assumed to be constant. Thus growth increases profits to the elite class of owners of capital and technology and not the urban sea of a low-wage proletariat.

In the model, Lewis identifies the sources from which labor flows towards capitalist employment. The economic system is composed of "capitalist" and "subsistence" sectors. According to Lewis the "capitalist" sector, which may be private or state-owned, includes manufacturing and estate (commercial) agriculture. In the "subsistence" sector, labor is considered as being self-employed in mainly subsistence agriculture or small-scale unstructured economic activity.

Lewis argues that at an early stage of the development of nations, the supply of labor to the "capitalist" sector will exceed demand at a wage rate which can be maintained at the opportunity cost of the surplus unskilled agricultural labor force. This wage rate, determined by the alternatives provided by the capitalist sector, can thus remain relatively constant, although, in practice, it may be set above the minimum to induce labor transfer.

Within the capitalist sector, Lewis's explicit interpretation of the motive for employment corresponds to the capitalist employer's desire to generate profits and to fuel further growth. He is classical in distinguishing between "productive" and surplus or "unproductive" labor. Furthermore, he assumes the savings ratio will rise in the capitalist sector along with capital accumulation. Thus, given the wage and technology, the Lewis model attempts to explain the relationship between, first, the capital-labor ratio and the rate of profit, and second, the size of capital stock and employment. In his desire to explain the mechanics of economic development, he leaves room for defining the capitalist employer as the state in appropriate circumstances. Additionally, he admits that, although the dynamic force is capitalist accumulation and the expansion of capitalist employment, the stimulus for growth could be located in the expansion of the self-employed sector, for example, the expansion of peasant agricultural employment and output through technological innovation.

In many respects, the Lewis model resembles the Kaldor-Robinson model of the Cambridge school. Both anticipate a rate of growth determined by a product of the rate of profit and the propensity to save out of profits. Depending on the nature of technical change, the accumulation of capital and with it, rising national income, will be constrained by exhaustion of the labor reservoir. That is, rising living standards in the traditional sector and/or rising real wages may check the rate of growth

during this first phase of economic development. From this point onwards, Lewis concedes the neoclassical model is the relevant approach for explaining the approximate uniformity of wages in the integrated labor markets of a relatively developed industrial economy.

# Critics of the Model

The methodology of Arthur Lewis shows his lack of confidence in the established paradigms. His skepticism of the scientific method for example, is demonstrated by statements in *The Theory of Growth* like "Most predictions are no more than exercises in method," or, "To be able to predict what will happen we have to be able to know how all the variables are going to behave . . . no single brain could ever set up a system of equations which could embrace all the millions of variables which determine the future." As a renegade of economic science, Lewis therefore attracts critics in the same way honey attracts flies.

An explosion of criticism of the "dual economy" model occurred soon after the publication of the 1954 article. However, in retrospect, the broad philosophical leanings of the critics and the range of attack have contributed immeasurably to the theoretical refinement, empirical testing, and policy relevance of economic development as a discipline.

Lewis's suggestion that there is a perfectly elastic supply of labor at a given real wage drew early attention. Critics were quick to point to the proposition's potentially damaging impact on the view of rational economic behavior in the traditional sector if, in fact, zero marginal product of labor exists, so as to encourage labor transfer without a loss of output. But, in the original Lewis model, the real wage in the "capitalist" sector is distinctly determined by the opportunity cost of labor in the "traditional" sector. Thus, theoretically, a perfectly elastic supply of labor at a given real wage can be envisioned if the marginal and average product of labor is assumed to be the same in the relevant range. This scenario is plausible in egalitarian societies with abundant land held under communal ownership.

On the other hand, if marginal product rose in response to increases in the labor input, then the wage schedule should rise as well. This is a plausible interpretation fitting the neoclassical model of the labor market and the scenario in developing countries with extremely little land per capita. The compromise with the neoclassical approach whereby real wages in the modern sector are determined by exogeneous forces is valid only if the rise in real wages is due to excess demand at the original level of wages. However, as has been pointed out, it is difficult to reconcile this conclusion with the chronic unemployment in urban areas and the scarcity of rural labor at critical periods in most developing countries today.

Furthermore, the gap between subsistence and capitalist (industrial) incomes has widened considerably when viewed in terms of Lewis's logistic process of transition from a traditional to modern industrial economy based on the "dual economy" model. Critics say that the model overemphasizes the "Big Push," that is, the desire to accelerate growth of the industrial sector at the expense of the agricultural sector. In his 1972 variant of the model, Lewis clarified his definition of the capitalist sector to include the investment of physical as well as human capital in peasant agriculture. However, critics still insist that more emphasis on agriculture and small-scale enterprises presents a greater opportunity for the rapid elimination of inequality and poverty. In this vein, the assumption of stagnation in the subsistence sector gives the model a static bias which can be misleading.

The policy implication that free enterprise and the development of a market economy are desirable leaves the issue of distributional inequalities and the potential impoverishment of the subsistence sector unresolved. Economists who work within the political-economy paradigm criticize the Lewis model for assuming that profits made in the capitalist sector will automatically be reinvested and that whatever the capitalist sector produces can be sold. On the contrary, the development of the so-called modern sector has, except in a few cases, entailed the disruption and restructuring of the economies of the present-day underdeveloped countries. While weakening the traditional economy, the structure of international relations has prevented most developing countries from generating viable capitalist development. Furthermore, the existing evidence reveals a long history of exploitative relations with the metropolitan countries and/or dependent relations benefiting only an elite minority in each country.

Finally, the rise in savings associated with the expansion of the capitalist sector causes the income of the savers to increase relative to the national income. Thus the potential for further exploitation of the peasantry through the emergence of monopoly and other market imperfections may further exacerbate the problems of underdevelopment. Thus, with the exclusion of the masses from the capitalist sector, some have concluded that the Lewis process has failed the Third World.

It is fair to say that, in responding to his critics, Lewis has made refinements, some of which have been viewed as concessions. However, the dual-economy model continues to receive evaluative treatment in textbooks on development. In addition, Lewis's mode of presentation draws on the antagonism of the existing paradigms. This makes his work an easy target for critics and others desirous of more rigorous reformulation and extension of his ideas. For example, criticism of Lewis reflects the current concern with urban unemployment, migration, and declining agricultural incomes in developing countries. Furthermore, the essentially heuristic Lewis model has been more fully developed in formal analyses on development by a number of renowned economists. For example, A. K. Sen (1966) presents an outstanding analysis of dualism in traditional economies "with or without

surplus labor." Reference to the "Lewis-Fei-Ranis" model or the "Lewis-Jorgenson" model in discussions on industry, agriculture, and growth reflects the link between Lewis and others in the methodological perspective of today's mainstream economist.

# Lessons from History

In 1945, Lewis dropped industrial economics to teach a course on the survey of world economy between the wars. Four years later, he published his interwar *Economic Survey* and his first official paper, *Industrial Development in the Caribbean*. These were soon followed by *Report on Industrialisation and the Gold Coast* (1953), and *Aspects of Industrialization* (1953), which was written for the National Bank of Egypt. Thus, Lewis turned from the economic history of the "core," the developed industrial economies of the North, to its relations with the "periphery," the underdeveloped agricultural economies of the tropics and the South.

A good deal of Lewis's work has focused on developing models that utilize evidence from economic history to explain the connections between the agents of change and the policy prescriptions for selecting and nurturing the desired change. He argues in *The Theory of Economic Growth* that the limitations of specifying the parameters of a model make it realistic to call on history to explain the model just as much as the model is needed to simplify reality. From his perspective, therefore, it easy to "write with fair confidence on how society changes, but with little or no confidence on the directions in which it is likely to change" (p. 16).

Such humility, however, vitiates Lewis's impact on development planning in Africa, the Caribbean, and Latin America. In another sense, the "Lewis strategy" has come to suggest a criterion for evaluating both the process and results of change, an appelation that one cannot sidestep in any post-1950 discussion on industrialization in underdeveloped countries.

## Industrialization

In a number of ways, Lewis was concerned about the gap between industrial wage and incomes in the subsistence sector. With his insights from earlier works as well as more recent writings, including the essay "The Dual Economy Revisited," (1979), he employs the whole historical perspective in explaining the propensity for wages in the "modern" or urban sector to be well above those in the subsistence sector. Lewis extends this proposition to link the problems of development suggested by the study of segmented labor markets in closed static economies to the shifts in terms of trade of open economies.

In "Reflections on Unlimited Labour" (1972), Lewis outlined the three versions of his model. In the closed-economy variants, growth is constrained by rising wages or adverse terms of trade with the noncapitalist sector. It is in the third version that Lewis explores the growth potentials of an open econ-

omy whose capitalist sector trades with the outside world.

The mechanisms outlined in his earlier models define the subsistence sector as the part of the economy which is not using reproductive capital. His open-economy model, however, implies that the primeval state of the subsistence sector could have been caused by prior history; the conditions for surplus labor and low incomes may have been generated by customary land tenure constraints on production and/or the absence of opportunities for technical advance, education, and investment. While these constraints are obvious, his research on colonial development policies may have reinforced his conviction that by the use of such mechanisms as monopoly over markets, forced taxation (to keep rural incomes down) and declining terms of trade (in generating agricultural exports), the preservation of rural poverty is linked to relations with the metropole.

Lewis envisaged an unacceptably slow pace of structural transformation via the indigenous sector. By emphasizing the accelerated growth of the capitalist sector, he implied that the noncapitalist sector, by its very character, lacks the "pull" to transform its functioning units to possess the characteristics of a fully operating capitalist economy.

Furthermore, Lewis chose industrialization as the principal strategy for economic development. In so doing, he also identified and employed the "center-periphery" theories for which Raoul Prebisch is noted. His prognosis for development was, in part, motivated by the historic association between Western political and economic power and the growth of industry. On the other hand, the need for Third World nations to avoid economic specialization that leaves them vulnerable to the adverse effects of economic fluctuations in industrialized countries serves as the other major motivation. These observations underlie his call for a departure from the prior history of relationships with the metropole and for investment in indigenous capitalism.

Through numerous official papers and commission reports, the Lewis strategy became a reality in Latin America and the Caribbean and in Africa. For example, mindful of Puerto Rico's attempt to industrialize in the 1940s, Lewis argued, that establishing industries in underdeveloped areas may involve considerable sacrifice. To achieve the desired level of capital accumulation and capitalist enterprises would require an inflow of foreign capital and capitalists and a period of "wooing and fawning" to win such investment.

In Jamaica, Lewis first discovered and later wrote about the "Dutch disease," his description for the condition in which one dominant industry employs a few people and earns considerable foreign exchange but also causes unemployment by paying high wages, forcing up salaries in other industries beyond what they can pay. In *Politics in West Africa* (1965), he made proposals to improve the efficiency of state-owned enterprises by highlighting management reforms and minimizing corruption and nep-

otism. While attacked at the time, the analysis is now regarded as obvious.

Lewis on the whole preferred a balanced growth strategy oriented towards the home market. This strategy, which came to be known as Import Substituting Industrialization (ISI), consists of developing the domestic manufacturing capacity to substitute for imported goods. He argued that by merely exporting manufactures instead of primary products, developing economies "exchange one dependence for another."

# Accent on Change

Until the twentieth century, the regions of Latin America, Asia, and Africa fit into the world division of labor as exporters of raw inputs for industrial production in the "core." There was little desire to interrupt Third World exports that sustained "the engine of growth" in the metropole and also benefitted local elites in the colonies. Devoid of manufacturing activities, other than a few workshops, small refineries, and food processing factories, Latin America and Africa entered the post-World War II era with almost no entrepreneurial class, skilled labor force, economic infrastructure, market size, or administrative capacity to cope with industrialization.

As consultant and adviser to the governments of various newly independent Commonwealth Caribbean and African countries in the 1950s and 1960s, Lewis saw the role of government as principally to create the conditions necessary for stimulating the economic activity of entrepreneurs. Without forgetting the historical examples of the mischief done to economic life by governments which fail either because they do too little or because they do too much, Lewis concerned himself with asking what is the proper contribution of government to the promotion of individual initiative in a free-enterprise system.

Historically, all governments, regardless of their democratic character, face a strong temptation to scatter investment funds far and wide in an effort to gain support from all constituents. The most pervasive tendency of governments of developing nations in making investment decisions is not so much the obsession with large, highly visible projects as the allocation of funds among a large number of politically justified but economically inefficient projects.

In *The Economic Theory of Growth*, Lewis makes a case for optimal government intervention by identifying the categories of function relevant to economic progress. The framework for relating government and the economy as a whole to relations with the private sector is presented in the context of comprehensive production planning, prudent fiscal management, and public influence on the level of investment. He argues for the stimulation of domestic production capacity on the ground that investment in growth industries exerts a powerful pull on other sectors of an economy in the process of development, through external economies and, more importantly, through the demonstration effects of success.

Referring to the Latin American experience, Lewis once commented one can hardly speak of "industrialization." The lasting effects of the 1929–34 depression broke "the political resistance to industrialization—whether it had been the resistance of imperial powers or the resistance of domestic vested interest in primary production" (1978, p. 31). In Africa and most of the Third World, another thirty years elapsed before import substituting industrialization (ISI) came to be regarded as a necessary leading sector for encouraging pronounced structural changes.

Lewis's support for ISI reflected his deep-seated skepticism about the effectiveness of trade for stimulating development. In his earlier works, he clearly demonstrated that market instability for primary products and the slow growth of world demand for them have turned factorial terms of trade against primary-product exporters. He concluded that although a trade option is available to nations, the engine of growth has to be internally installed by promoting a balanced industrial and agricultural revolution of one's own. Critics part company with Lewis by arguing that although trade by itself may not be sufficient in promoting the development of backward areas, trade and technological imitation are mutually reinforcing and should not be viewed as alternatives. The experiences of Japan and, more recently, the emergence of Taiwan and Korea as newly industrializing countries provide additional evidence of the positive impact of trade on growth.

ISI policies attempt to gear

economies away from the traditional world division of labor because of its inimical implication for economic development. The emergence and growth of an industrialized sector, which may be privately owned or state owned, is consequently viewed as introducing a dynamic element into developing economies. The expected increase in the rate of growth is, accordingly, deemed necessary to accommodate both the natural population increase and the demands of rapid urbanization.

ISI proponents tend to assume import substitution would bring greater economic independence by promoting self-sufficiency in manufacturing. On the basis of this view others agreed that what looked like a puzzling preference for capital intensity on the part of capital-poor countries turned out to be, in effect, the incidental result of a perfectly commonsense way of "husbanding" capital. Because of this apparently vital role, Lewis and other economists extended ISI to include the case for intervention in the price mechanism to stimulate output expansion in domestic manufactures. Lewis did not provide a formula for optimal intervention, but he clearly found wage subsidies for manufacturing to be ideal and the use of output subsidies necessary only under appropriate circumstances. He also appeared to endorse tariffs to protect domestic manufactures. This argument for optimal intervention in the context implied by Lewis was further developed by Everett Hagen (1958) in his essay on the economic justification of protectionism

and extended by Jagdish Bhagwati, et al. (1963) as the theory of optimum subsidy.

Lewis's views on inward-looking industrialization, in sum, state that the imbalance between output and demand in the various sectors of a developing economy leads to trade deficits and sharp price fluctuations that are destabilizing because of their consequences for sustaining planned economic growth. Whatever the merits of these somewhat paradoxical views, the declining share of food and primary products in world trade is, perhaps, the best defense for his preference for capital-intensive lines of production, which many industrialized countries have used to sustain their own development.

The evidence on successful Third World industrialization indicates that a substantial influx of foreign capital, technology, management, and technical services play a key role. In the more pragmatic nations, formal and informal rules of operation have encouraged multinationals to function, with or without local participation, in a manner conducive to mutual interests. The decline of state enterprises as a notable feature of contemporary policy in developing economies merits further examination, with reference especially to resource conservation and long-term economic planning, the bargaining strength of governments in economically weak nations, development finance and debt management, decision-making autonomy of multinationals, and international competitiveness.

With respect to this pattern of

development, it is probably no exaggeration to concede that, although Lewis's balanced-growth strategy has its social and economic stresses, it has compensating advantages and represents an alternative framework for minimizing Third World dependence on primary-goods exports as the principal engine of growth.

## Lewis's Place in Economic Theory

Like Keynes, but unlike the large majority of his colleagues, Lewis chose social relevance—raising the level of living of the masses of people in the developing countries as rapidly as feasible—as the justification for a broader interpretation of economic theory. His stature as a student of economics and authority on the problems of the contemporary less developed countries largely stems from his ability to synthesize these problems in the context of the world's economic history. Indeed, he skillfully fuses many of the virtues inherent in the history of the developed core into his prognosis for accelerating the development of the periphery. His advice to statesmen and public officials recognizes that economics is not value free. As he suggests, the moral function of economics as pedagogy is to instruct humanity in how to improve the standard of living. In the last analysis, it is on the ethical plane that social problems have to be solved.

The pragmatism of his approach, however, exhibits Lewis's self-critical awareness of political-economic alternatives. For instance, in justifying the relevance of dualism as the appropriate mode of analysis in developing countries, he suggested in 1954 that intelligent government could be viewed as a substitute for the capitalist class. However, his model is used to legitimize capitalism, or the trickle-down theory of development. In *Economic Survey, 1919–1939* (1949); *Growth and Fluctuations 1870–1913* (1978), and *The Evolution of the International Economic Order* (1978), Lewis demonstrates his empirical skills and historical insights in support of his treatment of growth and development in today's interdependent world. In so doing, Lewis signals his belief that a general theory of economics exists.

However, in his 1984 article, "The State of Development Theory," Lewis noted that a search for the engine of growth is foredoomed. He had stated this view almost forty years earlier, citing negative terms of trade and unequal exchange as precluding international trade from serving as an engine of growth. Accordingly, John Wisman (1986) concluded that Lewis's appeal to inconsistent bodies of theory to explain economies at varying stages of their development is suggestive of the relativist view that since each society is unique and each stage of development is also unique, no general social laws are possible.

To a substantial extent, the methodology implict in Lewis's work and his pedagogical motivations are not often explicitly stated in terms of the narrow technical specializations that afflict the discipline of economics today. The typical stance of Lewis towards his col-

leagues is to maintain open dialogue. His argument for the inadequacy of both neoclassical and
Keynesian theory for dealing with
economies with unlimited supplies
of labor may have initiated his pedagogical stance, and since 1954 the
methodology implicit in his work
has been converted into a social
product, a product of tolerant and
intolerant viewpoints which have
propelled the paradigms of economic development to a highly visible status.

   Lewis's dedication to the ur-
gency of development places him in
the company of a small but growing
class of pragmatic economists who
willingly challenged the positivist
stance by their belief that different
societies have enough in common
for it to be possible to deduce some
general rules of human behavior
without resort to scientifically irresponsible puzzle-solving exercises in
logic in order to effect social change.

   In retirement at Cove Hill in
Barbados, Lewis has earned the
right to enjoy a leisurely pace of life
with his wife and the affluence
which development has bestowed on
the nations of his native Caribbean.
His students, no doubt, will attempt
to refine and extend the versions of
the Lewis model which have stood
the test of time. Reflecting on the
state of development theory, Lewis
believes that if conflict and dispute
are indices of intellectual activity,
the subject of economic development would seem adequately contentious. The discipline, though not
spectacular, is alive and well.

                REXFORD AHENE

# Selected Bibliography

## WORKS BY LEWIS

*Labour in the West Indies.* London: Fabian Society, 1939.

*Economic Problems of Today.* London:
   Longmans, 1940.

*Monopoly in British Industry.* London:
   Fabian Society, 1945.

*Economic Survey, 1919–1939.* London:
   Allen and Unwin, 1949.

*Overhead Costs.* London: Allen and
   Unwin, 1949.

*Report on Industrialisation and the
   Gold Coast.* Accra: Gold Coast
   Government, 1953.

*Aspects of Industrialization.* Cairo: National Bank of Egypt, 1953.

"Economic Development with Unlimited Supplies of Labor." *The Manchester School of Economics and
   Social Studies* 22 (1954): 134–91.

*The Theory of Economic Growth.* London: Allen and Unwin, 1955.

"Unlimited Labour: Further Notes."
   *The Manchester School of Eco-
   nomic and Social Studies* 1. 26
   (1958): 1–32.

*The Principles of Economic Planning,*
   London: Allen and Unwin, 1949, 2d
   rev. ed., 1963.

*Politics in West Africa.* London: Allen
   and Unwin, 1965.

"Reflections on Unlimited Labour." In
   *International Economics and De-
   velopment (Essays in Honour of
   Raoul Prebisch)*, edited by L. E. di
   Marco, pp. 75–96. New York: Aca-
   demic Press. 1972.

*The Evolution of the International Eco-
   nomic Order.* Princeton, N.J.: Princeton University Press, 1978.

*Growth and Fluctuations 1870–1913.*
   London: Allen and Unwin, 1978.

"The Dual Economy Revisited." *The Manchester School, of Economics and Social Studies* 47 (1979): 211–29.

"The State of Development Theory." *American Economic Review* 74 (1984): 1–10.

## OTHER WORKS

Barker, T. E., A. S. Downes, and J. A. Sackey, eds. *Perspectives in Economic Development: Essays in Honour of W. Arthur Lewis.* University Press of America, 1982.

Bhagwati, Jagdish and Ramsawami, V. K. "Domestic Distortions, Tariffs and the Theory of Optimum Subsidy." *Journal of Political Economy* 71 (1963), 44–50.

Fei, J. C. H. and Ranis, G. *Development of the Labor Surplus Economy: Theory and Policy.* Homewood, Il. Irwin, 1964.

Findlay, R. "On Arthur Lewis' Contributions to Economics." *Scandinavian Journal of Economics* 82: (1980): 62–76.

Hagen, Everett. "An Economic Justification of Protectionism." *Quarterly Journal of Economics* 72 (1958): 496–514.

Sen, A. K. "Peasants and Dualism with and without Surplus Labor." *Journal of Political Economy* 74 (1966): 425–50.

Wisman, John D. "The Methodology of W. Arthur Lewis's Development Economics: Economics as Pedagogy." *World Development* (1986): 165–80.

# JAMES MEADE   *1977*

James Meade was born in the small Dorset town of Swanage, in the southwest corner of England, on June 23, 1907, beginning a life which has spanned most of the twentieth century, and which saw him at various times at Oxford, Geneva, the heart of British government, the London School of Economics (LSE) and Cambridge. During his career he was a young member of the elite circle of associates which gave birth to Keynes's *General Theory of Employment, Interest and Money* (1936), a key player in the reconstruction of the post-World War II international economy, a refugee in wartorn France, and eventually, in 1977, one of only three English economists to receive the Nobel Prize in Economic Sciences. His research interests have been just as wide, and his writings have covered international trade, income distribution, population growth, domestic policy issues, producer cooperatives, unemployment, and inflation. He now lives in the high street of a small village just outside Cambridge, still a regular producer of thought-provoking books as he moves into his ninth decade.

## Training and Early Career

The young Meade moved to Bath in his first year. His education was provided by a private governess until the age of ten, after which he went to a private preparatory school and then, as a classical scholar, to Malvern College, a boarding school in the center of England. His interest in economics and social issues stemmed not from his formal education, but from a rather remarkable maiden aunt who numbered amongst her interests politics, Jung, Einstein, the running of a local musical festival, and the social credit economics of the somewhat eccentric Major Douglas. In 1926 he went to Oriel College, Oxford, where he continued his classical education in his first year. This concentration on classical studies he later found to be a nuisance, for he subsequently had to teach himself all the mathematics that he ever learned, and it partly accounts for his writing style, which has been the subject of subsequent criticism. In his second year he turned to his real love, economics. In this year he invited Dennis Robertson, then second only to Keynes in the academic firmament, to talk to an Oxford undergraduate economics society, staying in the undergraduate guest room in college. It might seem strange that this friendship between the eminent economist and the unknown undergraduate should develop, but Robertson was a great-nephew of the two sisters who had lived next door to Meade at Bath, and the young Meade had already been introduced to Robert-son as someone who "was interested in economics."

Meade graduated in 1930 and was appointed a fellow by Hertford College, Oxford, which sent him to Cambridge to learn a little bit about economics. Robertson invited him to Trinity College and introduced him to Richard Kahn, with whom he formed a close friendship and through whom he found himself an intimate in the "Circus" of young economists surrounding Keynes, initially formed to discuss the implications of his newly published *The Treatise on Money* (1930). Robertson did not often attend, the main members being, besides Meade himself, Kahn, Piero Sraffa, and Joan and Austin Robinson. After each meeting Kahn delivered an oral report to Keynes, who was engaged at that time with the Macmillan Report, only coming to Cambridge on weekends. Thus, within months of being an undergraduate, Meade was part of one of the most important and exciting developments in the history of economics; indeed, not just a part, for if Austin Robinson is to be believed, he was the most active member of the "Circus," not just in the Keynesian arguments but also in those surrounding the theory of value, leading up to Joan Robinson's book on imperfect competition.

The "Circus" quickly came to the conclusion that in many respects the *Treatise on Money* was inadequate. The first tangible product of their meetings was the publication of Kahn's famous paper that developed the multiplier relationship, which is the concept that an increase in government spending leads to an even greater increase in total spending. An important part of this development was what became known as "Mr. Meade's Relation," linking savings and investment. There are no formal records of these meetings, and it is in the main difficult to ascribe the authorship of any specific concepts or ideas to individuals. But it is clear that by the summer of 1931 the interplay between the "Circus" and Keynes had developed most of the ingredients which were to make up the *General Theory*. Keynes's role in this interchange was remote and has been likened by Meade's wife to that of God in a morality play, dominating the proceedings but rarely being seen on stage.

In fact Keynes' role was to receive the deliberations of the "Circus," incorporate them into his own thinking, although sometimes only after extensive discussion, and send back requests, via Kahn, for discussions on fresh topics. Thus a case has been made, and it would seem to me quite a strong case, for arguing that the *General Theory* should be correctly attributed to a collective authorship. The role of Keynes should then be seen as that of a master conductor, instigating discussion, listening to arguments, and fitting the various pieces of the jigsaw together. In this light it is interesting to reconsider his comments in the preface of the *General Theory* about his long struggle to escape from habitual modes of thought and expression. In this struggle the role of the young turks of the "Circus," of whom Meade was of course the youngest (but Kahn and Joan Robinson were only two and four years older, respectively), can be seen to be crucial to the whole affair. They would have had less attachment for both the prevailing orthodoxy on macroeconomic analysis and the luminaries such as Pigou and Marshall with which it was linked. It is worth noting, however, that Meade attended Pigou's lectures while at Cambridge and was a great admirer of his work on microeconomic problems, as developed in the *Economics of Welfare* (1920).

After a single year at Cambridge, Meade returned to Hertford College as a fellow, where he stayed until 1937. It might appear that Oxford would have been something of an anticlimax after the heady year spent at Cambridge. But the Ph.D. degree had been introduced only a few years before. Partly to teach at that level, a young faculty group had been assembled, and Meade felt that this too was a challenging time. In 1933 he published his first paper in the form of a Fabian pamphlet, and the following year saw his first *Economic Journal* paper. But Meade has always been a writer of books rather than articles, his first also being published in 1933. There followed many more, including in 1936 *An Introduction to Economic Analysis and Policy*, which was the first textbook to systematically set out the Keynesian approach to economics. This was followed by a somewhat neglected *Review of Economic Studies* paper in 1937 which formalized the *General Theory* in algebraic form, although, it was, of course, Hicks's formulation which became standard. However, after a lag of some fifty years, Meade's paper has been rediscovered and is beginning to be seen by some as superior to this standard version. In addition, he kept up his links with Cambridge and was part of a group of young Cambridge economists who, together with a similar group from the LSE, established the *Review of Economic Studies.* During this time he also worked closely with Hugh Gaitskell, Evan Durbin, Roy Harrod, and others in drafting papers on Labour party policies which helped to lay the foundation for the subsequent postwar Labour government. Perhaps his main contribution was to convert many of the Labour Party leaders to Keynesianism.

## Public Service

In 1937 Meade temporarily left Oxford and academic life to take up a position at the League of Nations in Geneva, although with the mutual understanding that he would subsequently return to Hertford. He was responsible for the League's reports on the world economy, work which was to influence Keynes in, for example, his 1939 article that looked at the relationship between real wages and unemployment in *The General Theory.* Meade had by this time a wife and two children, his third child being born in Geneva. This work was cut short by the Second World War, and in 1940 he was asked to work for the Cabinet Office in London. He and his family left Switzerland in May 1940, aiming to embark at one of the Channel ports. But the Germans had at this time launched their invasion of France,

and their rapid advance changed this plan. Traveling in their small car, and moving at first against a steady flow of refugees, they swerved southwards. To begin with they moved in accustomed comfort, and in Annecy they spent some time choosing a hotel less noisy than that found on the main street. But when they finally reached Nantes, which was crowded with refugees, they were lucky to find shelter for three days in a single room of a kindly worker's third-floor tenement flat. They were fortunate enough to leave on an RAF transport ship and after ten days at sea landed safely in a small port in South Wales.

Hertford agreed to waive its prior claim on his services and, still only thirty-three, Meade was brought into the Economic Section of the Cabinet Office, first as an assistant for the period 1940–45, and subsequently as director, 1946–47. These were exciting times. Prior to 1939 the government had employed few economists, whereas Meade was to work with an enormously talented group which included Lionel Robbins, Austin Robinson, Alec Cairncross, Dennis Robertson, and of course Keynes and Richard Stone. Meade evolved a framework for a set of national accounts in June and July of 1940, being joined by the enthusiastic Stone, who had previously been working for a bank, in August of that year. The general purpose behind this project was to provide a better basis to deal with the general problem of inflation, and as part of that process aid in the production of budget forecasts. Together with a hand (Monroe) calculator, a Japanese slide rule, a single desk, and several sheets of very large paper, which they covered with boxes, they set about the task. There was much confusion at the time as to the relevant concepts, and they first laid out the principles, based on double-entry bookkeeping, which formed the basis of the work. It was from this foundation that emerged the key distinction between gross national product (GNP) at market prices and factor cost, a distinction that explained many of the differences between the various unofficial guesses as to GNP.

By December 1940 the first results of their work were available. They were used in the presentation of the 1941 budget and published after the budget speech of April 7. It must be realized that prior to this work there were no official estimates of consumer spending, no data at all on profits and capital formation, and only the vaguest ideas as to the state of the balance of payments. From this time the government's annual financial statement ceased to be regarded as a mere forecast of the financial position of the government and instead was used to describe how the government was to preserve balance within the economy. To put this work in its historical perspective, it should be noted that it was in 1921–22 that the first detailed estimates of national income were published for the United States by the newly established National Bureau of Economic Research, while in 1935 the National Incomes Section of the U.S. Department of Commerce began to publish annual estimates of national income by factor shares and industrial origin. For the United Kingdom there was the work of Colin Clark in the 1930s and Keynes and Erwin Rothbarth in preparation for the former's pamphlet, entitled *How to Pay for the War* (1940). But there were apparently no official estimates, although it has recently emerged that in 1929 the Inland Revenue prepared and printed a *Report on National Income* for the fiscal year 1923/24 and for the two subsequent calendar years. This document was, however, marked confidential, never published, and until recently lay forgotten in the archives. The work of Meade and Stone transformed this situation by developing the broad conceptual framework which has formed the basis of national-income accounting ever since. They also set the precedent of calculating national income within the final product, $Y=C+I+G$, framework Keynes laid down in the *General Theory* and which all other countries were subsequently to follow. Of course much guesswork was involved in this work, and on one occasion Meade and Stone entered into a discussion on the cost of and frequency with which they had their hair cut, multiplying this by the number of men in the UK and entering the figures at the appropriate point on their grid.

After the 1941 budget Meade turned to other problems of economic policy and Stone became solely responsible for the national accounts, developing the concepts of social accounting for which he too was to obtain the Nobel Prize. In these subsequent years in the Economic Section of the Cabinet Office

Meade's influence was important in both domestic and international policy areas. His main concerns with respect to the former were with post-war unemployment policy and long-term planning. Meade was the first to attempt to turn the government's attention to these issues, with a memorandum dated February 1941. A later memorandum of July 8, 1941, was instrumental in setting up an interdepartmental committee on postwar internal economic problems. By 1942 Meade, helped by J. M. Fleming and others, had produced a number of proposals, including that for countercyclical variation in national insurance contributions. This amounted in effect to a specific, flexible policy rule aimed at injecting extra spending power into the economy if unemployment increased. In 1943 Meade was pushing for a more gradual postwar unemployment program and was the author of the first draft of what became the White Paper on Employment Policy published on May 26, 1944, which committed governments to managing the economy so as to secure full employment.

Meade was also responsible for pushing for an early consideration of international policy questions. By the autumn of 1942 he had put together a series of proposals embodying a laissez-faire approach to trade that the Board of Trade subsequently adopted as its own. These proposals were considerably more liberal than Keynes appeared to want. He apparently preferred tariffs to exchange-rate adjustment as a means for controlling balance-of-

trade problems and bilateral trading treaties rather than multilateral ones. However, by the beginning of 1944 he had, somewhat grudgingly, been persuaded not to oppose the proposals, in the belief that other countries would probably find them unacceptable. In this he was prophetic, for the ambitious free trade proposals laid down in the Havana Charter for an International Trade Organisation (ITO), which Meade had worked so hard on, failed to be ratified in 1949 by several countries, including the United States. Thus recourse was made to the less ambitious provisional agreement made in 1947, the General Agreement on Tariffs and Trade (GATT), which took on many of the functions and some of the features of the ITO, prohibiting the use of quotas, except for temporary balance-of-payments purposes, and providing a framework for the progressive reduction of tariffs.

The Bretton Woods conference in 1944 w⸗ more successful. The agreement reflected the liberal views Meade, Robertson, and Fleming had persuaded Keynes to support, which he then did with inexhaustible skill and energy. The agreement set up a system of adjustable, but pegged, exchange rates, each currency being pegged to the dollar and in turn to gold via the fixed gold price for the dollar. The International Monetary Fund was set up in 1947, as part of this agreement, with the general aim of promoting international monetary cooperation and the development of world trade. The agreement also laid out that exchange devaluation rather than tariffs and managed trade was the appropriate method for reconciling the full employment policies of trading countries with the danger of any country running too great a deficit or surplus on trade.

# The Years of High Theory

Meade left government service in 1947, going to the London School of Economics as professor of commerce, a position he was to hold for a decade. It was during this period that, in many people's opinion, he made his most important contribution to economic theory, a contribution which was subsequently to earn him the Nobel Prize. This work lay in the field of international trade and encompassed two major books, together with a number of subsidiary ones. The two major ones were the two volumes of *The Theory of International Economic Policy: The Balance of Payments* (1951) and *Trade and Welfare* (1955). The most important of the subsidiary ones were *A Geometry of International Trade* (1952) and *The Theory of Customs Unions* (1955).

Prior to 1951 economists had always treated income and price movements separately and had dealt with mainly automatic mechanisms to adjust balance-of-payments surpluses or deficits. It was part of Meade's contribution to treat them jointly within a general-equilibrium framework, integrating Keynesian analysis with a classical concern with relative prices. In this he was paralleled by the work of Arnold Harberger, Sven Laursen, and

Lloyd Metzler at Chicago, while Jan Tinbergen had simultaneously developed a theory of targets and instruments. In Meade's analysis the policy objectives are the twin aims of internal and external balance. Here internal balance refers to the full-employment objective, and external balance to balance-of-payments equilibrium. The mechanisms through which these might be achieved involve both income and price adjustments. Income adjustments occur when either fiscal or monetary policy, in this case the rate of interest, is used to change the level of spending in the economy. Price adjustments involve changes in either the exchange rate or relative wage rates. Meade showed that for two policy objectives to be simultaneously achieved, one needed the application of two policy instruments. If only one is to be used, conflicts between objectives arise, leading to what have later been called "dilemma cases." One of the main contributions here was to point out that, starting in internal balance, a devaluation would be inflationary unless it was accompanied by policies to reduce domestic expenditure. This lesson was successfully put into practice by one of Meade's political intimates, Roy Jenkins, when chancellor of the exchequer following the devaluation of sterling in 1967. Prior to Meade's book economists had also tended to ignore the impact of capital movements, which he had now integrated within the model. The book also contained the first steps of what was eventually to become known as the theory of optimum currency areas.

In the second volume of the series Meade examined the arguments for trade and factor controls. This concept of embracing trade and factor controls in a single analysis was again highly original. The analysis of the latter in particular was stimulating and included a model of the effects of migration on the terms of trade as well as work on optimal population theory. This book also introduced the "theory of the second best," later expanded upon by Richard Lipsey and Kelvin Lancaster. The basic principle is easily explained. The marginal conditions of the Pareto optimum, for example, hiring labor until its marginal product equals the wage rate, are not valid criteria for welfare increases unless all are simultaneously satisfied. Thus the belief that in the event that we cannot satisfy all of these conditions it is best to satisfy as many as we can is totally erroneous, and any attempt to do so may well reduce welfare rather than increase it. In its original use Meade argued the case for controls on trade and factors on the grounds that there are various constraints which must be taken as given, examples being those supplied by government policies (such as taxes) or in aspects of the private sector (such as a major monopoly). If one were to seek an optimum trade policy in the face of these constraints, then the result would be different from that which would apply in a first, best world with no distortions. Lipsey and Lancaster's presentation of this theory was somewhat pessimistic, suggesting that nothing could be said about the nature of optimal policies because of

the inevitable existence of distortions. Meade was more positive, outlining a method whereby, in theory at least, it is possible to establish in a second-best situation whether or not the removal of impediments will increase welfare. He argued that the optimal second-best tax or tariff will generally partially offset some other distortion, even though it creates fresh distortions in the process. However, it must be admitted that in practice it is rare that we can trace through the effects on welfare of second-best policies.

In analyzing second-best situations Meade also had to reformulate the theory of welfare. On the empirical side he provided a method of quantifying the impact of various policy changes, in a forerunner of cost-benefit analysis, although this has only been realized in retrospect, the subject having developed independently of Meade's early contribution. The original draft of the book was based on the work of Hicks, Nicholas Kaldor, Tibor Scitovsky, and others in the late 1930s, which examined welfare economics from the point of view of compensation rules. But this quickly led him to sterile results, as the whole approach comes close to the position that economists can say nothing about the implications of policy changes which have distributional impacts. He thus reverted to an older tradition that allowed him to make interpersonal comparisons, which was embodied in a paper by Fleming, "On Making the Best of Balance of Payments Restrictions on Imports," which appeared in *The Economic Journal* of 1951. In what

Harry G. Johnson calls "an act of great intellectual honesty and courage," Meade scrapped the original draft and reworked it, using this earlier approach. He calculated welfare as a weighted sum of individual welfares, assessing policy changes by whether such a change leads to a net gain or loss.

Meade's emphasis on factors also led to an important contribution to the analysis of the welfare economics of controls on international movements of factors of production—a subject which has since steadily gained in importance. A third major contribution of *Trade and Welfare* lay in the extension of the analysis of customs unions from a two-country framework to a multicountry one, thus permitting the analysis of policy discrimination among national sources of goods. One of the implications of this analysis is that a partial reduction in tariffs on a nondiscriminatory basis may have adverse effects on welfare through its repercussions on the volume of trade still subject to discriminatory taxation. This analysis includes within it the essential ideas of effective protection, which when subsequently developed by W. M. Corden, previously one of Meade's students, and Johnson, had a major impact upon the analysis of the effects of trade and welfare of protectionist policies.

The work on customs unions was expanded upon in *The Theory of Customs Unions* (1955). The initial work in this area had been done by Jacob Viner, who concentrated upon the production effects of customs unions. Meade changed the

emphasis to include the impact upon consumption. His formulation for both consumers and producers included substitution and complementarity relationships. He argued that by changing relative prices a customs union will change demand both between and within countries. Trade creation comes about by the substitution of low-cost foreign supplies for domestic production, and by the increase in real income, which results from a decline in import prices. The general-equilibrium framework he employed allowed the analysis of the welfare implications for participants and nonparticipants of the customs union, as well as for the world as a whole. This was a significant improvement on previous work, although in empirical terms the welfare effects for the world as a whole of a customs union have not proved easy to calculate.

The contribution of the *Geometry of International Trade* was more of the toolmaking kind and still figures as an almost mandatory appendix in most textbooks on international trade. The contribution followed on work done in the early 1930s by Wassily Leontief and Abba Lerner on providing a geometric technique for obtaining a country's offer curve from its social-indifference curve and production-possibility frontier, where the offer curve shows, for a two-country, two-good analysis, the combination of goods which a country is willing to import and export at alternative values of the terms of trade. Using the concept of a "trade-indifference curve," Meade was able in a single diagram to represent a free-trade equilibrium involving two countries, each with its own production-possibility frontier and consumption-indifference curves.

# The Cambridge Years

In 1957 Meade left the LSE, returning to Cambridge as professor of political economy, replacing his old friend Dennis Robertson, who retired in that year. He did so because, as he entered his sixth decade, he wanted to turn his attention to the problems of domestic policy making, and the LSE could not provide him with a suitable position. His ambition was to provide a theory of domestic economic policy analogous to the theory of international economic policy. In this he was unsuccessful, although an incomplete series of books in this general area did emerge, including *The Stationary Economy* (1965), *The Growing Economy* (1968), *The Controlled Economy* (1971), and *The Just Economy* (1976). The main theme of these books is to combine the efficiency of market forces with the need for government intervention, generally at the macro level, but also to correct for inequitable distribution of incomes. He strongly believes that if one can get the macro economy right, then most micro issues can be left to the individual economic agent. This belief, in what Samuelson has termed the "neoclassical syntheses," is a common thread throughout Meade's life and underlies almost all of his work. It stems from his initial year at Cambridge, where he came under the spell of both Keynes and Pigou. Indeed much of

his work can be seen as an attempt to combine Keynesian macroeconomics with Pigovian microeconomics.

The role of governments in the micro area should be mainly to provide the climate in which individuals can make optimal and mutually consistent decisions. In part this involves providing them with as much information as possible, in particular about intended future government policies. Thus, there is a case for governments making their intentions for levels of taxes, interest rates, and so on known in advance, although they should not then be tied to these plans but have the freedom to modify them to meet changed circumstances. This line of thought, which has been closely paralleled in monetarist thinking, has had some influence on government policy making, at least in the UK, where the government set policy targets for the future, although these have mainly related to the money supply and the public-sector borrowing requirement, and not, so far, to the levels of and structure of taxation.

These concerns, including the distribution of income, were evident as early as 1948, when Meade wrote *Planning and the Price Mechanism*. However, it is perhaps in *Efficiency, Equality and the Ownership of Property* (1964), that he made his most significant contribution from his time at Cambridge, in connection with the development of models of income distribution. Indeed, it is worth noting that Meade regards this as possibly his best book. In it he looks at the relationship between earned and unearned income and the forces underlying capital accumulation. This work stimulated a revival of interest in the area, particularly in the UK, although significantly, it has almost been ignored in America. On the policy side he argued against redistributory policies which would tend to reduce the size of the social pie, such as high rates of direct tax, or exclude from employment the least productive of workers, such as minimum-wage legislation. Again we see here his reluctance to interfere with the price mechanism. Instead he argued for the use of redistributive death and gift taxation. Meade himself later returned to this subject in the following decade with the publication of *The Inheritance of Inequalities* (1974) and *The Just Economy* (1976).

The aim of much of this work has been to translate sophisticated economic theory into a form which is accessible to the policy maker. However, apart perhaps from the work on income distribution, it did not meet with the success of his earlier work. Perhaps as a reaction to this, or possibly as a response to real-world conditions, he began to concern hinself more with the macro problems of inflation and unemployment. With respect to unemployment, he remains a Keynesian and believes that expansionary fiscal policies can still be used to expand monetary demand, but that these measures will only be fully effective in reducing unemployment if they are accompanied by policies to control inflation.

The problem arises because of the growth of imperfect competition in the economy from both demand- and supply-side monopolies. Faced with increased demand for their product, too many economic agents are in the position of raising their price instead of increasing supply. The problem is one of outsiders versus insiders, and Meade's solutions have varied from incomes policies to the hiring of new workers at wages less than those of existing workers. Meade's variant on the former requires the bargainers to make their final bids in the knowledge that if agreement is not reached, the dispute will go to arbitration. The arbitrator will decide in favor of the bid which will lead to most employment, thus tending to force both sides towards the competitive wage that would prevail in the absence of imperfections. There are many problems with this solution, not least the question as to how you "force" powerful labor monopolies to accept less than they can force out of the system. Presumably Meade might argue that, in the UK at least, this problem is less important than a decade ago, due to the recent decline in trade union power. But if this is the case, then any income policy would work, and Meade's contribution lies in suggesting a policy which would result in a shift in the system of pay bargaining towards that which would prevail in the absence of monopoly powers.

Meade's second solution, contained in his latest book, *Alternative Systems of Business Organisation and of Workers' Remuneration* (1986), lies with the choice of institutional structure most suitable for a modern economy, which he feels to be of basic importance to society. He favors a discriminating labor-capital partnership, by which new workers are issued with share certificates in accordance with their marginal value to the firm, in effect resulting in their being paid lower wages than existing members. This, he feels, will reduce the conflict between those with jobs and those without, that is, between insiders and outsiders. He prefers this solution to the Weitzman-type profit-sharing scheme, as he feels the latter, by reducing the return on capital, is likely to reduce investment. These ideas have their roots in an influential 1976 *Economic Journal* paper which built upon work on producer cooperatives by Barbara Ward and Jaroslav Vanek. In it he was the first to propose inegalitarian producer cooperatives, which solves some of the efficiency problems associated with this form of enterprise. He also made an important contribution in analyzing the problem of conditions of severance, using the concept of worker shareholders, previous work having assumed that members of the cooperative can be dismissed as in an ordinary firm. This whole area is now attracting considerable attention, and once more Meade's contribution has been critical.

## Flying Kites

Meade retired from the chair in political economy at Cambridge in 1968, although retirement hardly marked the end of his career. As has been noted, he continues to publish a stream of books and articles. He has also chaired a committee that produced *The Structure and Re-*

*form of Direct Taxation*, (1978), in which Meade also had the assistance of a talented young group of economists, John Kay, Mervyn King, and John Flemming, who subsequently became full members of the committee. The relationship between this group and Meade is reminiscent of the earlier relationship between Keynes and his young helpers, with Meade and others of the committee drawing the best from their talents. The committee's recommendation reflected Meade's lifetime concerns and beliefs with respect to the efficiency of the microeconomy and the need to avoid unnecessary distortions in the price mechanism, together with a passionate concern for equality. It recommended replacing the income tax with an expenditure tax, partly because the latter distorts incentives and the price mechanism less than the former. This tax could be made progressive, then being levied on the individual rather than as a sales tax; individuals would have to go on completing tax forms, working out their income, from which they deduct savings to arrive at their expenditure. The committee also recommended a progressive tax on wealth, coupled with a new Beveridge-style social-security program. The latter would substantially increase social benefits, including child benefits based upon the number of children in the family.

This was in fact the second committee Meade had chaired, having previously been chairman of an influential committee of inquiry which reported its findings in 1961 in *The Economic and Social Structure of Mauritius*. Mauritius at the time was an island economy based almost entirely on a single commodity, sugar, which fascinated Meade, leading to a number of additional publications of which the most important was the 1961 *Economic Journal* paper "Mauritius: A Case Study in Malthusian Economics."

In the 1950s and 1960s, Meade retained his strong ties with the Gaitskellite tradition of the Labour party, meeting regularly with Gaitskell, James Callaghan, Anthony Crossland, Jenkins, and others. More recently he has been part of the great divide on the left of British politics that saw a splinter group from the Labour party form the Social Democratic party (SDP). In alliance with the Liberal party, they attempted to replace the Labour party as the choice of most left-wing and center voters. Meade's influence on the SDP was very great, especially on economic issues, with proposals for Keynesian expansion coupled with incomes policies forming a central part of their program. The 1987 general-election result appears, however, to have dealt this new grouping a terminal blow.

Ideas are a strange currency, and it is often difficult to trace an individual's influence. However, the emphasis on the importance of the price mechanism is increasingly being echoed not just by the left in the UK, but also by left-wing parties throughout the world. Meade also appears to have had some influence on the Conservative government, which has gradually placed more emphasis on expenditure taxes at the expense of income taxes, and again it may be that this shift will

become internationalized, although it must be admitted that Meade's concerns with equality and control of the macroeconomy are not now shared with most Western governments. But it is only a matter of time before his concerns become fashionable again. It may then be that the metaphorical kites he has been flying these past decades, as opposed to the actual kites which are his hobby, are once more taken on board by the policy makers.

## A Matter of Style

Meade's career can be clearly divided into various stages, which are in fact closely linked with the decades of his life. It began with the extraordinary good fortune of his being one of the inner circle of those responsible for the birth of the *General Theory*, arguably the most single important event in the history of economics, with Meade, just one year after graduating, being a central part of it. There followed the years at Oxford, where he continued to learn his subject. On entering his fourth decade he left academic life for a decade in public service, first in Geneva and then in the Cabinet Office in London. Again Meade was fortunate in being in the right place at the right time. The immediate task was to give the theoretical notions built up in the *General Theory* empirical content. This he did, together with Stone, and their work at this time laid the foundations of national-income accounting. His subsequent years in public service saw him dealing more with international questions, such as those resolved at the Bretton Woods conference, and laying the foundations for what was eventually to become GATT. As he entered his fifth decade he moved back into academic life to begin his work on international economics, which many people see as the most successful of his career. Equally, his move to Cambridge at the beginning of his sixth decade and the simultaneous switch to domestic policy questions have been seen as a mistake, resulting in work of considerably inferior quality to what had gone before.

There are several points to note here. His working life appears to have been systematically and neatly subdivided into decades, although he is not explicitly conscious of it, giving force to Johnson's argument that Meade's approach to economics can be characterized as that of the single scholar working away in his study, pursuing successive research projects according to a more-or-less firm lifetime program. Johnson is a strong critic of the Meade style of writing, which consists in the development of a general mathematical model followed by a literary exposition, which many have found taxonomic in the extreme. In other words the argument proceeds by an enumeration of most, if not all, of the possible cases the model in question allows. This criticism was being made to Meade very early on, for example in a letter from Keynes dated 25 August 1942, relating to a draft of an employment paper. He argued that it should be cut in half, was unintelligible to the nonexpert, and that it was generally a waste of time to rebut arguments which have not been made. But the leopard does

not easily change his spots and, with respect to this same paper, in a letter to Lionel Robbins written in March of the following year, Keynes was still complaining that it was too long, indigestible, and unreadable. This style, which has changed only slowly over the years, is foreign to the modern economist, weaned on a diet of rigorous and extensive mathematical analysis largely beyond Meade's comprehension, coupled with only a sparse literary discussion. Neither is the reader helped by Meade's frequent failure to highlight the originality of what he has done. Sometimes, as with cost-benefit analysis, this originality is only perceived retrospectively. Partly as a consequence, perhaps, initial reviews of Meade's books have frequently underestimated their eventual impact, although, as Robert Mundell has observed, the initial tepid reception given to *The Theory of International Economic Policy* was due more to the state of confusion of economics in the early 1950s.

There may be other reasons why Meade's work on domestic policy has not been so successful. While at the LSE he was surrounded by a number of able young graduate students such as Corden, Robert Lipsey and Mundell, who were both a direct stimulus to him and able to translate his work into a form more easily recognizable by the profession. This was not the case at Cambridge, where he was never given a graduate seminar program to run. Moreover, Mundell and Lipsey had the enormous advantage of being from the North American continent, and thus carried more credibility with the American audience than perhaps someone from Britain would. Regrettably, the parochial nature of the American profession appears to have been growing over the decades, and books such as *Efficiency, Equality and the Ownership of Property*, which have had a substantial impact on British economists, have all but been ignored in America. Meade's tendency frequently to write with the problems of the British economy in mind has not helped, nor has his left-wing or interventionist bias. Many of the problems Meade has been concerned with, such as reducing the current high levels of unemployment in Europe, reducing the power of monopoly trade unions, and correcting market imperfections, are not of great concern to the average American economist.

Having said all this, it still must be admitted that the move to Cambridge was probably a mistake from a professional point of view. It is slightly surprising, too, in that Cambridge was not the most pleasant of places for an economist at this time and seemingly incompatible with the style of the man, as partially reflected by his almost total absence from the conference scene. It is also perhaps surprising that someone with socialist principles and so concerned with inequality could choose to teach and live in the bastion of privilege which was and is Cambridge. This can partly be explained by his great love of the place, something which is shared by many economists. Cambridge was also moving down the road of isolation and irrelevancy driven partially by the increasingly Marxist interpretation being given to the *General Theory* by Joan Robinson, Kaldor, Piero Sraffa, and others. Symptomatic of this tendency was the acrimonious debate between Robinson and Kaldor on one hand and Samuelson and Robert Solow on the other on the nature of capital and growth. Meade entered the "Cambridge controversies," as this debate was known, with *A Neo-Classical Theory of Economic Growth* (1961), which was rather scornfully reviewed by Robinson. Surely Meade would never have involved himself with this controversy if he had managed to avoid Cambridge.

The move from international issues to domestic policy issues was also probably a mistake. The former offered more opportunities for original thought and required the development of new tools of analysis. The questions of domestic policy which Meade mainly interested himself in were already well-worn tracks on which originality of approach was difficult, and instead he frequently ended up building intricate and complicated policy structures that stood little chance of being implemented. Meade himself has said that he is a toolsetter rather than a toolmaker, yet it appears that many of his most significant contributions, including the development of national-income accounts, the revision of welfare economics and his model of intergenerational transmission of wealth have been of the toolmaking variety. Moreover, the success of these tools then seems to have frequently allowed him to use them in new and imaginative methods of policy analysis.

Meade entered economics because he abhorred mass unemployment and wanted to know why society was failing to avoid the stupidity of idle men and machines combined with crying real needs for the products of those men and machines. He must have thought that, partially through his efforts in the 1930s, these problems had forever been resolved. Such is not the case, and it is somewhat ironical that as he enters his ninth decade he is still grappling with the same problem. In between, he has tackled an impressive range of subjects and brought to economics an impressive range of new tools, although it is again somewhat ironical that he may be remembered more as a toolmaker than the toolsetter he set out to be. He was fortunate in being in Cambridge in the 1930s when economics was in the melting pot, in the Cabinet Office in the 1940s when the rules of domestic and international policy were being rewritten, and in the LSE in the 1950s, when it was at the pinnacle of its prestige. Yet, if he was lucky to have the chances that came his way, he was able enough to make the most of them. His contribution to economics has been immense. The work he did at Cambridge in his youth alone would have been sufficient to place him in the forefront of British economics, and his work prior to 1947 was instrumental in securing the unrivaled decades of international and domestic prosperity which followed. Moreover, this work was achieved, as Herbert Giersch has commented, by combining rigorous reasoning with human kindness and fairness, embodied in a

scholar who is the prototype of an English gentleman.

JOHN HUDSON*

# Selected Bibliography

## WORKS BY MEADE

"The Amount of Money and the Banking System." *Economic Journal* 44 (March, 1934): 77–83.

*An Introduction to Economic Analysis and Policy.* London: Oxford University Press, 1936.

"A Simplified Model of Mr. Keynes' System." *Review of Economic Studies* 4 (February, 1937): 98–107.

*Planning and the Price Mechanism: the Liberal Socialist Solution.* London: George Allen & Unwin, 1948; New York; Macmillan, 1949.

*The Theory of International Economic Policy: I. The Balance of Payments.* London and New York: Oxford University Press, 1951.

*A Geometry of International Trade.* London: George Allen & Unwin, 1952, New York: A. Kelley, 1969.

*The Theory of International Economic Policy: II. Trade and Welfare.* London and New York: Oxford University Press, 1955.

*The Theory of Customs Unions.* Amsterdam: North-Holland, 1955.

*I would like to acknowledge the assistance of James Meade, Adrian Winnett and David Vines, who provided me with notes on Meade from his entry in the *New Palgrave Dictionary of Economics*. In this case it is particularly important to emphasize that the usual disclaimer applies. I also owe a large debt to Harry Johnson's earlier biography of Meade.

*A Neo-Classical Theory of Economic Growth.* London: George Allen & Unwin, 1961.

"Mauritius: A Case Study in Malthusian Economics." *Economic Journal* 71 (September, 1961): 521–34.

*Efficiency, Equality and the Ownership of Property.* London: George Allen & Unwin, 1964.

*Principles of Political Economy: I. The Stationary Economy.* London: George Allen & Unwin, 1965; Chicago; Aldine Press, 1965.

*Principles of Political Economy: II. The Growing Economy.* London: George Allen & Unwin, 1965; Chicago; University of Chicago Press, 1968.

*The Economic and Social Structure of Mauritius.* London: Cass, 1968.

*Principles of Political Economy: III. The Controlled Economy.* London: George Allen & Unwin, 1971.

"The Theory of Labour Managed Firms and Profit Sharing." *Economic Journal* 82 (March, 1972): 402–28.

*The Inheritance of Inequalities: Some Biological, Demographic, Social and Economic Factors.* London: Oxford University Press, 1974.

*Principles of Political Economy: IV. The Just Economy.* London: George Allen & Unwin, 1976.

*The Structure and Reform of Direct Taxation.* London: George Allen & Unwin, 1978.

*Alternative Systems of Business Organisation and of Workers' Remuneration.* London: George Allen & Unwin, 1986.

## OTHER WORKS

Fleming, J. M. "On Making the Best of Balance of Payments Restrictions on Imports," *The Economic Journal* 61 (March, 1951): 48–71.

Johnson, Harry G. "James Meade's Contribution to Economics." *Scandinavian Journal of Economics* 80 (March, 1978): 64–85.

Keynes, John Maynard. *A Treatise on Money.* London: Macmillan, 1930.

Keynes, John Maynard. *The General Theory of Employment, Interest and Money.* London: Macmillan, 1936.

Keynes, John Maynard. *How to Pay for the War.* London: Macmillan, 1940.

Pigou, A.. C. *The Economics of Welfare.* London: Macmillan, 1920.

# FRANCO MODIGLIANI   *1985*

In 1985 Franco Modigliani, a professor at the Massachusetts Institute of Technology, was the twenty-third recipient of the Nobel Prize in Economic Sciences. Born in June 1918 in Rome, Italy, Modigliani immigrated to the United States just before the outbreak of World War II and thus became the thirteenth American to win the prize. The Royal Swedish Academy of Sciences indicated that the award was in recognition of the professor's work on the construction and development of the life-cycle hypothesis of household saving and the formulation of the Modigliani-Miller theorem of the valuation of firms and of capital costs.

Modigliani is no doubt one of the great intellectuals of recent times. His contribution in the field of economics and his influence on public policies have been enormous. Ever since 1944, when he published a seminal article on the theory of interest and money, the economics profession has been almost continuously enjoying pathbreaking ideas or theories and procedures developed or improved by Modigliani. During the early 1950s, through a theoretical article that he coauthored, he provided a much-needed explanation for individual consumption behavior.

In the late 1950s the Modigliani-Miller theorem of cost of capital and firm valuation revolutionized the finance profession. Expounded in a classic paper in the *American Economic Review* (1958), along with another that the two coauthored in 1961, it provided strong analytical tools for financial problems and, indeed, created the modern field of corporate finance as we know it today.

It was during the late 1960s that the great controversy between "monetary economists" on one side and "Keynesian economists" on the other erupted with respect to the relative power of government fiscal and monetary policies. Modigliani was in the middle of this controversy; as a firm believer in Keynesian economics he fought to persuade people toward a sound mix of fiscal and monetary measures, which he insisted could create a more stable economy than a policy of passivity. Through his writings, testimony before congressional committees, and government consulting positions, he no doubt was instrumental in shaping government economic policies of the time.

## Early Career

As a youngster Franco Modigliani was brought up in a Jewish family in Rome. After finishing high school in Liceo Viscanti, he enrolled at the University of Rome to study medicine. His father was a good doctor, and young Franco thought he could easily become one, too. He soon discovered he was not cut out for medicine. He then studied law and went on to receive a law degree in 1939. While still a student at the University of Rome, he entered a national competition among university students by writing an essay on the subject of price control. The essay brought him first prize. In addition to the prize, though, the competition gave Modigliani something even more valuable—the direction to study economics. The judges who chose Modigliani for the prize advised him that he would make an excellent economist if he pursued the field.

In 1939, the year Modigliani married his wife, Serena, the couple decided to leave Italy, where the political ideology of the ruling Mussolini's fascist regime was in total disagreement with Modigliani's own liberal thinking. After a short stop in France, he arrived in the United States and quickly enrolled in the

New School for Social Research in New York. At this point in time the school was a refuge to all intellectuals fleeing the tyrant regimes of Europe. Its reputation earned it the nickname of "University in Exile."

There are always a few instrumental people in the lives of those who make a name for themselves in history, and Modigiliani's case was no exception. While at the New School for Social Research he had an economics teacher by the name of Jacob Marschak who, as Modigliani himself proudly confesses, took him in his hands and gave him a style. Marschak was truly both a great mentor and a dear friend to Modigliani. He taught Modigliani mainly macroeconomics, but perhaps the most important thing that Modigliani learned from him was research methodology. Marschak emphasized the importance of building testable hypotheses and, therefore, the importance of mathematics and statistics in economic analysis. The two would often meet each other outside the classroom and for hours discuss controversial economic issues. Sometimes the professor would even take the young student along with him to social get-togethers where Modigliani could meet and confer with the noted economists of the time.

In 1942, while Modigliani was still a graduate student, Marschak helped his friend get his first teaching job, at New Jersey College for Women. The job gave Modigliani the financial security that he needed to focus his attention on his studies and certainly helped him to secure his next teaching positions, with

Barnard College of Columbia University (1942–44) and New School for Social Research (1943–44).

In 1944 the New School for Social Research awarded Modigliani his doctorate in social science. Also in the same year, his first article, "Liquidity Preference and the Theory of Interest and Money," which was essentially the core of his doctoral dissertation, was published in the prestigious journal *Econometrica.*

The 1944 article was widely accepted by the profession and quickly became a classic work in Keynesian economics. The Great Depression of the early 1930s had puzzled economists all over the Western world. It seemed ironic that in spite of the availability of modern tools of production and massive unemployment no one would dare to embark on productive enterprises. The persistence of a high level of unemployment had prompted people to think that perhaps there was something fundamentally wrong with the capitalist system. Keynes's masterpiece, *The General Theory of Employment, Money and Interest* (1936), provided a rigorous and complete diagnosis of the unemployment plagued economy, along with some simple prognosis. According to him since the capitalist system was inherently unstable due to uncertainties and market frictions, in times of severe recession the government should intervene to stimulate the economy. The article by Modigliani was an attempt to iterate Keynes' arguments in the form of a mathematical model consisting of a set of simultaneous equations. In this way, the effects that a change in one variable has on the others could be precisely traced. His work quickly became a classic because it was one of the early attempts in building mathematical and, therefore, econometrically testable theories based on Keynes's book. After all, he was simply following Marschak's teachings of constructing testable hypotheses.

Modigliani's obsession with the construction of testable hypotheses and the empirical relevance of economic theories impelled him to accept a position with the Institute of World Affairs in 1945 in New York as research associate and chief statistician. A year later his application for U.S. citizenship was approved, and he became a naturalized American. He was with the Institute for three years, during which time he also taught at the New School for Social Research.

The year 1949 was the time to make a move. Modigliani could not pass up a joint appointment as a research consultant with the prestigious Cowles Commission for Research in Economics at the University of Chicago and associate professor with the University of Illinois, Chicago. A year later he was promoted to the rank of professor of economics by the University of Illinois, where he stayed until he moved back east to the Carnegie Institute of Technology in 1952. However, he continued his association with the Cowles Commission until 1954. By that time the professor had established himself as a research economist through several pathbreaking articles and one book (with Hans

Neisser), entitled, *National Incomes and International Trade* (1953). This work was an attempt to provide an econometric version of Keynesian theory in an open economy, with the aid of some sixty behavioral equations. The authors also painstakingly calculated the parameters of their model, using time-series data. It was one of the early econometric works of its kind.

In 1954 Modigliani published what was perhaps his most important contribution to the theory of consumption. Consumption spending is normally the biggest portion of the aggregate spending in any economy so it was only natural that Keynes had made individual consumption behavior the major building block of his general theory. He held that consumption is primarily dependent on current income. However, because of some "psychological law," the relationship is not proportional. In other words, as income changes by a given amount, consumption will change by less than the change in income. By the late 1940s, though, enough empirical evidence had been found to throw doubt on Keynes' version of consumer behavior. It was found, for example, that over long periods of time (50 to 100 years) there was, in fact, a proportional relationship between income and consumption, implying a constant ratio between the two variables. As a result, economists set out to build stronger consumption theories that would better fit the statistical realities.

Among the early pioneers in that endeavor were Modigliani and one of his students, Richard Brumberg. The product of their collaboration was the article "Utility Analysis and the Consumption Function: An Interpretation of Cross-Section Data," published in *Post-Keynesian Economics* (1954). Their theory received widespread recognition among scholars and was quickly given the name "life-cycle hypothesis of consumption." According to the theory, rational individuals would tend to maintain a normal level of consumption throughout their lives. Their income, on the other hand, starts from low levels at childhood, reaches a plateau at middle age, and declines thereafter. To maintain a smooth level of consumption throughout their lives individuals should, therefore, be dissaving at the early and later stages of life against the savings of the middle stage. This behavior would imply that the relationship between changes in current income and changes in current consumption is not proportional. Not every penny of an additional dollar of income would be spent; some would be saved. This conclusion was the same that Keynes had reached, but Modigliani and Brumberg explained it on the basis of logical economic assumptions rather than on the psychological law that Keynes claimed.

The other implication of the model is that the decision to consume in the current period has to do not only with the level of current income but also with future levels of income. Almost the whole lifetime income stream of a person is taken into account when deciding on current consumption. Since the present value of the future earnings

of a person is nothing but the person's stock of wealth (both human and physical), current consumption could also be said to depend upon the person's current wealth—something that the pure Keynesian consumption model did not explicitly take into account. This was an important feature of the new theory as it could explain the observed phenomenon that, unlike the short-run situation, over the long run the ratio of consumption to income is fairly constant. The reason for this is that over longer periods of time the increase in an individual's assets will increase the normal level of consumption so that it will offset the increase in income, thereby more or less holding the ratio of the two constant.

The Modigliani-Brumberg theory of consumption, as described in the original article, was a strong and sophisticated theory that had yet to undergo empirical tests. Unfortunately, the untimely death of Richard Brumberg in 1955 put a halt to the empirical exploration of the theory. It took a few years for Modigliani to get over the incident and start working on the theory again.

In the same year that the consumption theory was presented to the public, Modigliani also published the result of another brilliant collaboration. This time his partner was one of his colleagues at Carnegie Institute of Technology—Emile Grunberg. Their paper, entitled "The Predictability of Social Events," was published in the December 1954 issue of the *Journal of Political Economy*. It was about a subject whose time had not yet come—the impact that the announcement of the prediction of some social events by formal sources could have on the behavior of people and, therefore, on the actual event. At the time the idea did not receive much attention. However, some twenty years later it was recognized as one of the original works on the controversial issue of "rational expectations" and macroeconomic policy. The big issue was whether the public develops rational expectations and correctly anticipates changes in government fiscal and monetary policies. If this does happen, it could result in weakening or sometimes defeating the policies. The economics profession was divided upon the issue and, ironically, Modigliani found himself as the main spokesman of the camp that would play down the importance of rational expectations for macroeconomic policies.

Starting in 1955, the year that Modigliani became associated with the Department of Economics and Industrial Management of the Carnegie Institute of Technology, his interest more or less focused on the economics of firms, as many of his colleagues at the institute were involved in research in this area. Looking at the impressive record of Modigliani's contributions, one cannot escape the fact that most of his research was done in collaboration with his colleagues, which says something about the traits of the man. He was not only likable and easy to work with but was of such research caliber that he could augment his associates' productivity.

The field of business economics as we know it today was nonexistent at the time. It was, to a great extent, related to institutional and legal problems, and much was needed to be done in terms of rigorous economic analysis. In 1955 alone, three papers on different aspects of firm operation were coauthored by Modigliani. It was also during this busy year that the professor took a sabbatical and spent time as a Fulbright lecturer at the universities of Rome and Palermo.

A year later he edited a book entitled *Problems of Capital Formation: Concepts, Measurement, and Controlling Factors.* This work was actually the proceedings of a conference as attended by many wellknown economists. The articles in the volume centered around two subjects. One was the problem of accurately measuring a nation's capital stock, and the other was related to the exact nature of relationships among business investment, its determinants, and business cycles. Modigliani contributed one paper: "Business Reasons for Holding Inventories and Their Macro-Economic Implications." The volume was viewed by a reviewer as "an interesting blend of theory, quantitative testing, and studies in the nature of basic sources of data."

# The Modigliani-Miller Papers

His masterpiece on the theory of business finance, however, came while Modigliani was a visiting professor of economics at Harvard University during 1957–58. This time he teamed up with Professor Merton Miller in publishing "The Cost of Capital, Corporation Finance and the Theory of Investment," in the *American Economic Review* (1958). The theory presented in the paper was so novel and revolutionary that it shocked the profession, initiating such controversy among scholars and practitioners that still, after thirty years, its heat has not subsided. The "Modigliani-Miller Theorem," although presented in a rigorous manner, was a simple one: In a world of no taxes and perfect financial markets, the average cost of capital for a corporation is independent of its capital structure.

Traditionally, however, it was believed that as a corporation increases the borrowed portion of its total capital it will face an increase in the cost of financing the additional amount of capital. In other words, as the corporate debt increases, the investors will require a higher rate of return in order to provide additional funds to the corporation, the reason being that increased debt is perceived by the investors as an increase in the level of bankruptcy risk. Modigliani and Miller, on the other hand, argued that investors generally hold a portfolio of diverse financial assets ranging from low-risk government bonds to highly risky common stocks. The relevant investment risk to them is the average risk associated with their portfolio rather than the riskiness of each individual asset. Investors can always hedge against the increased riskiness of a certain com-

pany by simply including a greater amount of low-risk assets such as government bonds in their portfolio.

The "Modigliani-Miller Theorem" was valid and sound as long as the assumptions upon which it was built were correct. Most of the ensuing debate about the theorem was related to the significance of the proposed assumptions and the empirical relevance of the theory. Over the next several years a number of supplementary articles on the subject were published by the two professors in the hope of clarifying their position and settling disputes. But the consensus was clear: It was time for economists to treat the economics of the firm more seriously and look for some rigorous analytical tools. Modigliani and Miller's theorem was only a beginning.

The *Journal of Business* gave special recognition to Modigliani and Miller for a second theoretical paper they wrote. One of the most prestigious journals in the field of finance, it honored them with the award of "best contribution of the year" for the paper "Dividend Policy, Growth, and the Valuation of Shares" (1961). Again, this paper was an attempt at laying business finance on a sound theoretical foundation. The subject this time was the dividend policy of corporations and whether or not it has any impact on the share valuation. The paper's conclusion was that, contrary to customary belief, corporate dividend policy—that is, the amount taken out of total earnings for distribution—should not have any impact on the valuation of the stock of the

company. In other words, two corporations similar in every aspect but
their dividend-payout ratios must
command the same market value.

This conclusion was rigorously
arrived at by the authors through a
set of assumptions about the financial market, for example, the existence of perfect markets and nonex-
istence of taxes. The core of the
theory was that the price per share is
a function of the future stream of
income expected from the ownership of a share. However, the income stream could either be in the
form of dividends received earlier,
or in the form of capital gains
accrued to the owner if income were
retained in the company. As with
the first paper on the cost of capital,
this one, too, caused a flood of new
literature on the subject, both theoretical and empirical. On theoretical
grounds the major criticism leveled
against the theory was that, since
capital gains are to be received at
future dates, they entail a great degree of riskiness and uncertainty to
investors. As a result, price per share
of the companies with a high rate of
retention should be lower relatively
than that of the companies with a
high dividend-payout ratio.

To this Modigliani and Miller
cleverly responded that investors
normally reinvest the dividend
earned from their own company in
other companies and could, therefore, expose themselves to the same
kind of risk involved in the reinvest-
ing of dividends in their own company. On empirical grounds, the assumption of no taxes became a
center of controversy. Some economists argued that since the income-

tax rate on capital gains is lower
than that on dividends, the decision
to retain a higher portion of corporate income and produce more capital gains should mean higher after-
tax return to investors. In that case
the price per share of the companies
whose dividend-payout ratios are
lower than the others would be
traded at relatively higher prices. A
great deal of empirical research was
done in order to settle the issue, with
no success. However, with the 1986
tax-law revision, it seems that the
Modigliani and Miller position is
stronger than ever.

Although the two papers discussed above were directly concerned with business economics,
they produced a very important macroeconomic implication. In his
*General Theory* Keynes had given
special attention to the business sector as the main engine of the economy, responsible for investment and
growth. He went to great lengths to
prove that the most important factor in investment decisions is the
business outlook. A more scientific
version of business outlook involves, of course, the degree of uncertainty or riskiness attached to future expected profits. Being a
lifetime ardent disciple of Keynes,
Modigliani has always been engaged
in either clarifying or strengthening
Keynes's arguments. The macroeconomic message of the two papers
discussed above was that the market
value of the firm is determined
solely by capitalization of its expected stream of income at a rate
which differs from the riskless rate
(rate on short-term Treasury bills)
only by a risk premium reflecting

the riskiness of the firm. Other things equal, the greater the risk, the lower the market value of the business. Therefore, policies aimed at reducing the interest rate will not necessarily cause expansion of investment and business so long as the business outlook (business risk) is such that investors are wary of making strong commitments.

At the time that Modigliani published his article on dividend policy, he was on a one-year assignment as visiting professor of economics at the Massachusetts Institute of Technology (MIT). After spending the next year at Northwestern University, he returned to MIT in 1962 to begin an uninterrupted tenure to date. Perhaps the most important element in Modigliani's decision to stay at MIT was that he found himself at ease among the other economics faculty members, mostly mainstream economists. This type of economist is more or less in agreement with the basic tenets of Keynesian economics, is involved in the study of basic economic behavior, along with the institutions that underlie the functioning of the whole economy, and is concerned with research methodology. Judging by all the contributions he has made to economic literature one has to conclude that Modigliani himself is a mainstream economist. He is a Keynesian who has researched consumer behavior and firms. He has also done much in terms of econometric analysis of economic statistics. The same year that he returned to MIT, he was elected president of the Econometric Society, of which he was a long-time member.

# Keynesians and Monetarists

Modigliani's first article while at MIT was, in effect, a review of his first article, written back in 1944. Within a time period of nineteen years, every one of the building blocks of Keynesian theory had undergone revision or improvement: the consumption function, the demand-for-money equation, and investment theory. Further, much more had been learned about the overall functioning of the economy. As Modigliani notes, "the paper traces the major developments of lasting value in our understanding of the monetary mechanism and its role in the economy which have occurred since the early forties, when the process of digesting *The General Theory* and integrating it with the earlier streams of thinking had been more or less completed" (1963, p. 79). In addition to this paper, two more noteworthy papers were published during Modigliani's beginning year at MIT. One was "The 'Life Cycle' Hypothesis of Saving: Aggregate Implications and Tests," which he wrote with his colleague, Professor Albert Ando, who eventually became Modigliani's most frequent collaborator.

Like a true scholar, Modigliani was always the first to review his own works. Sometimes the review was in the form of empirical testing of an old theory, as in the case of the paper with Ando. Other times, the review would take the form of an improvement or even a correction. Of this type was "Corporate Income Taxes and the Cost of Capital: A

Correction" 1963), written with Merton Miller. One of the assumptions upon which the original work on the cost of capital was based was the assumption of "no taxes." However, it was evident that the U.S. tax system was definitely favorable to corporate borrowing, as corporate interest charges are tax deductible. In order to make a viable theory, this second paper was devoted to a discussion of the impact of taxes on the cost of capital. The conclusion reached this time was that if debt is substituted for equity, the average after-tax cost of capital will not stay constant. Rather, it will continuously decrease. Suddenly, the business world had all the theoretical support it needed to expand its borrowing. Indeed, the explosion of debt financing during the 1960s and 1970s was phenomenal, and the trend continues today.

The following year, 1964, marks the beginning of Modigliani's involvement in public policy, since he was called upon by the Treasury Department to work as a consultant. This was a golden opportunity for the professor not only to influence the economic decision making of the country but also to learn about the technical and political aspects of running the economy. In 1966 he was also invited by the board of governors of the Federal Reserve to act as their academic consultant.

Modigliani now had one hand in the fiscal policies and the other in the monetary policies of the U.S. economy. Ironically, however, at this time it was becoming fashionable among economists to recognize themselves, more or less, as either

monetarists or fiscalists, not both. But being a true scholar in the pursuit of real truth, Modigliani could not pass up any opportunity that would help him understand the world better. He definitely was not a dogmatic scientist. He never forgot the lesson of his teacher, Jacob Marschak, that building a theory is only the beginning; the theory should withstand the criterion of reality. Perhaps it was because of this special trait that in May 1968 the Joint Economic Committee of Congress summoned Modigliani to testify on standards for guiding monetary action. At the time there was great concern over the rate of inflation, and Congress was studying different viewpoints on how to check the upward trend in the price level. On one extreme there were views that a new mix of monetary and fiscal measures should be chosen, and on the other there was the new idea that discretionary monetary policy should be permanently replaced by a monetary rule.

Proponents of the monetary rule were the economists who belonged to an emerging school of thought in economics considered by many as Keynesian counterrevolutionary. That school of thought, now widely known as monetarism, had its roots in pre-Keynesian economic thought, or the classical economics which became the subject of Keynes's harsh criticism. Classical economists believed that the economy had a general tendency towards stability and full employment without government intervention.

As to the state of the economy in 1968, the monetarist position was that the ongoing inflation was the result of an irresponsible explosion of the money supply at a time when the economy was near full capacity. Therefore, since money was such an important economic stimulus and since it is hard to pinpoint the exact amount and timing of a monetary change, and above all since the economy has an inherent capability to adjust itself toward full employment with stable prices, there is no need for discretionary monetary policy; the Congress should legislate a fixed and permanent rate of growth for the money supply commensurate with the rate of growth of the economy.

The monetarist position was fiercely challenged by the economists who were sympathetic to Keynes. Their major argument was that Keynesian economics had produced almost three decades of prosperity. Besides, if some policy makers are not trained to find the exact amount and timing of a monetary change, that should not be treated as a weakness of Keynesian theory. It was this kind of schism among the economists in the face of a rising inflation that prompted the 1968 congressional hearing on standards for guiding monetary policy.

Judging by the Federal Reserve's monetary policy in the immediate years following the hearing it is safe to say that Modigliani's testimony had indeed impressed the lawmakers. Right at the beginning of his testimony, he set the record straight by saying that he hoped the hearings would "persuade the committee of the undesirability of imposing any precise rules of behavior on the Federal Reserve, particularly rules taking the form of a stated rate of increase in money supply" (1968, p. 8). When he was asked by Senator Everett Jordan of North Carolina as to the most prudent policy to relieve inflationary pressure, he put forward a contractionary fiscal package consisting of cuts in government expenditures accompanied by a permanent increase in taxes.

Modigliani did not testify before Congress again until 1971. Like many other Americans, the professor thought the Vietnam War was a horrible tragedy that should end immediately. As a sign of protest, he turned down every request by Congress to appear on economic matters. Meanwhile, he was quite busy with a new project—econometric simulation of the U.S. economy.

The development of powerful computers in the mid-1960s made it possible to do tremendous amounts of calculations within seconds. For empirical economists, this development was like manna from heaven, as they could now easily calculate the coefficients of their econometric models. It was time for Modigliani to do the ultimate in utilizing the new technology. He, Albert Ando, Frank deLeuw, and a few others began the construction of a large-scale econometric model which came to be known as the Federal Reserve-MIT-University-of-Pennsylvania (FMP) Econometric Model. It was basically a computer program that would simulate the functioning of the economy. It was now possible to gauge with precision the effect of monetary or fiscal policies on every aspect of the economy—something that the advocates of both policies badly needed to counter the ever-increasing strength of monetarists' arguments.

The economic situation in 1971 was not as favorable as during the preceding decade. Unemployment was hovering around 7 percent, while inflation was at an annual rate of 4 percent; both rates were unacceptable by the standards of the time. Moreover, it was widely believed that higher rates of inflation should accompany lower unemployment, as recent history had shown. The economic realities of 1971 just did not make sense to people. Appearing before the Joint Economic Committee, Modigliani blamed these conditions on the misguided economic policies of the Nixon administration. In his testimony he criticized the administration for giving up hopes on unemployment rates of lower than 6 percent. According to him, the Federal Reserve should have increased the money supply at a rate of at least 12 percent a year if a lower unemployment rate was to be achieved. On the other hand, he maintained, inflation could be curbed by a fiscal program of restraining price increases.

These recommendations were in contradiction to those given by monetary economists present at the hearings. The monetarists maintained their old argument that the government should become as neutral as possible in the economic affairs of the country. Accordingly, they suggested a much lower rate of growth of money supply in order to dampen inflation pressure. For the unemployment problem, they argued that only improvement in the supply side of the economy can provide more jobs. That meant improvement in the quality of labor force, the condition of business and trade, and generally improvements in the entrepreneurial climate. In other words, as long as the business and the economic institutions were the way they were, the 6 percent rate was a "natural" outcome.

Of course, the congressional hearings were not the only place where the monetarists and Keynesians would come to clash. Most of the macroeconomic literature of the early 1970s was occupied by papers, comments, replies, and rebuttals written by the two sides in trying to convince, criticize, or even ridicule each other. The great challenger on the monetary side was Milton Friedman of the University of Chicago, while the Keynesian side was spearheaded by Modigliani. The two used every occasion to attack the other's position.

The policies that were actually implemented over the next few years were more or less in line with those recommended by Modigliani. In spite of this, the inflation rate kept its upward trend, with no real relief on the unemployment side. By 1976 it was evident, at least in academia, that the unemployment problem was too complicated to be solved by the traditional demand-oriented policies of the government, which only supplied fuel for inflation to continue to ascend. Suddenly, the monetarist position was under the spotlight.

Friedman was awarded the Nobel Prize in Economics in 1976.

In the same year, Professor Modigliani was elected president of the American Economic Association. For his inauguration reception, the professor made sure that his old friend and mentor, Jacob Marschak, was present. The old teacher must have felt very proud of his student when he gave his presidential address, which was of a kind that only a real scholar in pursuit of truth could give. It was expectedly concerned with the great question of the time—"the monetarist controversy or, should we forsake stabilization policies?" The following excerpt from his speech reveals what he thought the answer should be:

The monetarists have made a valid and most valuable contribution in establishing that our economy is far less unstable than the early Keynesians pictured it. . . . they are wrong, however, in going as far as asserting that the economy is sufficiently shockproof that stabilization policies are not needed. They have also made an important contribution in pointing out that such policies might in fact, prove destabilizing. The criticism has had a salutory effect on reassessing what stabilization policies can and should do, and on trimming down fine-tuning ambitions. (1977, p. 17)

Obviously, Modigliani had recognized the contribution the monetarists had made to the understanding of economic problems. But it would take some time before the public, and especially the policy makers, fully appreciated those ideas.

By the late 1970s a new economic terminology, stagflation, was coined. It referred to a situation where economic stagnation was being accompanied by high levels of inflation: a one-word description of the U.S. economy during the Carter administration. The expansionary monetary policies of the previous administrations, combined with the ever-increasing cost of energy, had set off an inflationary spiral unprecedented in the history of the country. Naturally the most important question on the mind of every economist during those times was how to simultaneously curb inflation and maintain full employment. One thing, however, was becoming very clear— that the discretionary monetary and fiscal policies of the government had lost their alleged magic and could no longer provide quick answers to the questions at hand. Indeed, a group of monetary economists, calling themselves "rational expectationists," revived a rather old idea in their criticism of the government's "fine-tuning" of the economy. Ironically, the idea's origin went back to one of the early articles coauthored by Modigliani—"The Predictability of Social Events," in the *Journal of Political Economy* (1954). According to the rational expectationists, people are very rational in their economic decision-making—so rational that they could even predict the duration of a temporary monetary or fiscal policy and therefore temporarily change their own behavior. As a result, they would defeat the very purpose of such policies, which is to permanently change certain economic variables.

In 1979, Modigliani was given the Graham and Dodd Award by

the Financial Analysts Federation for the outstanding article of the year. This article, which he coauthored with Richard Cohn, was "Inflation, Rational Valuation and the Market." It concerned itself with the low performance of the stock market during the inflationary period of the early 1960s through the late 1970s. The market's performance during this time was far from echoing the common belief that stocks are a good hedge against inflation. The authors' hypothesis, a startling one considering the frame of mind ruling the economics profession during the late 1970s, was that stock market investors, as a whole, had been "irrationally" undervaluing their holdings by one half. More specifically, the authors were able to prove that investors had incorrectly double-adjusted the flow of expected nominal dividends for the inflation effect in their calculations of stock prices. This article was an example of the type that Modigliani published in the late 1970s and early 1980s in an effort to challenge the dogma of rational expectations in general, and the validity of their proposed policies of passivity in particular.

The beginning of the new decade coincided with the start of a new administration in the country. The runaway inflation of the earlier years, along with high rates of unemployment, had convinced almost everyone that it was time to try a different approach to the solution of economic problems. The economic platform upon which President Reagan was elected to office was quite revolutionary, given the standards of the time. Its call for minimal intervention of government in the market system would mean a swift reversal of four decades of active involvement of government in the management of the nation's economic affairs. Indeed, most of the policies that were later implemented by the new administration were in line with its agenda and were of the type that the monetary economists had been proposing for years.

When in 1985 the Royal Swedish Academy granted the Nobel Prize in Economic Sciences to Modigliani, the timing was perfect. After five years of laissez-faire economic policies, America was still in an economic crisis. For the first time in U.S. history the federal budget deficit had passed the $1 trillion mark, the trade deficit was the highest ever, the degree of income inequality was on an upward trend, and yet the dream of full employment and stable prices was far from being realized. The granting of the prize was, in a sense, a signal by the scientific world that Modigliani's ideology as to the practicality of economic management was still valid.

MOJTABA SEYEDIAN

# Selected Bibliography

WORKS BY MODIGLIANI

"Liquidity Preference and the Theory of Interest and Money." *Econometrica* 12 (1944): 45–88.

*Problems of Capital Formation: Concepts, Measurements and Control-*

*ling Factors.* Princeton, N.J.: Princeton University Press, 1956.

"The Monetary Mechanism and its Introduction with real Phenomena." *Review of Economics and Statistics* 45 (1963): 79–107.

"Standards for Guiding Monetary Action." In *Hearings Before the Joint Economic Committee, Congress of The United States* (May 1968), 8–13, 50–76. Washington, D.C.: Government Printing Office, 1968.

"The 1971 Mid-year Review of the Economy." In *Hearings Before the Joint Economic Committee, Congress of The United States* (July 1971), 111–27. Washington, D.C.: Government Printing Office, 1971.

"The 1974 Economic Report of the President. In *Hearings Before the Joint Economic Committee, Congress of The United States* (February 1974), 643–76. Washington, D.C.: Government Printing Office, 1974.

"The Monetarist Controversy or, Should we Forsake Stabilization Policies?" *American Economic Review* 67 (1977): 1–19.

*The Collected Papers of Franco Modigliani.* Edited by Andrew Abel. 3 vols. Cambridge, Ma.: MIT Press, 1980.

*The Debate Over Stabilization Policy.* Cambridge: Cambridge University Press, 1986.

Modigliani, Franco, and Ando, Albert K. "The 'Life Cycle' Hypothesis of Saving: Aggregate Implications and Tests." *American Economic Review* 53 (1963): 55–84.

Modigliani, Franco, and Brumberg, Richard. "Utility Analysis and the Consumption Function: An Interpretation of Cross-Section Data." In *Post-Keynesian Economics,* edited by K. K. Kurihara, pp. 388–436. New Brunswick, N.J.: Rutgers University Press, 1954.

Modigliani, Franco, and Cohn, Richard. "Inflation, Rational Valuation and the Market." *Financial Analysts Journal* 35 (March/April 1979): 24–44.

Modigliani, Franco, and Grunberg, Emile. "The Predictability of Social Events." *Journal of Political Economy* 62 (1954): 465–78.

Modigliani, Franco, and Miller, Merton. "The Cost of Capital, Corporation Finance and the Theory of Investment." *American Economic Review* 48 (1958): 261–97.

———. "Dividend Policy, Growth, and the Valuation of Shares." *Journal of Business* 34 (1961): 411–33.

———. "Corporate Income Taxes and the Cost of Capital: A Correction." *American Economic Review* 53 (1963): 433–43.

Modigliani, Franco, and Neisser, Hans. *National Incomes and International Trade.* Urbana, Il.: University of Illinois Press, 1953.

# GUNNAR MYRDAL   *1974*

Karl Gunnar Myrdal, the 1974 recipient of the Nobel Prize in Economic Sciences, was born on December 6, 1898, in Gustafs, Sweden. He was the son of Karl Adolf and Sofia (Carlson) Myrdal. On October 8, 1924 he married Alva Reimer, and they had three children—Jan, Sissela, and Kaj. His education included a law degree from the University of Stockholm in 1923 and a Ph.D. degree in economics, also from the University of Stockholm, in 1927. Myrdal died on May 17, 1987, in Stockholm, at the age of eighty-eight.

Upon graduating with his degree in economics, Myrdal accepted a teaching position in economics at the University of Stockholm. He applied for and received a Rockefeller fellowship for study in the United States, 1929–30. A good deal of his time was spent in traveling through the United States. It was a year of great upheaval in the United States as the stock market had crashed in October, the month that he arrived in New York City. The year 1930–31 was spent in Switzerland, where he served as an associate professor at the Post-Graduate Institute of International Studies in Geneva. The following year he returned to the University of Stockholm as an acting professor, and in 1933 he became the Laras Hierta Professor of Political Economy and Financial Science.

During the decade of the 1930s, Myrdal became both more politi-cally and policy oriented. He was appointed to the Swedish government's new housing and population commission, where he was able to exercise considerable influence with respect to both public housing and population policies. Moreover, he was a Social Democratic member of the Swedish Senate and served as a deputy member of the Board of the National Bank of Sweden. In 1938, he made another visit to the United States to lecture at Harvard University on the problems of population and its growth in a democratic society. It was during this visit that he accepted the invitation of the Carnegie Corporation to do a study of racial problems in American society.

This research activity resulted in a major publication in 1944—*An American Dilemma: The Negro Problem and Modern Democracy.* During the early part of the decade of the 1940s, Myrdal was back in Sweden, since World War II had begun. He was not without a position of policy influence, serving on the commission that had the responsibility of drawing up a new government budgetary system, based on some ability to predict future production and incomes. Although he made several trips to the United States during the war, he continued to serve on the faculty at Stockholm University in a teaching position. In the second half of the decade, he held an additional policy position, serving as minister of commerce from 1945 to 1947. His resignation from the ministerial post came about so that he could accept still another policy position, this time as executive secretary of the United Nations's Economic Commission for Europe, 1947–57.

Myrdal first visited Southeast Asia during the decade of the 1950s. Another visit was made there in 1955, during the period in which his wife was serving as Swedish ambassador to India. These trips exposed him to the enormous developmental problems of the region. Once he had completed his term as executive secretary of the Economic Commission for Europe, he began research work on the backwardness of this region. This project was not finished and published until the end of the 1960s as *Asian Drama: An Inquiry into the Poverty of Nations* (1968). In 1967, Myrdal was back in Sweden, occupying a professorship at the Institute for International Economic Studies, University of Stockholm. However, he resigned from that position in the same year. He was sixty-eight years old.

Myrdal continued professionally active in the 1970s and into the 1980s. It was while he was teaching at the Graduate Center of the City University of New York in 1974 that he was informed that he was to receive the Nobel Prize in Economics, to be shared with Friedrich von Hayek. Certainly, this was an interesting juxtaposition of recipients because of the extreme differences in their economic philosophies, their research interests, and their professional activities. Von Hayek, after all, was a firm believer in the efficiency of market forces with min-

imal restraint or intervention, while Myrdal had a firm commitment to planning and to what he liked to believe was rationalized intervention. Moreover, Myrdal, while not the first recipient to have an interest in the development of the Third World—Simon Kuznets was the 1971 recipient—was the first outside of the economics mainstream so engaged. (This was to make it easier, subsequently, for Sir Arthur W. Lewis from the West Indies to receive the award in 1979.)

# Political Economy and Economics

The field of economics started out as political economy—a concern for and a belief in economic policy formulation that was, after all, the area of the classical school. As the field developed, becoming more quantitative and abstract, it also became more objective and positivist. Political economy, as such, seemed appropriately better relegated to a separate field. This field, and its practitioners as well, came to be viewed as definitely less important and less precise than what came to be the mainstream of economics. It appears that Gunnar Myrdal was one of those rarities to the profession who, for most of his professional life, never made a distinction between economics and political economy. On the contrary, from his later writings it can be inferred that he came to believe such a distinction was impossible.

That the distinction was impossible was not a view which he had always held but rather one at which he arrived over the years. For example, in one of his earliest publications—certainly his first major one—*The Political Element in the Development of Economic Theory* (1928), in Swedish, he criticized the profession, in general, and Knut Wicksell, in particular, for failing to keep value systems separate from theory. However, when one looks at the preface to the English edition of 1953, some twenty-five years later, he appears to have concluded that he was mistaken. Quoting from that preface, Myrdal argues that:

This implicit belief in the existence of a body of scientific knowledge acquired independently of all valuations is, as I now see it, naive empiricism. Facts do not organize themselves into concepts and theories just by being looked at; indeed, except within the framework of concepts and theories, there are no scientific facts but only chaos. There is an inescapable a priori element in all scientific work. Questions must be asked before answers can be given. The questions are an expression of our interest in the world, they are bottom valuations. Valuations are thus necessarily involved already at the stage when we observe facts and carry on theoretical analysis, and not only at the stage when we draw political inferences from facts and valuations.

At the outset of his career, however, Myrdal defined the task of economics as to observe and describe empirical social reality and to analyze and explain causal relationships between economic facts. Myrdal pointed out that in observing and describing one should not be concerned with the desirability of the relationships nor the future which might be predictable from them. This nature and scope of economics contrasts with political economics in that politics involves the desire for the preservation of the actual state of society or its change in various ways and directions. Either preservation or change implies, of course, a basis on a set of social values. Myrdal argued that by contrast economics, if it is to be scientific, must be kept free of values.

While these conclusions suggest a strong divergence between the two fields, they are not substitutes for each other but, in fact, complements. Economics as a science whose tools are devoid of value judgments can help provide an objective or positive description of social conditions. Furthermore, once the political economist has arrived at a set of objectives based upon a particular value system, the economist can evaluate the likelihood and the cost of the policies to be implemented in order to achieve the desired objectives. Myrdal's argument, therefore, was that the relationship between the two fields of study is not one of inferior/superior or better/worse but rather of working together. His opinion notwithstanding, the mainstream position is that the field of political economy is less precise and less important.

As economics developed, two doctrines were paramount—utilitarianism and natural law. The former includes the neoclassical extension of marginal utility and the latter the notion of the general welfare. The

classical economists used these doctrines as a basis for their political
judgments. It was their contention
that only in the natural state of equilibrium could individual utility and
social welfare be maximized. Myrdal considered these two doctrines
to be the most prominent ones in the
history of economic thought. They
represented the biases of their adherents, even if not necessarily the
biases of society. These doctrines
were used to derive moral and political norms, giving these norms the
objective validity with which to formulate ideal political conditions and
to criticize the current social order.
As biases, they are values and, therefore, subjective rather than objective.

The natural-law philosophy
claimed that there was a natural
state of the economy, an equilibrium. This natural-law equilibrium
provides a kind of norm for economic policy formulation, since policy recommendations should recognize and strive for this natural state
of equilibrium. It follows from this
view that a most important law of
political economy is that less intervention is preferable to more intervention.

The utilitarian philosophy paralleled and reinforced this tendency
towards a natural-state equilibrium.
The emphasis, however, was on the
objective outcome of the actions
taken rather than on their deviation
from the natural state. The outcomes, since they are observable, are
objective. Consequently, these outcomes should be evaluated in terms
of their contribution to the benefit
of all of society. The community in-

terest, the benefit to all of society,
was defined as the arithmetic sum of
all individual benefits.

Myrdal has criticized both the
philosophy of natural law and that
of utilitarianism as being highly subjective, if not necessarily vague. Economic philosophers use these and
other value-laden systems as a basis
for their rationalizations without
specifying these value systems. This
gives to their arguments the appearance of being objective and absolute, when in fact they are neither.
Disagreements arise among economists because of the differences in
their value systems. Obviously, these
conflicts would not arise if all values
were shared. However, the unanimity of interests is something that has
to be proven and not merely asserted. In this context, Myrdal suggests that the main task of economics applied to the issues of social
choice (public policy) should be

> to examine and unravel the complex
> interplay of interests, as they some-
> times converge, sometimes conflict,
> . . . It would be of great practical im-
> portance to reconstruct precisely the
> social field of interests. In the first
> place, we should want to know where
> interests converge, for in these cases
> we could make at once generally
> valid recommendations. We should
> also want to ascertain where lines of
> interest intersect. In these cases we
> could offer alternative solutions, each
> one corresponding to some special in-
> terest. Both types of solutions can
> claim objectivity, not because they
> express objective political norms, but
> because they follow from explicitly
> stated value premises which corre-

spond to real interests. The solutions are of practical interest to the extent to which their value premises are relevant to political controversies, i.e., insofar as they represent the interests of sufficiently powerful social groups. (1953, p. 193)

Myrdal's primary concern in this work was to show that economic analysis is too often vague because value judgments are incorporated into the analysis without those values being explicitly stated. Frequently, these values are in conflict with one another, thereby vitiating the analysis. From Myrdal's point of view, a common error made by most economic philosophers is that their rationalization of the values in their analyses made the analyses appear objective and, therefore, correct, when in fact they were only subjective.

What Myrdal attempted in this work was a redefinition of political economy so as to reconstruct the field of economic interests, which he called the technology of economics. In essence, he was calling for a complete change in the nature and scope of economic analysis. Instead of trying to trace the evolution of prices, incomes, output, etc., he argued that economic theory should concern itself with those interferences which serve the interests of particular groups. He pointed out that in doing this one must not take the prevailing institutional arrangements as a given; to do so would mean to perform analysis based upon a set of interests or values not in harmony. On the other hand, studying the diverse interests as part of the analysis would

make it possible to treat the institutional arrangements as another endogenous, rather than exogenous, variable. In this way it would become possible to discover the relative strengths of the various groups in effecting institutional changes as well as to discover the importance of these relative strengths in price determination and in income distribution.

## Rationalizing Economic Policy

Some twenty-nine years later, in 1957, Myrdal had refined his thinking on the relative strengths of the various interest groups and their impact on price determination to the point that he believed it possible to harmonize their differences through the use of a national plan for economic growth. In *Rich Lands and Poor* (1957), Myrdal argued that "The action part of a national plan consists of nothing else than a system of interferences with the price system, which must be judged in terms of the practical contribution which they make toward the cumulative upward process which is the goal of the plan."

Interestingly enough, Myrdal points out that institutional changes are not necessarily systematic. Moreover, he argues that it is probably incorrect to view the socio-economic environment as a unified and consistent system. It should be possible, according to Myrdal's reasoning, to bring about institutional changes in such a way as to alter social factors by degrees without transforming the environment into something completely different.

Thirty-two years after his first major publication, Myrdal used this argument to criticize the United States and praise his native Sweden. In *Beyond the Welfare State* (1960) Myrdal points out that the essential difference between Sweden and the United States is not that one is a welfare state and that the other is not but that one, Sweden, recognizes it is a welfare state and rationalizes its interventions while the other, the United States, does not recognize it is a welfare state and, therefore, does not rationalize its interventions. It should be possible, following his argument, to harmonize our own interventions without a complete change in our institutional arrangements. The resistance of the United States and other Western societies to doing so is because of their belief in the value judgment in favor of individual contracts individually arrived at. This belief has to be viewed as an extension of the idea of a liberal or laissez-faire economy. Myrdal believed that the changes required to rationalize interventions are only marginal. This notion of marginality is reflected in the following quote from this work:

Generally, as levels of living and education rise, and as people's participation in the affairs of the national community through the regular political processes and through all the organizations within the institutional infrastructure increases, we may approach a situation where many important public policies can be put into effect without much direct state intervention in the ordinary sense, and particularly without necessitat-

ing more than a minimum of state administration, simply by activating, as a means of communal control, the pressure of enlightened public opinion, and the bargaining strength of the organizations. (p. 89)

## Third World Problems

In 1968, Myrdal published not his last, but his last major work, just six years before being awarded the Nobel Prize in Economics. This work was *Asian Drama: An Inquiry into the Poverty of Nations.* Not only its nature and scope, but even its title reflect its debt to the concerns of the classical economists in general and to Adam Smith in particular. Naturally, it has none of the philosophical superstructure of that school, that is, neither a labor theory of value nor a stationary state. In *Asian Drama* we have an excellent example of a modern political economist writing about the problems of the economic development of a geographical region.

In the years which had passed since the publication of Myrdal's first major work, he found that not only had political economy become more quantitative and precise, and therefore, in the eyes of mainstream economists, objective and positivist, but that it also increasingly reflected the norms and the concerns of Western industrial societies as well. While these qualities might well be appropriate for studying the problems of economic growth in industrial societies, they hardly could be applied to the study and the analysis of the problems of the development of the countries of the Third World, in particular, those of Asia. Even the use of, or the effort to, measure such standard economic aggregates as gross national product, real per-capita gross domestic product, savings, investment, and incremental capital/output ratios would be inappropriate not merely because of the lack of acceptable data but also because they are units of measure which originated in a culture with attitudes and institutions completely different from those of the less developed nations. The whole system of national-income accounting arises out of a culture geared to consuming and to producing, and therefore, inclined to a system for measuring what is produced and by which groups it is consumed. Myrdal would hasten to add that the use of such statistical concepts in a culture differently inclined gives the appearance of knowledge without, in fact, any substance.

Even though this position is neither unique to Myrdal nor one of his contributions to economics, it is a quite logical extension of his 1928 attack on the values of the profession, that is, the natural state and utilitarianism. If these two concepts are culturally biased, and to be recognized as such, then the elegant system of quantifying economic activity arising out of the industrial West is also culturally biased and should be recognized, therefore, as inapplicable to Third World problems. He goes so far as to reject the standard definition of economic growth as a sustained increase in real per-capita income. Instead he argues that the entire economic

system deals with changes in a number of areas at the same time: output and incomes, the conditions of production, the levels of living, attitudes toward life and work, the institutions of society, and the political economy. These are all interrelated through a process of upward circular causation, a process which Myrdal described as early as 1928 and which he continued to use.

But the use of this concept of upward circular causation does not mean that a society is always progressing. In this respect Myrdal is pessimistic about the development of Third World countries in Asia. His examination of the data—what he criticized as knowledge without substance—shows that the living standards of large portions of the populations were either lower than before World War II or not substantially higher. This lack of development can be explained by the kinds of rigid institutions prevalent in the region and their inefficiency resulting from their rigidity. Not the least important impediment was the prevailing philosophy on equity, or its lack, leading to persistent and increasing inequality in the distribution of income.

A second group of attitudes had to do with size of the family and the value of children, particularly males. In all of the areas of Asia, rates of population increase were high, and in several countries were rising, after the conclusion of World War II. While children might be negatively related to increases in income in Western industrial societies, they are positively related to such increases in most Asian countries. With respect to population growth, Myrdal considered high rates of increase to be detrimental to economic improvement. In this he is probably correct. While there is disagreement as to the actual relationship of high rates of population growth and economic growth, it is generally conceded that high rates of population growth are less favorable rather than more favorable in the early stages of economic growth.

It is quite possible that Myrdal was a believer in the "low-level equilibrium trap"—that high rates of population growth constantly push down the marginal physical product of labor, particularly in agriculture, so that with only very low rates of increase in the level of technology, real per-capita incomes cannot rise. Lest there be some confusion on this point, this is not the equivalent of the natural state of equilibrium which Myrdal had criticized in his initial attack on the mainstream of economics in his earliest major work in 1928. The "low-level equilibrium trap" was, in Myrdal's mind, not natural. It could be altered by appropriate economic policies.

# The Limits of Industrialization

Whatever the specific policies to be followed, gradual change would fail to accommodate the rapidly increasing population. A high percentage of the labor force would have to be used in industry—the capitalistic sector—and in other nonagricultural occupations. This does not constitute an acceptance of the labor surplus/savings short model of

J. C. H. Fei and G. Ranis ("A Theory of Economic Development," in *American Economic Review*, 1961), nor of the labor surplus/entrepreneurial short model of W. A. Lewis ("Economic Development with Unlimited Supplies of Labour," in *The Manchester School of Economic and Social Studies*, 1954). In the Fei-Ranis and Lewis models, large capital inflows into the secondary or capitalistic sector, given the high rates of population increase generating rising demand for outputs from both agriculture and industry, would serve to stimulate capital formation and increase the demand for labor more rapidly in industry than in agriculture. These stimuli would facilitate the movement of labor from agriculture into industry.

Myrdal argues that this analysis reflects what is presumed to have happened in the economic development of those countries which today form the industrial West—a more rapid development of the secondary sector attracting and absorbing labor from agriculture into industry. However, the countries of today's industrial West had much lower rates of population increase at the time of their industrial transformation than the countries of the Third World, and, in particular, those of Asia. Furthermore, these transformations took place over a much longer period of time. Not only is population growth a completely different variable in Asia, but so are the cultures, attitudes, and the institutional arrangements which exist in these countries. They are lacking in the indispensable material, human, and institutional infrastructure for economic growth. Large inflows would only result in creating significant bottlenecks, and these bottlenecks (unlike those salubrious ones of Albert O. Hirschman, *The Strategy of Economic Development*, 1958), with their "backward" and "forward linkages," would not be resolved by the workings of the market. Since the existence of bottlenecks creates equity problems, they are to be avoided and can be avoided only by the planning process.

Myrdal does agree that, with the high rates of population increase and the very slow changes in technology in both agriculture and industry, labor in agriculture is surplus, or excessive. In the countries of his study in Southeast Asia, both large population and high rates of increase result in very high man/land ratios, at least relative to those in the United States, perhaps as much as four times as high. As a consequence, both the output per unit of land cultivated and the output per unit of labor input is very low, so low that the result is mass poverty. While both Fei-Ranis and Lewis see this ratio as indicative of a labor surplus which would aid industrial development if the surplus moved into secondary-sector employment and the remaining agriculturalists did not increase their food consumption, Myrdal disagrees. He views the opportunities for employment in the secondary sector as too limited to absorb much of this excess labor, were it to move from the rural area to an urban area. The migration of this population to the urban areas only results in changing

the venue of its poverty, with the distinct possibility that the actual food intake of these new urban immigrants will be less than it was in their rural setting.

Additionally, while Fei-Ranis and Lewis argue that the productivity of labor in industry is higher than it was in agriculture because of the higher capital/labor ratio in industry, Myrdal argues that this result need not be the case. In urban areas, the inadequate housing, the low level of private hygiene, and the lower level of food consumption all interact to cause productivity to decline below its level in agriculture. The low level of productivity in agriculture results not so much from the low capital/labor ratio as it does from attitudes and institutions which discourage initiative and which fail to provide incentives. It is these attitudes and institutions which have to be changed to provide incentives and to stimulate individual initiative. Myrdal believes that the current set of attitudes and institutions block all of the spread effects that could result from more saving and investment.

A number of Third World nations have argued that import-substitution-industrialization is an effective policy to increase employment opportunities in the industrial sector, thereby absorbing some of the excess population in agriculture. Many Third World countries have followed this policy, either to achieve this objective or to correct for persistent deficits on the current account in their balances of payments. In the latter case, the policy is viewed as a way of reducing imports relative to exports, thus slowing down the capital outflow or, at the very least, reducing the need for borrowed capital inflows. In fact, once implemented, this policy frequently seems to lead to even larger deficits, at least in the short run. The reason for this undesirable result is that many of the new substituting industries, or even some of the already existing ones, now able to expand because of protection, find that they have large import components in their manufacturing processes.

Did Myrdal endorse import-substitution-industrialization? He recognized it as an absolute necessity because of the serious foreign-exchange shortages which exist for the Third World countries of Southeast Asia. Aside from necessity, it is not an economically efficient policy, since it encourages high-cost activities resulting from protection from foreign competition. But he did, nonetheless, believe that there was no alternative. He adhered to the conviction that planning was superior to no planning, because it permitted the rationalization of intervention. This planning for protection and the resulting controls used to foster the development of domestic industries should be of the nondiscretionary than discretionary type. This is the preferred methodology implementing protection and controls because of both the incompetence and the corruption of public officials. The adverse effects of incompetence and corruption, however, could be minimized by limiting the discretion of public officials.

# Growth or Development?

Aside from its length and impressive scholarship, the importance of *Asian Drama* may not be all that obvious. According to Nicholas Balabkins ("Myrdal Versus the 'Armchair Economists': His Asian Drama," in *Il Politico*, 1972), its importance lies in showing the difficulty of building realistic theories of economic development while concentrating only on economic variables. So much of what has to change for growth to take place is among the noneconomic rather than the economic variables, that is, the attitudes and institutions of the society. It is for this reason that mathematical models deductively arrived at, with a focus on savings and investment, are inadequate. Myrdal's approach in arguing the inapplicability of mathematical models and the absolute necessity of examining attitudes and institutions makes his achievement both institutional and historical. *Asian Drama* is the work of a political economist, a modern political economist outside of the mainstream with a large debt to institutionalism and to the German historical school.

From Mydral's first major publication to his last, he took a position outside the mainstream of the profession. In his first major work, he attacked the lack of recognition of the political element in economic theory. The mainstream writers like Wicksell were guilty of confusing what they viewed as objective and positive with what was actually subjective and normative. Their writings were really subjective and normative because they rested upon a foundation of a set of values. In *Asian Drama*, his last major work, Myrdal attacked the profession for its lack of recognition of both the political and the sociological in the developmental process. While the conventional wisdom accepted and even insisted upon the use of mathematical models and dealt with purely economic variables in the growth process, Myrdal focused upon the attitudes and the institutions of the countries as the primary obstacles to economic development. Myrdal would argue that the mainstream of the profession seems to be dealing with merely the process of economic growth. He felt that what really mattered was not economic change or growth but economic development. As has been argued subsequently by other writers, such as Robert A. Flammang, "Economic Growth and Economic Development: Counterparts or Competitors?," in *Economic Development and Cultural Change* (1979), in the long run, these are not competitive processes. Growth and development are not only distinct but are complementary processes.

ALVIN COHEN

# Selected Bibliography

BY MYRDAL

*Population: A Problem for Democracy.* Cambridge, Ma.: Harvard University Press, 1940.

*An American Dilemma: The Negro Problem and Modern Democracy.* New York: Harper, 1944.

*The Political Element in the Development of Economic Theory.* London: Routledge & Paul, 1953.

*Economic Theory and Underdeveloped Regions.* London: Duckworth, 1956.

*An International Economy, Problems and Prospects.* New York: Harper, 1956.

*Rich Lands and Poor: The Road to World Prosperity.* New York: Harper, 1958.

*Value in Social Theory: A Selection of Essays on Methodology.* London: Routledge & Paul, 1958.

*Beyond the Welfare State: Economic Planning and Its International Implications.* New Haven, Ct.: Yale University Press, 1960.

*Asian Drama: An Inquiry into the Poverty of Nations.* 3 vols. New York: Twentieth Century Fund, 1968.

ABOUT MYRDAL

Angresano, James. "Gunnar Myrdal as a Social Economist." *Review of Social Economy* 44 (1986): 146–58.

Assarsson-Rizzi, Kerstin, and Bohrn, Harald. *Gunnar Mydral, A Bibliography, 1919–1981.* New York: Garland, 1983.

Dykema, Eugene R. "No View Without a Viewpoint: Gunnar Myrdal." *World Development* 14 (1986): 147–63.

Hume, L. J. "Myrdal on Jeremy Bentham: Laissez-Faire and Harmony of Interests." *Economica* 36 (1969): 295–303.

Rex, John. "Plural Society in Sociological Theory." *British Journal of Sociology* 10 (1959): 114–24.

Sherman, Howard. "Veblen-Commons Award: Gunnar Myrdal." *Journal of Economic Issues* 10 (1976): 210–16.

# Bertil Ohlin   1977

Bertil Ohlin was born on April 24, 1899, the son of a district attorney. He enrolled at the University of Lund at the age of sixteen and studied economics, statistics, and mathematics, receiving his undergraduate degree in 1917. He obtained his Ph.D. in economics at the University of Stockholm in 1924 and was appointed full professor at University of Copenhagen in January 1925. He moved to a chair in political economy in Handelshögskolan (The Stockholm School of Economics) in Stockholm in 1930—a chair he held until he retired in 1965. During 1938–67 Ohlin was one of the leading politicians in Sweden and was the leader of the Liberal party for 24 years. In 1977 he shared the Nobel Prize in Economic Sciences with James Meade for their pathbreaking contributions to the theory of international trade and international capital movements. After retiring from politics Bertil Ohlin returned to the economic sciences where he was active to the very last minute. Early on the morning of August 3, 1979, he was found dead in bed, sitting up and obviously having been writing an article on economics.

Ohlin married Evy Kruss in 1931. In 1933 they had their first child, a daughter. In 1934 they had a son, and in 1943 a second daughter. The latter has followed in her father's footsteps; that is, she started out as an economist but is presently one of the leading figures in the Liberal Party.

## International Economics

Having finished his undergraduate education at the University of Lund, Bertil Ohlin enrolled at Handelshögskolan (the Stockholm School of Economics), where he studied under Professor Eli F. Heckscher. In 1919 he moved on to the University of Stockholm, where he studied under Professor Cassel and Professor Gösta Bagge.

It seems safe to assume that Heckscher's seminars, which Ohlin attended during his two years at Handelshögskolan, contributed to Ohlin's strong interest in international economics, and also to his Ph.D. dissertation. However, the seminars also resulted in one of Ohlin's first scientific contributions, which was in an entirely different field than his later works. A dispute with Heckscher on the correct principles for the right time to cut trees in forestry resulted in the article "Till frågan om skogarnas omloppstid" (On the Question of Forestry Rotation Time), published in *Ekonomisk Tidskrift* in 1921. As shown by Paul Samuelson in 1976, Ohlin's article made a contribution to capital theory by deriving the Faustman-Ohlin theorem. Cassel's influence was probably of a different kind than Heckscher's, more on the format of the analysis. Cassel had constructed his famous general-equilibrium model, and Ohlin took great care to formulate his theories in this framework.

In 1919 Heckscher published his paper "Utrikeshandelns verkan på inkomstifördelningen" (translated and published in English in 1949 as "The Effect of Foreign Trade on the Distribution of Income" in the American Economic Association's *Readings in the Theory of International Trade*). This paper, and previous seminar presentations, inspired Ohlin in his work in international economics which in 1933 resulted in the publication of his opus magnum, *Interregional and International Trade*. Judging from his dedication in the copy of the book which he presented to Heckscher, Ohlin started to work on this project in 1921.

Ohlin's thesis for the lower doctor's degree, which he obtained in 1922, dealt with material that since has been termed the Heckscher-Ohlin theorem. His 1924 Ph.D. dissertation, "Handelins Teori" (The Theory of Trade), extended this analysis. Thus, the core of the material contained in *Interregional and International Trade* had been presented in Swedish by Ohlin about ten years before the publication of the book.

Ohlin's writings contain a wealth of valuable and insightful discussions of various topics in international economics. It is, to some extent, a matter of taste as to which contributions should be singled out. However, we have decided to describe the following four achievements: a restatement of the pure theory of trade in general equilibrium terms; the Heckscher-Ohlin theorem; a test of this theory; and the transfer problem. Many would probably regard the Heckscher-Ohlin theorem as the major contribution. Ohlin himself, however, thought that the restatement of the trade theory in general equilibrium terms was his most important contribution.

## Restatement of the Trade Theory

From Ricardo's days, trade theory had been mainly built on the labor theory of value. It was also set in a partial-equilibrium framework. Ohlin had studied under Cassel and had a thorough understanding of the interdependencies in the economy, both within a country and between countries. Thus, Ohlin was the first one to state the trade theory using a general-equilibrium context, and where prices of goods are determined not only by cost considerations but also by the structure of demand. For economists having obtained education during the last three or four decades, it is natural to work within a general-equilibrium framework. In the 1920s, however, it was an achievement to formulate the trade theory in general-equilibrium terms as well as he did. This reformulation of trade theory should probably be regarded as Ohlin's most important contribution to international economics. It has probably inspired many later scholars to use the general-equilibrium framework.

## The Heckscher-Ohlin Theorem

There is a strong consensus in the economics profession that one important reason for international trade is that under autarky, relative prices vary between countries. However, there are many theories why this is so. It can, for example, be because of differences in endowments, technology, scale economies, or preferences. So far most attention has been on differences in technology and endowments.

Ricardo's classical theory built on the labor theory of value and the assumption that different countries had different technology. In his famous example, the input of labor to produce one unit of cloth and wine differed, respectively, between England and Portugal. In England a gallon of wine cost 120 and a yard of cloth 100 hours of work, while in Portugal the labor cost of wine and cloth amounted to 80 and 90 hours, respectively. Although in his example Portugal had an absolute cost advantage in producing both wine and cloth, England had a relative cost advantage in producing cloth and Portugal a relative cost advantage in producing wine. The differences in relative labor costs induced the trade, with at least one country specializing completely in one product.

Heckscher, in his 1919 paper, analyzed how differences in factor endowments can cause differences in autarky relative prices. In this paper he formulated what later became called the Heckscher-Ohlin theorem. This theorem comes in a weak and a strong version. According to the weak version, a nation tends to export those goods which would be relatively cheap in the absence of trade. According to the strong version of the theorem, a country tends to export those commodities

which require large quantities of its relatively abundant factor, and to import those which require large quantities of its relatively scarce factors, given that the demand patterns are similar in the two countries. Heckscher also studied the conditions under which factor prices would be equalized by trade and provided an almost complete proof of the factor price-equalization theorem.

Heckscher formulated the basic idea that trade patterns might be caused by differences in relative factor endowments. Thus, Ohlin's contribution to the Heckscher-Ohlin theory is not the original concept but rather the fact that he presented the idea in a general equilibrium framework. It is a fruitful synthesis of ideas from his two teachers, Heckscher and Cassel. Also, Heckscher thought that differences in relative factor endowments were necessary for trade. Ohlin noted that demand conditions can make a factor scarce in the sense that its relative autarky price becomes high. Thus, one can say the weak version of the Heckscher-Ohlin theorem originates from Ohlin. Since Heckscher's article was not published in English until 1949, the basic concept was first presented in English in 1933 in Ohlin's *Interregional and International Trade.*

Heckscher stated conditions under which factor prices would be equalized in the trading countries. Ohlin opposed Heckscher's argument and claimed that, in general, there would be only a *tendency* towards factor-price equalization, but that factor prices would not be equalized. As later studies have shown, the conditions for factor-price equalization are quite stringent and would in practice not be satisfied. Thus, from a practical point of view, Ohlin's intuitive argument that there would only be a tendency towards factor-price equalization seems to be quite correct.

## Empirical Tests

The latter part of *Interregional and International Trade* is concerned with various tests of the trade theory put forward in the earlier part of the book. These tests are not formulated as tightly as present-day empirical tests, and statistical procedures are not used. Instead Ohlin uses causal reasoning and a wealth of empirical observations assembled during a long period of time. The tests are carefully done, and the efforts to test the theory should be an example for younger generations of economists. (In his later days Ohlin thought that trade theory was tested much too little. He wanted an operational theory with clear empirical predictions.)

## The Transfer Problem

After the First World War, Germany had to pay reparations, mainly to France and Great Britain. Germany was badly hurt by the war, and there was a general worry how Germany possibly could succeed in paying the reparations. John Maynard Keynes argued in an article in the *Economic Journal* (1929) that it was not likely that the transfer of real resources could possibly work. Keynes thought that the generation

of a trade surplus was a prerequisite for a real transfer to be possible, and thought it unlikely that a sufficiently large surplus could be generated.

Ohlin, in his famous exchange with Keynes, viewed the problem from an entirely different angle. According to Ohlin the transfer of purchasing power (say in German marks) should be regarded as the initiating disturbance to the economic system. This financial transaction would generate a real transfer, that is, a transfer of commodities. Besides emphasizing the financial transaction as the initiating disturbance Ohlin also noted an adjustment mechanism hitherto largely neglected. Previously the direct income effect of a transfer on imports and exports had been noted and that changes in the exchange rate would affect the trade surplus. Ohlin also noted that a transfer of purchasing power from country A to country B would shift the demand schedules for "home market" goods and "international" goods in the two countries. In country A the demand schedule for home market goods would shift inwards, implying a transfer of resources from the "home market" industry into the export goods industry. In country B it would be the other way around. Taking this effect into consideration, one could be more optimistic about the transfer problem. Thus, Ohlin's contribution is to point both to the monetary transfer as the initiating disturbance that will generate the real transfer and to an adjustment mechanism earlier overlooked.

# Macroeconomics

During the 1930s Bertil Ohlin made important contributions to the development of employment theory. In certain respects Ohlin, and other Swedish economists such as Erik Lindahl and Gunnar Myrdal, were predecessors of the Keynesian employment theory. Ohlin himself gave the name Stockholm School to the group.

However, Ohlin's first published macroeconomic paper was written within the realm of "classical" macroeconomics. It was published in 1919 and had the title "Kvantitetsteorin i den svenska litteraturen" (The Quantity Theory in the Swedish Literature). In this article Ohlin summarized the Swedish discussion during the eighteenth and nineteenth centuries about the problem of inflation. It was very well-written and showed both wide reading and great knowledge of and maturity in economics, especially considering that Ohlin was twenty years old at that time. Ohlin himself stands out as a nuanced quantity theorist. He consequently characterized the quantity theory of money of the time in the following way: "The modern quantity theory that nowadays is maintained by Swedish economists, is nothing else than a combination of the simple basic truths of the quantity theory [changes in nominal prices are almost always the result of changes in the supply of money] and a theory of the means of credit and its regulation."

Ohlin was, however, to become very critical of the quantity theory.

One reason was that it represented an older way of thinking that had to be abandoned in connection with the development of the theory of employment during the 1930s. But more important was possibly the heritage from Knut Wicksell. After Wicksell, the Swedish economists were accustomed to assuming that the quantity of money was endogenously determined. The quantity of money was partly determined from the demand side. This meant that the simple causal connection between an increased quantity of money and a rising price level was no longer at hand.

The Wicksellian analysis of the transmission mechanism of the quantity theory of money was, at the end of the 1920s and the beginning of the 1930s, both criticized and further developed by Lindahl (1930, 1939) and Myrdal (1931, 1939). Myrdal's contribution is perhaps the better known, because it introduced the terminology of an ex ante and ex post. As a part of this discussion, Ohlin in 1933 published an article in *Ekonomisk Tidskrift*, "Till frågan om penningteorins uppläggning" (On the Question Formulation of Monetary Theory, published in English in 1978).

What has made this article famous is that Ohlin here suggests monetary disturbances will not only influence the price level cumulatively, but income and production as well. In many places in the article one can find reasonings of a primitive multiplier type. Ohlin also stresses that disturbances may not only come from the demand for capital goods. It is aggregate demand (in comparison with aggregate supply), investments, and consumption that are important. It was not the rate of interest, or the price level, that would coordinate investments and savings; this would instead be brought about by variations of production and employment. This means, for example, that an increase in the demand for consumer goods (less saving) in the final analysis does not need to imply less saving, but could even lead to more saving (the paradox of thrift).

Ohlin's article was a preparation for his 1934 monograph *Penningpolitik, offentliga arbeten, subventioner och tullar som medel mot arbetslöshet* (Monetary Policy, Public Works, Subsidies, and Custom Duties as Means Against Unemployment), written within the framework of a Swedish government investigation of unemployment. Even if Ohlin's objective mainly was of a practical nature—to propose means of dealing with the severe unemployment of the time—his book had great scientific value. In the two first chapters he gave a theoretical background to the applied analysis that followed in the rest of the book. It essentially contains what was to become the Keynesian employment theory, but it was extended to cover an open economy and gave due respect to the fact that not only real production and employment will be affected during the process of expansion/contraction, but prices and wages as well. The book has an example of multiplier analysis for an open economy, where he works with a marginal propensity of consump-

tion for home commodities and services equal to 0.5. He only follows the expansion process for three steps and does not analyze the final equilibrium.

Ohlin further combined the multiplier and the accelerator in a discussion of the causes of the business cycle. None of the two components was new at the time. Richard F. Kahn had introduced the multiplier in a famous article a few years earlier. The accelerator, as a theory of investments, was for the first time suggested by John M. Clark in 1917. In spite of this, Ohlin's idea to combine the two components in an explanation of the oscillation movement of national income and employment was new and fruitful. Ohlin's discussion was verbal and nonmathematical, however. The final mathematical analysis came with Paul Samuelson's article in 1939.

Ohlin's monograph on the whole gives an overview of economic policy measures against unemployment that became standard during the 1950s and 1960s. This means that the book does not offer any great news for the reader of today. But fifty years ago the situation was different. His task was both to develop economic theory in a new direction and to break with earlier lines of thought about sound public finances and the role of saving in the business cycle.

Ohlin did not believe that monetary policy would be an effective measure against unemployment during depressions. He based this conclusion partly on an argument that was close to the Keynesian liquidity trap. The other side of the coin was, however, that Ohlin (and other members of the Stockholm School) were optimists about increasing employment by expanding government expenditures (for example with the help of public works), even if they were financed by public borrowing. They did not believe that the issuance of bonds would cause any severe crowding-out effects.

The primary aim of Ohlin's 1934 book was not to develop new theory. It was rather a question of analyzing the effects of different economic policy measures against unemployment, starting from what was at the time very advanced economic theory. This aim naturally influenced the presentation so that it became informal and directed to practical economic policy issues. Nevertheless, his way of reasoning had certain characteristics that have influenced the later evaluation of his achievement.

For example, Ohlin consistently tried to describe the interaction between different markets. He had a great ability to see the interdependence between different events. However, this also meant that he seldom focused his discussion on a main issue. There is a plethora of interesting observations that often intrudes so that the reader does not always know what is important and what is unimportant. He thought that as soon as one treated important dynamic problems it was necessary to analyze special cases. Since different effects could work in different directions, and since velocities of reaction were so important for the final outcome, it was not possible to work

with general models. The best strategy of research was instead to start from concrete and well-specified examples. Ohlin called this casuistics. It is true that casuistics was a pedagogical method in connection with problems of stabilization policy, but as a result the theoretical structure was not presented in an efficient way.

Contrary to Keynes, Ohlin assumed that interest rates are determined in the credit market, not in the "money" market. He thus worked with a loanable-funds theory, not with liquidity-preference theory, a natural consequence of working in the Wicksellian tradition and partly due to his critical attitude to the quantity theory of money. This starting point had, however, the consequence that his analysis was less aggregated than the Keynesian analysis and that the connection between interest determination and transaction demand for money was less obvious. However, in a debate with Keynes in 1937, Ohlin stated that it did not make any great difference if one assumed that interest rates were determined in the money market or in the credit market, since it was a matter of an interdependent system.

Like the other members of the Stockholm School, Ohlin stressed the importance of the expectations of firms of an uncertain future. In connection with his analysis of Wicksell's cumulative process, Myrdal had developed the ex ante-ex post terminology. One of the first applications was the identity between investment and saving. In the beginning of the relevant period, that is, ex ante, there is no reason to assume that planned saving will be equal to planned investment. In a modern society it is not the same agents that make the saving decisions and the investment decisions. Neither is the rate of interest a dependable regulator. The reason is partly that neither saving nor investment needs to be very sensitive to the rate of interest, partly that saving does not necessarily take the form of purchases of bonds—it can also be in the form of increased cash holdings. On the other hand, saving and investment will always be equal ex post, that is, at the end of the period. This is due to a mere accounting identity of the same type as the requirements that registered purchases at the end of a period must be equal to sales.

However, Ohlin stressed more than did Lindhal or Myrdal the significance of basing the analysis on ex post values. In other words, Ohlin thought that the information on which firms base their expectations and decisions to a large extent consists of accounting material, meaning an absence of very sophisticated expectations of the future. Thus, Ohlin did not consider Lindahl's and Myrdal's assumption that permanent income determined consumption plans to be very realistic.

Ohlin made a very important interpretation of the ex ante concept. He stressed that *expectations* must be conceived of as being probabilistic. Different events may happen with various probabilities. The *plans* must be regarded as an alternative, depending on the uncertain outcome of the expectational variables. This means, in turn, that the ex ante con-

cept was partly another way of describing behavior equations. Like the other members of the Stockholm School, Ohlin was more interested in following developments over time than in equilibrium analysis. This tendency was a heritage from Wicksell, but the reason was also that the Swedish economists did not regard it as especially meaningful to analyze the business cycle with equilibrium methods.

Ohlin's monograph was never translated into English. If it had been, it is possible that Keynes's *General Theory of Employment, Interest and Money* (which appeared two years later) would not have been regarded as so new and pathbreaking. Keynes's work was viewed as a breakthrough in the scientific community. The year after, Ohlin wrote two articles in the *Economic Journal*, in which he partly presented the employment theory of the Stockholm School and partly discussed its relation to Keynesian macroeconomics. His 1937 articles stressed that the theory of Keynes was not unique. A group of Swedish economists had already developed similar thoughts. Ohlin was also critical of certain parts of the Keynesian theory, particularly in that it was an equilibrium theory and that employment depended on the volume of investment. Ohlin did not think that it was realistic to analyze the employment problem with equilibrium models, since the business cycle in itself was a dynamic phenomenon. Moreover, one could not expect that the central relationship and parameters (for example the marginal propensity to consume) would be stable. The volume of investment could furthermore not be regarded as exogenous.

Ohlin's critique of Keynes and his stress on the limited degree of originality of the Keynesian employment theory was perhaps partly based on a natural disappointment. Ohlin thought that he and the other members of the Stockholm School had essentially developed the theory for which Keynes received the credit. The Stockholm school had both preceded, and to a certain extent, been more advanced than the theory of Keynes. It was however Keynes's General Theory, not the Stockholm school, that would dominate the development of macroeconomics for several decades. The Swedish economists presented important pioneering work with value of its own. They were not able to put their imprint on the development of macroeconomics that followed, partly due to basic traits in their analysis (for example, that they studied the development of the economy over time, but not the final unemployment equilibrium), but also due to relatively trivial circumstances, such as that many of the important works were published only in Swedish.

## Politics

It was not unnatural that Ohlin, as a social scientist, was to become increasingly interested in the possibilities of applying the new theoretical ideas about the business cycle on the employment problems of the 1930s. From an early age, he was interested in social questions, and from the beginning of the 1930s he wrote editorials in *Stockholms Tidningen*—a leading Liberal daily paper in Stockholm—and more elaborated articles in *Index*, a journal of one of the Swedish banks. In these forums Ohlin applied the new scientific results to actual employment problems. He also discussed social questions from the point of view of a wider perspective. Ohlin called himself a social liberal. First of all he cared for those who lived under the worst conditions, combining this perspective with a strong skepticism towards socialism, central planning, and bureaucracy. The politician Ohlin believed in the market economy but one with a social concern. On this point he was critical of the Social Democrats, who he thought mainly fought for industrial workers—a middle class—while those who really had a difficult situation ("the forgotten Sweden") were neglected. With regard to actual policy making, Ohlin's position in the 1930s was not very far from that of the Social Democrats, the reason being that the employment issue was central.

In 1934 Ohlin was elected president of the FPU (the youth organization of the Liberal party), and in 1938 he became a member of parliament. As such, he very soon became one of the most influential members of the Liberal parliamentary group. In 1944 he became chairman of the Liberal Party and at the same time was appointed minister of trade, serving in the latter post up to the dissolution of the coalition government nine months later. He remained leader of the Liberal party until 1967.

During the Second World War
the Social Democrats, "Bon-
deförbundet" (the Farmers party),
"Folkpartiet" (the Liberal party)
and "Högerpartiet" (the Conservative party) had formed a coalition
government. Of the parties with parliamentary representation, only the
Communists were not included in
the government. With the war coming to an end, the tensions within the
coalition government were brought
to life again. The Social Democrats
talked about a socialist "harvest
time" in the postwar program of the
labor movement.

Ohlin held a leading position in
the nonsocialist opposition against
these plans. Without exaggeration
one can say that it was due to Ohlin's energetic opposition that the
thought of socialization and a
planned economy partly faded out.
In the elections to the second
chamber of parliament in 1948, the
Liberal party more than doubled its
representation, and Ohlin emerged
as the natural leader of the nonsocialist opposition.

Similarly to his position during
the 1930s, Ohlin stressed a combination of a market economy and social
responsibility. When it came to social reforms, there were hardly any
great differences between the Social
Democrats and the Liberal party.
The differences were, however, large
as to the question of a market versus
a planned economy. One can also
say that Ohlin's own emphasis had
changed since the 1930s. Now he
emphasized the importance of the
market economy. He thought that
welfare would most effectively be
brought to the general public by

economic growth. The possibilities
of helping the poor by redistributing
income through taxation were limited, since a strong progressive tax
system would have negative effects
on work effort and saving, and consequently on growth.

Ohlin never became prime minister of Sweden, but he played an
important political role. It is probable that the degree of socialism
would have been much larger in
Sweden without Ohlin's energetic
and well-informed opposition. His
important political achievement was
the reason why his scientific production was accomplished before the
age of forty. But the reason why he
received the Nobel Prize in Economics was his fundamental achievements realized prior to the 1930s.

In summary, Bertil Ohlin was
both a scientist and a politician. His
important contributions to economics notwithstanding, he gave the
larger part of his working life to politics. Without doubt, Ohlin was one
of the most prominent and influential Swedish politicians during this
century. The judgment is, of course,
subjective. However, it is our view
that because of Ohlin's forceful opposition, combining knowledge of
facts, clear logic, and a strong sense
for honesty, the ruling party (parties) often had to rethink and rede-
sign their policies. Thus, during the
late 1940s, the 1950s, and the 1960s,
Ohlin forced (helped) the Social Democrats to perform better policy by
weeding out badly thought out suggestions and improving others. To
Swedes in general, Ohlin is not remembered for his scientific contributions but for his political work.

Ohlin's development of employment theory during the 1930s was a major achievement, but it was Keynes who made the impact on the development of macroeconomics. As an economist Ohlin will be remembered for his contributions to international economics—putting trade theory in a general equilibrium framework and, together with Eli F. Heckscher, developing the Heckscher Ohlin model, which stressed the importance of relative factor endowments for the pattern of international trade. His book *Interregional and International Trade* is still, more than fifty years after its publication, a standard reference work in textbooks on international trade.

SOREN BLOMQUIST and
CLAES-HENRIC SIVEN

# Selected Bibliography

## WORKS BY OHLIN

"Kvantitetsteorin i den svenska litteraturen" (The Quantity Theory in the Swedish Literature). *Ekonomisk Tidskrift* 21 (1919): 45–81.

"Till frågan om skogarnas omloppstid" (On the Question of Forestry Rotation Time). *Ekonomisk Tidskrift* 22 (1921): 89–113.

*Handelns teori.* Stockholm: Centraltryckeriet, 1924.

"The Reparation Problem: A Discussion." *Economic Journal* 39 (1929): 172–78.

"A Rejoinder from Professor Ohlin." *Economic Journal* 39 (1929): 400–04.

*Interregional and International Trade.* Cambridge, Ma.: Harvard University Press, 1933.

"Till frågan om penningteorins uppläggning." *Ekonomisk Tidskrift* 35 (1933):48–81. Translated into English by Hans J. Brems and William P. Yohe and published in *History of Political Economy* 10 (1978): 353–88.

*Penningpolitik, offentliga arbeten, subventioner och tullar som medel mot arbetslöshet* (Monetary Policy, Public Works, Subsidies, and Custom Duties as Means Against Unemployment). Stockholm: P. A. Norstedt & Söner 12 (1934): monograph.

"Some Notes on the Stockholm Theory of Savings and Investment." *Economic Journal* 47 (1937): 53–69 and 221–40.

"Alternative Theories of the Rate of Interest." *Economic Journal* 47 (1937): 423–27.

## OTHER WORKS

Clark, J. M. "Business Acceleration and the Law of Demand: A Technical Factor in Economic Cycles." *Journal of Political Economy* 25 (1917): 217–35.

Heckscher, Eli F. "Utrikeshandelns verkan på inkomstfördelningen." *Ekonomisk Tidskrift* 21 (1919): 497–512. Reprinted in English: "The Effect of Foreign Trade on the Distribution of Income," in Ellis, H. S. and L. A. Metzler, eds., *Readings in the Theory of International Trade.* Philadelphia: Blakiston, 1949.

Kahn, R. F. "The Relation of Home Investment to Unemployment." *Economic Journal* 41 (1931): 173–98.

Keynes, J. M. "The German Transfer Problem." *Economic Journal* 39 (1929): 1–7, and "The Reparation Problem: A Rejoinder." *Economic Journal* 39 (1929): 179–82.

Lindahl, Erik. *Penningpolitikens Medel.* Malmö: Förlagsaktiebolaget, 1930.

———. *Studies in the Theory of Money and Capital.* London: George Allen and Unwin, 1939.

Lundberg, E. *Studies in the Theory of Economic Expansion.* London: P. S. King & Son, 1937.

Myrdal, Gunnar. "Om Penningteoretisk Jämvikt." *Economisk Tidskrift* 32 (1931): 191–302.

———. *Monetary Equilibrium.* London: William Hodge & Company, 1939.

Samuelson, Paul A. "Interactions between the Multiplier Analysis and the Principle of Acceleration." *Review of Economic Statistics* 21 (1939): 75–78.

———. "Economics of Forestry in an Evolving Society." *Economic Inquiry* 14 (1976): 466–92.

# PAUL ANTHONY SAMUELSON *1970*

Paul Samuelson was awarded the Nobel Prize in Economic Sciences in 1970 for his many papers. They consist of hundreds of titles and thousands of pages, presently gathered in four volumes, with no end in sight. Unlike many academic economists, who devote their careers to pursuing the evolution of one major idea or at least the ideas in one narrow branch of economics, Samuelson took all of economic theory as his domain and set about re-examining vast areas, using the language of mathematics. The result is that Samuelson is not associated with a breakthrough in one particular area of economics, but any search of the literature in vast areas of economics requires one to consider Samuelson's written contribution to the discussion.

Paul Anthony Samuelson has earned an incredible number of honors. A complete listing would leave little space for a discussion of his contributions to economics. But a few highlights include the David A. Wells Prize for the best Harvard dissertation in 1941; innumerable honorary doctorates; Guggenheim and Ford Foundation fellowships; the presidencies of the American Economics Association, the Econometric Society, and the International Economics Association; the John Bates Clark medal; the Albert Einstein medal; and, of course, the Nobel Prize for economics in 1970.

## Early Training and Career

Samuelson was born on May 15, 1915, in Gary, Indiana. His parents, Frank, a druggist, and Ella (Lipton) moved their family to Chicago a few years later, and Samuelson received his undergraduate education at the University of Chicago. After finishing his B.A. in 1935, he went to Harvard University and earned his masters in 1936 and his doctorate in 1941. He accepted an assistant professorship at MIT in 1940, quickly moved through the academic ranks, and has maintained his faculty status there ever since.

Samuelson attended public schools in Chicago and Hyde Park High School. It was quite common for Hyde Park graduates to enroll at the nearby University of Chicago, and Samuelson decided to follow this custom. "In those simple days of the Depression, you went to college near your home, or your father's college." Samuelson's father did not want his sons to follow in his footsteps and go to pharmacy college. "I think he saw the chain store trend . . . so I went to the University of Chicago" (1976, p. 7).

While at Chicago, Samuelson made the decision to major in economics, a definite gain to economics but a terrific opportunity lost to sociology:

Although there was a minute in my sophomore year when I toyed with the notion of becoming a sociologist, my real stimulation came from an old-fashioned course in elementary economics . . . By luck, my teacher was Aaron Director, a strong libertarian of the Knight-Hayek school . . . Director was also an analyst and an iconoclast, whose cold stare terrorized the coeds in the class but captivated me. In any case, even if I had had Mr. Squeers for a teacher, the

first drink from the economics textbooks of Slichter and Ely would have been like the Prince's kiss to Sleeping Beauty. It was as if I were made for economics. . . . Possibly I would have done well in any field of applied science or as a writer, but certainly the blend in economics of analytical hardness and humane relevance was tailor-made for me or I for it. (*Paul Samuelson and Modern Economic Theory*, 1983, p. 5)

By choosing economics at Chicago, he was to study under the faculty of the best-known school for classical, laissez-faire economics, the brand of economics that was to be so strongly attacked by the Keynesians.

Samuelson did not stay at Chicago for graduate work, as he was one of the recipients of a Social Science Research Council Fellowship. Those fellowships were experimentally awarded in 1935 to the eight most promising graduates in economics. The fellowships would subsidize the doctorate, but they carried the stipulation that the recipients could not carry out their graduate studies in the same institution in which they had done their undergraduate work.

It is rather surprising that Samuelson's choice of Harvard was not based upon its academic reputation. In fact, most of his teachers recommended Columbia. He made his decision on "quite nonscholarly grounds." He decided to go to Harvard "in search of green ivy."

Never having been east (I don't consider Florida as east) before the age of twenty, I picked Cambridge over

New York in the expectation that Harvard Yard would look like Dartmouth's Hanover Common. Expecting white churches and spacious groves, I almost returned home after my first view of Harvard Square, approached by bad chance from the direction of Central Square. (1983, p. 8)

Also, Samuelson's famous first encounter with the economic chairman Harold Burbank was not amiable. Samuelson annoyed Burbank by telling him that he would not take E. F. Gray's famous course in economic history; rather he would take E. H. Chamberlin's course for second-year graduate students. Also, he informed Burbank that he intended to "skim the cream" of Harvard, as he was not certain if he would stay longer than a year. Moreover, when asked why he had not applied in advance, Samuelson said that "an anointed Social Science Research Council Pre-Doctoral-Training Fellow could get in anywhere." Samuelson observed that "it was not love at first sight" (1983, pp. 8–9).

Samuelson soon decided Harvard was the place to be, as it took him from a solid foundation in free-market classical theory to the American university that was to have the most important role in the initial adaptation of Keynesian ideas for the American academic community. Among his instructors at Harvard was Alvin Hansen, who was to do much of the initial explanation of Keynes to the American audience, and Samuelson was to work with Hansen.

... my transfer from Chicago to Harvard put me right in the forefront

of the three great waves of modern economics: the Keynesian revolution . . . , the monopolistic or imperfect-competition revolution, and finally, the fruitful clarification of the analysis of economic reality resulting from the mathematical and econometric handling of the subject—including an elucidation for the first time of the welfare economic issues that had concerned economists from the days of Adam Smith and Karl Marx to the present.

Much of Harvard analysis was crude and unrigorous, as I discovered to my intense surprise. But it had life and lacked closure. The mistakes one's teachers made and the gaps they left in their reasoning were there for you to rectify. You were part of the advancing army of science. (1983, p. 10)

# Mathematical Models

Samuelson began his prolific writing career before he finished his doctoral studies. In 1937 he published his first two articles: "A Note on Measurement of Utility" in *The Review of Economic Studies* and "Some Aspects of the Pure Theory of Capital" in *The Quarterly Review of Economics*. Five more appeared the following year, and he produced in the neighborhood of twenty before he wrote his dissertation.

Probably the most important of his predoctoral articles, "Interactions Between the Multiplier Analysis and the Principle of Acceleration," came out of his association with Hansen. He used Hansen's model, in which additions to national income come from three components: government deficit spending, private consumption expenditures induced by previous public expenditures, and private investment, which was assumed to be proportional to the increase in income. He tried different values for the marginal propensity to consume and for the accelerator, and he found that varying oscillating economic systems could be generated.

The article established his reputation in dynamic analysis. It had special importance, however, in that it used a mathematical model demonstrating various results from changing assumed values of a variable. It did not attempt to take data from the economy to create functional relationships. The article ended with a statement of Samuelson's firm belief in the importance of expressing economic models through mathematics. He argued that contrary to common impression, if mathematical methods were properly employed, rather than "making economic theory more abstract" they would "serve as a powerful liberating device enabling the entertainment and analysis of ever more realistic and complicated hypotheses" (1966, p. 1110).

His doctoral dissertation, largely conceived and written in 1937, was awarded the David A. Wells prize for the academic year 1941–42 for the best essay in economics by a Harvard student. Because of World War II, Samuelson did not have it published until 1947, under the title *Foundations of Economic Analysis*. It was very successful and has been printed in many

languages. He began the book by quoting the mathematician E. H. Moore: "The existence of analogies between central features of various theories implies the existence of a general theory which underlies the particular theories and unifies them with respect to those central theories."

Samuelson argued that conditions of equilibrium in theory involving single economic units involved the maximization or minimization of some magnitude. Furthermore, he argued that the "correspondence principle" between comparative statistics and dynamics could be used to derive operationally meaningful theorems. By meaningful theorems, he meant "hypotheses about empirical data which could conceivably be refuted." Samuelson went through many of the major areas in economic theory and reexpressed the concepts in mathematical relationships. He felt that Marshall had been wrong in writing that it was dubious if "anyone spends his time well in reading lengthy translations of economic doctrines into mathematics, that have not been made by himself." Rather, Samuelson felt just the opposite. He attacked writers of modern economics theory for the "laborious literary working over of essentially simple mathematical concepts." He believed that such activity is "not only unrewarding from the standpoint of advancing the science, but involves as well mental gymnastics of a particularly depraved type" (1947, p. 6).

Samuelson certainly carried out his beliefs, as the book covered many areas of economic theory and reexpressed those ideas in mathematical formulas. Unlike many dissertations whose readership is limited to the writer's doctoral committee, Samuelson's *Foundations* was widely read by the scholarly community and established his reputation in the profession. Samuelson was not the first to express economic theories in mathematical form, but he made an extraordinary contribution in pushing economics exposition in that direction.

Years and hundreds of equations later, Samuelson was to exhibit his wit and good humor about his reputation for using mathematics in his 1961 presidential address to the American Economics Association:

I could give a sermon tonight on the use and misuse of mathematics in economics. This subject is the only commodity in the world that seems not subject to Gossen's law of diminished marginal utility. It was only yesterday that three successive presidential addresses touched upon this delicious topic: and the strongest of these attacks on mathematics led to so resonant a response with this annual audience as to give rise to a standing ovation to the speaker.

Thomas Hardy remarked, "If the Archbishop of Canterbury says that God exists, that is all in a day's business; but if he says that God does not exist, then you have something that is really significant." What a Daniel-come-to-Judgment I would be, if I, the lamb that strayed fustus' and mustus' to the fold from the fold, were to testify before God and this

company that mathematics had been a terrible mistake; that right along, it has all been there in Marshall, Books III and V; and that the most one needs for life as an economist is a strong voice, and a compass and ruler.

I wish I could be obliging. Yet even if my lips could be brought to utter the comforting words, like Galileo I would hear myself whispering inside, "But mathematics does indeed help." (1966, p. 1500)

No contemporary economist has contributed to so many areas of economics. In his words:

My own scholarship has covered a great variety of fields. And many of them involve questions like welfare economics and factor-price equalization; turnpike theorems and osculating envelopes; nonsubstitutability relations in Minkowski-Ricardo-Leontief-Metzler matrices of Masak-Hicks type; or balanced-budget multipliers under conditions of uncertainty in locally impacted topological spaces and molar equivalencies. My friends warn me that such topics are suitable merely for captive audiences in search of a degree—and even then not after dark. (1966, p. 1499)

In reality, Samuelson's writings have captivated his colleagues throughout his long and unsurpassed career. John S. Chipman credits him with setting up welfare economics as a separate discipline, writing that Samuelson succeeded in "setting up a formal framework for the description of value judgments and the analysis of their relationships to economic systems and policies" (*Samuelson and Neoclassical Economics*, 1982, p. 152). Lawrence J. Lau has written that "Samuelson's influence on the modern development of production theory can be found everywhere," adding that "Samuelson was the first economist to recognize and emphasize the critical role of the assumption of maximization (or equivalently minimization) in the derivation of theorems in comparative statistics" (*Samuelson and Neoclassical Economics*, 1982, p. 83).

Richard Musgrave has written that Samuelson really began the modern theory of public goods with this 1954 paper, "Pure Theory of Public Expenditures." It was only a three-page paper, but Musgrave argues that "never have three pages had so great an impact on the theory of public finance." His writings led to a vast literature with contributions by many people, and the basic model had been determined by his expansion of the Pareto optimality condition to include public goods (*Paul Samuelson and Modern Economic Theory*, 1983, p. 141).

# Advancing Keynesian Economics

One could continue through most of the categories of economic theory and find the top names praising Samuelson's contributions to each particular area. But in addition to being the economist's economist, Samuelson has a reputation with the public which is largely based upon his involvement with the development of Keynesian economic theory in the United States.

Soon after Keynes's death in 1946, Samuelson wrote on his contributions in a piece that points out the profound effect that Keynes had on economists of Samuelson's generation:

I have always considered it a priceless advantage to have been born an economist prior to 1936 and to have received a grounding in classical economics. It is quite impossible for modern students to realize the full effect of what has been advisably called "The Keynesian Revolution" upon those of us brought up in the orthodox traditions. What beginners today often regard as trite and obvious was to us puzzling, novel, and heretical.

To have been born as an economist before 1936 was a boon—yes. But not to have been born too long before!

Bliss was it in the dawn to be alive,
But to be young was very heaven!

The *General Theory* caught most economists under the age of thirty-five with the unexpected virulence of a disease first attacking and decimating an isolated tribe of south sea islanders. Economists beyond fifty turned out to be quite immune to the ailment. With time, most economists in between began to run the fever, often without knowing or admitting their condition. (1966, pp. 1517–18)

Fifteen years later Samuelson made a good summary of the importance of Keynes's *The General Theory of Employment, Interest and Money* (1936):

I myself believe that the broad significance of the *General Theory* to be in
the fact that it provides a relatively
realistic, complete system for analyzing the level of effective demand and
its fluctuations. More narrowly, I
conceive the heart of its contribution
to be in that subset of its equations
which relate the propensity to consume and to saving in relation to
offsets-to-savings. In addition to
linking saving explicitly to income,
there is an equally important denial
of the implicit "classical" axiom that
motivated investment is *indefinitely
expansible or contractable*, so that
whatever people try to save will always be fully invested. (1966,
p. 1523)

Classical theory insists that a
capitalist economy will tend towards
full employment. Natural market
forces will ensure sufficient spending
so that all production can be sold.
With this view that the economy
corrects its own spending problems,
there is no need for government interventions to bring about full employment. Samuelson points out
that Keynes destroys the idea that
there is an "invisible hand" to guarantee that individual self-centered
decisions with respect to savings and
investment will somehow result in
full employment. Rather, Keynes is
arguing for "rules of the road" to
guide people's actions. Samuelson
insists that Keynes's approach is not
a way to destroy the capitalist
system. Instead, it is the means to
make it work.

Left to themselves during depression,
people will try to save and only end

up lowering society's level of capital
formation and saving; during an inflation, apparent self-interest leads
everyone to action which only aggra-
vates the malignant upward spiral.

Such a philosophy is profoundly
capitalistic in its nature. Its policies
are offered "as the only practical
means of avoiding the destruction of
existing economic forms in their entirety and as the condition of the successful functioning of individual initiative." (1966, p. 1523)

Keynes had argued that there
was no guarantee of full employment in a capitalist system. There
would be times of insufficient spending leading to recession and times of
excessive spending pushing prices
up. The government through its fiscal and monetary tools could attempt to bring spending back on
track when it started to fluctuate
away from the optimal level.

Samuelson was among the first
to use the emerging Keynesian ideas
to recommend government policies.
In 1943 he wrote an essay called
"Full Employment After the War."
He argued that when the soldiers
returned to the civilian labor force
and the government cut back its military spending, there would be a
major depression. The only way to
avoid economic suffering would be
for the government to adopt a
Keynesian expansionary fiscal-policy approach. Without such an approach, he was convinced that there
would be the "greatest period of unemployment and industrial disloca-
tion which any economy has ever
faced" (1980, p. 102).

Fortunately for the economy, Samuelson's prediction this time was not as good as his ability to advance theory. There was no depression, in spite of the end of the war and the failure of the government to engage in Keynesian-inspired intervention. In fact, the economy did quite well.

This boom after the war did not cause Samuelson to lose faith in economic forecasting. In 1956 he wrote an essay on economic forecasting in which he recalled the inaccurate forecast of a slump after the war, while in reality there was a boom. He felt that the postwar period had been one in which policy makers had been successful in diagnosing the trends and needs for the economy. He did not believe that forecasting was accurate in providing detailed quantitative estimates of gross national product (GNP) and inflationary and deflationary gaps, but he did believe that the economy changed slowly enough that a six-month forecast would likely be accurate enough to allow policymakers to select policies that would lead to economic stability (1966, pp. 1331).

During World War II, Samuelson engaged in other activities besides his writings and teaching. He served on the War Production Board and was a consultant for the National Resources Planning Board. And at MIT he helped the university's Radiation Laboratory develop computer techniques for tracking airplanes.

The year 1947 was an especially good one for Samuelson. Besides having his *Foundations* published, he was promoted to full professor and received the John Bates Clark award for the most distinguished work by an economist less than forty years old.

His teaching duties at MIT included, by his own choice, introductory economics. His decision to share in the teaching of introductory economics, in spite of his risking reputation and abilities, was to lead to the writing of the book that has made his name so well known to college students. When Samuelson began teaching, the existing textbooks were rather institutional in approach and did not pay much attention to mathematics and the emerging Keynesian ideas. Samuelson decided to write his own introductory textbook. *Economics: An Introductory Analysis*, published in 1948 soon captured much of the market, inspired many clones, has been translated into over twenty languages, and, after twelve editions and three million copies, is still very popular. Since so many students in the last thirty years began their studies of economics with that textbook, and since so many college professors under the age of fifty began their own learning of economics with it, one might argue that Samuelson has written the most important English-language book on economics since Keynes's *General Theory*.

The book's content is important for two reasons. The first is that it began the process of incorporating Keynesian concepts into the introductory-economics classroom. Since

Samuelson had studied at both Chicago and Harvard, he was well-prepared to carry out the transition in his text. Secondly, since Samuelson was a strong believer that mathematics was a precise means of explaining economic relationships, he wrote a textbook that started the move toward exposing even beginning students to theory via graphs and equations.

The book continues to be successful, and every edition addresses contemporary issues. Therefore, a review of successive editions of Samuelson's textbook would give anyone a thorough grounding in the economic issues that have faced the United States during his time.

# Political Activities

Samuelson became political during the 1950s. He testified before Congressional committees on current economic issues, and in a 1955 hearing he took the stand that with "proper fiscal and monetary policies, our economy can have full employment and whatever rate of capital formation and growth it wants" (*The Collected Scientific Papers of Paul A. Samuelson*, 1966, p. 1329). He could not resist closing that testimony with an equation and a comment that "I do not recall ever seeing mathematical economics in congressional committee hearings. This drought can be ended by the following brief proof. . . ." He then proceeded to introduce a simple equation for national-income determination.

Samuelson was using the mathematics for a purpose. His message was very clear: macroeconom-

ics in the post-Keynesian era had progressed to the point that economic activism could be successful in ensuring both full employment and economic growth in a capitalist economic system. Once the political process had arrived at some conclusion as to the desired level of economic activity, economics could be used to make the levels a reality.

Samuelson was eager for government to pay more attention to the issue of economic growth. Achieving full employment does not guarantee economic growth. The potential GNP today is the amount of output that can be produced with all job seekers employed. However, the amount of output (GNP) that they can produce is to a large extent a function of the capital goods, namely machinery and tools, that the workers have. If more capital goods are produced in the future, then the economy will be able to have more output per worker and hence a higher living standard. Samuelson felt that the government could determine the growth in capital-goods production and hence the growth in output and employment. The problem is that at any given time the amount of goods that can be produced with full employment is fixed. Care must be taken to see that the economic-output pie is not cut with such a large slice for consumer goods that too small a slice is left for capital goods.

In a demand-driven economy, the way to achieve the shift from consumer to producer goods is by restraining consumers from demanding too many goods. In addition to consumer savings or thrift,

Samuelson argued that there could be public thrift. In 1962 he wrote:

> For a half dozen years I have been preaching the doctrine that a mixed-enterprise economy can raise its rate of capital formation and hence the growth rate of potential GNP by public thrift. Just as people decide their day-to-day decisions about consuming and non-consuming in the marketplace for goods, for bonds and savings accounts and for political polls and vote for an additional rate of capital formation to be brought about through government action, I do not have in mind here merely that people may vote for durable dams, school buildings and other forms of social capital, even though such programs may well be desirable for their own sake and for growth. What I mean is that we may all democratically vote that our full-employment mix of output should be shifted toward more capital formation and less consumption. (1966, p. 1725)

Samuelson's scenario calls for political representatives who would carry out an agenda of an expansionary monetary policy coupled with an austere fiscal policy. The idea is that the Federal Reserve System should engage in a monetary policy that is sufficiently expansionary to keep interest rates low. The lower that interest rates are for borrowed funds, the more likely business firms will be to borrow funds and invest in capital goods. The danger is that the increased spending for capital goods, added to consumer spending, will result in a greater demand for goods than can be produced at a given time—an in-

flationary gap. To avoid this demand-caused inflation, the government should be willing to step in and raise taxes to cut consumer spending sufficiently to avoid triggering inflation.

The scenario Samuelson has set up has three requirements. First, the public must be sufficiently economically sophisticated to arrive at some majority feeling as to the desirability of economic growth and some understanding of the mechanism for achieving it so that it can elect politicians who will carry out its will. Second, the politicians must have sufficient economic knowledge to be able to design appropriate legislation. Third, economists must be able to provide useful recommendations as to the technical decisions that must be pursued in any given time period to make the policies work.

This scenario also explains much of Samuelson's use of his professional energies. A considerable amount of his efforts has been devoted to furthering the development of economic theory down the Keynesian path for enlightened decision making regarding stabilization and economic growth. His willingness to advise political candidates and testify in Washington to educate the political establishment may be seen as a necessity rather than some gratuitous attempt to achieve political clout behind the scenes. And the need for an economically sensitive, if not economically literate public provided a strong rationale for Samuelson to write his textbook and articles for the laymen in popular magazines. Throughout his career, Samuelson's writings in scholarly journals have been accompanied by a steady stream of articles on contemporary economic issues. These popular writings distinguish him from the majority of academic economists, whose works appear only in academic journals.

Samuelson feels that these popular efforts are important, even if they did not bring professional prestige. Yet he is well aware of the "split, between the 'inside look' of a subject in terms of the logic and experience of its professional development and its implication for the man-in-the-street. . . ." Moreover, he has written: "until academic tenure has come, you are best advised not to write for *Harper's* or the *Manchester Guardian* (to say nothing of the *National Review* or the *New Republic*) lest you be indicted for superficiality." Since he has had no worries about academic tenure or his reputation, he has been able to indulge himself in the popular press without risking his career (1966, pp. 1503–4).

This willingness to speak out in the popular press with advice on contemporary economic issues has been based on a continuing faith in the viability of Keynesian economic theory. In a 1958 essay, "What Economists Know," Samuelson maintained his optimism about the ability of economists to provide policies that could wipe out persistent slumps. He was not arguing that recessions could be avoided, but he continued a firm belief that they could be kept mild and that there would no longer be the need to fear a 1930s-type downturn. Because of the progress that had been made

with respect to recessions, he believed that the major remaining problem was inflation. "From the standpoint of society at large, perhaps the greatest problem still facing the student of political economy is the threat of long term inflation" (1966, p. 1647). The events of the late 1960s and 1970s were to prove Samuelson quite correct.

Samuelson's belief in the desirability of intervention in the economy has resulted in a willingness on his part to be an advisor to the Democratic party. In 1958, two years before his successful presidential campaign, John F. Kennedy added Samuelson to his group of advisors, and after his election he made Samuelson the head of a task force to develop the economics agenda for the new administration. The final report was written by Samuelson, but it was fairly conventional and did not contain much in the way of a Keynesian agenda. Most noticeably, there was no call for a tax cut to stimulate the sluggish economy. This was not because Samuelson did not believe a tax cut necessary but because he was sensitive to political reality. He knew that it was politically "out of the question," since Kennedy "had run on a program that asked sacrifices of the American people. How could he begin by giving them what many would regard as a handout?

Samuelson also indicated that he was sensitive to the need to educate Congress: "He [Kennedy] also has something that his economic experts naturally lack, namely, an appreciation of the degree to which congressmen have to be educated and re-educated" (1966, p. 1494). Here he was revealing the difficulty in getting economic recommendations turned into a succesful legislation.

This appreciation of the political process probably explains why he turned down the chairmanship of the Council of Economic Advisors when Kennedy offered it to him. As he had learned in writing the task force report, he could not speak as an economist and make recommendations based upon economic theory and at the same time be a spokesman for the administration. Samuelson chose to maintain his ability to make independent recommendations as a professor at MIT. However, he was willing to put his energies into the economic debates of both the Kennedy and Johnson administrations.

In his own words, "As with Moses, it was not given to me to enter into the promised land of the White House. Other duty called. But I was able to serve as out-of-town designated hitter, backing up the magnificent on-the-site all-star Council of Economic Advisors" (*Economics from the Heart*, 1983, p. 35).

He often came down to Washington to support the fight for a tax cut to stimulate the economy, which was eventually passed after Kennedy's death, and he served on a task force on prosperity for the Johnson administration and strongly lobbied for the surtax during the Vietnam War.

For fifteen years, from 1966 until 1981, Samuelson wrote a column on a regular basis for *News-week*, in which he worried about the problems of "stagflation" and inflation in the 1970s. However, he remained moderate in his recommendations and did not join the group in the Democratic party that was calling for price controls at the time of the 1980 elections, as he felt that such controls would only be effective for one year and then would lose the ability to continue to deal with inflation.

E. Carey Brown and Robert M. Solow have written a warm tribute to Samuelson, based on their years of association with him at MIT. They refer to him as a comrade in arms, as a helpful and supportive colleague, and as a warm and generous friend. They point out his dedication to MIT and praise his concern for the students, his minimizing of competition among faculty and students, and his interest in and support of others in their professional and personal problems. They note the quality of his verbal skills, which have been amply visible in the preceding quotations:

> As a companion Paul is simply superb. His conversational and writing styles are very similar: trenchant, vivid figures of speech, extensive historical references, illuminating comparative situations or ideas. He loves to improve on conventional wisdom by rephrasing, sometimes standing it on its head. For example: "The exception that improves the rules." (1983, pp. xii–xiii)

They finish with a final tribute to the amazing breadth of Samuelson's contribution to the evolution of modern economic theory: "Alfonso the Wise is supposed to have said that if he had been present at the Creation, he would have done a better job. Paul was, and did . . ."

This tribute by his colleagues is well-deserved. The field of economics has changed rapidly in the last fifty years, and in almost any area one picks to do a review, the name of Samuelson appears over and over. No other person has written in so many areas of economics with such depth and perception. Samuelson stands alone.

TOM STALEY

# Selected Bibliography

## WORKS BY SAMUELSON

"A Note on Measurement of Utility." *Review of Economic Studies* 4 (1937): 155-61.

"Some Aspects of the Pure Theory of Capital." *Quarterly Review of Economics* 51 (1937): 469-96.

"The Gains from International Trade." *Canadian Journal of Economics and Political Science* v (1939): 195-205.

"Interactions Between the Multiplier Analysis and the Principle of Acceleration." *Review of Economics and Statistics* 21 (1939): 75-78.

(with Wolfgang Stolper). "Protection and Real Wages." *The Review of Economic Studies* ix (1941): 58-73.

"Full Employment after the War." In *Postwar Economic Problems*,

edited by S. E. Harris, pp. 27-53. New York: McGraw-Hill, 1943.

*Foundations of Economic Analysis.* Cambridge, Ma.: Harvard University Press, 1947.

Economics: An Introductory Analysis. New York: McGraw-Hill, 1948.

"Pure Theory of Public Expenditures." *Review of Economics and Statistics* 36 (1954): 387-89.

"What Economists Know." In *The Human Meaning of the Social Sciences*, edited by Daniel Lerner. New York: Meridian Books, 1959.

*The Collected Scientific Papers of Paul A. Samuelson.* 2 vols. Edited by Joseph E. Stiglitz. Cambridge, Ma.: MIT Press, 1966.

*Economics from the Heart.* Edited by Maryann O. Keating. San Diego: Harcourt Brace Jovanovich, 1983.

## OTHER WORKS

Arrow, K. J., "Samuelson Collected." *Journal of Political Economy* 75 (5) (1967:730-37).

Brown, E. Carey, and Solow, Robert M., eds. *Paul Samuelson and Modern Economic Theory.* New York: McGraw-Hill, 1983.

Feiwel, George R., ed. *Samuelson and Neoclassical Economics.* Boston: Kluwer-Nijhoff, 1982.

Lindbeck, A. "Paul Samuelson's Contribution to Economics." Swedish Journal of Economics 72 (1970): 341-54.

Silk, Leonard. *The Economists.* New York: Basic Books, 1976.

Sobel, Robert. *The Worldly Economists.* New York: Macmillan, 1980.

# THEODORE SCHULTZ  *1979*

In 1979, at the age of seventy-seven, Theodore W. Schultz was awarded The Nobel Memorial Prize in Economic Sciences along with Sir Arthur Lewis, for his work on the problems of development in Third World countries. According to his Nobel citation, Schultz was the first economist to systematize how investments in education affect the productivity of the agricultural sector and the overall economy.

## Career and Achievements

Theodore W. Schultz was born on April 30, 1902, to Henry E. and Anna E. (Weiss) Schultz in the German farm community of Arlington, South Dakota. Schultz has characterized the early part of his life as a period of tremendous turmoil, uncertainty, and confusion, mostly reflecting the depressed economic circumstances surrounding his birth and childhood. From this life experience, Schultz developed the desire to study economics so that he could "know about the circumstances he was living under."

In 1924 Schultz, without having ever attended secondary school, entered South Dakota State College, where he received a Bachelor of Science degree from the School of Agriculture in 1928. He then attended the University of Wisconsin, where he was awarded both a Master of Science degree in 1928 and a Ph.D. in agricultural economics in 1930. Schultz's doctoral dissertation dealt with the effects of tariffs on grain imports and exports. His dissertation served as the basis for his first book: *The Tariffs on Barley, Oats, and Corn* (1933).

In 1930 Schultz married Esther F. Werth (with whom he had three children: Elaine, Margaret, and Paul) and joined the economics department of Iowa State College. In 1934 Schultz achieved the rank of professor and was appointed head of the Department of Economics and Sociology at Iowa State.

One of Schultz's lesser known contributions to agricultural economics was his work in transforming the field into an area of study within general economics. At the time of Schultz's appointment as department chairman, agricultural economics fell into various specialized areas (for example, farm management, marketing, etc.) as the subject lacked a firm footing in price and value theory. His desire to integrate agricultural economics into general economics guided his tenure as chairman at Iowa State, both by the way he organized the program and in attracting such young theoreticians to the department as George J. Stigler, Albert G. Hart, and Kenneth Boulding. Schultz also improved the quality of empirical research at Iowa State by encouraging close cooperation between economic theorists and statisticians.

During World War II Schultz and his colleagues initiated a study on the ways that agriculture might contribute to the war effort. This project culminated in a series of papers on war, food, and the farm. One of the studies from this series, O. H. Brownlee's *Putting Dairying on a War Footing* (1943), suggested that the artificial taxes and coloring restrictions imposed on margarine be removed. Iowa's dairy farmers, feeling financially threatened by this suggestion, exerted political pressure on the University and the bulletin was removed from circulation. Schultz, in face of this violation of academic freedom, resigned his position in 1943.

Schultz then joined the economics faculty at the University of Chicago as a professor of economics. In 1946 he was appointed departmental chairman. Many of the organizational skills he demonstrated at Iowa State also served him well at Chicago. One of Schultz's major contributions during his tenure as chairman was the encouragement of workshops—especially in human capital theory—that took place from the 1940s onward. Schultz served the department in this capacity until 1961. In 1952 he became Charles L. Hutchinson Distinguished Service Professor. In 1972 Schultz retired from the University of Chicago. He has remained professionally active and still maintains an office in the economics department at Chicago.

Schultz is the author of almost 300 publications, including approximately thirteen books. Some of the more important titles of his voluminous output include *Agriculture in an Unstable Economy* (1945), *Pro-*

*duction and Welfare of Agriculture* (1949), *The Economic Organization of Agriculture* (1953), *Transforming Traditional Agriculture* (1964), *Economic Growth and Agriculture* (1968), *Investment in Human Capital: The Role of Education and of Research* (1971), and *Distortions of Agricultural Incentives* (1978).

Schultz has also been the recipient of many honors in addition to his Nobel Prize. He is a fellow of the American Farm Economic Association, the American Academy of Arts and Sciences, and the American Philosophical Society. He is also a member of the National Academy of Sciences. Schultz has served as a past president of the American Economic Association (1960) and has received its highest award (1965): the Francis A. Walker Medal. Unlike many other American social scientists, Schultz has also been honored for his work by the socialist world and has served as a guest of the Soviet Academy of Sciences (1960).

Schultz's nonacademic offices have included membership and chair positions with the National Bureau of Economic Research (1949–73) and advisory and consulting positions with the U.S. government (Department of Agriculture, Federal Reserve Board, President's Economic Council of Advisors, National Science Foundation, various World War II boards and administrations, etc.), the United Nations, nonprofit corporations (Rand, Ford Foundation, Carnegie Foundation, Rockefeller Foundation, etc.), and missions abroad.

## Intellectual Development

During the 1930s and 1940s Schultz directed his attention towards the objective analysis of agricultural policies. Schultz was interested in studying the effects of President Franklin D. Roosevelt's New Deal programs on farm output and income. One important conclusion, which still has relevancy today, was that farm programs which attempted to firm up agricultural prices or distribute input cost or output subsidies did little to improve the economic position of the low-income farm producers. Schultz's explanation was that the primary function of prices is to allocate resources, and any policy that attempts to use prices to effect a fairer income distribution is doomed to fail.

A second theme which began to emerge in Schultz's work during the 1940s dealt with the economics of development and growth. Many economists consider Schultz's *Transforming Traditional Agriculture* (1964) to be his most significant contribution in this area of research. Schultz argued the then-heretical ideas that traditional farmers in poor countries are rational economic agents, that the marginal productivity of farm workers is above zero, and that poor agriculturalists would adopt new techniques if in fact they were superior to the old. Schultz's account of the apparent unwillingness of poor farmers to innovate emphasized the uncertainties surrounding economic returns from farming, the lack of agricultural extension services, and the discriminatory price and tax policies pursued by many low-income governments against agriculture in the name of industrial development.

Beginning in the late 1950s, Schultz began to write on human capital theory. Schultz's interest in this topic began after World War II, while he was serving as an agricultural economist with the U.S. occupation army in Germany. Schultz was impressed with the rapid reconstruction of Germany and the other European countries. His explanation of this phenomenon was that while the physical capital stock of Europe had been destroyed, its human capital—in terms of knowledge and skills—had actually grown.

While Schultz is sometimes wrongly thought to be the father of human capital theory, he may be credited with reviving an interest in this topic with his article in *Social Service Review*, "Investment in Man: An Economist's View" (1959), and his American Economic Association presidential address, "Investment in Human Capital" (1961).

What stands out in Schultz's overall intellectual development is what has been called his "uncanny knack for asking relevant questions" (Sills, p. 708), and his willingness to extend, widen, and integrate his research interests. These qualities can be seen both in the new lines of research he has inaugurated (such as questions dealing with the unexplained residual in the growth of output) and his own more recent works dealing with the economic analysis of fertility, which combines human capital theory and population dynamics to explain the returns to agricultural research, entrepreneurship, and donor community policies.

## Food Production in Developing Nations

If there exists a center of gravity to Schultz the man—that is, if there exists a place which brings together both the many threads of his scientific analysis and his own personal life experiences to provide energy for his intellect and imagination—it must be in the area of development.

Following World War II, many economists, planners, and politicians involved in economic development understood Europe's rapid material advancement as the by-product of a large industrial sector financed out of domestic savings and capital transfers from abroad. The global significance of this interpretation of European reconstruction was in its application to poor nations. To the question, "What should underdeveloped nations do to foster their own development?," the stock answer became, "Invest in physical industrial capital." To the question, "From where does a poor nation obtain physical industrial capital?," the development community responded, "From savings generated by selling raw materials and agricultural goods to the industrial world and capital transfers from abroad."

As might be expected, Schultz's development program is quite dif-

ferent from those who wanted to create the equivalent of a Marshall Plan for the underdeveloped world. Schultz's plan for eradicating world poverty emphasizes changes in existing agriculture policies and the development of human capital.

Schultz begins his enquiry into the wealth of developing nations by noting that most of the people in these nations are poor, and that most poor people in these countries earn their livelihood through agriculture and that the poor spend on average half or more of their income on food. From this observation Schultz deduces that if we understood the economics of agriculture we would know much of the economics of being poor. Schultz thus sets as his object of study the agricultural sector in developing countries.

Schultz initiates his analysis of poverty by first arguing that agriculture production has the potential to grow significantly in underdeveloped countries. The importance of this proposition is that it implies the possibility of profoundly improving the income levels of the world's existing poor people. Schultz is even willing to extend his argument to say that the food-production potential of the planet can comfortably handle growing populations.

What is so engaging about Schultz's position is that it is so contrary to the dismal food forecasts that appear in the popular press. Schultz argues that these pessimistic food predictions are made mostly by rich urban people who know the least about agriculture. And besides, these dire food forecasts have mostly turned out to be wrong during the past century.

Given this immense possibility to increase food production, Schultz's analysis begs the question, What in fact has constrained poor nations from feeding their own populations? Schultz's position is that the decisive factors in depressing world food production are a lack of population and other input qualities, and economic distortions generated by government policies. Regarding the former, population qualities refer to acquired skills, health, longevity, and so on, while other input qualities refer to fertilizer quality, farm-implement quality, etc.

How exceptional is his analysis? Consider the following traditional explanations of deficient food production by imagining a conference attended by four agriculturalists on the food shortage problem of nation X. Expert one: "Too little food is produced in X because of poor soil conditions." Expert two: "No, that's not right! X's food-shortage problem is due to inadequate space." Expert three: "You're both wrong. X's problem has to do with an inadequate supply of energy." Expert four: "All three of you are missing the point totally. X's problem has nothing to do with food production at all. The real problem in X is too much population growth."

The basis for the above statements can be found in the natural-earth philosophies of David Ricardo and Robert Malthus. What makes Schultz's food-production ideas unique is that they represent a move away from this position. Schultz favors the socio-economic perspective which believes that humankind has the ability to lessen its dependence on the physical aspects of the production process through its intellect. Ricardo's concept of land as the original and indestructible powers of the soil is wrong in a world in which soils have been augmented by research and new discoveries, while Malthus's "iron law" of population growth has been circumvented by many nations as a result of parents' choosing to have fewer children as their income levels have risen.

Schultz provides an empirical attack on the natural-earth argument by documenting and comparing areas of the world that have good soil quality and poverty with areas of the world that had poor soil quality and managed through modern agricultural techniques, research, and cropland substitution to improve their soils dramatically and with an area of the world in which good-to-excellent-quality soil was made even more productive through human capital.

The alluvial lands along and at the mouth of the Nile River and the soils of south India represent examples of the first case. In both of these geographical areas, soils are rich but people are poor. Schultz uses Europe and Japan as examples of the second case. According to Schultz, "The original soils of Finland were less productive than the nearby western parts of the Soviet Union, yet today the croplands of Finland are superior. [And] Japanese croplands were originally much inferior to those of northern India; [yet] they are greatly superior today" (1980, p. 642). The United States is illustrative of the third case, in which good to excellent soils were made even better by improving input qualities—especially human quality. Schultz cites the U.S. statistic that from 1933 to the present corn acreage dropped by 33 million acres while corn production increased threefold.

The second factor stressed by Schultz to account for low food production in developing countries is government-induced distortions in agriculture. Schultz asserts that governments in developing countries actively retard the development process by creating distortions in their economies. These distortions take such forms as "cheap" food policies (aimed at placating urban populations) and nationalizing the pricing of fertilizer by controlling its importation, production, and distribution.

Subsidized food policies are frequently rationalized on the ground that agriculture plays an insignificant role in the development process, while industrialization is viewed as the key to economic progress. Also, farmers are viewed as being indifferent to economic incentives on the ground that they are strongly committed to traditional ways of cultivation. Hence, "cheap" food policies are supposed to support industrialization by providing industrial workers with a relatively inexpensive input in their household production function while doing very little damage to food production. Unfortunately, as Schultz points out, food policies that decrease the relative price of food create incentives for rational farmers to cut back on their food production and thus disrupt the industrialization process.

Schultz argues that while the relative price of food in developing countries is kept low, the relative price of fertilizer is kept high. He attributes the high price of fertilizer in many poor regions of the world to inadequate domestic competition caused by trade barriers and government-sponsored fertilizer monopolies. While governments defend such fertilizer policies in the name of protecting some domestic producer, the end result again is the creation of a disincentive to produce food.

These examples of government-induced distortions highlight an important assumption in Schultz's analysis: that farmers in developing nations are rational, calculating entrepreneurs who are sensitive to costs, returns, and risk. This assumption also includes farm wives in their role as allocators of farm income. The radical implication of this assumption, in a world of government-induced distortions, is that the unrealized potential for additional food production is enormous if only farmers were given the incentive to produce.

But governments in developing countries are not alone in creating disincentives for farmers in poor countries. Schultz also criticizes the international donor community. He argues that this community—best represented by donor agencies and the U.S. government—has an anti-market bias and a propensity to support government intervention at the expense of economic productivity.

Schultz places the problems created in poor countries by the donor community into several categories. One is dumping and tying. The former he calls "a convenient way for a donor country to dispose of its own burdensome surpluses" (1981 symposia, p. 485). Tying refers to donor countries insisting that part of the aid given be used to purchase supplies from the donor country. According to Schultz, the United States has been one of the more guilty parties of dumping through its P.L. 480 programs, which use the rhetoric of "Food for Peace." In reality, according to Schultz, they allow the government that receives "such aid to continue discriminating against its agriculture whether it be by means of procurement of food grains from farmers by marketing boards, or by other means to maintain a 'cheap' food policy that distorts agricultural incentives" (p. 185).

A second type of distortion created by the donor community is the insistence by donors that their own experts be used in projects. Schultz considers this requirement a waste of development finance in those cases where there exist host-country experts of equal caliber who would work for lower salaries.

A third type of distortion imposed on developing countries by donors is their overemphasis of equity considerations as opposed to production. Schultz views this as a mistake given the great needs the developing world has for more output.

For Schultz, though, the most serious distortion imposed by inter-national donors on host countries is their bias against using markets for the allocation of resources and goods and services. Schultz: "Donor agencies with few exceptions are strongly biased against markets. They thrive on the rhetoric of market failure" (p. 487). Therefore, the economic effect of a good deal of foreign aid is to strengthen the capacity of the host governments to discriminate against agriculture.

Schultz's arguments may be summarized as follows: (1) Given that most of the world's poor people earn their livelihood in agriculture, the way out of world poverty is by increasing world food production; (2) The planet has the capacity to greatly increase food production. World poverty is a correctable problem; (3) What is presently preventing more food from being produced is a lack of population and other input qualities, and economic distortions created by developing and donor governments and international agencies.

These three points constitute the essence of Schultz's arguments surrounding the development question. Some of these points Schultz also raises in terms of the U.S. economy, especially emphasizing the role of input qualities and government farm policies.

# Errors and Solutions

Schultz believes that development economists committed two primary errors: they rejected the standard neoclassical paradigm in favor of specialized development models, and they neglected economic history in both its theoretical and empirical forms.

In Schultz's judgment, the specialized models in economic development that have evolved since World War II have proven barren. Even worse, from his perspective, is that some economists, in response to the apparent failure of these models, have opted for models that emphasize cultural and social variables. Schultz prefers the use of orthodox models to guide policymakers in the design, analysis, and implementation of economic policy in poor countries. His case in support of mainline models is that the poverty predicament is primarily a problem of resource scarcity, which standard theories were designed to solve.

Schultz's second criticism deals with what he perceives to be gaps in the education of development specialists: their lack of knowledge concerning past economic doctrines and their lack of knowledge concerning past economic trends. Schultz notes that classical economics evolved at a time when the people of western Europe were themselves very poor. He believes that development economists should be familiar with the ways that earlier economists in the West attempted to grapple with many of the same problems that underdeveloped nations presently face.

But, more important than understanding past economic theories, those working in development should also be familiar with the achievements of past impoverished peoples in order to develop an understanding of the possibilities of low-income countries today. An ex-

cellent example of how an inadequate grasp of history caused many scholars to form misguided views of the future is the so-called "population problem." During the 1960s and 1970s, a common exercise amongst development scientists was the simple extrapolation of world population statistics into the future. The results were horrifying. Those concerned with economic development came to the conclusion that people in poor countries were reproducing at a rate that no amount of development could ever sustain.

Schultz points to this experience as an example of how a lack of knowledge of past trends caused many to misread the implications of population statistics. An "over-the-shoulder" view of population dynamics, he contended, results in an entirely different assessment. What in fact has occurred historically is that as family incomes have risen, parents have chosen to have fewer children, which has reversed population-related problems.

What contributes to Schultz's uniqueness as an economist is his desire to place the human mind (in the form of knowledge, imagination, etc.) at the center of economic development. Schultz believes that "while land per se is not a critical factor in being poor, the human agent is: Investment in improving population quality can significantly enhance the economic prospects and the welfare of poor people" (1980, p. 643).

Schultz's emphasis on population quality follows from his belief in it as the single most important input in agricultural production functions. To the extent that labor is

healthy, educated, and skilled, it becomes more productive. For example, an increase in health care generates a flow called health-time, or
sickness-free time, which acts as an
input into labor time. An increase in
labor time will cause overall societal
production and welfare to increase.
Furthermore, there will be multiplier effects following an increase in
food production. Also, as health-
time increases, populations will have
a greater incentive to acquire additional education as an investment in
their future earnings. Parents will
also invest more in their children's
future. More on-job training will become available. Longer life spans result in more years of labor-force
participation. All of these factors
contribute to labor's productivity in
agriculture.

Schultz also suggests an indirect
benefit flowing from greater population quality. He posits that an important condition for agriculture to
reach its peak production is for government to remove itself from certain aspects of the agricultural economy. Unfortunately, a short-run
consequence of government's withdrawal from the agricultural economy will be to throw the system into
a disequilibrium state, a condition in
which the economy is going through
many changes. During this adjustment time, new relative resource and
product prices will come into being,
risk factors will change, and new institutions might arise. What does
this have to do with population
quality? Schultz maintains that the
ability of farmers to take advantage
of this period of disequilibrium is a
function of their entrepreneurial

skills, and that entrepreneurship itself is a function of population quality. Therefore, the ability of the agricultural sector to take advantage of
government reforms is itself a function of population quality.

Although Schultz has been critical of government's attempts to
manage the agricultural sector of the
economy by limiting the role that
markets play in the allocation of
agricultural inputs and outputs, his
analysis should not be interpreted as
a bias against the role of government in the improvement of the
economy. Schultz sees seven areas
where government has an important
role to play in the development of
agriculture: (1) collecting and reporting agricultural statistics; (2) creating
and maintaining standards of measurement; (3) determining and en-
forcing property rights; (4) com-
bating animal and plant diseases;
(5) maintaining a stable price level
through macroeconomic management techniques; (6) reducing economy-wide inequalities; (7) aiding the
creation of an agricultural research
establishment.

In all seven of these areas government has a comparative advantage over the private sector. In addition, all seven of these areas support
the existence of a market-style economy. Schultz believes that the empirical evidence weighs heavily
against the possibility of government substituting itself for the marketplace. In his words, "The Soviet
Union, with all of its farm machinery, fertilizer, and other large investments in agriculture, continues to be
incapable of developing a modern
efficient agricultural sector. . . .

Orders from Moscow are poor substitutes for market prices" (1981 article, p. 11). What is true of the Soviet Union is also true for poor nations. Nevertheless, Schultz's seven points do provide a broad landscape for creative and market-enhancing activities on the part of government.

## The Future of Agriculture

Schultz's position is to be neither pessimistic nor optimistic about future agriculture production (and human welfare) in low-income countries. Given his rejection of the natural-earth view, the decisive factor in determining food production is population quality and the role of the government in agricultural markets. On both of these accounts, Schultz believes the possibilities are open-ended. Schultz reminds us that "Robert Malthus could not have anticipated the substitution by parents of quality for quantity of children. Nor could David Ricardo have anticipated the results of modern agricultural research that have become substitutes for land in agricultural production" (1981 article, p. 7). Therefore, it is not really possible to anticipate what will occur in the future.

Schultz does believe that many favorable developments are presently taking place in developing countries that if continued will lead eventually to the alleviation of world poverty. Primary among these is the wide recognition of the economic value of agricultural research. "Real progress is being

made," he says, "in financing and in increasing research that is oriented towards the requirements of low-income countries" (p. 7). Schultz also sees the narrowly focused commitment to industrialization with little concern for agriculture as a thing of the past. He argues that though "cheap" food policies are still present in the world, fewer nations rely on this type of policy than during the 1950s and 1960s. Also, life expectancy is higher in many poor nations, with some countries showing increases upwards of 50 percent over the past three decades. Schultz believes that the implications of this achievement are favorable for agricultural development. In addition, other standards of population quality have improved worldwide. Young adults in underdeveloped nations have more human capital than their forebears had.

Of great importance for poor nations has been the recent reduction in the gap between rich and poor countries in terms of agricultural productivity changes. The gap had begun to widen during the 1930s, when food production began increasing dramatically in high-income countries, and therefore the comparative advantage in growing food had shifted towards the wealthier nations of the world. Schultz believes that the comparative advantage lost by the less developed world is slowly being regained as a result of research oriented towards the requirements of poor nations.

But all is not well. On the negative side of the ledger, many governments in poor nations still refuse to allow agricultural markets an op-

portunity to do what they do best—
which is to perform their allocative
function. Compounding this difficulty is the antimarket bias of donor
agencies. The end result of this
stunting of markets is reduced agricultural production and increased
world poverty. And finally—again
on the negative side—there are still
many unstable governments in
Africa, which does not bode well for
agricultural development in that
part of the world.

MARK A. NADLER

# Selected Bibliography

Brownlee, O. H. *Putting Dairying on a War Footing.* Ames, Iowa: Iowa State College Press, 1943.

Ranis, Gustav. "The 1979 Nobel Prize in Economics." *Science* 206 (1979): 1389–91.

Schultz, Theodore W. *The Tariffs on Barley, Oats, and Corn.* Madison, Wisconsin: Tariff Research Committee, 1933.

———. "Scope and Method in Agricultural Economic Research." *Journal of Political Economy* 47 (1939): 705–17.

———. *Agriculture in an Unstable Economy.* New York: McGraw-Hill, 1945.

———. *Production and Welfare of Agriculture.* New York: Macmillan, 1949.

———. *Measures for Economic Development of Underdeveloped Countries,* with D. R. Gadgil, Arthur Lewis, George Hakim, and Alberto Balta Cortez. New York: United Nations Department of Economic Affairs, 1951.

———. *The Economic Organization of Agriculture.* New York: McGraw-Hill, 1953.

———. "Investment in Man: An Economist's View." *Social Service Review* 33 (1959): 109–17.

———. "Investment in Human Capital." *American Economic Review* 51 (1961): 1–17. (American Economic Association Presidential Address.)

———. *Transforming Traditional Agriculture.* New Haven, Ct.: Yale University Press, 1964.

———. *Economic Crisis in World Agriculture.* Ann Arbor: University of Michigan Press, 1965.

———. *Economic Growth and Agriculture.* New York: McGraw-Hill, 1968.

———. *Investment in Human Capital: The Role of Education and of Research.* New York: Free Press, 1971.

———, ed. *Economics of the Family: Marriage, Children, and Human Capital.* Chicago: University of Chicago Press, 1974.

———. *Distortions of Agricultural Incentives.* Bloomington: Indiana University Press, 1978.

———. "Nobel Lecture: The Economics of Being Poor." *Journal of Political Economy* 88 (1980): 639–51.

———. "Knowledge Is Power." *Challenge* 22 (1981): 4–12.

———. "Distortions by the International Donor Community." *Promoting Increased Food Production in the 1980's,* Proceedings of the Second Annual Agricultural Sector Symposia, January 5–9, 1981. Washington, D.C.: World Bank, 1981.

——. *Investing in People: The Economics of Population Quality.* Berkeley: University of California Press, 1981.

Sills, David L., ed. *International Encyclopedia of the Social Sciences: Biographical Supplement.* Vol. 18. New York: Macmillan and Free Press, 1979.

# HERBERT ALEXANDER SIMON *1978*

*Advances in human knowledge, even more than other events, cast very long shadows before them.*

HERBERT ALEXANDER SIMON

Few in the field of economics have cast longer shadows than Herbert Simon. In 1978, he was awarded the Nobel Prize in Economic Sciences for his lifetime study of organizations, with particular reference to the limits of human rationality in the decision making process. The award came over thirty years after the publication of *Administrative Behavior* (1947), Simon's pioneering work on decision making. While thirty-one years may seem like an unusually long time to come to appreciate the importance of Simon's seminal work, we are now in truth only beginning to realize the significance of his thinking and the impact his insights have had on a number of fields of which economics is but one.

For Simon, born June 15, 1916, the Nobel Prize came late in life and was a genuine surprise. Considered a heretic by many conventional economists, Simon was an uneasy visitor to the field, passing through the discipline on his way from public administration, his research interest as a young man, to his present work on artificial intelligence. His broad training in psychology and organizational behavior led him early on to reject the economist's narrow concept of rationality in favor of a broader rationality based on empirical studies of how people in fact make decisions. Simon believed that economists could make better use of their time observing how people in organizations actually make decisions rather than modeling behavior based on an idealized view of rationality, and he put his preaching into practice in his doctoral dissertation.

In that research, Simon initiated empirical studies of decision making, then supplemented this analysis with firsthand observations and interviews with decision makers within organizations. The cumulative result of this work led to his magnum opus, *Administrative Behavior* (1947), which contains two of Simon's most notable contributions to decision theory. One is the concept of "bounded rationality," which refers to the limited ability of decision makers to compare alternatives in the face of uncertainty; in short, to process information. The second contribution, "satisficing," is Simon's observation that human beings, because of their cognitive limitations, identify with subgoals and are willing to settle for "good enough" solutions to problems instead of optimal ones.

The quest to understand decision making as it really is, is a recurring theme throughout much of his scientific career. Simon is determined to base his work on empirically valid assumptions and to describe economic decisions made by real people who analyze problems the way his psychological studies have shown real people to think. His position is that economics is a behavioral science and should have an empirical content. He rejects the economic assumption that people behave as if they were solving sets of differential equations in their heads. He continues to work instead on developing mathematical and computer models that simulate human thinking as that process has been revealed through observation and empirical studies.

## Simon's Life and Work

Herbert Alexander Simon was born on June 15, 1916 in Milwaukee, Wisconsin. His parents, Arthur and Edna Merkle Simon, nurtured in him an early attachment to books and other things of the intellect. Simon's father had come to the United States from Germany in 1903, after earning an engineering diploma from Technische Hochschule of Dormstadt. He was an electrical engineer, an inventor of electrical control gear, a patent attorney, and an active leader in professional and civic affairs in Milwaukee. He received an honorary doctorate from Marquette University for his many activities on behalf of the Milwaukee community. Simon's mother was a third-generation American and an accomplished pianist. She was a piano teacher until her marriage in 1910 and was always very active in local musical clubs.

Simon grew up in a middle-class extended family on the German west side of Milwaukee. The family provided for Simon and his older brother, Clarence, a home rich in music, intellectual discussion, and debates. Simon was an introverted, bookish child who took great pride in his ability to learn, not by asking others but by his ability to master learning independently. He was a good listener who was often sought out as a confidant, even by the adults in his family. He says that before he was twelve he had learned that quite reasonable and truthful people could perceive the same sets of events in remarkably different ways.

The recipient of an excellent general education from the public schools in Milwaukee, Simon supplemented his formal learning with an ambitious, self-directed reading program. Many of the books he read, especially in the areas of economics and psychology, once belonged to his mother's younger brother, Harold Merkle. Although he died at age thirty, when Simon himself was only five years old, Uncle Harold had a profound influence on the intellectual development of his nephew.

Harold Merkle had studied economics at the University of Wisconsin with the famous institutional economist, John R. Commons, and he later graduated with distinction from the University of Wisconsin law school. An ardent formal debater, Harold worked for the National Industrial Conference Board prior to his untimely death. While not physically present to guide and shape his young nephew's intellectual growth, Uncle Harold left Simon a legacy of books and the burning desire to find out what was in them.

In high school Simon followed his uncle's footsteps and became an active debater. In order to defend such unpopular causes as free trade, disarmament, and the single tax, Simon was led to a serious study of his uncle's library, where he found works by Richard Ely, Norman Angell, and Henry George. When Simon first entered high school he was interested in the hard sciences, especially physics, mathematics, chemistry, and biology. By the time he left high school, the combination of vigorous debating and his uncle's library had cultivated in Simon a deep interest in the social sciences.

When Simon, age seventeen, en-

tered the University of Chicago in 1933, he had a definite sense of mission. He would study the social sciences, not as an extension of the humanities, but with the same kind of rigor and mathematical underpinnings that had made the hard sciences so successful. He decided to become a mathematical social scientist. With that as his goal, Simon set out on a course of study that treated human behavior as a scientific discipline. Through formal training and self-study, he was able to gain a broad base of knowledge in economics and political science, together with considerable skills in advanced mathematics, symbolic logic, and mathematical statistics. Only his unwillingness to take a required course in accounting, which he thought dull, kept him from majoring in economics as an undergraduate. In 1936, Simon earned his bachelor's degree in political science, although he was for all practical purposes a quantitative social scientist.

His most important mentor at Chicago was Henry Schultz, an econometrician and mathematical economist. Simon also studied with economists Frank Knight, Henry Simons, and Paul Douglas. Other mentors were Rudolf Carnap in logic, Nicholas Rashevsky in mathematical biophysics, and Harold Lasswell and Charles Merriam in political science. Simon made a serious study of graduate-level physics in order to strengthen and practice his mathematical skills and to gain an intimate knowledge of what a "hard science" was like. An unexpected byproduct of this study has been his lifelong interest in the philosophy of physics, an area in which he has published several papers.

Upon graduation, Simon started working as a research assistant to Clarence Ridley, whose field of interest was municipal governments. Simon's economic training suggested to him that one could approach the issue of evaluating government activity as a problem in utility maximization, subject to budget constraints. Although he continued to attend a few classes, Simon devoted increasing amounts of time and effort to his research work for Ridley, especially the idea of evaluating government performance. This research led to his first published work, "Measurement Standards in City Administration" (1937, 1938), a series of articles coauthored with Ridley.

Simon soon became a staff person in Ridley's organization, The International City Managers Association, which was geared to help local governments become more effective. At age twenty-two, Simon served as assistant editor of the monthly journal, *Public Management* and the *Annual Municipal Yearbook.* He gradually assumed responsibility for the statistical section of the yearbook, and he wrote numerous chapters for the training manuals for city executives. It was here that Simon mastered the technology of the IBM punch card, tabulator, plugboard equipment, and enjoyed his first experience with computers.

This time at Chicago was also significant in a more personal way. It was here on June 14, 1937—one day before his twenty-first birthday—that Simon had his first date with Dorothea Pye. Simon had met the lovely, red-haired girl in the political science department office; she was the departmental secretary and a graduate assistant. Simon was too shy to ask her out, but instead asked a friend, economist Bill Cooper, to arrange a double date. Dorothea Pye and Herbert Alexander Simon were married just six months later, on December 25, 1937. The parents of three children, Simon and his wife have shared a wide range of experiences, even publishing together in two widely separate fields: public administration and cognitive psychology.

In 1939 the Simons moved to California, where Herbert assumed the directorship of a research group at the University of California at Berkeley, carrying out work similar to the kind he had started with Ridley. Here he learned to manage a staff and an organization of considerable size. At the same time he found time to finish his Ph.D. dissertation on administrative decision making that would ultimately become the foundation of his classic work, *Administrative Behavior* (1947).

Acute color blindness and his family responsibilities preempted a military service during World War II. When his Berkeley grant was exhausted in 1942, Simon secured a teaching position in political science at the Illinois Institute of Technology. Back in Chicago, Simon worked in an engineering climate at Illinois Tech, but he also maintained close contacts with scholars at the University of Chicago.

Looking back, Simon would characterize these times as intellectually stimulating and dramatic in terms of the ideas that were born then: operations research and management science, the theory of games, information theory, feedback theory, servomechanisms, control theory, statistical decision theory, and the stored program computer. These ideas intertwined with Simon's work in decision making, helping him to become part of this network of scientists who, he said, had a real sense of community that transcended their individual areas of specialization. The scholars he worked with came from physics, statistics, biology, mathematics, engineering, philosophy, psychology, political science, and economics, and each contributed in his or her own way to the intellectual environment in which Simon's ideas were nurtured.

At that time, the Cowles Commission for Research in Economics was located at the University of Chicago. Its staff included Jacob Marschak and Tjalling Koopmans, who were then directing the graduate work of such students as Kenneth Arrow, Leo Hurwicz, Lawrence Klein, and Don Patinkin. Oscar Lange, Milton Friedman, and Franco Modigliani frequently participated in the Cowles Commission seminars, and Simon became a regular participant.

Simon's association with the Cowles Commission did not diminish his preoccupation with human decision making; rather it introduced him to a host of new research topics to explore. One of the discussion topics was Paul Samuelson's famous essay on comparative statics and dynamics, which proposed a promising new systematic approach to the prediction of shifts in the equilibria of dynamic systems. Another topic was the estimation of supply and demand elasticities—the root of what came to be known as the "identification problem." As part of his work with the commission, Simon wrote a theoretical piece on the economics of urban migration and collaborated with Jacob Marschak on a study of the *Economic Aspects of Atomic Power* (1950), to which Simon contributed two chapters on the macroeconomic aspects of atomic power.

During these Chicago years, Simon revised his Ph.D. thesis and circulated it for comment. Macmillan accepted the work for publication, and Simon's thesis appeared in print as *Administrative Behavior* in 1947. In that same year, he accepted the chairmanship of the Department of Political and Social Science at Illinois Tech, where he had been teaching for five years. For Simon, this appointment marked the beginning of nearly a quarter of a century of departmental and deaning activities. But despite his commitment to administration, he still found time for research and other work. In the late 1940s, he teamed up with colleagues Don Smithberg and Victor Thompson to write the textbook *Public Administration* (1950), and in 1948 Simon participated in the formation of the Economic Cooperation Administration, the agency created to administer the Marshall Plan.

Simon's work at Illinois Tech came to an end in 1949. That year, the Carnegie Institute of Techology (which later merged with Mellon Institute to form Carnegie Mellon) in Pittsburgh received a $5-million endowment and funds for a building to house the new Graduate School of Industrial Administration. The GSIA would provide business education for students with degrees in science and engineering. Bill Cooper, the old Chicago friend who had arranged his first date with Dorothea Pye, asked Simon to become part of this new venture. Cooper was on the economics faculty at Carnegie Tech, and invited Simon to join the GSIA as a professor of administration. Although initially reluctant to leave Illinois Tech, Simon accepted the position, as it gave him the opportunity to launch a program of empirical research in organizations, expanding on the research he had done in administrative behavior.

Simon recalls these years devoted to forming the new school as a lively, entertaining "three-ring circus." With Lee Bach, formerly chair of the Economics Department at Carnegie Tech, installed as dean, Cooper and Simon worked to develop a faculty and curriculum for the new school. Within the school there were two major areas of extensive research activity: organizational behavior and management science. Simon headed the area of organizational behavior and simultaneously found himself serving as an organization theorist, management scientist, and business-school administrator.

Since 1949, Simon has been at Carnegie, where he is now the Richard King Mellon University Professor of Computer Science and Psychology. During his tenure, Simon has become known as its foremost intellectual strategist. As associate dean, he was instrumental in helping the Graduate School of Industrial Administration become one of the leading business schools in the United States. His own research into the cognitive basis of decision making led him into two fields of study: psychology and computer science. Each of these areas at Carnegie Mellon has benefited from Simon's involvement. His work in psychology has made the psychology department a world leader in the field of cognitive psychology. Through his interest in computers, Simon provided a major impetus to the establishment of a computer-science department at Carnegie Mellon—the first such department at an American college and now widely recognized for its pioneering work in artificial intelligence, a field Simon virtually invented.

While his work in educational innovation would represent a career in itself, Simon has always found time for research and writing. The author or coauthor of nearly 700 books, monographs, and articles, Simon is one of those few Nobel laureates whose scientific productivity has not decreased since winning the award. His books include *Models of Man* (1957), *The New Science of Management Decision* (1960), *The Sciences of the Artificial* (1969), *Human Problem Solving* (1972), and *Reason in Human Affairs* (1983). He has published articles in many fields, his works having appeared in such diverse journals as *Management Science, The American Scholar, Science, The Journal of Philosophy, The American Psychologist, Econometrician,* and the *American Political Science Review.*

As the list of his publications illustrates, Simon has made over the span of his career significant contributions to the fields of political science, sociology, psychology, computer science, public administration, management, and philosophy. While his Nobel Prize in Economics can be seen as a recognition of his contribution to economics, it can also be seen as a result of his lifetime goal of "hardening" the social sciences. He approaches all his research in the same manner, with intellectual rigor. He has been described as the consummate intellectual, a man who has lived the life of an adventurer in the world of knowledge. Since early childhood he has shown the ability to learn for himself, and he established early on his lifetime pattern of intellectual excellence.

# Simon's Contributions to Economics

The announcement that Herbert Alexander Simon was the 1978 Nobel laureate in economics caused consternation among many of the discipline's intellectual leaders, as they considered him a heretic. Still, mainstream orthodoxy had to put on a happy face, even if some in the profession believed that Simon's choice was inappropriate. So, rather than focus on the differences between Simon's thoughts and con-

ventional neoclassical theory, mainstream economists tried to create the impression that Simon was one of them.

In the *Scandinavian Journal of Economics* (1979), noted economists William J. Baumol and Albert Ando were given the task of writing scholarly valentines about Simon's work and its impact on modern economics. To his credit, Baumol begins the essay with a particularly cogent passage about Simon's contributions to organizational behavior, describing in succinct terms the fundamental difference between optimizing and "satisficing" behavior. Having done that, Baumol then devotes an equal amount of space and praise to the Hawkins-Simon Theorem, the mathematical conditions that guarantee none of the outputs in an input-output process will be assigned a negative value. However important to input-output analysis the Hawkins-Simon Theorem may be, it hardly represents the sort of breakthrough that would warrant a Nobel Prize.

If Baumol aimed his *Journal* remarks at the marginal, Ando chose to focus his on the obscure. Like Baumol, Ando begins by acknowledging the real essence of Simon's contributions to economics. Indeed, in the introduction to his essay, Ando penned what could very well be the single best one-sentence precis of Simon's life work: "to construct a comprehensive framework for modeling and analyzing the behavior of man and his organizations faced with a complex environment, recognizing the limitation of his ability to comprehend, describe, analyze and to act, while allowing for his ability to learn and to adapt." Having so stated, Ando proceeds to describe several of Simon's "minor" contributions that have some significance to mainstream economics but are only tangential to the true meaning of Simon's work. Ando writes about Simon's simplified criterion function and his work on near decomposability, hierarchical structures, and causal relationships, relegating to a footnote the following observation:

. . . Probably the most ambitious undertaking by Simon to model human problem solving behavior is reported in his monumental book with Allen Newell entitled *Human Problem Solving*. Although his findings reported in this book are of major potential importance to economists, they are at such a micro level that most economists are likely to find them somewhat remote from their everyday concern. (p. 84)

It was these and other equally "remote" results that earned Simon his Nobel Prize and have made him one of the most frequently cited students of modern management in the world.

In and of themselves, the so-called significant contributions about which Baumol and Ando wrote would not have warranted a Nobel nomination for Simon, let alone the actual award. No, it was not his contributions to mainstream economics for which Simon received the prize, but rather his frontal assault on that most cherished of neoclassical theories, optimizing behavior.

At the heart of modern economics is a theory of choice that contends individual decision makers, be they consumers or producers, consciously choose among alternative strategies or patterns of behaviors so as to maximize some singular goal or objective, be it utility or profit. Developed by mathematical statisticians and economists, this expected utility/profit model is critically dependent on four basic assumptions. First, each economic agent has a well-defined utility or profit function. This function allows an analysis of decision making that bypasses the impact values have on human behavior by loading all values into a single function that effectively finesses the issue. Second, each decision maker is completely knowledgeable of all alternative patterns of action available and is free to choose any option, be it a commodity basket of goods and services or a specific input-output combination. Third, each economic agent has a joint probability distribution of all potential outcomes and thus is working within an environment characterized by complete certainty. Finally, every decision maker is driven by the universal desire to maximize expected utility or expected profit.

Within the context of these four assumptions, neoclassical economists have fashioned a theory of human behavior that is logically consistent, complete, and mathematically elegant. But is it right? Is it relevant? When it comes to an analysis of personal consumer behavior, their theory of subjective expected utility, as Simon calls it, is virtually unassailable, for the individuality of preference preempts the designation of any action or choice as irrational, that is, suboptimal. No matter how bizarre or idiosyncratic behavior may be, its rationality is determined solely in terms of the value structure of the decision maker and not society at large. Hence, all consumer behavior is perfectly rational. This conclusion is the consequence of a theory of choice that ignores the question of values and is a principal reason economists have little of substance to say about consumer behavior. Is it any wonder that profit-making organizations turn to marketing professionals and not economists when wishing to pursue a sales-expanding strategy that does not involve changing price?

When it comes to an analysis of decision-making behavior within organizations, be they profit-making or social-welfare oriented, the conventional theory of choice is not just innocuous, it is simply inaccurate. That was what a young Herbert Simon concluded after observing the activities of decision makers in several public agencies he studied during the 1930s. In those situations where performance is evaluated in terms of quantifiable output targets, such as the number of clients served, and not something as ephemeral as a utility function, Simon discovered that decision makers behaved quite unlike the predictions of classical choice theory.

For starters, decision makers were confronted by the need to optimize several, often competing, goals, not just one objective such as utility. Secondly, most decision makers were seldom aware of all the possible alternatives in the solution sets to the problem confronting them but had a bounded knowledge of viable solutions, limited by their own experiences, education, and intelligence. Thirdly, decision makers operated within a realm of uncertainty when evaluating the present and future consequences of alternative policy choice, and not the situation of risk as pictured in neoclassical theory. Finally, decision makers almost always sought "satisficing" or "good enough" solutions to problems, not optimal or "best" alternatives.

As Simon saw it, conventional decision theory merely approximated, and then only poorly, actual behavior. He sought to correct these obvious deficiencies by developing a behavioral theory of choice consistent with the observation that the knowledge and computational abilities of humans are far more modest than the neoclassical theory demands. Mainstream economists had created a theory of decision making that served as a model of the mind of God; he would make a theory that would be a model of the mind of humans. That was the primary motivation behind Simon's magnum opus, *Administrative Behavior: A Study of the Decision-Making Process in Administrative Organizations* (1947).

One of the two major themes that would become the cornerstone of Simon's theory of choice was his concept of bounded rationality. Conventional choice theory assumes perfect rationality, decision makers having complete knowledge of all the possible choice options available to them and anticipating with certainty the consequences of any decision they make. In fact, decision makers seldom entertain more than a few of all possible alternatives when resolving a problem, and knowledge of consequences is almost always fragmentary, not exhaustive as mainstream economists presuppose. These restrictions or bounds on individual rationality are the results of the skills, habits, conscious and unconscious behaviors, and knowledge, or lack thereof, unique to a given decision maker. In concert, these limitations produce a bounded rationality which is, in effect, a subset of perfect rationality.

The upshot of this bounded rationality is that optimizing behavior may not be possible because: (1) the optimal solution to a problem is not in the subset of alternatives the decision maker is considering; or (2) even if it is, the decision maker may not possess the wherewithal to differentiate the optimal solution from others nearly as good but clearly suboptimal in a world of perfect knowledge and foresight. Under these conditions, "satisficing," not optimizing behavior becomes the norm. The decision-making process does not involve a comprehensive comparison of all alternatives in terms of some objective function. Rather, candidate solutions are tested serially in terms of some acceptability criterion, and the first solution considered that passes the acceptability test is adopted. This is the essence of "satisficing," the second of the two major themes that form the foundation of Simon's theory of choice.

For Simon, decision making is hierarchical and adaptive. Decision makers prioritize objectives, "satisficing" most important ones first, then considering other goals if time and resources permit. After encountering similar problems repeatedly, decision makers begin to internalize the decision-making process, learning from past experience so that the selection of viable solutions to familiar problems becomes almost intuitive. With maturity, decision makers learn to narrow the search for options, exploring only a small fraction of the immense number of possible solutions to recurring problems. The process becomes so institutionalized that, in most instances, the selection of the "good enough" solution is not governed by foolproof, systematic procedures, but by rules of thumb or decision-making heuristics that evolve over time. If the whole process of identifying alternatives and choosing the "best" solution results in the optimal decision, that is strictly a matter of chance, not design.

In deference to mainstream economics, it should be noted that the classical/neoclassical tradition of optimization was an accurate description of decision-making behavior through much of the nineteenth century. In a world of small, owner-operated farms and shops, each producing a single product, selling in a limited geographic area, under conditions of near-perfect competition, decision-making theory and decision-making practice meshed. Indeed, with entrepreneurs producing nearly identical products, buying inputs at comparable prices, employing like technologies, and selling to the same consumer at the going market rate, what option did decision makers have other than to maximize profits?

Profit maximization became by default the universal objective function most decision makers sought to optimize. Competitive market conditions provided all the price and cost information producers needed to select the optimizing output, while preventing any one firm or factory from so dominating the business environment as to thwart the will of the market. The preconditions necessary for the neoclassical theory of choice to be operational were satisfied. In such a world, the theory provided a good, almost perfect, predictor of human decision-making behavior. However, by the end of the nineteenth century, as Alfred D. Chandler, Jr. noted in his book *The Visible Hand* (1977), the business environment began to change.

Major changes in the processes of production and distribution, including changes in transportation, communications, and finance, diminished the importance of one-person or small-group operations in favor of the multiunit enterprise. The end result of all these changes was a business environment that rendered conventional decision theory obsolete. The decline of agriculture, the growth of large-scale manufacturing, the emergence of oligopolies, and the globalization of commerce and finance that took place during the end of the nineteenth century and into the twentieth century did not go unnoticed.

An immensely rich analysis of the changing business environment chronicled the demise of the invisible hand of the marketplace and the ascendancy of the visible hand of managerial capitalism. John R. Commons and Thorstein Veblen contributed greatly to the formation of institutionalism, a school of economics that emphasized inductive methodology in the study of the economy as a whole, with particular reference to the economic impact of institutions. Joan Robinson advanced a theory of imperfect competition, John von Neumann and Oscar Morganstern developed the theory of games, and Herbert Simon devised the concepts of bounded rationality and "satisficing." These breakthroughs, coupled with the emergence of psychology as a genuine science of mental processes and behavior, provided all the ingredients necessary to build a new science of choice, one grounded in the positive realities of observation and not the normative ideals of the heroic.

Instead of shaping these innovative ideas into a new theory of choice, orthodox economists tried to preserve the old, disguising the substantive shortcoming of conventional decision analysis in ever more exotic mathematics until procedure triumphed over content. By so doing, economists fell victim to a variant of what Simon calls mathematicians' aphasia. In this ailment, which usually afflicts theoreticians when a problem turns out to be too complex to handle with the tools available, the victim abstracts the original problem until the mathematical intractabilities have been removed (and with them, all semblance to reality), solves the new simplified problem, then claims that this was the problem to be solved all along. The hope is that in the dazzle of the mathematical results, no one will notice that nothing of consequence has been done to resolve the original problem. This is precisely what happened to conventional choice theory which, despite a profusion of mathematical elegance over the last half century, is as hollow today as it was when Simon began writing *Administrative Behavior*.

The behavioral economics that lies within their grasp but so far has eluded mainstream economists rests on the following intellectual tripod. First, economic theory must be consistent with the body of knowledge accumulated in the other social sciences. Contradictions between existing ideas and new discoveries, such as the classical concept of perfect rationality and the new theories of learning advanced in cognitive psychology, cannot be ignored. Rather, these discrepancies must be addressed directly and theory modified accordingly. Second, economic theory must be able to explain observed behavior. It makes no sense to perpetuate a theory of optimizing behavior when "satisficing" is clearly what decision makers do. Finally, economic theory must be empirically verifiable with field or laboratory surveys or other microdata generating techniques. Armchair theoretizing about perfectly rational beings operating under conditions of risk makes for poor science, espe-

cially when such an obviously simplistic approach leads to predictions of behavior so at odds with actual observations.

The opportunity that mainstream economists failed to seize management theorists embraced wholeheartedly. Indeed, modern management, as revealed in the discipline's major scholarly journals, is the behavioral science economics might have become if Simon's work had had the impact on economics it has had in the fields of psychology and the science of the artificial. Management professionals have constructed a field whose principles of behavior are consistent with the findings of all the major social sciences and explain behavior with a high degree of operational accuracy. Moreover, they are constantly reevaluating basic precepts through empirical analysis and testing.

Of course, contemporary management is not solely the product of Simon's work. A variety of scholars in a number of fields have made the study of management what it is today. Still, management owes a special debt to Simon, and in recognition of this debt holds him in the highest regard, equating his breakthroughs with those of Chester I. Barnard, who is to twentieth century management what John Maynard Keynes is to twentieth century economics.

While mainstream economists have not embraced Simon, they haven't rejected him either. Being a Nobel laureate in economics, Simon has a professional attachment to this discipline which requires conventional economists to recognize his achievements no matter how much they fly in the face of contemporary thinking. Simon also has a personal attachment to the discipline in virtue of his friendships with Kenneth Arrow, Lawrence Klein, and other economics Nobel laureates he worked with on the Cowles Commission. Finally, his published works in the *American Economic Review, Quarterly Journal of Economics*, and other prestigious economics journals give him bona fide credentials as an economist. Still, despite the professional, social, and intellectual ties Simon has to mainstream economists, the fact remains that, epistemologically, he is not of their ilk.

JAMES AND JULIANNE CICARELLI

# Selected Bibliography

Ando, A. "On the Contributions of Herbert A. Simon to Economics." *Scandinavian Journal of Economics* 81 (1979): 83–93.

Baumol, W. J. "On the Contributions of Herbert A. Simon to Economics." *Scandinavian Journal of Economics* 81 (1979): 74–82.

Chandler, A. D., Jr. *The Visible Hand.* Cambridge, Ma.: Harvard University Press, 1979.

March, J. G., and Simon, Herbert A. *Organizations.* New York: John Wiley, 1958.

Newell, A., and Simon, Herbert A. *Human Problem Solving.* Englewood Cliffs, N.J.: Prentice-Hall, 1972.

Ridley, C. E., and Simon, Herbert A. "Measurement Standards in City Administration" (series of thirteen articles). *Public Management* 19–20 (1937–38).

Simon, Herbert A. *Administrative Behavior: A Study of the Decision-Making Process in Administrative Organizations.* New York: Macmillan, 1947.

———. "The Effects of Atomic Power on National and Regional Economics." In *Economic Aspects of Atomic Power,* S. H. Schurr and J. Marschak, editors. Princeton, N.J.: Princeton University Press, 1950.

———. "Atomic Power and the Industrialization of Backward Areas." In *Economic Aspects of Atomic Power,* S. H. Schurr and J. Marschak, editors. Princeton, N.J.: Princeton University Press, 1950.

———. D. W. Smithberg and V. A. Thompson. *Public Administration.* New York: Alfred A. Knopf, 1950.

———. *Models of Man.* New York: John Wiley, 1957.

———. *The New Science of Management Decision.* New York: Harper and Row, 1960.

———. *The Shape of Automation for Men and Management.* New York: Harper and Row, 1965.

———. *The Sciences of the Artificial.* Cambridge, Ma.: MIT Press, 1969.

———. *Models of Discovery.* Boston: D. Reidel, 1977.

———. "Rational Decision Making in Business Organizations." *American Economic Review* 69 (1979): 493–513.

———. *Reason in Human Affairs.* Stanford, Ca.: Stanford University Press, 1983.

# ROBERT MERTON SOLOW  *1987*

Economics was labelled the "dismal science" in the first half of the nineteenth century, when the findings of some of its leading practitioners suggested that there was a little prospect for permanent improvement in the material circumstances of mankind. Two memorable economists of the British "classical" school—David Ricardo and Thomas Robert Malthus—argued that economic growth, when accompanied by population expansion (which they held to be virtually unavoidable), was likely to produce a redistribution of income that would choke off further net capital accumulation. In their view, a "stationary state"—a situation in which further economic expansion would be halted—was a real and present danger. But, though economic growth might stop, population growth would not. It was small wonder that their message was widely read as foreshadowing a "dismal" outcome.

Born in Brooklyn, New York, in 1924, Robert Merton Solow was exposed in his boyhood to some of the realities of the Great Depression. Few sensitive observers of any age in the 1930s could fail to sense that something was out of joint in the functioning of the American economy. In some currents of opinion at the time, it was suggested that the "stationary state" anticipated by Ricardo and Malthus had at last arrived. The fact that its emergence had been delayed for more than a century could be explained by extraordinary bursts of technological creativity in the late nineteenth and early twentieth century (phenomena which economists of the British classical school had not foreseen). In the case of the United States, long-term economic growth over that period had also been sustained by a unique set of circumstances—the abundant availability of land and the investment opportunities associated with the taming of a continent. By the 1930s, however, it was apparent that this "frontier" had closed. From the perspective of a number of prominent economists of the day, the American economy was confronted with a situation not unlike the classical stationary state (though it was renamed as "secular stagnation"). This diagnosis suggested that the long-standing American confidence in the capacity of the economy to generate sustained growth was misplaced.

Much of Solow's work as a professional economist has been focused on the tasks that preoccupied the British classical economists, especially developing an understanding of the mechanisms of economic growth, and it was for this work that he received the Nobel Prize in Economic Sciences in 1987. As an economic theorist and empirical investigator, he has provided new answers to some old questions. But both the substance of his analysis and the style in which it is communicated are anything but dismal.

By Solow's own account, he took up the serious study of economics almost by "pure accident" (Klamer [1983], p. 128). Though his personal observation of depression conditions had sparked an interest in social questions, he entered Harvard College in 1940 intending to study such subjects as biology and botany. He soon discovered that these fields were not to his taste. Before he had settled on an alternative program of study, the war intervened. In 1942, he entered the United States Army, serving in the Signal Corps in North Africa, Sicily, and Italy. Returning to Harvard in 1945, he was still uncertain about his academic niche. At the suggestion of his bride—who had just completed a degree in economics at Radcliffe College—he tried economics and discovered that he liked it. He received the B.A. degree at Harvard in 1947 and the Ph.D. in 1951.

In 1949, Solow joined the economics faculty of the Massachusetts Institute of Techology, which was then being built up by Paul A. Samuelson, who was subsequently to be the first American recipient of the Nobel Prize in Economics in 1970. Apart from leaves of absence for government service and stints as a visiting professor at Oxford and Cambridge, MIT has been his regular address. Commenting on his ability to resist recruitment by other universities, Solow has observed: "A man would have to be a fool to go elsewhere just for money when instead he could sit and talk with Paul Samuelson every day" (*Science* [1987], p. 755).

# Analysis of Economic Growth

In announcing the award to Solow, the Nobel Prize Committee drew particular attention to his contribution to the reorientation of economic debate in the late 1950s. The topic of economic growth was again at the forefront of professional discussion, both in the more advanced industrial economies and in the less developed ones. Two rather different approaches to the problem were dominant. The first had its conceptual roots in Keynesian economics and was organized around a question that John Maynard Keynes had not addressed in *The General Theory of Employment, Interest and Money* (1936). The central concern of that pathbreaking book had been the analysis of the conditions under which a depressed economy could reach full employment. But a further question remained: once full employment had been achieved, how could it be maintained over time? The analysis of this issue, which was explored independently by Roy Harrod in Britain and Evsey Domar in the United States, involved a deeper probing into the properties of investment. In the study of an underemployed economy, Keynes had been concerned primarily with its income-generating effects in stimulating aggregate demand through multiplier effects. The broader issue of keeping a fully employed economy on course also meant, however, that the capacity-creating effects of capital spending needed to be taken into account. A full-employment equilibrium through time was thus seen to require that aggregate demand would have to grow at a rate sufficient to absorb the increment in aggregate supply resulting from investment spending in preceding periods. The upshot of this line of argument was that an economy's growth rate was determined by the percentage of gross national product (GNP) allocated to saving and by a capital-output ratio (which was usually taken to have a constant value).

For Third World countries, an alternative route to the analysis of growth was presented in 1954 by Arthur Lewis (who later was to be awarded the Nobel Prize). This model was inspired by a rereading of the works of the British classical economists of the early nineteenth century. Much of their argument turned on a linkage between the distribution of income between various social classes, such as capitalists, landlords, and workers. As it was presupposed that only capitalists had both the will and the ability to save and invest, the rate of capital accumulation and the prospects for economic growth thus depended on the share of capitalists' profits in the national income. Lewis adapted and modified this insight by analyzing the differing characteristics of two sectors (rather than classes) in the typical underdeveloped economy. In this scheme of things, the central feature of the growth process in the Third World was the interaction between a capitalist sector (organized on modern lines and usually initiated by foreign capital) and a subsistence sector (built around tradi-

tional agricultural practice). As no saving could be expected to arise from the subsistence sector, the momentum of growth depended on investment from the ploughed-back profits in the capitalist sector, which would, in turn, create wage-employment opportunities for workers who would otherwise be trapped in subsistence agriculture. This line of argument had the merit of concentrating attention on structural characteristics of underdeveloped economics that differentiated them from the more advanced ones. Even so, the Harrod-Domar and Lewis approaches had one thing in common: both interpreted capital accumulation as the key determinant of the rate of economic growth.

In two fundamental papers—"A Contribution to the Theory of Economic Growth," in the *Quarterly Journal of Economics* (1956), and "Technical Change and the Aggregate Production Function," in the *Review of Economics and Statistics* (1957)—Solow challenged doctrines assigning primacy to capital formation as an explanation of the growth process. Working with data on the performance of the American economy between 1909 and 1949, he argued that only about one-eighth of the increase in output per man-hour over that period could be attributed to an increased use of capital, while roughly seven-eighths could be assigned to technical change. Some might quibble about the use of the term "technical change" to describe the phenomenon under investigation, but what this exercise really captured was the unexplained gap between the observed growth in output and the amount of that growth that could be linked to additional capital inputs.

Strictly speaking, this residual might also be interpreted as an "ignorance coefficient." Solow recognized that a lot more than technological innovation, as conventionally understood, was involved. Thus, his use of the phrase "technical change" was a shorthand expression for any kind of change in the production function and might include all sorts of things such as speedups and improvements in the education of the labor force. But the fact that there was more work to be done in isolating the noncapital contributions did not diminish the significance of his central finding: that the accumulation of physical capital was not the fundamental regulator of a nation's rate of economic growth. Improvements in the quality of inputs mattered more than enlargements in their quantity.

Solow's work at this time changed the agenda of research on economic growth. Economists were increasingly alerted to the significance of research, technological innovation, and education for improvements in factor productivity. In at least forty countries, Solow's techniques have formed the basis for empirical studies and have confirmed the fundamental validity of his original insights. Indeed, "growth accounting" along the lines he pioneered has become a staple of the literature in development economics. The impact of his work for the study of the less-developed economies, however, could hardly have

been anticipated in 1956 and 1957. As Solow has noted, he was not thinking about the underdeveloped countries at all when he embarked on his sources-of-growth analysis. His motivation instead was to extend the theory set out in the Harrod-Domar growth model which, after all, had been formulated in the context of the advanced industrial economies (Solow [1983], p. 892).

# An Economic Agnostic

While Solow's career has been prominently identified with the analysis of economic growth, his work on this topic has by no means bounded his professional interests. On the contrary, he has made important contributions to the discussion of a wide range of issues. Versatility is one of the hallmarks of his career.

In the early 1960s, Solow served on the staff of the Kennedy administration's Council of Economic Advisers under Walter Heller, James Tobin (Nobel laureate in 1981), and Kermit Gordon. This illustrious group of economists—which also included Kenneth Arrow (Nobel laureate in 1972)—was responsible for orchestrating a Keynesian-style approach to demand management in the American economy. The council's 1962 Report—to which Solow contributed—was, in fact, a textbook in applied Keynesian macroeconomics, and it did much to educate the Kennedy White House, the Congress, and the general public on the wisdom of a demand-side tax cut to stimulate the American economy.

Solow also participated in the council's formulation of wage-price guideposts, intended as an instructional tool to labor and management on the form of wage and price behavior compatible with price stability in a high-employment economy.

Though his earlier work had been focused primarily on macroeconomic issues, Solow turned attention to another set of topics in the early 1970s. His papers at that time included writings on urban economics and on environmental pollution. When the OPEC oil crisis raised public consciousness on energy problems, he took up the analysis of the economics of exhaustible resources. The environment of "stagflation" in the late 1970s prompted papers on the productivity slowdown and on employment policy in inflationary times.

Solow's impact on the profession and the prestige he enjoys within it cannot, however, be measured solely in terms of the substantive content of his scholarly production, impressive though that is. Other dimensions of the man are also important: among them, his conception of the nature of economics as a discipline. In his view, there is no single "true" economic model that can be applied universally throughout time and space. He is critical of those who proceed from the premise that economics can be regarded as the "physics of society" and suspects that an attempt to construct economics as an axiomatically based hard science is doomed to fail. His reply to such a question as "what then should economics do?" proceeds as follows:

To my way of thinking, the true functions of analytic economics are best described informally: to organize our necessarily incomplete perceptions about the economy, to see connections that the untutored eye would miss, to tell plausible—sometimes even convincing—causal stories with the help of a few central principles, and to make rough quantitative judgments about the consequences of economic policy and other exogenous events. In this scheme of things, the end product of economic analysis is likely to be a collection of models contingent on society's circumstances—on the historical context, you might say—and not a single monolithic model for all seasons. (Solow [1985], p. 329)

Many in the community of professional economists like to categorize their colleagues by assigning them to "schools." Solow's intellectual posture resists tidy labeling. He has characterized his approach as follows:

I suppose I am myself a neoclassical economist—at least people who don't like me keep telling me so. But it is equally clear that I am a Keynesian economist. When the dichotomy under discussion is Keynesian vs. neoclassical, I am almost always on the Keynesian side. But I don't feel any conflict with my neoclassical self. There are problems where the neoclassical apparatus seems better suited, and problems where the Keynesian apparatus seems better suited. . . . As it happens, I am also a strong believer that social and economic institutions, attitudes and motivations, widely held standards of fairness, and all that sort of thing, have a lot to do with the observed behavior of advanced economies, even in the context of short-run macroeconomics. Does that make me an institutionalist? I confess that in theological disputes (dichotomies again) between neoclassicals and institutionalists I tend to feel like a neoclassical, without giving an inch on my belief that institutions matter a lot. I think that is mostly because I am by temperament a theorist. I don't feel that I understand something until I have a (usually mathematical) model of it. But in disputes *among* theorists, I feel the same frustration *real* institutionalists must feel with me. (Solow [1983], pp. 892–93)

Solow is prepared to draw insights from more than one analytic tradition when addressing complex economic problems—indeed he insists on the importance of doing so. At the same time, he can be outspoken in attacking economists who make claims that are overly simplistic. In his view, the "hard-core" version of monetarist doctrine promoted by Milton Friedman (Nobel laureate in 1976) can be faulted on this score. The monetarist argument holds that the money supply is the single driving force underlying the behavior of the macroeconomy and prescribes that monetary policy should be conducted in accordance with a preannounced fixed rule. From Solow's perspective, this view is misguided because of the cavalier treatment it gives to the multiplicity of forces affecting economic activity. Moreover, he holds its approach to policy to be mistaken. In his judg-

ment, economic performance would probably be worse under a regime in which the hands of central bankers were tied than it is under one in which policy makers are afforded discretion.

Similarly, Solow finds little merit in the work of the "new classical" economists. Adherents to this position are inclined to build models around the presuppositions that wages and prices are flexible and that market-clearing equilibrium is the normal state of the economic system. Solow recognizes that these exercises may have some intellectual appeal on the ground that they are analytically tidy. He questions, however, their utility and validity, believing that the findings refer to an imaginary world from which economic frictions are banished. In consequence, he feels they have little to contribute to the understanding of the world in which we actually live.

One further aspect of Solow's style sets him apart from most of his fellow economists: his lively and spontaneous sense of humor. On some occasions, he has been known to use it tellingly in the context of professional debate. In a dialogue with Milton Friedman on their divergent views on monetary theory and policy, for example, he remarked: "There is a difference between Milton and me, but not as big as you might think. For Milton, everything reminds him of money. Everything reminds me of sex. The difference is that I keep it out of my writing" (*Science* [1982], p. 755).

He also pokes fun at the procedures of the "new classical" economists. In defense of that tactic, he has observed:

Suppose someone sits down . . . and announces that he is Napoleon Bonaparte. The last thing I want to do with him is to get involved in a technical discussion of cavalry tactics at the battle of Austerlitz. If I do that, I am getting tacitly drawn into the game that he *is* Napoleon. Now ["new classicists"] like nothing better than to get drawn into technical discussions, because then you have tacitly gone along with their fundamental assumptions; your attention is attracted away from the basic weakness of the whole story. Since I find that fundamental framework ludicrous, I respond by treating it as ludicrous—that is, by laughing at it. (Klamer [1983], p. 146)

With the selection of Robert M. Solow, the Nobel Prize Committee has honored a decidedly undismal economist. This honor, however, was but the capstone to many others that he has received, among them the American Economic Association's John Bates Clark Medal (1961), MIT's Faculty Achievement Award (1978), and the presidency of the American Economic Association (1979). In addition to his work as a scholar and teacher, he has also continued to take on the public-service assignments that began with his tour in Washington as a member of the staff of the Kennedy administration's Council of Economic Advisers. In 1964 and 1965, he was a member of President Johnson's Committee on Technology, Automation and Economic Progress. Between 1968 and 1970, he served on President Nixon's Commission on Income Maintenance. From 1975 to 1980, he was a director of the Federal Reserve Bank of Boston.

There was a touch of irony in the timing of the announcement of Solow's receipt of the Nobel Prize in Economics. It coincided with the stock market crash of October 1987. When asked to comment about the significance of this event, Solow replied characteristically, "It may make engineers out of some yuppies. Sweet are the uses of adversity" (*Wall Street Journal,* October 22, 1987).

WILLIAM J. BARBER

# Selected Bibliography

## WORKS BY SOLOW

"A Contribution to the Theory of Economic Growth." *Quarterly Journal of Economics* 70 (1956): 65–94.

"The Production Function and the Theory of Capital." Review of Economic Studies 23 (1956): 101–08.

"Technical Change and the Aggregate Production Function." *Review of Economics and Statistics* 39 (1957): 312–20.

"Substitution and Fixed Proportions in the Theory of Capital." *Review of Economics and Statistics* 29 (1962): 207–18.

*The Nature and Sources of Unemployment in the United States.* Stockholm: Almqvist & Wiksell, 1964.

*Capital Theory and the Rate of Return.* Chicago: Rand McNally, 1965.

"The Economics of Resources or the Resources of Economics." *American Economic Review* 64(2) (1974): 1–14.

Solow, Robert, and Ginzberg, Eli, eds. *The Great Society: Lessons for the Future*. New York: Basic Books, 1974.

"Economic Development and the Development of Ecnomics: Comment." *World Development* 11 (1983): 891–93.

"Economic History and Economics." *American Economic Review Papers and Proceedings* 75 (1985): 328–31.

"Insiders and Outsiders in Wage Determination." *Scandinavian Journal of Economics*, 1985.

## OTHER WORKS

Klamer, Arjo. "Robert M. Solow." In Klamer, *Conversations with Economists*, pp. 127–48. Totowa, N.J.: Rowman and Allanheld, 1983.

Marshall, Eliot. "Nobel Prize for Theory of Economic Growth." *Science*, November 6, 1987, pp. 754–55.

Robinson, Joan. "Solow on the Rate of Return." In *Collected Economic Papers of Joan Robinson*, vol. 3. Cambridge, Mass.: MIT Press, 1980.

# GEORGE J. STIGLER    *1982*

George J. Stigler has long since settled into the comfortable and unique stimulation of the academic life, thoroughly enjoying the pleasures of teaching, research, and intellectual exchange associated with the renowned University of Chicago. Although currently in semi-retirement, Stigler continues to direct the Center for the Study of the Economy and the State, which he founded in 1975 to study the role of government intervention in the marketplace.

The "dismal science" of economics has been illuminated by the dynamic lecture style of Dr. Stigler. His curiosity as to how the world works is pervasive in his writings and conversation. His witticisms and good-natured sharp tongue manage to entertain his audience as well.

Here is a man who knows the limitations of his field. He does not believe that economists can successfully preach to the world to advocate change in economic policies, nor does he believe in building complex, multiple-equation models of a hypothetical economy. He is content simply to study the world, try to understand its inner workings, and use straightforward but usually very clever empirical methods to test his theories. This effort has led him to create a new field, the economics of information, force the profession to take a new view of public regulation, and help shape the direction of studies on market structure and the role of public policy in the marketplace. For all this he was awarded the Nobel Prize in October 1982.

# Early Career

Stigler was born in the Seattle suburb of Renton, Washington, on January 11, 1911. His father, Joseph, emigrated from Bavaria at about the same time his mother, Elizabeth Hungler, left Austria-Hungary. They married in the United States. In Stigler's words, his father's skills as a brewer were devalued greatly by Prohibition, and he went into the business of buying, repairing, and selling real estate. George attended schools in the Seattle area and enjoyed student life. He described himself as a relaxed student but voracious and promiscuous reader. With the Great Depression looming, he enrolled at the University of Washington, where he earned a B.B.A. degree in 1931. In his selection of courses, Stigler felt he lacked good judgment as well as guidance from his parents. He ended up taking many "applied" business courses but little in the way of mathematics or the physical sciences.

The University of Washington at that time lacked any standout economists. It wasn't until graduate school that Stigler received the stimulation that attracted him to an academic career with his enrollment in the Northwestern University M.B.A. program and his association with Coleman Woodbury. After graduation he enrolled at the University of Chicago, where he studied under three great economists: Frank Knight, Henry Simon, and Jacob Viner. Knight's specialty was the history of economic thought, and he delighted in exposing errors of such well-known early economists as David Ricardo. Both Viner and Knight taught their students not to respect academic reputations and titles but to examine critically the arguments being presented by the speaker. Henry Simon was a passionate spokesman for rational, decentralized organization of the economy. Stigler's later writings showed he learned his lessons very well.

His dissertation, *Production and Distribution Theories: The Formative Period*, was written under Knight. This survey of nineteenth and early twentieth century scholarship was completed in 1938 and published by Macmillan in 1942. Stigler now complains that the work embarrasses him because it is full of excesses and immaturity.

Having finished all his doctoral work except for the completed dissertation, Stigler left Chicago in 1936 to become assistant professor at Iowa State College in Ames. The chairman of the Economics Department—and later, like Stigler, a Nobel laureate—Theodore W. Schultz, had gathered together a small group of vigorous economists, and Stigler knew he would thrive in such an environment. The task of teaching, however, was a new responsibility.

I still remember my first class, in economic principles. I had prepared the first few weeks of the course in an outline, so I entered the class with confidence. Forty minutes later I had covered all the material in my outline, and there remained ten minutes, not to mention ten and a half weeks, still to go! (1986, p. 98)

In December of his first year of teaching he married Margaret L. Mack, a former graduate student at Chicago. They had three children: Stephen, a statistician; David, a lawyer; and Joseph, a social worker.

The beginning of Stigler's career was marked by changes and important initiatives. He was just settling in at Ames, finishing his dissertation, when he accepted an offer from Frederic Garver at the University of Minnesota. His colleagues there included Francis Boddy and Arthur Marget.

In 1938, he published his first article, "Social Welfare and Differential Prices," in the *Journal of Political Economy*, one of the prestigious journals of the University of Chicago. Shortly thereafter he wrote his first book, *A Theory of Competitive Price* (1942). In 1946 he followed this effort with *A Theory of Price*. This volume covered both perfect and imperfect competition as well as multiple products, capital theory, and labor theory. When published the book was one of the first comprehensive texts on the workings of a stationary economy. Reviewers noted that although he analyzed complex topics with considerable clarity and detail, a reader needed a background in higher mathematics to receive the full benefit of Stigler's work. The book has now gone through several revisions and is considered a minor classic among microeconomics theory textbooks.

In 1942 Stigler, now an associate professor, took leave to work at the National Bureau of Economic Research (NBER) in New York City. He was hired to study the service industries as part of a program of studies on the trend of output, employment, and productivity in the U.S. economy. Studies and essays were published in pamphlet form on employment in science, service industries, and other sectors, and the relationship of that employment to other factors, including federal minimum wage legislation. In one publication, *Trends in Output and Employment* (1947), Stigler constructed the first total productivity index, relating industrial output to a combination of all inputs. One of his best known studies, *The Demand and Supply of Scientific Personnel* (1957), was, in the words of Jacob Mincer, a "pioneering attempt at empirical diagnosis of the popular but slippery concepts of shortages (or surpluses) in manpower . . . the book punctured the notion of a long-term shortage of engineers in the U.S. and did a great deal to stimulate manpower analyses by economists, which are now proliferating" (p. 73).

Another myth that needed exploding was the notion that the minimum wage had only beneficial effects on labor. One of Stigler's NBER employment studies, "The Economics of Minimum Wage Legislation" (1946), included the analysis of the federal minimum-wage legislation's distorting effects on resource allocation, its creation of unemployment, and its inconsequential effect on the elimination of poverty. Subsequent empirical studies by others would confirm his initial theoretical conclusions.

Much later, during President Johnson's Great Society era of pervasive federal social legislation, Stigler related the minimum wage to civil rights in a way that was in sharp contrast to the prevailing liberal view. He noted that the Great Society efforts to increase employment opportunities for unskilled youths, particularly black youths, centered on the direct legislation of the 1964 Civil Rights Act. However, despite the fine intentions of the lawmakers, discrimination continued to exist. Stigler proposed that black youths be helped by increasing their skills (through a program of educational grants). Stigler argued that the marketplace would increase their wages as a result of their training. Recognizing that minimum wage legislation led to unemployment among the unskilled, Stigler irked the liberals of the day by suggesting that it was better to be working at a wage below the minimum wage than not to be working at all.

While at the bureau, Stigler worked with Arthur Burns (later to be chairman of the Federal Reserve Board), Geoffrey Moore, and Milton Friedman. The bureau continued to support him after his departure, funding empirical studies on pricing behavior and rates of return in manufacturing industries, particularly among oligopolies. Before World War II ended, Stigler moved across town to the Statistical Research Group at Columbia University. He contributed to the groups applying statistical analysis to military problems. "I learned a little statistics there, and I did not seriously delay the nation's victory" (1986, p. 99).

In 1945 Stigler briefly returned to Minnesota, then taught at Brown University. In 1946 he was offered a job at the University of Chicago but he later said he alienated the president, Ernest Colwell, in an interview. He did not get another chance until another eleven years passed.

*Roofs or Ceilings?* (1946), one of his more widely read and controversial books, was published by the Foundation for Economic Education. In this work, coauthored with Milton Friedman, Stigler argued that governmental rent controls were counterproductive, leading to decreased construction activity and housing shortages. He noted the difference between the short run, in which the original tenants benefit, and the long run, in which property values decline through owner neglect. The book caused some outcry at the time, particularly, again, among liberals, since it was becoming more common for the public to support government intervention to achieve the greater good. Stigler's work suggested the opposite.

# Industrial Competition

In 1947 Stigler began an eleven-year stay at Columbia University, where he taught industrial organization, history of economic thought, and economic theory. His colleagues were Arthur Burns, William Vickrey, Albert Hart, Regnar Nurske, and Carl Shoup. Before his first year at Columbia was completed, Friedrich A. von Hayek invited him to join a group of free market-oriented scholars at a meeting in Vevey, Switzerland. While there he helped found the Mont Pelerin Society, a group dedicated in defending a free society, and he later served as its president during 1976–78. At his first meeting he met Aaron Director, with whom he developed a close relationship over the years. Stigler acknowledged Director's influence on his ideas on industrial organization and regulation with an eventual book dedication.

In the early 1950s, Stigler devoted much of his writing and speaking to the nature of industrial competition. In a 1950 appearance before the House Judiciary subcommittee that was reviewing the nation's antitrust laws, he discussed the stifling effects on competition caused by monopoly elements in the economy and argued that the biggest steel companies should be broken up. His appearance supported a new legislative initiative against the current horizontal-merger wave, the Celler-Kefauver Anti-Merger Act of 1950. He continued his fight in the May 1952, issue of *Fortune* magazine, "The Case Against Big Business," which called for the government to break up large firms in other industries as well. This flexibility in his conservatism no doubt surprised those who would have placed Stigler firmly in the laissez faire school.

One far-reaching aspect of the nature of competition is the determination of efficient sizes of enterprises. Engineering estimates of the optimal size have always been unreliable. Stigler proposed an innovative "survivor method" to measure the optimal size of a firm. He showed that if a survey of the existing sizes of firms in an industry are taken at two or more points in time, then the size that survives (that is, continues to exist) must be optimal. Sizes that are too large or too small will be seen less frequently over time, as they are failing the market test. This test application led to the striking conclusion that in many industries no unique optimal size exists—that is, a wide range of sizes can be optimal. A formal study on the controversial survivor method, sponsored by the NBER but not published in their series, resulted in a 1958 article, "Economies of Scale." Critics of this technique have noted that the survivor test is not free of ambiguities, puzzling patterns, and instability over time. Tests on the same industries by other economists have yielded different measurements of efficient scales. It is perhaps best used as an alternative method to check on more direct approaches rather than the sole approach to analyzing optimal scales.

Another important contribution to the industrial competition area was Stigler's 1964 paper, "Theory of Oligopoly," in which he examines the difficulties faced by oligopolists attempting to collude on prices. The main problem is the enforcement of price agreements, as cheating (through secret discounts to large customers) is highly profitable if it goes undetected. Stigler's quantitative approach led to the conclusion that (1) the gain in sales from any one rival by secret price concessions is not sensitive to the number of rivals; (2) the incentive for price-cheating falls as the number of customers per producer rises; and (3) the incentive for covert price-cutting increases as the probability of repeat purchases to the same customer falls. Although this theory lacks the complexity needed to be applied in real markets, it nonetheless is regarded as the earliest and most influential of the works using the mathematical approach to study dynamic secret price-cutting, detection, and deterrence.

Another aspect of collusion associated with oligopoly is the behavior of cartels. Stigler's 1965 article "The Dominant Firm and the Inverted Umbrella" gave important insights into cartel behavior and applied it to the steel industry. He showed that United States Steel's strategy of high prices and declining market shares was quite profitable. Well before its time it also explains the oil pricing behavior of Saudi Arabia in the Organization of Petroleum Exporting Countries.

Stigler's many contributions to the field of industrial organization continued in the 1960s, with important works on the theory of oligopoly, dominant firms, administered prices, mergers, and antitrust policy. This culminated in the publication of twenty-two articles (mostly reprints) in *The Organization of Industry* (1968).

The publication also led to his appointment as chairman of President Nixon's Task Force on Competition and Productivity. This committee was set up to respond to outgoing President Johnson's request for a law that would restructure highly concentrated industries (based on the recommendation of a special task force). The Stigler Report contradicted Johnson's task force, noting that there are a number of ways that an oligopolistic industry would behave in a competitive manner and that factors other than structure play important roles in determining an industry's performance. As such, it was argued that antitrust policy should be based on a great deal more than just the proposition that high concentration is associated with poor performance. The "Concentrated Industries Act" later proposed in revised form by Senator Philip Hart of Michigan died a quiet death in the late 1970s.

# The University of Chicago Years

In 1958, the same year of the publication of his "survivor method" article, Stigler was named the Charles R. Walgreen Professor of American Institutions at the University of Chicago's Graduate School of Business. Thus began his long tenure at the university, during which time, together with Milton Friedman, he helped guide the Chicago school of free-market economics, with its emphasis on monetarism and a reduced role for government known throughout the world.

In 1957–58 Stigler took a one-year leave to work at the Center for Advanced Study in the Behavioral Sciences in Stanford, California, sharing what he recalls as a "splendid year" with Kenneth Arrow, Melvin Reder, Milton Friedman, and Robert Solow. All but Reder were later to become Nobel laureates.

In 1961 his most famous work, "The Economics of Information," was published by the *Journal of Political Economy*. This study developed from Stigler's curiosity about the existence of different prices for nearly identical products. He concluded that the price dispersion resulted from the "expensiveness" of knowledge. Stigler argued that information is like any other commodity. It has its cost, and different agents will be led to acquire different amounts of it when "shopping," as they match the marginal cost of additional information with the marginal benefit. As such, (1) frequently purchased goods vary less in price than infrequently purchased goods of the same value; (2) the more expensive the good or service, the more worthwhile it is to search for the lowest price; and (3) the value of knowledge declines over time.

Stigler's model of the supply and demand for information found immediate application in the labor market and other fields and, unlike other new ideas, was quickly accepted by the profession. After twenty-seven years and hundreds of articles, studies are still forthcoming, and the *Index of Economic Articles* had long since given it a classification of its own. That the new area was accepted without controversy, Stigler observed in his Nobel lecture, "certainly was no tribute to the definitiveness of my exposition, but was due instead to the fact that no established scientific theory was being challenged by this work [and to the fact that] the theory immediately yielded results which were intuitively or observationally plausi-

ble. Here was a Chicago theory that didn't even annoy the socialists!"

In the late 1950s Stigler began formally to question the usefulness of government imposed regulations on businesses. In his pathbreaking article on the electric utility industry, "What Can Regulators Regulate?" (1962), he found that regulation failed to have any effect on consumer prices or producer profits. This finding raised serious questions about the impact of regulation and made the topic a legitimate area of research as well as a serious concern for public policy. Together with another significant contribution, "The Theory of Economic Regulation" (1971), he changed thinking about public regulation by suggesting that it often served the producers (for example, by limiting the entry of new competitors) and the regulators themselves rather than the consumer. He went on to examine those factors that led industries to embrace regulation as a means of acquiring benefits.

Even popular laws as the Clean Air Act of 1972 are not immune to special interests. Stigler has noted that this law is an example of the government's good intentions gone awry as, in his view, it serves a special interest group as much as the general welfare. In *U.S. News and World Report* (January 31, 1983), he declared:

It [the Clean Air Act] says that if a community's air is wonderful, it can't accept a factory that is going to degrade the air quality. That's really a device to prevent the migration of industry from the Northeast to the

Southwest. So, though I'm willing to pay for clean air, I resent having to pay the greater price that extraneous regulation, combined with all these schemes to redistribute income and bail out declining companies and industries, exacts—that is, a less efficient economy. We haven't lost all our resiliency, but we are slower, creakier, and less able to adapt to changing circumstances than we once were. The human race existed for several million years without governmental rules; now we suddenly need so many of them. That's a little paradoxical to me.

In 1975, Stigler published *The Citizen and the State*, a collection of studies and essays on the mistrust of government policies, the effectiveness of regulation, and the intended and unintended side effects of regulation. He dedicated the volume to his close friend and colleague, Aaron Director. These studies encouraged the study of the forces that gave rise to regulation, and eventually this new approach became known as the "public choice" school, represented by Gordon Tullock and James Buchanan.

Stigler had the opportunity to apply his academic observations on regulation to public policy while serving as vice-chairman of the Securities Investor Protection Commission during 1971–74 and as advisor to President Nixon on regulatory reform in 1969–70. Stigler was cited even earlier, during the Kennedy administration, when the chairman of the Council of Economic Advisors, Walter Heller, explained that he used "Stiglerian the-

ory" to help win Kennedy's approval to reduce transportation regulations despite the desire of the Commerce Department to increase them. Stigler was among the first and certainly the most eloquent and forceful to argue for deregulation. Presidents Ford and Carter subsequently made regulatory reform a top priority in their administrations, and the deregulation legacy, so prominent in President Reagan's program, can be traced to Stigler's initial efforts.

A number of important professional appointments and elections followed, all made in recognition of his contributions. In 1964 he was elected president of the American Economic Association. In 1974 he was named editor of the prestigious *Journal of Political Economy*, a post he still holds. One year later he was elected to the National Academy of Sciences. The greatest achievement, of course, came with his award of the Nobel Prize on October 20, 1982.

At the White House reception for Stigler's prize, the press was not so interested in his scholarly contributions as it was in hearing him evaluate President Reagan's new economic initiatives in the area of tax reduction and government spending. The year 1982 was the year of supply-side economics, the first year of an enormous three-year tax cut. Presidential aides assumed the conservative economist would have kind words for the president's program, and hopes ran high for some favorable publicity on network news. Stigler's comments, however, sounded more like complaints than praise. He dismissed supply-side economics as "a gimmick or . . . a slogan," and he described the economy as "bumping along" at the bottom of a full-blown "depression." Asked to grade the president, Stigler thought "an incomplete" would be appropriate, since he wanted to wait two years to see how the economy performed. Two months later, in a *U.S. News and World Report* interview, he changed the grade to a "B," because a president always faces a thousand pressures to act and has very little command over events. "In contrast, when I look at former President Carter's record, I am reminded of a student who complained about the grade I gave him. 'That's impossible to change,' I said. 'Why?' he asked. And I told him, 'F is the lowest grade I'm allowed to give.'"

Nobel Prize fame provided numerous outlets to express his views. In the same interview with the *U.S. News and World Report*, Stigler argued that economic stability would be reached if large swings in the money supply, such as those occurring in 1982, could be eliminated. But Stigler was on firmer footing when he stood on the platform of government noninterference:

Equally important, the government should stop tinkering with the tax law, price controls, business regulations, and things like that. Less of that would contribute greatly to a stable investment climate. When I say 'government,' I really mean people, including the media. I don't blame the politicians as much as I do the public and the press for making unrealistic demands on government to

'do something' about every problem that comes along. Next the government will be expected to prevent earthquakes and meteoric showers. There's really no limit to the pretended competence of the state.

When asked how he felt on winning the Nobel Prize (worth $157,000 that year), he replied, among other things, "richer." As *National Review* (November 12, 1982) noted, it "was a wry example of his characteristic mode of economic analysis: precise, unsentimental, and above all verifiable."

At age seventy, Stigler eased into semiretirement, allowing more time to pursue his hobbies as book collector, photographer, woodworker, and golfer. He relinquished his chaired position in the university and was named Charles W. Walgreen Distinguished Professor Emeritus.

THOMAS H. BRUGGINK

# Selected Bibliography

WORKS BY STIGLER

"Social Welfare and Differential Prices." *Journal of Political Economy* 20 (1938):573–86.

*A Theory of Competitive Price.* New York: Macmillan, 1942.

*A Theory of Price.* New York: Macmillan, 1946.

"The Economics of Minimum Wage Legislation." *American Economic Review* 36 (1946): 358–65.

*Trends in Output and Employment.* New York: National Bureau of Economic Research, 1947.

"The Case Against Big Business." *Fortune*, May 1952, pp. 3–12.

"Economies of Scale." *Journal of Law and Economics* 1 (October 1958): 54–71.

"The Economics of Information." *Journal of Political Economy* 69 (June 1961): 213–25.

"Theory of Oligopoly." *Journal of Political Economy* 72 (February 1964): 44–61.

"The Dominant Firm and the Inverted Umbrella." *Journal of Law and Economics* 8 (October 1965): 167–72.

*The Organization of Industry.* Homewood, Il.: Irwin, 1968.

"The Theory of Economic Regulation." *Bell Journal of Economics and Management Science* 5 (Autumn 1971): 59–65.

*The Citizen and the State.* Chicago: University of Chicago Press, 1975.

"George J. Stigler." In William Breit and Rogert W. Spencer, eds. *Lives of the Laureates: Seven Nobel Economists*, pp. 93–111. Cambridge, Ma.: MIT Press, 1986.

Stigler, George, and Friedman, Milton. *Roofs or Ceilings?* Irvington-on-Hudson, N.Y.: Foundation for Economic Education, 1946.

Stigler, George, and Blank, David. *Demand and Supply of Scientific Personnel.* Princeton, N.J.: Princeton University Press, 1957.

Stigler, George, and Friedland, Claire. "What Can Regulators Regulate? The Case of Electricity." *Journal of Law and Economics* 5 (October 1962): 1–16.

**OTHER WORKS**

Leube, Kurt R. "George J. Stigler: A Biographical Introduction." In Kurt R. Leube and Thomas Gale Moore, eds. *The Essence of Stigler*, pp. xiii–xix. Stanford, Ca.: Hoover Institution Press, 1986.

Mincer, Jacob. "George Stigler's Contributions to Economics." *Scandinavian Journal of Economics* 85:1 (1963): 65–86.

Moore, Thomas Gale. "Introduction." In Kurt R. Leube and Thomas Gale Moore, eds. *The Essence of Stigler*, pp. xxi–xxvii. Stanford, Ca.: Hoover Institution Press, 1986.

Moritz, Charles, ed. *Current Biography Yearbook.* New York: H. W. Wilson, 1983, pp. 372–75.

*National Review.* "Nobel Prizes." November 12, 1982, pp. 1392–93.

"Report of the Task Force on Productivity and Competition." *Antitrust Law and Economics Review* 2 (Spring 1969): 13–52.

Schmalensee, Richard. "George Stigler's Contributions to Economics." *Scandinavian Journal of Economics* 85:1 (1983): 77–86.

Shepherd, William G. "What Does the Survivor Technique Show About Economies of Scale?" *Southern Economic Review* 34 (July 1967): 113–22.

*U.S. News and World Report.* "Government Really Can't Do Very Much About the Economy." January 31, 1983, pp. 68–69.

# RICHARD STONE  *1984*

Richard Stone was born on August 30, 1913, educated at Westminster School and Gonville and Caius College, Cambridge University, and graduated with his M.A. in 1938. After working for a brokerage firm, he served in the Ministry of Economic Warfare in 1939–40 and the Office of the War Cabinet in 1940–45. He became director of the Department of Applied Economics at Cambridge in 1945 and resigned in 1955 to become P. D. Leake Professor of Finance and Accounting at the university. He married Feodora Leontinoff in 1941, and after her death in 1956 he married Mrs. Giovanna Croft-Murray in 1960. He was awarded the C.B.E. in 1946 and knighted in 1978. He retired in 1980 and was awarded the Nobel Prize in Economic Sciences in 1984.

Stone was awarded the Nobel Prize for his work on the development of national income accounting. As the Royal Swedish Academy of Sciences stated when it announced the winner of the 1984 prize, Stone was "a pioneer and the driving force with respect to both the theoretical underpinning and practical application of different systems of national accounts [which] formed the basis for economic analysis of the prevailing lack of balance in Britain and for economic policy recommendations." It continued, "In today's perspective, presentations of national accounts, with their rows of interlinked balance calculations for the different sectors of the economy, are regarded as a self-evident and necessary part of systematic reporting of countries' financial position and pattern of development. . . . But then, in the early 1940s, reporting and analysis in the form of a logically connected system of national accounts constituted an epoch-making innovation, the breakthrough of a new methodology. And it was Stone who was primarily responsible for the breakthrough" (p. 2).

Apart from his role in the development of national accounts, which is generally considered to be his main contribution to economics, Stone has also been a major contributor to other areas of applied economics. Principal among these are the analysis of consumer demand and the Cambridge Growth Project.

## The Development of National Accounting Systems

Stone's work on national accounting problems began in 1940, when he and James Meade (Nobel laureate in economics, 1977) began the task of collecting, processing, and making systematic the vast amount of data needed by John Maynard Keynes in his attempts to plan the British war effort. They worked under the stimulus of Keynes's ideas for running the war economy and Colin Clark's earlier work, which established the basis on which national accounting was to develop. Their objective was to produce a complete account of the nation's resources to assist in the war effort, and they set out to do this by obtaining a full integration of the United Kingdom's accounts for different subsectors. These subsectors included the household sector, businesses, the public sector, national savings and investments, and transactions with the outside world. The basic approach was to apply and modify the ideas of double-entry bookkeeping, in which each item was to appear as an item of revenue on one side of the account and an item of expenditure on the other. The fact that the same item appeared on both sides of the ledger meant figures had to agree with each other, and while this specification involved a massive amount of work, it also provided an important check on the reliability and consistency of the data. When completed, this exercise was to produce an overview of the interplay and interdependence of the entire economy, and a full account of its resources.

Stone's starting point was the notion of *transactions* between different sectors. Apart from the relatively obvious problems of collecting data and ensuring that they were reliable, Stone had to face the problems of how the immense number of transactions within the economy should be consolidated and aggregated in a meaningful way in sectoral accounts, and how these accounts should be presented. Stone's approach to the problem went far beyond the routine application of bookkeeping rules, and he insisted that economic theory had a major

role to play. As the Royal Swedish Academy of Sciences put it, he saw the "theoretical analysis of national economic balance problems . . . as the starting point and justification for national accounts" (p. 3). One might add that while this analysis was motivated by Keynesian ideas of economic imbalance and the need for appropriate policies to counteract it, national accounts are in fact neutral in a policy sense and imply support for no one particular philosophy of economic policy over another.

Stone had to deal with three major problems in order to arrive at a system of national income accounting. The first problem was to develop a set of definitions and practical conventions to measure the main types of economic activity in the economy. These are production (or output), accumulation, and consumption. (Note also that these factors are related by the identity that states that all output is either accumulated or consumed, so that output is the sum of accumulation and consumption.)

Let us consider first the problem of developing a suitable measure of output. The essential problem is to "collapse" the outputs of heterogeneous goods into a single measure of "output." To do that requires assigning appropriate price "weight" to each particular good produced to arrive at a figure for the value of aggregate output. The obvious procedure, and the one Stone adopted, was to value the output of different goods at market prices, although this still leaves problems where market prices have been distorted (for example, by rationing or by taxes). A more basic problem, however, was what to do with output that is not sold on a market. Stone's approach to this problem was essentially pragmatic. Where data were available, as with government expenditures, for instance, then his approach was to assess the value of output by the value of the inputs that produced it. Where no data were available (for example, with household production), then his approach was to ignore it. The essence of Stone's approach was that one did the best one could with the data one had. Household production was ignored and government "output" measured at cost, not for any theoretical reason, but because at the time there was little else that could be done. If data on household production or government input-output indices became available, however, then one would usually want to use them.

We now consider the issue of measuring accumulation. Again, the approach was fundamentally a practical one. Where the only data available were on private-sector asset accumulation, then one had little alternative but to make do with that. However, if one had data on "infrastructure" accumulation (for example, roads, schools, bridges) one ought to include that as well. A lot of work went into trying to get such data, but one encounters similar problems here as with the valuation of output. Much infrastructure output is not sold on a market—although there are exceptions (for example, toll bridges)—so one is often forced to value such accumulation

by the expenditures on them. An additional problem, however, is how to deal with depreciation. Ideally, one would infer the depreciation of an asset from the price of similar assets on second-hand markets, but such markets frequently do not exist, and one is often forced to rely on relatively ad hoc procedures instead. The usual procedure is to assume that a commodity has a given expected life and depreciates in a given way, but this sort of procedure is obviously fraught with problems. Estimates of depreciation tend to be very sensitive to the precise assumptions one makes, and in any case they tend to correspond more to "physical" estimates of depreciation rather than to "economic" estimates of it that take into account relevant changes in relative prices. One also has to deal with the related problem of valuing stocks. In principle, one might want to value stocks at their replacement value, but much of the data one is likely to get would refer only to their initial cost. Where prices are relatively stable, of course, this might only cause minor problems, but one is likely to encounter more severe problems in periods of inflation.

Thirdly, there is the problem of measuring consumption. The problem here is that one typically has data on consumer expenditures, and one has to figure out some way of extracting estimates of actual consumption from them. Consumption expenditures and actual consumption differ, of course, because of current and past consumer expenditures on durable goods. A proper estimate of consumption would therefore subtract from consumer expenditures the amount spent on durable goods but add in the value of the services consumers currently enjoy from past and present expenditures on durable goods. It is then necessary to derive implicit estimates of the stock of consumer durables and be able to estimate the flow of services they yield. (One must also be able to model their depreciation, and that takes us back to some of the problems encountered in measuring accumulation.) This problem is particularly acute when dealing with housing services: in that case, it is necessary to estimate not only the stock of housing (which is difficult enough), but also to estimate the service flow it yields.

Once settled on suitable conventions to measure the basic categories of activity in which one is interested, one then has to put one's data set together. This is a massive undertaking and involves solving a number of specific problems, such as the collection of data, filling in the gaps, resolving inconsistencies, and standardizing the data to make figures comparable. Stone put much effort into trying to find reliable ways to resolve these types of problem. A way to handle gaps in the data is to fill them "residually" (that is, by using accounting identities in which all terms except one are measured, and inferring the missing one). This is frequently done, for example, to obtain estimates of savings which are not generally observed directly. Unfortunately, obtaining data residually has the disadvantage of using up an identity that could otherwise have been used to check on the con-

sistency of one's data. Another practice sometimes used is to add in all the discrepancies to one side and arrive at some "balancing item" that can be considered as "measurement error," but this procedure is often unsatisfactory since it presupposes that the errors all take place on that side of the balance sheet. One can also "adjust" data in line with prior assessments of their reliability and thereby assign putative "errors" to them. Stone wrote several papers indicating how this might be done.

Finally, once the data are sorted out, one has to find a way to represent them. This is where Stone's work went far beyond a routine bookkeeping approach. As Leif Johansen put it:

> Stone's early work on national accounting problems [illustrates] the fact that his perspectives and advanced analytical ideas aimed far beyond a systematic, although rather conventional bookkeeping approach to describing the economic conditions and development in a country. Even if he did invest considerable effort in working out practical details and a seemingly conventional means of presenting national accounts, it was because this was a prerequisite for initiating the practical work involved and ensuring the reliability of data at an early stage. Concurrently, he worked on more advanced theoretical ideas which pointed towards the subsequent development we have witnessed in the national accounts literature and the use of national accounts data for analytical purposes. (1985, p. 10)

Stone's intention was to use accounting conventions to develop a representation of national accounts in the form of "transaction matrices" which provide a more or less aggregated account of all the transactions taking place within an economy. His attitude towards aggregation was a flexible one: the appropriate level of aggregation depends on the kind of data one has and the purpose for which one wants to use it. Consequently, a system of national accounts needs to be flexible enough to accommodate most potential users of it. This means that a system of national accounts should be organized in large matrices and aggregated as needed. However, to aggregate two sets of transactions into a larger set raises some difficult issues. Each of the two smaller aggregates would need to be weighted by a "convertibility multiplier" to construct the overall aggregate. In principle, problems like this are index-number problems of a conventional sort, and Stone put a considerable effort into solving them. His approach to solving them was typically pragmatic, however, and relied at least as much on ensuring that data were consistent as on the economic theory of index numbers.

Stone's work during the war consisted of laying out the groundwork of what later evolved in national accounting and in compiling preliminary national accounts for the United Kingdom and United States. After the war his work expanded to cover other countries as well. Immediately after the war, Stone headed a group of experts working first under League of Nations and then under United Nations

auspices to prepare standardized forms of national accounts for general international use. The work of Stone and his team was widely accepted and forms the basis of many other countries' national accounts and international comparisons between them. The methodology was still relatively rudimentary in 1945, of course, and it was constantly revised and updated in the following years. Problems were gradually ironed out as time went on, however, and it eventually reached a reasonably mature form in the 1968 United Nations handbook *A System of National Accounts.* Regular revisions continue to be made as more data become available and more problems are sorted out, but the essential methodology remains as it was set out then, and it is generally agreed that the UN definitions of production, consumption, and accumulation, and the many subsidiary conventions that go along with them, are sufficiently flexible to be useful in most practical situations. As the Royal Swedish Academy of Sciences put it: "National accounts have . . . created a systematic data base for a number of levels of economic analysis, including the analysis of different types of economic activity, inflation analysis, the analysis of economic structures, growth analysis and, particularly, international comparisons between countries" (p. 3).

Much of Stone's later work on national accounting was devoted to extending the basic methodology to provide accounts for new and less conventional areas. Among these sectors are the financial sector, the education system, and the population. In each case, the objective was to provide a complete representation of available resources with a view to the possible use of such information for public-policy purposes. This extension of the scope of national accounting reflected Stone's view that a system of accounts was much more than a mere inventory of the number and type of goods traded in markets and should take into account all forms of economic activity, nonmarketed as well as marketed. Indeed, the scope of national accounting went well beyond the purely economic to embrace sociodemographic and environmental factors as well. As Stone put it in his Nobel Memorial lecture:

> The three pillars on which an analysis of society ought to rest are studies of economic, sociodemographic, and environmental phenomena. Naturally enough, accounting ideas are most developed in the economic context . . . but they are equally applicable in the other two fields. By organizing our data in the form of accounts we can obtain a coherent picture of the stocks and flows, incomings and outgoings of whatever variables we are interested in, whether these be goods and services, human beings, or natural resources, and thence proceed to analyze the system of which they form part. (p. 5)

He then elaborated on the role of accounting systems in that analysis of society. Such an analysis should begin with:

> our *facts*, organized as far as possible into a coherent set of accounts. Given

this quantitative framework, we can formulate some hypotheses, or *theories*, about the technical and behavioral relationships that connect them. By combining facts and theories we can construct a *model* which when translated into quantitative terms will give us an idea of how the system under investigation actually works. (p. 5)

# Analysis of Consumer Demand

Stone also carried out a considerable amount of work on consumer-demand analysis while he was working on the development of national accounting. Apart from a handful of papers published in the late 1930s, his work on consumer demand really began during the war, when he and his co-workers put together the most comprehensive and detailed data set yet assembled for U.K. consumers' expenditures and the price, income, and other data needed for an empirical analysis. The data set covered the period 1920–38 and was to be used extensively in Stone's later work.

While Stone was well aware even at an early stage that demand functions for different commodities form a coherent system and ought in principle to be treated as such, such treatment was effectively precluded by practical considerations at the time, and so equations for each commodity or group of commodities were estimated separately. A typical equation had demand for the good or goods in question depending on total consumption expenditures, the price of the commodity or a price index for the commodity group, other relevant prices, a time trend, and occasionally other variables. Elasticities were taken to be constant. Economic theory was used in a relatively loose way to suggest what other prices or miscellaneous variables might be relevant in any particular equation. Stone went to enormous efforts to ensure that his data were as reliable as possible and to correct for sources of error in his empirical work.

This work produced some papers in the 1940s and early 1950s, but the main result was the monumental study *The Measurement of Consumers' Expenditure and Behaviour in the United Kingdom, 1920–1938*, which was published in two volumes in 1954 and 1966. More effort went into collecting and revising data for this study than went into the empirical estimates which it presented. It was characterized by a careful treatment of data problems, a loose but insightful use of economic theory, and a practical approach to methodological problems, and it was the first major comprehensive empirical analysis of U.K. consumer demand. The methodology used was similar to that used in earlier studies but provided a much more thorough treatment of the dynamic problems caused by serially correlated residuals. It was one of the first studies to make use of the Durbin-Watson test that later became so widespread. Stone's results indicated that equations estimated with data in levels tended to exhibit high residual serial correlation, but the serial correlation was reduced considerably when equations were estimated in first-dif-

ference form. This study also broke new ground in combining time-series data and data from cross-section household budgets which take account of family size, social class, and other such sociodemographic variables, and this combination helped to reduce the errors in time-series estimates.

Also in 1954, Stone began to publish estimates of simultaneous systems of demand equations instead of relying only on equations estimated separately. Stone was a pioneer in this field. The advantage of estimating systems of equations simultaneously was that it allowed one to make full use of economic theory that imposes restrictions on the system as a whole as well as on individual equations. (For instance, theory tells us that the matrix of Slutsky substitution effects should be negative semidefinite, and this requires simultaneous estimates of demand equations. The prediction that a consumer-demand equation should exhibit no "money illusion," on the other hand, can be tested with single-equation estimates.) One can use such restrictions either to test the theory by investigating whether they are refuted or else one can use them to derive more efficient estimates.

In this paper Stone worked with the linear expenditure system (LES) in which expenditure (that is, price times quantity) is a linear function of income and relevant prices. He showed that the LES could be interpreted as a system in which each household needed to buy certain minimum "subsistence" levels of each good and then choose additional amounts of goods to maximize utility once "subsistence" has been assured. He made a major contribution in deriving the restrictions imposed on the linear expenditure system by the hypothesis that the consumer maximizes utility, and he showed that the LES that satisfies these conditions has far fewer parameters than an unrestricted LES, and that these "overidentified parameters" can be used to test the theory or improve one's parameter estimates. The system had to be estimated simultaneously, however, because some of the parameters of the LES were common to each equation. Stone developed an iteration procedure to estimate the system and estimated it using his U.K. data set for 1920–38 to obtain quite reasonable estimates. The paper also presented some results of experiments that attempted to forecast consumption for 1920 and 1952.

We might also mention two other issues in consumer analysis to which Stone made useful contributions. One was in the handling of the dynamic problems caused by durable goods. In his work with D. A. Rowe (1957), Stone developed a framework that emphasized the distinction between the flow of consumption services derived from a durable good and the "capital stock" of the good itself. This framework allowed researchers to handle both durable and nondurable goods and led to a distinction between the long-run and short-run elasticities of demand for durable goods, the difference being that stocks of durable goods are at their "desired" levels in the long run but not necessarily in the short run. However, the frame-

work did not explain how "desired" stocks of durable goods were themselves determined.

The other area was in the econometric analysis of saving behavior. In the early 1960s Stone developed models which improved on simple Keynesian explanations of saving behavior by incorporating wealth as well as income as explanatory variables, and by distinguishing between their temporary and permanent values. His models also investigated the differential effects of labor and nonlabor income on consumption, the effects of government policy on saving, and the distinction between the saving of consumers and that of firms.

# The Cambridge Growth Project

In the 1960s, Stone's main efforts were devoted to a project intended to shed some light on the prospects for more rapid British economic growth. This was the "Program for Growth" carried out at the Department of Applied Economics at Cambridge under Stone's leadership. The motivation behind the project was the concern aroused by Britain's relatively slow growth rate in the postwar period and the sense of economic failure which that inadequate growth rate aroused. The project worked on the basis of a mixed economy with a competitive private sector and various forms of state intervention or control. The underlying philosophy behind the project was expressed as follows:

We should approach the economic system as an engineer approaches a complicated piece of machinery or as a doctor approaches his patient. Any adjustment or treatment depends on a sound diagnosis. Only in this way can we meet the arguments of the reactionary who can say with some plausibility that things might be worse and that tampering with them will probably make them more so, and those of the revolutionary who can say with equal plausibility that things might be better and invites us to follow his particular nostrum. The common link between these very different types is their utter disregard for the economic facts of life, a disregard they would never think of showing if their car broke down or if they contracted pneumonia. By exaggerating differences in political and social objectives, they obscure the fact that the main reason why we do not have a more successful economic policy is that we not understand the economic system sufficiently well, and that what we should be doing is to study anatomy and physiology instead of endlessly debating quack prescriptions. . . .

So let us follow the normal course of action: analysis, diagnosis, prescription, treatment. We shall get nowhere if we continue to shortcircuit the first two stages. (1962)

The objective of the Growth Project was not to give specific policy advice or to give detailed scenarios of the consequences of different policies. It was rather to look more generally at ways in which economic policy affected British economic growth. It was hoped that it might be able to identify potential growth sectors and give a rough idea of the effects

that different policies might have on them. The Growth Project examined both explicit "policy instruments" (for example, changes in the tax regime, changes in the exchange rate), and ways in which the government might indirectly be able to influence the private sectors. The latter would include, for instance, the effects of government policies on private-sector expectations and the effects, if any, of "indicative planning," in which the government tries to encourage the private sector to achieve its targets but does not coerce it.

The project consisted of two models which coexisted in an uneasy kind of way. One was a model of the economy in a steady state, and the other was a transient model which tried to explain how the economy could reach its steady-state path, taking into account the problems of capital adjustment and capacity constraints on available labor and capital. A considerable amount of work went into developing algorithms to carry out the very extensive computations involved, but much of Stone's earlier work was used as "building blocks" as well. Consumers' expenditures were modeled using the LES, for instance, and the model of saving behavior borrowed much from his earlier work in that area. The project also saw an extension of the scope of national accounting and some new uses made of it. Work was done to add to existing national accounts a more sophisticated treatment of financial transactions, and a more sophisticated treatment of labor issues that included health, education, and demography. Stone also extended his earlier work linking national accounting to input-output tables by developing a methodology to allow limited changes in input-output coefficients. This methodology helped to overcome the main drawback of input-output work and marked a notable advance in the field. As Johansen says:

The overall method . . . has been used to a large extent in subsequent input-output analyses. Indications of this type of changes in the coefficients may be found in some of Leontief's early work and a parallel method has been used in earlier statistical contexts. But Stone and his colleagues have carried out the most fundamental and thorough work on this method with respect to input-output analysis and have thus provided support for a means of treating changes in input-output coefficients which has been applied in many countries. (p. 27)

The Growth Project also broke new ground in modeling the economy sector by sector rather than by the fashionable procedure of modeling by broad output categories such as consumption, investment, and saving. This method was considerably more difficult—especially when one recalls the primitive computing facilities the Cambridge group would have used—but perhaps more sensible. It was always difficult providing even remotely "robust" microtheoretic foundations to highly aggregated models, and such models do not appear to have shown much stability in face of the various "shocks" that have hit Western

economies since the mid-1970s. Stone's disaggregated approach may therefore prove to be the more fruitful one in the end.

We have seen that Stone's principal contribution to economics was the development of national accounting, but that he also made valuable contributions to the empirical analysis of consumer demand and to large-scale empirical modeling. Stone's work has become so much a part of the modern economist's "working capital" that we tend to take it for granted. Perhaps the best way to appreciate its significance is to try to imagine what it would be like to work in a world where we did not have the benefit of national accounts. A great deal of modern empirical work could never have been carried out. Not only that, but Stone's national accounting methodology may yet set the groundwork for further developments in fields like demography and the study of the environment.

KEVIN DOWD

# Selected Bibliography

"Bibliography of Richard Stone's Works, 1936–1984." *Scandinavian Journal of Economics.* 87(1) (1985): 33–43.

Houthakker, H. S. *Richard Stone and the Analysis of Consumer Demand.* Cambridge, Mass.: Harvard Institute of Economic Research, 1985.

Johansen, Leif. "Richard Stone's Contributions to Economics." *Scandi-*

*navian Journal of Economics* 87 (1985): 4–32.

Royal Swedish Academy of Sciences, Press Release for the Nobel Memorial Prize in Economics 1984, reprinted in the *Scandinavian Journal of Economics* 87 (1985): 1–3.

Stone, Richard (with D. A. Rowe and others). *The Measurement of Consumers' Expenditure and Behaviour in the United Kingdom, 1920–1938.* Vol. 1. Cambridge: Cambridge University Press, 1954.

Stone, Richard (with D. A. Rowe). "The Market Demand for Durable Goods." *Econometrica* 25 (1957): 423–43.

Stone, Richard (with D. A. Rowe). "Dynamic Demand Functions: Some Econometric Results." *Economic Journal* 68 (1958): 256–70.

Stone, Richard (with D. A. Rowe). "The Durability of Consumers Durable Goods." *Econometrica* 28 (1960): 407–16.

Stone, Richard (with D. A. Rowe). "A Post-War Expenditure Function."

*Manchester School of Economic and Social Studies* 30 (1962): 187–201.

Stone, Richard, *et al. A Programme for Growth.* Vol. 1: *A Computable Model of Economic Growth.* London: Chapman and Hall, 1962.

Stone, Richard (with D. A. Rowe). *The Measurement of Consumers' Expenditure and Behaviour in the United Kingdom, 1920–1938.* Vol. 2. Cambridge: Cambridge University Press, 1966.

Stone, Richard, and Peterson, William, eds. *Econometric Contributions to Public Policy: Proceedings of a Conference Held by the International Economic Association at Urbino, Italy.* New York: St. Martin's Place, 1979.

Stone, Sir Richard. "The Accounts of Society" (1984 Nobel Memorial Lecture). *Journal of Applied Econometrics* 1 (1985): 5–28.

United Nations. *A System of National Accounts.* New York: United Nations, 1968.

# JAN TINBERGEN *1969*

Jan Tinbergen, a Dutch economist born in 1903, shared the first Nobel Prize in Economic Sciences, awarded in 1969, with his Norwegian colleague, Ragnar Frisch. Both Tinbergen and Frisch were cited for their pathbreaking development of quantitative, dynamic models for the analysis of economic processes. Tinbergen, studying the Dutch economy, had developed the first large-scale econometric model in 1936. Shortly thereafter, he constructed similar models for the U.S. and British economies. His application of mathematical and statistical methods to economic analysis built on his background in physics, in which he earned a doctorate from the University of Leiden in 1929. His thesis dealt with problems in both physics and economics, and since completing his education, Tinbergen has devoted his life to the advance of economic theory and economic policy analysis.

Tinbergen's family background clearly fostered excellence in intellectual pursuits. He had one sister and three brothers, one of whom is also a Nobel laureate, having received the prize in biology in 1973. As a young man, Tinbergen was a member of a socialist youth association and an active member of the Social Democratic Labour party who refused to serve in the army, performing alternate service in the Rotterdam prison administration. His intellectual pursuits, always rigorous and frequently highly technical, have consistently been directed by his social and political beliefs. One of his broad professional goals has been to use the analytical tools developed by free-market economists to show that pure laissez faire is not the optimal economic system.

It is difficult for an overview of Tinbergen's exceptionally prolific professional career to do justice to the depth and breadth of his creativity and intellectual acumen. Writing in many languages, including Dutch, English, French, German, and Danish, Tinbergen has published more than fifteen books, over two hundred journal articles, and numerous pamphlets, reports, and essays. His work has spanned a broad spectrum of subfields in the discipline of economics, including development planning, international

trade, the theory of economic policy making, comparative economic systems, and income distribution, in addition to the econometric modeling of business cycles for which he was awarded the Nobel Prize. The connecting threads through all of Tinbergen's work are a deep-seated concern for human welfare and a conviction that scientific, mathematical analysis can be combined with a broader, humanistic approach and applied to theoretical issues which arise out of and inform practical economic policy decisions.

Tinbergen embarked on his professional career by heading up a new unit for business cycle research in the Dutch Central Bureau of Statistics, beginning in 1929. He maintained his association with the bureau until 1945, with a short interlude working for the League of Nations in Geneva from 1936 to 1938. In 1945, he moved to the Netherlands Central Planning Bureau as director. Tinbergen engaged in an academic career alongside his government service. In 1931 he became a part-time lecturer in statistics at the University of Amsterdam, and two years later he joined the faculty of the Netherlands School of Economics in Rotterdam as a full professor. He became a full-time academic there in 1955. In 1973, Tinbergen was named professor of international cooperation at the University of Leiden, a post from which he retired in 1975.

Tinbergen's career can be divided into several distinct stages. From the late 1920s to World War II, he was involved in the pathbreaking work in econometric modeling which won him the Nobel Prize. The second major stage of Tinbergen's career was his focus on the theory of short-term economic policy making, from 1945 to 1955. From the 1950s to the 1970s, he immersed himself in the problems of developing nations, contributing both to the theory of development and to the current political processes of international cooperation and development. The fourth stage of Tinbergen's career encompasses his work on the nature and determinants of the personal distribution of income. In the 1970s, he extended his field of inquiry from the inequality between nations and the poverty of developing countries to include the study of inequality within industrialized nations. He has also written extensively on the comparison of alternative economic systems in the later phases of his career.

A continuous feature throughout Tinbergen's career has been his integration of major social and economic problems with practical recommendations and scientific work. Tinbergen's intense devotion to social issues, which is never overshadowed by his brilliant mathematical and statistical contributions, is a natural outgrowth of his basic nature. He is known by friends and associates for his gentleness and modesty and for his selfless dedication to the cause of human welfare. His personality is reflected in his tendency to focus on the accomplishments of his colleagues and to play down his own pathbreaking contributions. Tinbergen lives a simple lifestyle, eschewing the pursuit and consumption of wealth. He

chose to use his share in the Nobel Prize for a study on the introduction of a progressive land tax in developing countries, not for personal purposes. Tinbergen lives in a modest neighborhood and takes the bus or tram to work rather than driving a car. His personal lifestyle, like his professional endeavors, reflects a highly principled, powerfully motivated nature.

## Econometric Modeling

Early in his career, Tinbergen concentrated on the development of methods for empirical testing of mathematically formulated economic theories. He pursued this goal through the construction of econometric models of the economy. His first major effort in this direction was the development of a model for the Dutch economy in 1936, when he built a system of twenty-four equations. Tinbergen was convinced that a system of simultaneous equations was the best way to depict the interdependence of the numerous variables characterizing the level of economic activity.

The model he constructed at this early date included equations for income formation and consumption expenditures compatible with Keynesian theory. He modeled consumption as a function of disposable income and saw the demand for goods and services as a critical determinant of the overall level of economic activity. He included exports and imports, split money flows into prices and quantities, and introduced lags into a number of the equations. This early model also suggested the inverse relationship between wage inflation and employment which received widespread attention when it was depicted by the Phillips Curve in the late 1950s. In his own descriptions of this and later models, Tinbergen has been careful to point out that the economic processes described are not purely neoclassical in nature. Rather than assuming consistent profit-maximizing behavior, for example, Tinbergen incorporated "satisficing," or cost-plus pricing, into his supply equations. Despite its innovations and the impact it was to have on the profession in the long run, Tinbergen's model received no international attention at the time it was developed, and an English version did not appear until 1959.

In the mid 1930s, The League of Nations requested that Tinbergen develop empirical tests of an assortment of existing business cycle theories. No reliable method for validating competing explanations for the ups and downs of economic activity had yet been found. This project culminated in the publication of a two-volume work, *Statistical Testing of Business Cycle Theories* (1939). In the first volume, focused on the theory of investment activity, Tinbergen explained his empirical method and gave examples of its application. He found little evidence to support the prevailing acceleration principle of investment cycles and formulated alternative principles. His analysis used standard multiple-regression analysis as well as new methods which had been developed

by Frisch. Tinbergen's contribution was not in the development of new statistical methodology but in the application of existing methods to macroeconomic problems.

The second volume, the first attempt at building a macroeconomic model to explain business cycles in the United States economy, contained a system of forty-eight equations which constituted a complete macromodel for the United States economy. Tinbergen did not look at each phase of the economy separately but constructed a unified dynamic model. He formulated a quantitative analysis which allowed prediction.

Although Tinbergen's macromodeling work received a lukewarm reception at the time, he persevered in his attempts to perfect the technique. His 1951 book, *Business Cycles in the United Kingdom, 1870–1914*, extended his work to the British economy. Macromodeling did not receive wide respectability within the economics profession until the 1950s, but it was to revolutionize the economics profession in later years. In recent decades the predictive powers of econometric macromodels, while still of uneven reliability, have become highly valued by professional economists, business people, and government officials.

In 1930, Tinbergen had founded the Econometric Society together with Ragnar Frisch and Irving Fisher. They conceived the organization with the goals of advancing economic theory in its relation to statistics and mathematics and of promoting unification of empirical and theoretical quantitative approaches. They hoped to encourage constructive, rigorous thinking in the mode of the natural sciences. Although it was two decades before their approach prevailed, these pioneers in the field of econometrics eventually saw their ideas and methodology become established as the dominant technique of economic policy analysis.

In the field of econometrics, Tinbergen is known particularly for his contributions to dynamic theory and his attempts at statistical testing of business cycle theories. He pioneered the use of difference equations for dynamic analysis, a technique which had become standard by the end of the 1930s. Tinbergen is also credited with the discovery of the cobweb theorem, an explanation of cycles in individual markets. The theory explains the short-term fluctuations of prices and quantities, particularly in agricultural markets. He argued that supply reacts to changes in prices with a one-year time lag, whereas demand reacts immediately. More generally, Tinbergen's initiatives in building econometric models which would permit reliable short-term forecasting, leading to more rational policy choices, make him a key founder of the econometric method.

## Economic Policy Analysis

Having laid the groundwork which would revolutionize the approach of professional economists to macroeconomic policy, Tinbergen left the refinement of technical methodology to others and turned his attention to new but related areas. In 1945, he became director of the new Netherlands Central Planning Bureau. At this juncture, he became involved with general theoretical questions of economic policy making. In addition to many shorter pieces, Tinbergen wrote several books on this subject. They included *On the Theory of Economic Policy* (1952), *Centralization and Decentralization in Economic Policy* (1954), and *Economic Policy: Principles and Design* (1956).

Attempting to deal systematically with the problems of economic policy, Tinbergen divided policy variables into the three categories: targets, data, and instruments. He argued that policy could be effective only if the number of instruments was at least equal to the number of targets. For example, it would be impossible to adjust both the unemployment rate and the rate of inflation to desired levels if the rate of growth of the money supply were the only policy instrument available. This notion has become a basic premise of all economic policy analysis, but at the time policy targets were usually thought of separately. His approach of viewing economic policy as consisting of multiple related targets which had to be tackled with a sufficient number of policy instruments was an innovative one.

In his early work in this area, Tinbergen addressed policy issues by beginning with a given economy described by a certain number of economic variables and the same number of structural equations. Given the targets of economic policy with an equal number of policy instruments, he asked how the instruments should be fixed to attain the targets. Later, Tinbergen introduced flexible targets. That is, he was concerned with goals such as maximizing real income or minimizing unemployment, rather than with attaining a particular target level of unemployment.

Instead of treating economic policy as though there were always one policy maker with unilateral decision making power, Tinbergen also addressed the more complicated situation of decentralized policy making. He investigated the advantages and disadvantages of centralized, as opposed to decentralized, policy making under particular circumstances. An interesting theoretical twist involved in decentralization was the need for policy makers to be concerned with the decisions being made by others, in a manner parallel to decision making under oligopoly conditions.

Tinbergen made the distinction between analytical problems and policy studies explicit. In analytical problems, policy instruments are given and economic variables such as income, employment, and the balance of payments are to be determined by the model. For policy studies, by contrast, Tinbergen developed "decision models." Rather than beginning with the policies and predicting their outcomes, these models take targets such as desired levels of unemployment and inflation as given and derive the optimal policies for attaining those targets.

Tinbergen developed a quantitative framework for policy analysis

and concluded that the optimal regime was a mixture of decentralized and centralized policy making. Decentralization was optimal in principle, but externalities and economies of scale dictated that more central decision making was required. Tinbergen was particularly concerned about the paucity of supranational decision-making institutions, which he thought were necessary for survival, in light of the considerable impact policies of one nation often have on other nations.

Tinbergen aimed at the mathematical expression of the types of problems involved in economic policy decisions. He emphasized the value of the precision attainable through mathematical formulation of economic issues but was careful to stress that these issues cannot be isolated from institutional, juridical, technical, and psychological factors. Tinbergen's policy theory was not abstract welfare economics but was concerned with actual policies in actual economies. He was intent on developing theory which could be readily used to facilitate current economic policy design and implementation.

His 1956 book, *Economic Policy: Principles and Design*, was one of a series of books by various authors concerned with theoretical problems encountered in practical research. All of the books took a primarily quantitative, rather than qualitative, approach. Tinbergen described his work in this book as drawing on two main facets of his experience—his work at the Central Planning Bureau and his participation in discussions with friends and colleagues about wider aspects of economic policy. Much of his involvement with these issues has been through the Netherlands Labor party. His basic goal was to bring controversies often dealt with in a superficial, knee-jerk manner into the realm of objective, scientific analysis.

## Problems of the Developing World

Beginning in the mid 1950s, Tinbergen turned his attention to problems of long-term growth and development in the developing world, as well as to questions of international cooperation and integration. He was acutely aware of the problems of poor countries and was also motivated in part by the creation of Benelux and the European Economic Community. His work in the field of development was a natural outgrowth of his devotion to humanitarian activities and his idealistic view of mankind. He hoped to help repair some of the evils created by colonial repression.

In 1955, Tinbergen resigned from the Central Planning Bureau and became a full-time professor of development planning at the Netherlands School of Economics. He began to write extensively on development issues as well as serving as an adviser to the governments of a number of developing countries and as a consultant to UN agencies. From 1966 to 1972, he chaired the UN Committee for Development Planning, an advisory group of independent development experts.

Tinbergen immersed himself in the practical problems of the developing nations, traveling widely and lecturing on policy options. He was determined to work towards the closing of the gap between rich and poor nations.

Increased international cooperation and economic integration were high on Tinbergen's list of policy priorities. In his 1954 book *International Economic Integration*, Tinbergen discussed international economic integration as the essence of international economic relations between autonomous nations. He combined policy recommendations with economic science but was careful to warn the reader when he crossed the boundary. Tinbergen recommended more planning for international cooperation and saw serious political problems with the national focus on short-term interests. He advocated reductions in import restrictions, unification of indirect taxes, easy convertibility of currencies, an international policy of development, and a higher degree of centralization in financial policy, which would allow other policy instruments to be more decentralized. Tinbergen was not satisfied with purely theoretical discussions of economic integration and urged that future work on the issue be more quantitatively based.

In addition to his concern with relations among nations, Tinbergen devoted extensive efforts to understanding and promoting long-term development in Third World countries. The extensive writings which emerged from this phase of Tinbergen's career include *The Design of Development* (1958), *Mathematical Models of Economic Growth* (1962, with Hendricus Bos), *Econometric Models of Education* (1965, with Bos), *Development Planning* (1967), and *Reshaping the International Order* (1976).

Tinbergen's development models were designed with the assumption that only minimal data are available in developing countries and that the skills of the planners, administrators, and politicians involved in development planning are limited. He constructed three main types of models. One was a simple macro model based on three planning stages. In the first stage—the macro stage—overall levels for economic variables would be targeted. Plans would be made for output, savings, investment, capital, and export and import levels on a national basis. In the middle stage, the economy would be broken down by geographical regions and by industries or sectors. Using an input-output model and sectoral capital-output coefficients, the aggregate activity levels would be divided among sectors. Finally, in the micro stage of planning, individual projects would be appraised and planned.

By contrast, a second type of model Tinbergen constructed started from individual projects and constructed a macro plan which was essentially the sum of many micro plans. He also developed large systems of simultaneous equations that incorporated policy instruments more explicitly. These development models derived from the economet-ric-modeling methodology Tinbergen had used in business cycle studies.

Tinbergen recommended that the less developed countries (LDCs) focus on labor-intensive industries and technologies, while the developed world should concentrate on more capital-intensive endeavors. This would maximize employment and income opportunities in LDCs. He urged governments to create general conditions favorable to development, to acquaint the business community and the public with the potentialities and advantages of development, to make ample basic investments, and to take measures to facilitate and stimulate private investment. He expressed the conviction that governments had a responsibility to respect the preferences of their citizens but contended that in cases where the public view was shortsighted, government should override those sentiments.

Consistent with his usual approach, Tinbergen's goal was to apply quantitative scientific analysis to development issues. He thought it was vital that these social issues be removed from the realm of emotional discourse as far as possible and subjected to rigorous analysis. Nonetheless, in his closing comments in *The Design of Development* (1958, p. 69), Tinbergen stated that "It should not be forgotten, however, that the role to be played by scientific knowledge and insight in the field of development policy will for a long time to come be only a modest one. The relevant facts of life are too many and too varied to make it possible to reach decisions without a strong intuitive feeling for human relations." He was determined to promote quantitative scientific economic policy analysis, but not at the expense of a broader, humanistic approach to social and economic conditions.

Tinbergen's commitment to a broad-based approach is evidenced in his involvement in *Reshaping the International Order* (1976), a report to the Club of Rome coordinated by Tinbergen, with contributions from several other social scientists. The study addressed the question of what new international order should be recommended to meet the urgent needs of present and future generations. It posed as its goal the furthering of the prospects for removal of the injustices endemic in the present system of international relations.

The authors contended that "the construction of a better world implies acceptance by society of the responsibility to ensure the satisfaction of the individual and collective needs of people and the creation of international and national systems in which opportunities and the means to use those opportunities are much more equitably distributed than at present" (pp. 4–5). The three most urgent problems listed were the armaments race, population control, and food supply. Tinbergen's deep concern for human welfare and his integrated approach to the study of economic conditions are reflected here. Unlike many modern-day economists, Tinbergen has consistently avoided a narrow conception of economic issues as isolated from their social context.

# Distribution of Income

Tinbergen's deep-seated concern for the economic well-being of individuals and societies has continued to guide his professional interests. In the 1970s, he turned his attention to questions of the personal distribution of income in developed countries. He had written a pamphlet on equitable income distribution in 1946, and a fundamental theoretical article, "On the Theory of Income Distribution" in 1956. More recently he has written many articles in this area and a book, *Income Distribution: Analysis and Policy* (1975). In the latter, he attempted to give a positive explanation of the existing distribution of income among individuals as well as a normative statement of what would constitute an equitable distribution of income.

Tinbergen stated clearly his goal of reducing inequality within Western nations, characterizing this as a generally accepted aim of socioeconomic policy, but he focused on analyzing the determinants of inequality more than on philosophies of economic justice. He has, however, defined equity as implying equal welfare for all individuals, where welfare is a function of income, occupation, and schooling. He has argued that there is tension between actual and required levels of schooling which should be minimized.

Tinbergen's analysis of the distribution of income was based on the theory of supply and demand. He estimated price equations for the factors of production and investigated the distribution of the incomes corresponding to these prices. Treating labor as heterogeneous, he dealt with the supply of labor as based on individual utility functions, which he attempted to specify. The demand for labor was based on production functions, which determine job characteristics and requirements. A main theme of Tinbergen's work is that inequality cannot be explained by inequality in the distribution of productive capacities but by imbalances in the supply of and demand for particular types of productive services. It is excess supply, not any absolute lack of particular skills, which creates low wages. He has argued that the solution is for education to outpace technological development, reducing the pool of labor lacking skills compatible with current productive requirements. He contended that a deliberate creation of an oversupply of skilled labor and a shortage of unskilled labor could reduce income inequality.

Tinbergen's analysis of distribution relied on complete but simple economic models. He emphasized the interdependence of economic variables and criticized other approaches to distribution, such as human-capital theory, for focusing too much on supply to the exclusion of demand. He also criticized the stochastic approach of some early economic work that formulated mathematical expressions for the personal distribution of income, arguing that it had no economic interpretation and thus no policy implications. Without reducing inequality to an abstract problem, Tinbergen subsumed many noneconomic factors under the rubrics of supply and demand. Supply depended on personality traits, performance characteristics such as IQ and education, and noncognitive characteristics, all expressed mathematically. He considered quantification an essential step on the road to making the analysis of distribution scientific rather than emotional.

In order to express his model mathematically, Tinbergen has tempted to quantify utility, specifying functional forms. From his perspective, future progress in defining and approaching equitable distributions depends on advances in the ability of economists to specify individual-preference functions quantitatively, allowing comparisons of utility among individuals. He advocates assuming the measurability of utility on the pragmatic grounds that this approach allows economists to give substance to the concepts of equity and distributive justice and facilitates the formulation of policy conclusions.

In addition to his technical analysis, Tinbergen has made explicit policy recommendations aimed at reducing income inequality. In addition to his number-one priority of extending the educational system, he has promoted the redirection of research to further development of concepts of equity and of the measurement of welfare. His ideal tax system would tax individual capabilities rather than outcomes. Until the appropriate measurement techniques required for a capability tax can be developed, higher taxes on wealth, capital gains, and inherited estates win Tinbergen's approval.

# Welfare Economics

Throughout the various stages of his career, Tinbergen has dealt with issues of optimal policy in the various aspects of the economy he has studied. Thus, he has maintained a continuing interest in welfare economics—the branch of economic theory which formulates the conditions for the maximization of social welfare. In the *American Economic Review* (1957), Tinbergen argued that a successful welfare economics should have concrete influence on practical political thought and that this goal had not been realized. Results of welfare economics were not widely understood and not very relevant to practical policy. He outlined what he thought welfare economics could do about income distribution and social justice, arguing that these issues had not so far been adequately addressed. He wanted an explanation, not just a statistical description, of the distribution of income because this was the only way to approach changing that distribution.

In his own work in welfare economics, Tinbergen has attempted to define the shape of plausible social-welfare functions. The general notions of welfare economics underlie his approach to the study of comparative economic systems. In his search for the optimal regime, Tinbergen has taken his own advice and applied welfare economics to practical issues to derive concrete results. He sees all economic systems as sharing the same basic goal of maximizing the average sense of psychological satisfaction. The search for an optimal regime is the search for a set of institutions which can be described by behavioral equations and which create the conditions for optimal welfare.

Tinbergen prefers what he has called the "direct method" of determining an optimal regime. This involves expressing the conditions for maximizing social welfare in mathematical equations. The equations are then interpreted as representing the operation of a regime which would be optimal. The more indirect method would be to specify equations for the institutions of several alternative regimes and compare the resulting levels of social welfare.

Despite the apparent rigor of this methodology, Tinbergen admits that the optimal regime depends on the structural data of the particular society. The optimal size of the public sector, for example, depends on the extent of externalities and increasing returns in the economy, and the optimal tax rate is a function of the dispersion of productive capacities within the society.

Tinbergen has criticized the view that market economies and command economies represent a dichotomy in the structure of economic systems. He sees many shades between these two extremes, and it is in this territory of the mixed economy where Tinbergen's ideal lies. He perceives reality approaching such an ideal in the sense that capitalist and socialist economies are "converging"—compromising extreme principles and becoming increasingly alike.

Tinbergen considers the more black-and-white view as rooted in ideology and wants to use a welfare economic framework to move the issue into the sphere of scientific analysis. He is convinced that no system is morally better than any other and that the choice should be made on the basis of efficiency considerations. He calls the concepts of complete market freedom and of complete state regulation utopias and sees them as based on misconceptions of human nature.

Tinbergen has concluded that the optimal regime lies between the two extremes of a totally free market and a completely planned economy. He envisions increasing tasks for public authorities, a less unequal distribution of disposable income, and redistribution based on a tax system which does not seriously dampen incentives. Although he would institute more central planning, he has opposed public ownership of most of the means of production and sees economic incentives as the driving force of the economic system.

## Other Work and Overall Legacy

Tinbergen has also written on many other aspects of economics, including the theory of imperfect competition, tariff unions, balance-of-payments problems, national accounting, and numerous other areas. He has used his econometric modeling methodology to study a wide array of issues. He has, for example, constructed a model to estimate the influence of productivity on social welfare (which he found not to be consistently positive) and

has studied a variety of international trade issues using this technique.

Tinbergen's work has received wide acclaim. Nonetheless, hidden within it are many ideas which went unnoticed and for which his colleagues later received recognition. For example, as mentioned above, he anticipated John Maynard Keynes's notion of the short-run cyclical consumption function. In the 1950s, he understood that the flow of international capital was related to changes in interest rates rather than to the level of interest rates, an idea that was worked out later by other economists. He also anticipated some of the elements of prominent growth theories developed in later years.

Tinbergen's legacy is as the father of the field of econometrics and the first to develop empirical macroeconomic models. He also contributed to modern forecasting techniques and to the theory of economic policy. He laid foundations for scientific modern development planning and has contributed to the theoretical literature on income distribution and the international flow of goods and capital. He has done important work on comparative economic systems and questions of the convergence between planned and market-oriented economies.

In all stages of his career, Tinbergen has been concerned with practical problems and empirical analysis. The reforms that rank highest in Tinbergen's priority list are increased international integration, international redistribution of income, built-in monetary stabiliz-

ers, family planning, industrial democracy, and the equalization of
opportunity. More generally, he sees
the most pressing problems today as
the need to organize a peaceful
world, strengthen solidarity with
those living in poverty, and take the
welfare of future generations into
consideration.

Tinbergen has sought relatively
simple methodologies that work, not
highly sophisticated technical methodologies. For him, quantitative
techniques are a means to the end of
understanding social and economic
issues, not an end in themselves. Tinbergen's focus on mathematical formulation of economic events and
tendencies has become deeply entrenched in the economics profession. His concern with the broader
context in which these forces operate
is more often neglected.

Jan Tinbergen has provided a
model which deserves the emulation
of future generations of economists.
He believes firmly in the central role
of mathematical expressions and
statistical technique in economic
analysis. He is committed to the
scientific study of economic issues
but has never allowed concern for
technique to obscure the basic purpose of economic analysis as a tool
for social progress. He is intensely
aware of the complex nature of economic issues and of the impossibility
of understanding them without a
broader interdisciplinary approach.
He recognizes the interdependence
of positive and normative aspects of
economic analysis and engages comfortably in both, without neglecting
the distinction. Few of his followers
can hope to match his intellectual

prowess, but all should aspire to his
social conscience and to his use of
economic theory to solve practical
problems.

SANDRA R. BAUM

# Selected Bibliography

## WORKS BY TINBERGEN

*Statistical Testing of Business Cycle
Theories*. 2 vols. Geneva: League of
Nations, 1939.

*Redelijke Inkomensverdeling*. Haarlem:
DeGulden Pers, 1946.

*Business Cycles in the United Kingdom,
1870–1914*. Amsterdam: Elsevier-
North Holland, 1951.

*On the Theory of Economic Policy*.
Amsterdam: Elsevier-North Holland, 1952.

*Centralization and Decentralization in
Economic Policy*. Amsterdam: Elsevier-North Holland, 1954.

*International Economic Integration*.
Amsterdam: Elsevier-North Holland, 1954.

*Economic Policy: Principles and De-
sign*. Amsterdam: Elsevier-North
Holland, 1956.

"On the Theory of Income Distribution." Weltwirtschaftliches Archiv
77 (1956): 155–73.

"Welfare Economics and Income Distribution." *American Economic Review* 47 (1957): 490–503.

*The Design of Development*. Baltimore:
Johns Hopkins University Press,
1958.

Tinbergen, Jan, and Bos, Hendricus.
*Mathematical Models of Economic
Growth*. New York: McGraw-Hill,
1962.

*Central Planning.* New Haven: Yale University Press, 1964.

and Bos, Hendricus. *Econometric Models of Education.* Paris: Organization for Economic Cooperation and Development, 1965.

*Development Planning.* New York: McGraw-Hill, 1967.

*Income Distribution: Analysis and Policy.* Amsterdam: Elsevier-North Holland, 1975.

*Reshaping the International Order: A Report to the Club of Rome.* New York: Dutton, 1976.

*Production, Income, and Welfare: The Search for an Optimal Social Order.* Lincoln: University of Nebraska Press, 1985.

OTHER WORKS

Haveman, Robert H., "Tinbergen's Income Distribution." *Journal of Human Resources* 12 (1977): 103–14.

Mulligan, Gordon F., "Tinbergen-Type Central Place Systems." *International Regional Science Review* 7 (1982): 83–91.

Osberg, Lars, "Tinbergen and the 'Blurring' of the Human Capital Paradigm." *Review of Income and Wealth* 22 (1976): 93–97.

Thanawala, Kishur, "Tinbergen's Contribution to Social Economics." Rivista Internazionale di Scienze Economiche e Commerciali 34 (1987): 751–89.

# JAMES TOBIN 1981

James Tobin was the 1981 Nobel laureate in Economic Sciences. His major work cited by the Nobel Committee centers on the link between financial markets and markets for real goods and services. There are many related contributions in portfolio and investment theory that swirl around this creative core. Tobin was born in Champaign, Illinois, in 1918. His academic training was at Harvard University, where he received his bachelor's degree in 1939 and master's degree in 1940. His education was interrupted by naval service during World War II. After the war, he returned to Harvard and completed his Ph.D. in 1947. Tobin remained at Harvard after finishing his doctorate but was lured away by Yale University in 1950, where he has resided as Sterling Professor of Economics since 1957. He directed the Cowles Foundation for Research in Economics from 1955 to 1961. His stewardship of the foundation resulted in major, innovative research in economic theory and econometrics.

When asked by President Kennedy to serve on his Council of Economic Advisers, Tobin demurred, replying that he was an ivory tower economist. But Kennedy persevered, responding that he was an ivory tower president, an argument that was sufficient to induce Tobin to serve on the council during 1961–62. Despite his short tenure as a policy maker, Tobin has been one of the most influential commentators on national economic policy since the early 1960s. He remains the respected dean of American economists who stand squarely in the Keynesian tradition, believing that proper economic policy implemented by an activist government can have a significant impact on the quality of people's lives.

This essay explains Tobin's economics, paying most attention to the body of work recognized by the Nobel Committee. Any short essay on Tobin's contributions must pick and choose; these selections convey the general intellectual assumptions and analytic style Tobin brings to his examination of economic reality. In the end, a great economist is identified by his vision more than his technical skill. Tobin's vision has remained remarkably consistent throughout his career, both in terms of his assumptions concerning how the economic system functions and his focus on the empirical relevance of economic analysis.

# The Formative Years

The formative years of a creative life are a significant starting point for understanding the contributions of any economist discussed in this book, but in Tobin's case these years merit special attention. Paul Samuelson has remarked that

"Tobin had to win the Nobel Prize because he can't help winning any prize that's out there" (*Science* [1981], p. 520). From the start, Tobin was recognized as being special. His father, a journalist who was publicity director for athletics at the University of Illinois, was a highly intelligent man who loved to read and argue the liberal side of political issues and instilled a lifelong passion for intellectual pursuits in young James. That Tobin's abilities were up to the rigors of such a life was obvious to his peers and teachers at University High School, where Tobin remembers that he was "so unfailingly an A student that it was boring even to me" (1986, p. 113). As luck would have it, the Conant Prize Fellowships to Harvard University were established the year Tobin was applying for admission to the University of Illinois. Tobin's father read about the new fellowships in the *New York Times* and encouraged his son to apply. One can only guess at the father's feelings as he watched his son pack his bags to journey to Harvard and become a member of Conant's new "meritocracy."

But it was more than raw ability that formed the quiet, shy young man from Illinois into one of the leading economists of the twentieth century. Two additional influences were of crucial importance. First, Tobin was raised in a liberal family during the Great Depression. The efficacy of an activist government was one of the values imbued by the Tobin household, and the image of government defined by social responsibilities was etched into Tobin's mind before he had any notion he could make his living thinking about economics. While the Tobin household did not directly suffer as a consequence of the depression, Tobin's mother returned to her social-work career to help ameliorate the human suffering caused by the economic collapse. Tobin saw, through her eyes, the graphic day-to-day consequences of poverty. Second, he was a developing scholar during a time when the new economics of John Maynard Keynes was beginning to establish a foothold in the American academic community. The lure of Keynes was irresistible to an idealistic young scholar trying to understand what had happened during the 1930s and how such a terrible, dehumanizing collapse in the economic system could be avoided in the future. In Tobin's own words:

I went into economics for two reasons. One was that as a child of the Depression I was terribly concerned about the world. It seemed then that many of the problems were economic in origin. If you thought that the world should be saved, and I did, then economics looked like the decisive thing to study. The second thing was that you could have your cake and eat it too, because it was an intellectually fascinating subject. (*Conversations with Economists* [1983], pp. 97–98)

Despite his university-town upbringing, Tobin had no early ambition to be an academic. When he enrolled in Harvard he was not thinking about economics; he was inclined toward law, or perhaps journalism. His sophomore economics course changed all that. Tobin was introduced to Keynes's *General Theory of Employment, Interest and Money* by his tutor and introductory-economics teacher Spencer Pollard. Tobin has remarked that he was too young to know how difficult the book was and just "plowed into it." Both the controversy and political significance surrounding the book were intensely interesting to the Harvard sophomore.

With the exception of Seymour Harris, the senior faculty generally were not sympathetic to Keynes, but most of the younger faculty and graduate students rapidly became advocates. Tobin eagerly joined in their debates. With the arrival of Alvin Hansen, the young advocates gained a senior mentor to channel their enthusiasm. Hansen was 50 years old when he joined the Harvard faculty. He was an early critic of *The General Theory*, but he also prized intellectual honesty. This quality caused him to scrutinize ideas he had held all his professional life. More and more, Keynesian arguments seemed to provide superior explanations. Hansen changed his mind, and in so doing became the leading American Keynesian of his generation. To Tobin, Hansen was at first a hero and mentor, and later a good friend.

With the support and encouragement of the Harvard faculty, Tobin's choice of profession was inevitable. By the time he had to write his senior honors thesis, his skill as an economist had evolved to the point that he could challenge a central conclusion of the *General Theory*. In classical theory, prices adjust to ensure market equilibrium. Excess demand in a market causes market price to rise. Excess supply in a market causes market price to fall. The wage rate is the price of labor, and it increases or decreases to remove excess demand or excess supply in the labor market. Because wages adjust to remove any excess supply of labor, any observed unemployment must be voluntary. Labor-market equilibrium thus must be synonymous with full employment. In stark contrast, Keynes argued that an *underemployment equilibrium*, an equilibrium with involuntary employment, is possible. An underemployment equilibrium comes about because money wages do not adjust to restore full employment as predicted by classical theory. In Keynes's world, money wages are rigid in a downward direction. They are administered prices, prices not immediately subject to market forces.

Tobin argued that the significance of Keynes's conclusions did not rest on the existence of an underemployment equilibrium. The essence of Keynesianism remains intact if money wages are simply slow to adjust. If money wages are slow to adjust, output has to adjust to restore equilibrium. The slower the change in money wages, the larger the change in output. This disequilibrium fall in output can be sustained and long term. Thus long-run equilibrium issues are of little consequence. Tobin's honors thesis **was** revised and published in the *Quarterly Journal of Economics* in

1941. It was his first professional publication.

Tobin's undergraduate intuition touched what would become a major debate in the post-World War II period: What are the relative speeds of adjustment of prices, wages, and output to disequilibrium shocks in the modern industrial economy? The vision of a sluggish economy with sticky wages and prices, an economy where output gives way before prices in response to economic downturns, is shared by all economists who consider themselves followers of the Keynesian tradition. Over the years, the most eloquent, persuasive spokesman for this vision has been James Tobin. He has fended off several waves of revised classical thinking that have attempted to reestablish flexible market adjustments. His economy cannot be relied upon to correct itself through flexible wages and prices. It is also significant that Tobin's first attempt to explain the stickiness of money wages was developed by speculating on how workers determine their labor supply. Throughout his career, he has consistently formulated explanations of macroeconomic behavior in terms of such microeconomic-choice models.

Tobin had only to complete his doctoral dissertation when his education was interrupted by World War II. He spent nine months in the Office of Price Administration and Civilian Supply, dealing with the rationing of scarce materials, before he joined the Navy, where he served as an officer on a destroyer until the end of 1945. As with all other aspects of his life, Tobin's performance as a naval officer did not go unnoticed. Novelist Herman Wouk and Tobin attended the same officer's training school, and Wouk used Tobin as a model for the character Tobit, who makes a brief appearance in *The Caine Mutiny*:

> Willie stuck to his resolve to improve his shaky position with high marks, and he rose gradually to a place among the leaders in the school. In the first hours of fiery determination he had set his goal at Number One, but he soon saw that that would be denied him. A mandarin-like midshipman named Tobit, with a domed forehead, measured quiet speech, and a mind like a sponge, was ahead of the field by a spacious percentage. (1951, p. 58)

Immediately following the war, Tobin returned to Harvard and finished his dissertation. The students and faculty at this time were people of exceptional ability, and they created a special learning environment. Tobin remembers, "I see in retrospect that our professors left most of our education to us. They expected us to teach ourselves and learn from each other, and we did. They treated us as adult partners in scholarly endeavor, not as apprentices" (1986, p. 119).

It is doubtful, however, that even this gifted assemblage of talent could have foreseen the crucible of intellectual life that would form at Harvard in the postwar years and mold a new approach to economics. It was a time of intense theoretical development in economics. By the end of the war, the *General Theory*

was recognized as having defined macroeconomics as a new subject within economics. Macroeconomics centers on explaining the aggregate level of output for an economy. While previous theorists occasionally dealt with the overall level of economic activity, aggregate output had never been placed at the center of a body of economic theory and given the major emphasis of explanation.

It was not only the acceptance of Keynesian macroeconomics that created the postwar excitement; econometrics was a newly emerging field. Econometrics deals with applying statistical methods to estimating the parameters of models. As the Harvard macroeconomists developed models of the aggregate economy, econometrics provided the tools to estimate the parameters of the models. Keynes had sought to explain real-world economic variables through theoretical speculation. With the advent of econometrics, macroeconomic theory and empirical validation became inseparably linked. The new statistical methodology supported and refined the empirical basis of the new economics. The young economists, however, did not learn their econometrics in the Harvard Economics Department, which was suspicious of the new methodology. Other programs in the university, namely mathematics and agricultural economics, were interested. These programs, combined with the availability of visiting professors from Europe, allowed the young economists to hone their statistical skills. But it required more than econometric methods to estimate macroeconomic models. In order to estimate models, economists need data. Here again, the young economists were lucky. The newly implemented national-income accounting procedures were beginning to generate the necessary data. For the first time, consistent measures of aggregate output and income were available on a quarterly basis.

All these ingredients—gifted peers, macroeconomic theory, econometric techniques, and national-income data—fused together during the formative years of Tobin's intellectual life. By the time Tobin finished his education, the economics profession had been transformed. He had entered Harvard as an undergraduate and was fascinated by a new but highly suspect approach to economics. By the time he finished his doctorate, the new economics was well on its way to being conventional wisdom.

By the time he finished his doctorate, it was also obvious to all around him that James Tobin would become one of the leading economists of his generation. Yale University quickly recognized his talents with a better offer than Harvard. Yale was rewarded for its initiative when the faculty Tobin assembled moved the university to an eminent position in economics. A key ingredient in the transformation was the Cowles Commission move to Yale. The Cowles Commission for Research in Economics, then located at the University of Chicago, was the center of academic research in mathematical economics and econometrics in the postwar period. In 1954,

Tobin was approached to succeed Tjalling Koopmans as its director, but he declined the offer, choosing to remain at Yale. Unknown to Tobin, Koopmans was dissatisfied with the arrangement between the commission and the University of Chicago and was seriously considering relocating it. If Tobin would not come to the commission, the commission would come to Tobin. The fact that the commission's founder was a Yale graduate smoothed the transition, as did a name change to the Cowles Foundation.

The Cowles Foundation move provided the resources needed to recruit and develop a gifted faculty. During his tenure as director, Tobin assisted many young economists. His unselfish furthering of other economists' careers earned him the affection of his colleagues, just as his technical brilliance had earned him their respect. The high regard for Tobin within the economics profession reflects respect for a gracious, unassuming gentleman. Few Nobel awards have been met with such genuine good wishes.

The formative years of Tobin's professional life thus set in place the intellectual assumptions that would guide his economic and professional vision throughout his career: government is a protector of the common good; proper macroeconomic policy can maintain full employment; wages and prices are sticky, often resistant to market forces; macroeconomic theory should rest on choice models of individual behavior; and, economic research is a collegial undertaking of dedicated scholars.

The remainder of this essay examines Tobin's analytic style as an economist, especially considering one of Tobin's seminal contributions, the justification for a downward-sloping liquidity-preference function.

# The Demand for Money

In his *General Theory*, John Maynard Keynes challenged the foundations of classical economics. While economists still debate over which of these challenges were the most significant, the formulation of the demand for money in terms of liquidity preference is recognized by most as a major break with past thinking. What is liquidity preference and why was it important to Keynes? What were the problems in Keynes's formulation? How did Tobin correct these problems?

To answer these questions, we review how economists derive an individual's demand curve for a good. Consider a world in which an individual can only buy two goods, oranges and bread. The individual is assumed to have a given money income, and the prices of oranges and bread are assumed to be constant. This information forms the individual's *budget constraint*, which reveals all possible combinations of oranges and bread that can be purchased given the individual's money income. The individual also has a *preference function*, often called a utility function. The preference function indicates the relative desirability of various combinations of oranges and bread. The individual's *choice problem* is to purchase his or her most preferred combination of oranges and bread, given the budget constraint.

An individual's demand curve for a good shows the relationship between price and quantity demanded, all other variables being held constant. As the price of bread drops, the individual typically increases his or her quantity demand of bread. A smooth downward-sloping demand curve results. The sum of all individual demand curves gives the market demand curve for bread.

When a market demand curve is combined with a market supply curve, the equilibrium market price for the good is determined. The supply curve for the good has a positive slope: quantity supplied increases as the price of the good rises. The demand curve has a negative slope: quantity demanded decreases as the price rises. The equilibrium price for the good is indicated by the intersection of the demand and supply curves. At the point of intersection, quantity demanded is equal to quantity supplied. There is no excess demand or excess supply and no tendency for equilibrium price to change. A change in supply changes the equilibrium price and quantity. An increase in supply lowers equilibrium price. A decrease in supply raises equilibrium price.

If the market for money resembles this standard market model, the price determined by the interaction of the demand for money and supply of money is the interest rate. Changes in the supply of money, viewed as shifts in the supply curve, change the interest rate. The interest rate is one of the most important variables in determining the level of investment spending. The level of investment in turn affects the level of income and employment. Because the supply of money can be controlled by a nation's monetary authority—the Federal Reserve System in the case of the United States—the money supply is one of the most significant policy tools available to economic policy makers.

This sequence of events is a short-run scenario, ignoring the interaction of crucial macroeconomic variables. To understand the long-run issues, assume that the economy is currently at full employment. The Federal Reserve Board decreases the money supply, raising interest rates, which reduces investment spending and lowers the level of income and output. The economy is now underemployed, causing a decrease in money wages and consequent reductions in prices. The reduction in prices increases the real money supply, lowering the interest rate and increasing investment spending. This process continues until the economy is once again back at full employment. The long-run scenario depends on flexible money wages and prices to restore full employment, while the short-run scenario stresses a disequilibrium decrease in output and income. We have already seen that Tobin believes that such a disequilibrium can be sustained and long term. For Keynesian economists, it is thus exceptionally important to understand the short-run workings of the market for money.

Does the market for money resemble the standard market model? While there is some disagreement about the slope of the supply curve, it is generally accepted that the monetary authorities can control the money supply. In contrast, the slope and position of the demand for money have been the center of intense disagreement within the economics profession since the publication of the *General Theory*. Economists have argued about the stability of the demand curve and the inverse relationship with respect to the interest rate. If the demand for money is unstable or if the inverse relationship with the interest rate does not exist, the short-run market scenario sketched above must change in fundamental respects. An unstable demand function makes it impossible for the monetary authorities to influence the interest rate in a predictable manner through changes in the money supply. A demand function that is insensitive to the interest rate implies that demand and supply can only be brought into equilibrium by some variable other than the interest rate. This other variable is the level of income.

Prior to the *General Theory*, classical economists argued that the level of income was the single most important determinant of the demand for money. A very diverse group of economists fit uncomfortably under the general heading of classical economists, and not all of these economists thought about the relationship between the demand for money and income in the same manner. Some focused on the transaction needs of the aggregate economy. Others focused on the motives of individuals to hold money. Keynes's discussion of the demand for money followed directly from the Cambridge University tradition.

In this Cambridge approach, money is not a good consumed for any inherent utility like oranges or bread, and it does not yield a flow of services like a durable good such as an automobile or washing machine. You can't eat money or wear money or ride money to work. Cambridge economists prior to Keynes argued that individuals demand money to buy goods and services. Money is a medium of exchange that must be held for some period of time because people cannot instantaneously receive paychecks and buy goods and services. The demand for money arises from the need to coordinate receipts and expenditures: No rational consumer or business firm would ever hoard idle cash. The Cambridge economists went on to assume that each individual's demand for money in nominal terms was proportional to the individual's nominal income. They concluded that the nominal demand for money for the aggregate economy $M_d$ must be equal to the nominal level of income for the aggregate economy:

$$M_d = kPY, \qquad (1)$$

where P is the aggregate price level and Y is real income. The proportion k depends on payment periods and spending habits. When both sides of the equation are divided by the price level, the demand for money is written in real terms.

Economists often refer to the real demand for money as the demand for real balances:

$$\frac{M_d}{P} = kY. \qquad (2)$$

The discussion from this point on assumes that both the demand for money and the supply of money are represented as real magnitudes. The real money supply is indicated by the nominal money supply divided by the price level.

Although Keynes was well schooled in the Cambridge tradition, he departed from the analysis of these earlier Cambridge economists by looking much more carefully at what exactly individuals gain from holding money. Like the earlier economists, he believed that money is held for a "transaction motive." He considered the transaction motive to arise solely from the need to coordinate planned receipts and planned payments. Keynes also believed that individuals hold cash for unplanned needs; unexpected bills, a surprise drop in the price of a good, expenses connected with an accident, etc. Money held to cover such unexpected expenses is held for a "precautionary motive." Keynes considered the precautionary demand for money, like the transaction demand for money, to be determined by the level of income.

To this point, Keynes's discussion was squarely in the Cambridge tradition, but he went considerably beyond previous formulations when he posited a third motive for holding money that was directly related to *uncertainty* about the future. This third motive *liquidity preference*, suggested that the interest rate should be included in the demand function for money. While Cambridge theorists had speculated that the interest rate could affect the constant k, they never viewed the interest sensitivity of the demand for money as being of major importance.

To see how Keynes developed his analysis, consider a special type of British government bond called a consol. An individual buys a bond in return for a promise to receive a fixed amount of income per annum. Consols have no maturity date but yield a perpetual return. When an individual buys a consol, he or she buys a claim to this future perpetual income stream. How much is an individual willing to pay for a consol? Suppose that a consol pays its purchaser $50 per year in perpetuity and the current interest rate is 5 percent. It can be shown that the individual should be willing to pay $1,000 ($50/.05). Let the interest rate rise to 10 percent. An individual will no longer pay $1,000 to receive $50 per year in perpetuity. The individual will be willing to pay something less than the $1,000, $500 to be exact ($50/.10). The contractual nature of bonds thus determines an inverse relationship between bond prices and interest rates. A rise in the interest rate causes bond prices to fall. A fall in the interest rate causes bond prices to rise. (This relationship does not change if we introduce a bond with a maturity date.)

What does this inverse relationship have to do with the demand for money? A bondholder suffers a capital loss if interest rates rise and a capital gain if interest rates fall. Assume that an individual expects the rate of return on consols to be $r_e$ at the end of one year. Given this expectation, there is some current critical interest rate $r_c$ where the capital loss associated with $r_e$ just offsets the revenue yield of the bond. In contrast, the value of money does not change with a change in the interest rate: $1,000 is still $1,000. Under these conditions, an individual will choose to hold only money or only bonds. When the current interest rate r is above $r_c$, the individual holds only bonds. When the current interest rate r is below $r_c$, the individual holds only money. Individuals thus have a "speculative motive" for demanding money that is unrelated to income or the need to buy goods and services. They have a liquidity preference.

This analysis rests on a simplified view of an individual's investment portfolio. It considers only that portion of the portfolio that is held in monetary assets and reduces the individual's choice to two types of monetary assets, an interest-earning asset (consols) and a noninterest-earning asset (money). In order to focus on the demand for money, it is assumed that the individual has already allocated his or her portfolio between monetary assets and nonmonetary assets such as land, stocks, gold, etc.

Keynes wanted to argue that the demand for money for the aggregate economy is a smooth inverse function of the interest rate. How did he go from the individual discontinuous functions to the smooth inverse function? He assumed that different individuals in the economy have different expectations about changes in the interest rate $r_e$, the rate of return on consols one year hence. He further assumed that these different expectations are held in just the right way to generate the downward-sloping function. When the current interest rate is "high," most individuals feel that a fall in r is likely in the future and will want to hold bonds. But a few individuals will assume that further rises are likely and choose to hold money. On the other hand, when the current interest rate is "low," most individuals feel that the interest rate is likely to rise in the future and will hold money, and so forth and so on. This causality explained why low interest rates during the Great Depression were associated with large holdings of idle money balances.

Keynes's argument yields a smooth downward-sloping demand for money function, but it depends critically on accepting his view of how expectations are formed. Many economists were troubled by both his reasoning and its empirical implications. The argument assumes that individuals have a normal interest rate fixed in their minds and requires that this normal rate differ across individuals in a very specific manner. Moreover, an implication of Keynes's analysis is that the speculative demand for money, the component responsible for establishing the inverse- or negative-interest sensitivity to the demand for money, must by the nature of the argument exhibit a high degree of instability.

The demand for money may shift dramatically as individuals adjust their "normal" interest rates. A necessary implication of the analysis is that the speculative demand for money could be so unstable as to make invalid any predictions for the demand for money based on transactions or precautionary motives. The instability of the demand for money function thus could prove to be the Achilles heel of policy makers' ability to predict and hence control interest rates. Finally, the typical real-world investor does not hold only money or only bonds in a portfolio: Most individuals' portfolios contain some combination of money and bonds.

# Tobin and Liquidity Preference

Despite the troubling aspects of Keynes's liquidity-preference function, early Keynesian economists accepted the notion of liquidity preference as a key relationship in macroeconomic models. The concerns about the instability of the liquidity-preference function were minimized. The discontinuous, all-or-nothing individual function strained credibility, as did the assumption that individuals would hold different expectations about future interest rates in just the right way to generate the liquidity-preference function. But the function was intuitively reasonable to the early Keynesians. It explained the large cash balances held during the Great Depression and seemed consistent with post-World War II behavior.

The function also provided a solid foundation for monetary policy. It was, in short, exceptionally useful if not theoretically reasonable. As Tobin noted:

Nearly two decades of drawing downward-sloping liquidity preference curves in textbooks and on classroom blackboards should not blind us to the basic implausibility of the behavior they describe. Why should anyone hold non-interest bearing obligations of the government instead of its interest bearing obligations? The apparent irrationality of holding cash is the same, moreover, whether the interest rate is 6 percent, 3 percent or ½ of 1 percent. What needs to be explained is not only the existence of a demand for cash when its yield is less than the yield on alternative assets but an inverse relationship between the aggregate demand for cash and the size of this differential yield. (1958, p. 65)

Many economists felt that an improper use of uncertainty was the key difficulty with Keynes's formulation. As economists examined Keynes's arguments, they realized that he was not really talking about uncertainty. Keynes's individual investor clearly believed that his or her expected rate $r_e$ would exist in the future. It was the additional assumption that people differed in their expectations that accounted for the smooth inverse liquidity-preference function. Thus the Keynesian liquidity-preference function rested not on uncertainty in a probabilistic sense but instead on sticky expectations about future interest rates. Was it possible to base the liquidity-preference function on a set of more satisfying assumptions about human behavior?

Tobin addressed himself to this question in his classic 1958 paper. He agreed with Keynes that if an individual holds money as an investment balance and not as a transaction balance, it must be because the individual fears a loss in the value of other assets. But Tobin developed a much different and more rigorous explanation. Consider an individual who is truly uncertain about the future interest rate on consols. The interest rate may rise or fall. Holding consols thus involves some risk. The larger the proportion of investment-balances-held consols, the larger is the degree of risk assumed by the individual. A rise in the interest rate causes a much larger capital loss if the individual holds a high proportion of the investment portfolio in consols than a low proportion. The larger the proportion held in consols, however, the greater the expected return on the portfolio. A portfolio held solely in money has a zero expected return.

The individual must therefore trade off the degree of risk and the expected return on the portfolio. The outline of a choice problem, similar to the choice problem for oranges and bread, begins to emerge. But how can this intuitive perception be formulated into a rigorous argument that allows for the derivation of liquidity preference? What is the preference function? What is the constraint? The specification of the constraint is especially difficult. An individual can be assumed to have a probability distribution for the expected return on the portfolio. This probability distribution must be defined to be sensitive to changes in the interest rate and the proportion of consols held in the portfolio. Can any meaningful statements about an individual's constraint be derived from such a complex statement of probability?

It is on this key point that Tobin broke major theoretical ground in addressing the derivation of an argument to support liquidity preference. Consider an individual who is uncertain about the capital gain or loss g associated with his or her portfolio. The individual is able to indicate a probability distribution for g. This distribution is assumed to have an expected value of zero, meaning that on average capital gains balance capital losses. The expected value of the return for the portfolio then depends on the amount of the portfolio held in consols and a given interest rate. Tobin also argued that the *risk* associated with the portfolio can be measured by the standard deviation of the return.

This simple, clever formulation implies the powerful analytic conclusion that an individual's choice of consols determines *both* the expected return on the portfolio and the risk associated with the portfolio. The probability distribution for the portfolio's return is described by the expected value (mean) and standard deviation (or variance) of the distribution. Given the fixed interest rate, varying choices for consols are defined. Tobin called this set of choices the *opportunity locus*, which

serves the same role for the investor deciding on the optimal allocation of a portfolio as does the budget constraint for the consumer deciding on the optimal purchase of oranges or bread.

What portion of the portfolio will the investor choose to hold in consols? Just as preference information is needed to decide on the optimal purchase of bread, preference information is needed to decide on the optimal choice of consols. Assume that the individual has a preference function for the expected return and risk. Tobin argued that most individuals are risk-averse. Consider a game in which a fair coin is tossed. If the coin comes up heads, the individual must pay $100. If the coin comes up tails, the individual receives $100. The expected value of this game is zero, but a risk-averse individual values the $100 to be lost more than the $100 to be gained. A risk-averse individual has to be given a possible return greater than $100 to induce him or her to play the game. Risk-averse individuals will only accept more risk if the increase in risk is associated with a greater expected return. Tobin further argued that most risk-averse investors must be given increasing increments in the expected return to assume more risk as risk increases.

The combination of the opportunity locus and the preference function determines the optimal portfolio allocation. Tobin wanted to know how this allocation would change as the interest rate increased. He was able to show that a rise in the interest rate is generally associated with an increase in the proportion of the portfolio held in consols. Individuals assume increased risk at higher returns, precisely the result for which Tobin hoped. The liquidity-preference function could now be based on reasonable assumptions about how real people in the real world deal with risk aversity. The solution also generated the diversification associated with real-world portfolios. Harry Markowitz, working independently of Tobin, developed a similar portfolio model.

Tobin's solution to the liquidity-preference function problem requires gross simplifications of complex alternatives. The use of the standard deviation and expected return as the arguments in an individual's preference function requires a restriction on the probability function of the expected return and the preference function. This mean-variance approach to portfolio analysis remains a subject of controversy among economists concerned about the qualifications and restrictions that must be assumed to justify the approach. What is significant for purposes of this essay is not the controversies generated by mean-variance analysis but what the use of this methodology tells us about Tobin as a practicing economist.

Tobin's economics is the economics of parsimony. He is interested in isolating the critical variables and the crucial causality associated with economic reality. His vision is clear and crisp, cutting through the ambiguous results often found in theoretical discussions. Analytically elegant arguments that yield nontestable propositions not clearly related to economic reality

are of little interest to him. According to Tobin, it is not the restrictive assumptions underlying the mean-variance portfolio model that should concern us. The model yields statements of great power in understanding observed behavior, and critics must show that they have something better. Thus it is the focus on the essentials that marks Tobin's work as an economist.

The essentials of the mean-variance model are indeed revealing of observed economic behavior. Most individuals are averse to risk. Most individuals do have to be compensated with larger and larger rewards to assume greater degrees of risk. Such individuals do generally diversify their portfolios. All this is captured in Tobin's analysis. When a reporter asked Tobin why he had won the Nobel Prize, Tobin responded that he supposed it was because he had shown that people "don't put their eggs all in one basket."

It is, of course, not riskless to hold money if the price level is allowed to vary unexpectedly. While Tobin recognized this possibility, he did not deal with its implications in the 1958 paper, but he explored the impact of unanticipated inflation on asset-market equilibrium in subsequent papers. Generally, Tobin's economic intuition stresses the primacy of real phenomena. He recognizes that inflation has a large uncertain component, but he consistently considers unanticipated changes in the real rate of return to be more significant than inflation in terms of investor risk. Tobin also believes that the modern economy has an inflationary bias at full employment, but he forcefully argues that policy makers should give first priority to maintaining full employment. To Tobin, creating a recession to lower inflation is unacceptable. The strength of his feelings on this issue has caused him to call for incomes policies to control inflation, a decidedly minority position in the economics profession.

Tobin made other contributions to the demand for money. Concurrently with William Baumol, he showed that the transaction demand for money is also sensitive to the interest rate. The holding of transactions balances was modeled as an inventory problem, with individuals and businesses assumed to hold money as an inventory to be used to pay bills at specified times. It is not difficult to show that individuals and businesses economize on their inventory of money as the interest rate increases. The inventory approach thus suggests a second reason for some interest sensitivity in the demand for money.

Following his resolution of money-demand issues, Tobin concentrated on assets-market equilibrium and the link between financial markets and the markets for real goods and services. Once again, his modeling focused on restricted models that yield empirically relevant results. Some have been concerned that Tobin did not build these new models directly on his earlier portfolio model for the demand for money, but he was more concerned with explaining economic reality than with the universality of the models. If he could see the economic

landscape more clearly by moving to another hill—that is, by using a different model—such a move was desirable.

Tobin's investment theory is both intuitive and operational, the distinguishing characteristics of much of his work. The ratio of the market value of a firm's capital to the replacement cost of the firm's capital, known as Tobin's q, can be used to evaluate investment incentives without complex measurement problems. The stock market provides a market value for the firm's capital stock. A firm will invest more in capital when the value of the capital to the firm is greater than the price the firm must pay for the capital ($q > 1$).

If the explanation of observable economic behavior is one of the pillars that supports Tobin's economics, the other must be his sense of the obligations of the national government. His position on government policy choices flows from his belief in the relevance of short-run Keynesian income-determination models and has made him one of the most forceful spokesmen for discretionary government policy of his generation. Tobin's discussion of discretionary policy tools has always been balanced. He has given as much weight to monetary policy as to fiscal policy in the task of maintaining full employment. He has also steadfastly resisted single causal policy prescriptions, most notably those of the monetarists, and tenaciously argued against those who suggest that discretionary policy is ineffective at best and destabilizing at worst.

This faith in the efficacy of an activist government, the component of the *General Theory* that so attracted the idealistic Harvard sophomore, is perhaps the most controversial aspect of Tobin's economic vision. While he recognizes that problems of policy implementation have turned out to be much more difficult than predicted by early Keynesians, he continues to believe that past policy errors represent avoidable errors. Wrong policies result from imperfect information, bad judgment, or institutional rigidity.

Tobin has been sharply criticized for not making the behavior of government itself a subject of his economic analysis. It is alleged that government is not to be understood as Tobin's "protector of the common good" but rather as a set of economically motivated agents involved in a political or bureaucratic process. If Tobin understood this argument, it is suggested, he would be more sympathetic with arguments to limit the discretion of policy makers through fixed monetary and budgetary rules.

Discretionary policy has undeniably failed on many occasions in the postwar period, and an understanding of the motives of government agents is essential to an understanding of how the political process molds economic policy. But can it really be denied that the central concern of government remains the common good? The ancient Greeks recognized that the essence of man is societal. The very legitimacy of government rests on the acceptance of collective motives. Tobin's faith is that of a man who understands this principle.

BETTY J. BLECHA

# Selected Bibliography

## WORKS BY TOBIN

"Liquidity Preference and Monetary Policy." *Review of Economics and Statistics* 29 (1947): 124–31.

"The Interest Elasticity of Transactions Demand for Cash." *Review of Economics and Statistics* 38 (1956): 241–47.

"Liquidity Preference as Behavior towards Risk." *Review of Economic Studies* 25 (1958): 65–86.

"Money and Income: Post Hoc Ergo Proctor Hoc?" *Quarterly Journal of Economics* 84 (1970): 301–17.

*Essays in Economics: Macroeconomics.* Chicago: Markham Publishing Company, 1971.

"Friedman's Theoretical Framework." *Journal of Political Economy* 80 (1972): 852–63.

"Inflation and Unemployment." *American Economic Review* 62 (1972): 1–18.

*The New Economics One Decade Older.* Princeton, N.J.: Princeton University Press, 1974.

"Are New Classical Models Plausible Enough to Guide Policy?" *Journal of Money, Credit, and Banking* 12 (1980): 788–99.

*Asset Accumulation and Economic Activity: Reflections on Contemporary Macroeconomic Theory.* Chicago: University of Chicago Press, 1980.

"James Tobin." In William Breit and Roger W. Spencer, eds., *Lives of the Laureates*, pp. 113–34. Cambridge, Ma.: MIT Press, 1986.

## OTHER WORKS

Grossman, Hershel I. "Tobin on Macroeconomics: A Review Article." *Journal of Political Economy* 83 (1975): 829–847.

Klamer, Arjo. *Conversations with Economists.* Totowa, N.J.: Rowman & Allanheld, 1983.

Samuelson, Paul A. "1981 Nobel Prize in Economics." *Science* (October 30, 1981): 520–22.

Wouk, Herman. *The Caine Mutiny.* New York: Pocket Books, 1951.

# Index

*335*

For Product Safety Concerns and Information, please contact our EU representative GPSR@taylorandfrancis.com or Taylor & Francis Verlag GmbH, Kaufingerstraße 24, 80331 München, Germany